Amazing American Women

Amazing American Women

40 Fascinating 5-Minute Reads

Kendall Haven

with a Foreword by
Molly Murphy MacGregor

1995
LIBRARIES UNLIMITED, INC.
and its division
Teacher Ideas Press
Englewood, Colorado

To Roni Berg
the love of my life,
who first created the idea,
who lit the fires of inspiration,
who held this book true to its course and purpose,
and who helped me steer each story in a meaningful direction.

LIBRARIES UNLIMITED, INC.
and its division
Teacher Ideas Press
P.O. Box 6633
Englewood, CO 80155-6633
1-800-237-6124

Library of Congress Cataloging-in-Publication Data

Haven, Kendall F.
    Amazing American women : 40 fascinating 5-minute reads / Kendall Haven.
    xxi, 305 p. 17x25 cm.
    Includes index.
    ISBN 1-56308-291-8
    1. Women--United States--Biography.   I. Title.
CT3260.H38   1995
920.72'0973--dc20
[B]   95-16035
                                                                              CIP

Contents

1 Stories About Women's and Civil Rights

v

1 Stories About Women's and Civil Rights—*continued*

2 Stories About Politics

3 Stories About Sports

4 Stories About Science and Exploration

5 Stories About Education

6 Stories About Medicine

6 Stories About Medicine—*continued*

7 Stories About Military Service

8 Stories About Business

9 Stories About Visual, Written, and Performing Arts

Foreword

People's lives are the fabric of history. What they did and why and how they did it becomes our heritage, our lessons, and hopefully, our strength to continue the work they have begun. The stories of women's lives are often missing from the lessons of history. The engaging stories in this book help to remedy that omission. And in doing so, they challenge some of the most basic and long-held stereotypes about the nature of women. These are stories about an extraordinary array of women of different classes, ethnicities, and regions, whose lives span three centuries. Women who created their own lives in their own ways with gusto and joy and hard work. Women who challenged the social mores of their times, not necessarily because they were intent on changing the world, but because they were intent on living meaningful and purposeful lives.

What I most appreciate in reading the stories of these women's lives is the sense of joy and the possibility of making one's life better. The determination of taking on challenging and sometimes daring tasks also prevails. Story after story is a lesson in setting goals, and persisting until the goal is accomplished.

These stories take on an even more remarkable quality given the status of women during the times in which these women lived. Laws, customs, and traditions are often formidable barriers to accomplishment. From early colonial times to the present, women have actively worked to challenge and change customs, traditions, and laws that define them as inferior. In early colonial times, women assumed the role of "deputy husband" to carry out the work that needed to be done. In this capacity, they were able to participate in a variety of occupations. Women's opportunities to participate in the public sphere changed dramatically as the thirteen original colonies became the United States. With the adoption of the Constitution, and the codification of laws, the Blackstone Code was used to clearly define the status of women as inferior. According to the Blackstone Code, a married woman was considered to be the property of her husband, with no legal rights of her own. In addition to being unable to enter into legal agreements, women could not inherit money, or even gain custody of their own children. The first U.S. women's rights meeting held in Seneca Falls in 1848 challenged the restrictions established by the Blackstone Code and even argued for women's right to vote.

By the end of the nineteenth century, women had successfully eliminated many occupational barriers, but women's political and legal spheres were still very strictly defined in the courts, and women's participation in public life was severely criticized by the press, politicians, and preachers. In 1920, after a seventy-two-year campaign conducted by hundreds of thousands of women who created the largest nonviolent movement in U.S. history, women finally won the right to vote. Even with this victory, some legal and political sanctions continued. Today, it is often the unspoken rules of appropriate behavior and appearance that hinder women's full participation in creating their own lives.

The women featured in these stories lived lives of such determination and conviction that they overcame and often helped eliminate the barriers created by such laws, customs, or social conventions that existed during their lifetimes. Their stories help dispel the myth of women's fear of success. On the contrary, story after story demonstrates that in every sphere—politics, science, art, exploration, medicine, education, athletics, and military service—women have created strategies for success and accomplishment. These women, who were often the "first" in their fields of endeavor, did not see being first as an obstacle or a burden, but as an important opportunity to "do it first" and to "do it right." Using moments taken from very complicated, full lives, these stories help illustrate each woman's spirit of adventure, dedication, and· purposefulness. These are important stories filled with the human experience of the joy of discovery, success, and achievement. Knowing the stories of these women's lives helps fill in the gaps so often left in the traditional telling of our history. These stories give us the inspiration to create our own daring lives.

—Molly Murphy MacGregor
Executive Director and co-founder of the
National Women's History Project

Acknowledgments

I want to extend a very special thanks to the National Women's History Project (7738 Bell Road, Windsor, CA 95492, 707-838-6000). They have amassed an extensive and thoughtful archive on women in American history, and are a national treasure. I could not have successfully completed this project without their assistance and their resources.

I also want to thank three individuals. Geets Vincent, a veritable fountain of information and a good friend, graciously provided invaluable help and saved me countless hours of fumbling research. This is the second of my books for which Tama Serfoss has served as editor. It remains a delight to work with Tama. Her skilled and caring touch has greatly enhanced the clarity and readability of these stories. Last, a loving, "thank you," to Roni Berg for the many hours of review and the flashes of brilliance she cheerfully donated to this project.

Introduction

Stop for a moment and jot down the first five names from American history that pop into your head. How many of the five were women? I recently conducted this little experiment with two groups: a fifth-grade class of thirty-one students, and an adult (senior's) writing class of twenty-five students. Each individual wrote down five names, and we tallied the resulting composite lists for each class.

Of the 155 names listed by the fifth-graders, only eight women (5 percent) were included, and none more than once. Conversely, Washington and Lincoln were listed twenty-eight times each.

Surprisingly, the adults didn't do much better. Just over 15 percent of their names were women, even though women made up almost two-thirds of the class. Eighty-five percent of the figures in U.S. history that first came to their minds were men.

Look at U.S. history in textbooks, novels, or movies, and it often appears as though significant historical deeds have been reserved strictly for men. Studies show students are ten times more likely to read stories about American men than about American women.

The truth, of course, is that women played a great role in shaping this country and creating our heritage. However, the stories of women's contributions to our history aren't recorded, told, or taught. Their stories haven't been reported and publicized as have those of men.

This is a collection of stories about forty important American women. These stories celebrate and honor some of the incredible women who helped create, mold, and define this country. I admire and applaud their determination, bravery, perseverance, and fortitude, qualities that were essential in helping them overcome the dual challenges they faced: the struggle to complete their chosen work, and a complex web of gender restrictions unfairly holding them down.

I cheered when they triumphed. I felt enraged when petty societal roadblocks halted their progress. I felt awed by the grace and dignity with which they confronted senseless biases. Above all, I found these women and their stories thrilling and uplifting.

My hopes in writing this book are, first and foremost, that women and girls may be inspired by these models of feminine power and accomplishment and gain a greater pride in the heritage of their gender. These stories attempt to show girls that they can accomplish anything, if they set their goals and identify their dreams and then go out and make them happen. Second, I hope to increase general awareness of the women who represent such an important—and often overlooked—part of America's history and heritage. Finally, I want to encourage men and boys to tear off their blinders and acknowledge, applaud, and celebrate women's accomplishments.

I began my research for this book with a "short list" of just over 200 women, each more than worthy of inclusion in this collection. Probably the most difficult challenge I faced was reducing that list to the final forty. I am not suggesting that the women I chose are the forty most important women in American history. I do not believe it is possible to create such a list, or even that the concept is particularly relevant. There are hundreds of women who are important to our history at a national level, thousands more at regional and local levels. Here are forty women, each of whom *is* important, and whose stories I find fascinating. My criteria for this selection process are described in "How to Use This Book."

Each of the women in this book, and hundreds more not included in these pages, accomplished great deeds by any standard. More important, each of these American female heroes faced the additional burden of having to break through artificial, societally imposed gender barriers her male counterparts never had to face. These women had to do more than men to reach their goals. And still they succeeded.

These are individual stories, not complete biographies; they don't attempt to look at all of each woman's accomplishments, many of whom deserve "lifetime achievement awards." A score of stories could be written about most of these women. They each tore down barriers and expanded the options available to other women. It is my hope that these stories will inspire the reader to seek more complete biographies of these and other noteworthy women, and will remind us all of how unthinkable modern America would be without the contributions of women.

This book serves to honor the lives, efforts, and accomplishments of these women by presenting selected moments from their lives and flashes of insight into their character, strength, and contributions. It will serve to give the reader a better sense of the extent of the contributions of women to American history.

There are easily 400 or 4,000 more stories waiting to be told. Discover one or two of your own and share them. We all need to learn more about the women in America's past.

How to Use This Book

Women were selected as the subject of a story based on five criteria:

1. They had to be American women;

2. Their contributions had to have occurred in America and have significance to American history;

3. Strong preference was given to women who tore down some gender bias or barrier and expanded opportunities for other women;

4. The characters and stories in the book were selected to achieve temporal and racial balance; and

5. The resulting stories must have dramatic interest.

I began this project by creating a "short list" of women I wanted to consider for inclusion. That list contained more than 200 names. Each was worthy of a story. The process of narrowing the list to forty was a slow and difficult one. Using my criteria and a scoring system, I weighed each woman's story and its potential for this book to arrive at the final list. Another writer could easily start with the same list and the same criteria, and arrive at a different set of women for the final forty. What is paramount is that there are fascinating stories of countless women, all of which deserve to be told. Forty of these are told in this book.

The chosen stories are arranged into nine areas of activity and listed chronologically within each area. These areas weren't used to choose the stories; rather, they are a way of connecting the women who struggled along similar paths. The nine sections are: women's and civil rights; politics; sports; science and exploration; education; medicine; military service; business; and visual, written, and performing arts.

In addition to being arranged by area of activity, the stories in this book are cross-referenced both alphabetically and by date of occurrence. In many cases, the women described in these stories have made major contributions over a long period. The dates listed are for the specific event or events described in the stories of this book.

Before each story I have included a question or series of questions called "Library Links." These questions relate to a significant aspect of the following story, and are designed to stimulate student library research and class discussion, and to link these stories to other curriculum areas.

Library Links contains two types of questions. First are factual questions that lend themselves to direct library research and to gaining an expanded view of the types and variety of information our libraries contain. Second are philosophical or thought-provoking questions designed to spawn class discussion. Often the product of these discussions will be a list of questions and topics for student library research.

Bibliographic sources for further reading are listed at the end of each story. A key line of this section reads, "See your librarian for additional titles." Every library has a unique collection of reference material. Some of the resources I list may not be in your library. But other, even better resources, might. Your librarian is the person who can guide you to the best that your school or public library has to offer.

Following the stories in this book I have included two appendixes. The first is a timeline of some of the major events of U.S. history, putting the women in this book in historical perspective and creating an understanding of how these stories fall within the flow of our common history. The second appendix is a list of an additional 100 women from my original list of 200+. I have listed the year of each woman's birth and death and the general area of her major contribution. Encourage students to use these resources to research significant women and create their own stories.

Each of these stories is as historically accurate as available sources allowed me to make it. Each of the events and meetings included in my stories happened when and as described. My portrayal of each of the main characters is likewise historically accurate based on a comparison and compilation of available sources. Only the specific dialog is fiction, and even that is faithful to the personality, manner, and tone of the leading characters.

These stories are intended to act as classroom supplementary materials to enrich and enliven core curriculum teaching. They are a launching pad into a detailed study of a period, movement, or group of people. Above all, they are designed to spark the imagination and wonder of students, and to excite and motivate them to explore our thrilling common his- and her-story.

Alphabetical List of Featured Women

List of Stories by Year of Occurrence

17th Century

1607 . . . . . Pocahontas, "Indian and English"

18th Century

1778 . . . . . Mary Hays ("Molly Pitcher"), "Water and Fire"
1781 . . . . . Elizabeth ("Mumbet") Freeman, "Free and Equal"
1782 . . . . . Deborah Sampson, "Surrendering to a Woman"

19th Century

1805 . . . . . Sacajawea, "A Woman Led the Way"
1827 . . . . . Elizabeth ("Betsy") Ross, "Red, White, and Betsy"
1828 . . . . . Sojourner Truth, "The Travelin' Truth"
1840-1848 . Elizabeth Cady Stanton, "Property or Person?"
1844 . . . . . Dorothea Dix, "Out of Darkness"
1847 . . . . . Elizabeth Blackwell, "The Joke's on Them"
1849 . . . . . Harriet Tubman, "Conductor on the Train"
1850 . . . . . Sarah Winnemucca, "Not Our Way"
1851 . . . . . Amelia Bloomer, "The Right Dress"
1858 . . . . . Charlene ("Charley") Parkhurst, "Wild West Whip"
1862 . . . . . Clara Barton, "Barton's Bandages"
1862 . . . . . Sarah Edmonds, "Private Petticoat"
1862 . . . . . Harriet Beecher Stowe and Catherine Beecher,
              "Second-Best Sister"
1872 . . . . . Susan B. Anthony, "Vote to Win"
1875 . . . . . Annie ("Oakley") Moses, "Pigtails and Buckshot"
1879 . . . . . Fannie Farmer, "A Cup of Science"
1884 . . . . . Belva Lockwood, "Presidential Tracks"
1887 . . . . . Annie Sullivan and Helen Keller, "T-E-A-C-H-E-R"
1888 . . . . . Elizabeth Cochran Seamen ("Nellie Bly"), "A Pen for the Pain"
1890 . . . . . Jane Addams, "Coffee and a Roast Beef Sandwich"
1896 . . . . . Queen Liliuokalani, "Save the Fire"
1896 . . . . . Carrie Nation and Frances Willard, "Convention Halls and
              Cowtown Saloons"

20th Century

1903 . . . . . Isadora Duncan, "Chance to Dance"
1903 . . . . . Mary Harris ("Mother") Jones, "Go Ahead and Shoot"
1904 . . . . . Mary Bethune, "Ask Not; Get Not"
1915 . . . . . Sarah Breedlove ("Madam C. J.") Walker, "A Hair-Brained
              Idea"

1

Stories About Women's and Civil Rights

Free and Equal

A story about Elizabeth ("Mumbet") Freeman, who was the first person to challenge the legality of slavery

About This Story:

There was never a law legalizing slavery in America. Slavery was allowed because no one forbade it to start. While we think of slavery as a southern phenomena, it actually existed in all of the thirteen original colonies. Most of New England peacefully abandoned slavery by the beginning of the nineteenth century. The rest of the northern states soon followed. But it took the bloody American Civil War fifty years later to force the South to follow suit.

Not all the heroic struggles to end slavery took place in the South. One of the boldest confrontations with the institution of slavery occurred in Massachusetts, even before the final victory in the Revolutionary War that made Massachusetts a state instead of an English colony. This brave legal challenge to slavery was brought by a lone slave who was also a woman.

Overcast skies hung low on a bitter, slushy winter day in early 1781. It was one of those slushy days, with gloomy, overcast skies. A wet, penetrating cold stung the skin and drove straight through to the bone no matter what a person wore. It was a miserable day of old, crusty snow and heavy, black mud.

In spite of the weather, a lone black woman trudged the long four miles from Colonel John Ashley's estate to the town of Sheffield in the southwest corner of Massachusetts. A heavy cloak wrapped around herself and the young child she carried, the thirty-year-old woman struggled to keep her balance through mud and slippery snow.

Halfway to Sheffield, a thin, freezing rain began to swirl in the woman's face, matting her jet-black hair where it stuck out around the edges of the bandanna wrapped tightly around her head. The woman hardly noticed. One thought kept repeating in her mind and driving her feet: "I heard them write it into the state constitution. 'All are born free and equal'—'free and equal,' 'free and equal.' I'm gonna get me some of that free and equal."

The American Revolutionary War still raged across the country. American armies in the north under Ethan Allen and Nathaniel Green had met with considerable success. However George Washington's army in the mid-Atlantic colonies were struggling desperately, and the southern forces were all but crushed. While the war for American independence was still far from decided, and it was still not clear whether Masssachusetts would become a state in a free nation or remain an English colony, a group of Massachusetts leaders had already written a state constitution based on the approved Federal Articles of Confederation. This constitution stated that all men are created free and equal.

By noon the black woman knocked on the front door of Theodore Sedgwick, a young, eager lawyer who had been part of the committee that drafted the Massachusetts State Constitution at John Ashley's estate the previous fall. As the door opened, the woman introduced herself.

"Good day, sir. I'm Elizabeth Freeman from Colonel Ashley's."

"Ah, yes. I remember," answered Theodore, ushering her into his home and office. "They call you, 'Bet,' as I recall. Well come in, come in. Take off your wet things. You must be soaked. I'll have someone get towels for you and the baby."

Elizabeth's trim body and starched servant's uniform were soon perched on the edge of a chair before Mr. Sedgwick's long desk, a mug of hot tea steaming in her hand, her baby playing quietly on the floor.

Theodore settled into his high-backed chair and leaned forward. "For what important mission has John Ashley sent you out on such a miserable day? I hope everyone's all right."

"The Colonel didn't send me," answered Elizabeth. "I come on my own to get free." Her face was ordinary, even plain, but very alert. Her eyes sparkled with energy.

Theodore's eyebrows raised as if he hadn't heard correctly. "Excuse me, Bet, what was that you said?"

"I want to be free now." The words flowed across his desk—simple, powerful, and sincere.

Theodore rocked back in his chair as if struck hard in the chest by some mighty force and clasped both hands behind his head. Weakly he stammered, "Well now, I'm sure you do. Yes, indeed."

Bet continued to gaze, unblinking, into his face. "What's not to know, Mr. Sedgwick? The Massachusetts Constitution says that everyone is born free and equal. You were part of the committee that wrote it. I was serving in Colonel Ashley's house that day and I heard everyone say those words, 'free and equal.' "

Theodore's mind slowly regained its balance and raced through the enormity of her claim. "Yes, well certainly, that *is* in the constitution. But, Bet, you're a . . . a slave."

Bet nodded. "I've been thinking hard 'bout that, too. Is a slave free?"

Theodore chuckled, "Of course not. Not being free is the definition of slavery."

"And you say I'm a slave," continued Bet, " 'cause Colonel Ashley says that he owns me. That he bought me when I was a baby."

"That's right," agreed the lawyer.

"But, I *was* born, wasn't I?" she asked.

He laughed. "I presume so, Bet. How else would you be . . ."

She interrupted, "And I *am* a person, a human?"

"Yes," he agreed. "You're pretty safe on that one, too. But . . ."

Again she cut him off. "Now, does, or does not, the Massachusetts Constitution state that all men are *born* free and equal?" The lawyer thoughtfully tapped his fingertips together and started to answer when she added, "And I presume that when the constitution says, 'men,' it really means 'people.' I mean, white women aren't 'men.' But they're free. So it really says all *people* are born free."

Theodore gazed at the ceiling and gestured vaguely, stirring the air with his hands. "Bet, this is an intriguing—but very complicated—issue you raise."

"Why complicated?" she demanded, still gazing straight into his face. "It sounds simple to me. I am a person. I was born. I live in Massachusetts. So the state constitution says I am free and equal. Or does the constitution lie?"

"Oh, no," he reassured her. "The constitution is the most sacred legal document of the state. It certainly does not lie. It's just that . . . well, no one thought of slaves when we wrote those words. You see, Bet, slaves are property."

Again she cut him off. "Slaves are *people*."

Theodore leaned forward and patted her hand as a parent might pat a child who asks an innocent, but foolish, question. "But slaves are also *property*. And state law says that a man's property cannot be taken away without compensation."

Elizabeth nodded thoughtfully. "You say property isn't free. So be it. But the constitution says all people are free." Sedgwick nodded, trying to follow Bet's logic.

"Now the only way I can make those two fit is if no people can be property. Since I'm a people, I must not be property, and no one needs to compensate Colonel Ashley."

Theodore Sedgwick groped for a valid explanation, his mind whirling through volume and verse of Massachusetts law, his eyes slowly wandering along the walls. "But, Bet, why do you want to be free? Why upset the applecart that takes such good care of you? You live better at Colonel Ashley's than most free working white people in this part of Massachusetts. Why jeopardize that?"

Instantly she answered, "Why do you want to be free from the good life provided by England?"

Theodore spluttered, "Oh, that's a different situation entirely."

"Is it?" she asked. "What law says it's right to own people without their consent?"

"Where did you get all these fancy words and ideas?" he asked, both astounded and impressed by the forceful way she argued her case.

"I do my job in the Ashley house, and I listen close, and I think hard," she answered.

Theodore sat upright, again tapping his fingertips together, and began to seriously consider her claim. "While it's true, Bet, that no specific law authorized, or created, slavery in Massachusetts, no law specifically forbade it, either. Moreover, because slavery has existed in Massachusetts for a hundred years, legal precedent and custom have both been set that acknowledge slaves as property, and laws have been written *about* slaves—many, I should remind you, to require humane treatment of slaves."

Still Elizabeth Freeman gazed straight at the young lawyer. Her voice was quiet, but filled with power and conviction. "Three years ago my husband, who was also a slave, joined General Washington's army to fight this war for freedom for America. Just over one year ago he died fighting for America's freedom. The Declaration of Independence says all men have a right to freedom. The state constitution says all are born free. My husband died to make me free. Now I want that freedom for me and for my daughter."

Theodore realized it had never occurred to him that black people might want freedom as much as whites. He had always thought blacks struggled, sacrificed, and sweated just because some white person told them to. But in the determined face of this black woman before him, Theodore saw that black people were suffering and struggling through a long, hard war—much longer and harder than the one white colonists fought against England—dreaming of their own rights of life, liberty, and the pursuit of happiness.

For the first time he gazed straight back into her strong, black eyes. "I'll do what I can, Bet. I'll research it. But there are very complex legal issues here." Sedgwick's mind swirled with a thousand uncertainties. How would his neighbors react? What arguments could he use? What legal precedents could he rely on? What judge and court would hear him? How could he convince a judge and jury to free a slave when a number of them owned slaves of their own?

"Is that what lawyers do," Bet asked, "take a simple thing and make it complicated?"

He laughed and slowly shook his head. "Unfortunately, Bet, this is anything but simple. Still, I will do my utmost to . . ."

There was a fierce pounding on the front door that froze Theodore mid-sentence. Before Theodore could rise from his chair the door burst open. Cold, wet wind swirled into the room with Colonel John Ashley, eyes blazing.

He stood in the doorway fists and jaw tightly clenched, the wind moaning behind him, glaring at the two people huddled around Theodore Sedgwick's desk. Slowly his gaze focused solely on Elizabeth. His words were measured and clipped, as if he were struggling to control his rage. "Come home with me now, Bet."

Her eyes turned pleadingly to the lawyer. "Make me free," she whispered.

Colonel Ashley strode forward and slammed his fist on the desk. "You have deeply embarrassed me and my family, Bet. Reverend Reeve saw you walk through town to Mr. Sedgwick's and rode all the way out to my house to see what was the matter. Can you imagine my embarrassment at that moment?"

He began to pace as he spoke, his hand ripping at the air for emphasis. "I didn't even know one of my slaves had left my property. Can you imagine how foolish that made me look in front of one of the most esteemed members of our community? I don't know what foolishness has brought you here to waste good Mr. Sedgwick's time, but you come home now!" Again he slammed his fist on the desk for emphasis.

Elizabeth Freeman rose out of her chair, standing as tall and proud as she dared. A long skirt hid her trembling knees and churning stomach. She forced herself to look straight into John Ashley's eyes. "No, sir. I will not go home a slave. I came here to be free."

That Bet was able to actually say such brave words to her powerful owner greatly surprised herself and shocked John Ashley.

"To be what?" he demanded, shaking his head to clear his hearing. "You came here to be *what*?"

"I came here to be free and equal, sir, like it says in the Massachusetts Constitution."

Ashley turned to the young lawyer. "What is this nonsense she's babbling about, Theodore?"

Sedgwick gulped and pulled at his collar. "She does have a case, John."

Ashley exploded. "A case! A case? She's my property. Could my chair suddenly decide not to be my chair any more and walk off? Could my trees decide they liked my neighbor better and move there?"

In frustration he ran both hands through his thick, graying hair. Then he let out a deep breath and turned to Bet. "Haven't we given you a good home?"

"Yes, sir," she answered.

"Good and sufficient food?"

"Yes, sir."

"Good clothing?"

"Very good, sir."

"Enough heat in the winter? Time to enjoy the cool afternoon breezes in summer?"

"Yes, sir."

"Bet, we have worked very hard over the years to ensure you lived free from want, need, or care. You live far better than most of the free white laborers in this valley. Doesn't that make you happy?"

"Happy doesn't matter, sir. I want to be free."

Exasperated, John Ashley threw his hands into the air and slumped against a bookcase stuffed with thick lawbooks. "This is ridiculous. There is no argument. There is no case. You are a slave, *my* slave."

Again he turned to Sedgwick. "For her own sake, talk her out of this foolishness, Theodore. Everyone knows blacks lack the capacity to support themselves. Where will she go? Where will she live? What will she do? Where will she ever find a home as good as ours?"

A faint smile crossed Theodore's lips as he thought, "He sounds just like King George talking about ignorant American colonists."

Elizabeth answered, "Maybe I won't find a home at all, sir. Maybe I'll live in rags and starve. But I'll do it free and equal and happy."

Now Theodore struggled to hold in a chuckle as he thought, "Bet sounds just like we stout colonists talking back to the good English King."

Ashley turned back to Elizabeth. "Gather up your child, Bet. I order you to come home *now*."

Elizabeth planted her feet. "The lawyer is going to make me free."

Sedgwick shrugged apologetically. "I can't do that, Bet. I'm only a lawyer, not a judge. You'll have to go with him, Bet. You're a slave until a court decides your case and passes a verdict."

Elizabeth Freeman felt empty and defeated on the long, silent walk back to the Ashley estate. It was as if the cruel joke was finally clear to her. Fancy words in laws, declarations, and constitutions only granted freedom to those who already had it, only helped those who didn't need the help. The future looked more bleak than the dismal sky. Bet was forbidden to leave the main house, and mechanically trudged through her duties all that long winter.

In March, the sheriff arrived with a summons and writ for both Elizabeth and John Ashley to appear at the Great Barrington Court on Tuesday, August 19, 1781, for the trial of Elizabeth's petition for freedom. Elizabeth's heart soared. Her knees were shaking so much she could hardly stand. Theodore Sedgwick had done it! He'd maneuvered her case onto the court docket.

As a steamy, August sun spread orderly patterns of light across the courtroom floor, an eager crowd jammed into the viewing benches. Theodore Sedgwick fidgeted nervously with notes and his coat. Elizabeth sat next to him feeling a great calm. She whispered, "The words 'free and equal' are in the constitution. There's no words about 'custom,' and 'precedent,' and 'subsequent laws,' in there. Just the free and equal words. You tell them that in fancy lawyer talk and everything will be all right."

Lawyers argued back and forth. The judge listened carefully and took notes. The jury leaned forward so that no word could escape them. The crowd murmured as each point was made, refuted, and then remade. The neat splotches of sunlight marched slowly across the floor and climbed the east wall. For three days Bet sat and watched the light march its way across the crowded room as lawyers argued and tempers flared.

A wave of soft contentment washed over her when she heard the final verdict. The legal community called it a great precedent for freedom. Newspapers claimed the case destroyed slavery forever in Massachusetts and other freedom-loving states. Elizabeth Freeman said simply that now everybody knew what she had known in her heart for some time: she was free.

John Ashley was ordered to pay back wages, damages, and court costs totaling 5 pounds, 44 shillings, and 4 pence.

Elizabeth stared at the money and whispered to Theodore, "All I wanted was my freedom. I never had money before. What do I do with it?"

"First," he answered, "pay your lawyer. Second, buy three new dresses. I am impressed with your keen mind and abilities. I want to hire you to run my household. You'll need something new to wear."

Bet had a natural gift for organization and efficiency, and brought order and joy to the Sedgwick home. Both before and after her hard-won freedom, most people called Elizabeth Freeman "Bet." Theodore Sedgwick's children often affectionately called her "mother Bet" or "mum Bet." His grandchildren never called her anything but "Mumbet."

When she died in 1829, Mumbet had faithfully run the Sedgwick household as a hired housekeeper for over fifty years. She brought order and joy to the house, and Theodore gave her much credit for his success as a lawyer. Her income supported her grandchildren and great-grandchildren.

Mumbet's victory is often viewed as the first shining blow in the great fight against slavery in America. She viewed herself simply as a lucky woman who lived at a time when a constitution was written and set her free. It was just that lots of people's memories needed a gentle nudge to make them remember to do what their words promised they would. Struggling with the great issues and inequities of the twentieth century, we could benefit from such a gentle nudge. But that is another story.

Questions to Explore

Why was slavery legal in the American colonies?

Why wasn't it challenged right away?

Why were so many Americans unwilling to give up slavery?

Has slavery been legal in other countries? Which ones and when?

References for Further Reading

- *In the Children's Library*

Felton, Howard. *Mumbet; the Story of Elizabeth Freeman.* New York: Dodd, Mead, 1970.

- *In the Adult Library*

McManus, Edgar. *Black Bondage in the North.* Syracuse, NY: Syracuse University Press, 1973.

See your librarian for additional titles.

The Travelin' Truth

A story about Sojourner Truth, who worked to promote the rights of women and slaves

About This Story:

Slavery was not practiced only in America's South. During the eighteenth and early nineteenth centuries slavery was also accepted in most northern states. Even though slaves were gradually emancipated (freed) in northern states through the early 1800s, freed slaves had few legal rights.

But few black people dared enforce even those few rights they did have. Black people quite understandably feared reprisals from a white society that had until recently treated them as property. Worse, they lived in constant fear of being abducted by roving slavehunters and dragged back into slavery in the South. Most black people struggled to live quiet, unnoticeable lives, believing that any attention was bad attention, and that being anonymous was their only safeguard.

But not all thought this way. A brave few believed black people were entitled to their full share of legal protection, and demanded the enforcement of laws written to protect their rights. This is a story of one such black woman, who was a runaway slave.

A massive walnut desk occupied one entire end of Jacob VanCroft's legal office. The remainder of the room was stuffed with two small writing desks, a file cabinet, and heavy shelves with rows of thick, identically bound lawbooks. The office's windows overlooked busy Front Street in Kingston, New York. It was April, 1828, and a steady flow of horses and riders, pedestrians, and loaded carts ambled by one floor below, enjoying the sunshine.

Jacob VanCroft leaned back in his high-backed chair so that the back of his head almost touched the windowsill behind him. "Thomas, are you taking notes on this conversation?" he called to one of the two assistants hunched over the writing desks.

Eighteen-year-old Thomas wiped his shaggy black hair out of his face as he scribbled furious notes in his journal with a quill pen. "Yes sir, Mr. VanCroft."

VanCroft nodded and turned back to the thin, almost frail-looking black woman seated straight as a board before him. He decided that her frailty was deceptive. There was a powerful, honest toughness about the woman that made her uncomfortably imposing.

"For the record," he began, "please tell us your name, madam."

The woman answered, "Isabelle. But all call me 'Belle.' "

"And your last name?" continued VanCroft.

Belle tightened her mouth and arched her eyebrows with impatience. "I was a slave. We were't given the last name."

Her broken English was spoken with a thick Dutch accent through a straight, wide mouth. Her nose reminded Jacob of an enormous teardrop: thin, long, and straight at the top spreading out into a wide bulb at the bottom. She peered intently at him through small wire-rimmed glasses.

"Very well, Belle," he said. "Suppose you tell me exactly what brings you to the district court in Kingston."

"I want my son back," she said. "I told you that afore."

"Quite right," said Jacob with a broad smile. "But please tell me again so Thomas can get it all noted in his log."

A look of annoyance flashed across Belle's face. "My son is sold to Alabama. But the law say that cannot be. This writ say it, too. But my son still be gone."

Jacob VanCroft rocked forward in his chair. "Let me be sure I've got this straight. Your son was sold to someone who shipped him off to Alabama?"

Again Belle's exasperated look. "I say that two times."

VanCroft thoughtfully touched his fingertips. "Did you talk to the man who sold your son and try to have him brought back?"

Belle's face tightened into a look of disgust. "I ask. But the man and his wife they laugh and spit and ask why do I care? They say it's only one child and I got more, so why bother?"

"And then you filed suit in district court here in Kingston to sue for his return?"

The look intensified. "I say that, too, two times."

Jacob realized her expression was exactly the same you'd use on a dog who couldn't learn the simplest trick. "I'm sure you're aware, Belle, of the New York Emancipation Law which says that no child can be born a slave in New York after July 4, 1827, that all male slaves must be freed at age twenty-eight, all female slaves at age twenty-five, and that no slave can be sold outside the state. Clearly, selling your son was illegal. Now, who sold your son to Alabama? That is, who did you sue?"

Belle forcibly tapped her finger on the court document she had placed on VanCroft's desk. "It say on that writ Solomon Gedney."

"And he owned you, too?"

"Never!" snapped Belle. "I was owned by lots of families and mostly by Mr. Dumont. But Gedney never."

Thomas flipped pages in his journal, struggling to keep up.

Jacob VanCroft continued. "I presume, then, that Mr. Dumont set you free on Freedom Day in 1827?"

Belle shook her head. "No. I ran away in August, the year ahead of that."

VanCroft shot forward in his chair, his feet and legs flailing to hold his balance. He looked with new respect at the small woman before him. "A runaway slave dared to sue a white man in district court? Weren't you afraid of being found out? Weren't you afraid of being arrested?"

Belle said, "Dumont broke a promise to me. So I tell him I'm going to leave. After I ran, Quakers, Mr. and Mrs. VanWagener, buy me to make me free."

"Ah, the VanWagener's," nodded Jacob with a wide smile. "How are they? It's been five or six months since I've seen them. I assume they also helped you file your suit and sent you to me."

Belle nodded.

Jacob steepled his fingers and added, "Still, going to court after you ran away is a braver thing than I think I would have dared to do. Tell me, Belle, what happened in court?"

Belle shrugged. "I say what all happened. The judge nod. The jury nod. They give me a paper called that writ. I ask what I want with this paper? I say I got no use for paper. I say I only want my son. They say I win. But I got only this writ, no son."

And again she angrily tapped the printed document on VanCroft's desk.

Jacob nodded as he scanned the writ. "I see. The judge awarded you this summary writ demanding that this . . ." He quickly thumbed through the court papers for a name. ". . . this Solomon Gedney return your son to New York and, in light of his violation of New York law, bring him to court for a final hearing and disposition."

VanCroft scanned through several attached papers. "It also appears that the courts are a bit embarrassed to be ordering a white property owner around in the name of a runaway black slave, and have been lax in enforcing this writ. In fact, it appears they decided not to enforce it at all."

VanCroft smiled and neatened the stack of paper on his desk. "I can fix that. It all looks simple enough. I can have your son away from Gedney and free in twenty-four hours. Gedney admitted breaking the law. The case is quite clear."

He handed Belle a printed piece of paper. "If you would please read and sign this agreement retaining me as your lawyer."

Belle's eyebrows arched. Her mouth tightened. The look made Jacob feel like a misbehaving dog. "I can't read writing. But I can read people. You I trust. Gedney I don't."

VanCroft rose and motioned toward the door. "Very well, Belle. You go home and relax. I'll take care of everything."

As the door closed behind her, VanCroft turned to Thomas. "That is one brave woman, Thomas. No slave woman has *ever* filed suit against a white man in *any* court in this state—ever! And she's a runaway! White men have always beaten her and treated her worse than an animal. And still she dared face a white judge and jury to save her son."

He slowly shook his head and watched her walk proudly down Front Street. "Either Dumont or Gedney could have snatched her away to Alabama, and the court would have been thankful that they'd gotten rid of an embarrassing problem. Heck, if someone had shot her dead, the authorities wouldn't have done anything. And she's still willing to create a fuss in court."

Then he added, "That is one brave woman. If she wins—and I'm going to make sure she does—she will have led her people in a giant step forward in their fight to be real citizens of this country."

At three o'clock the next afternoon, Jacob VanCroft knocked on the Van-Wagener's door. His face was pinched with embarrassment. "Is Belle in there?" he called. "We have a problem."

Belle raced from the kitchen wiping her hands on a towel, her small eyes bulging. "What do you mean we got trouble?"

Jacob held up his hands to calm Belle and to protect himself from her boiling anger. "Nothing we can't handle, Belle. It's just that your son claims not to know you. The judge has called a hearing for tomorrow morning. I can't free him until then."

Belle's eyes seemed to bore straight through VanCroft. "What do you mean he be not knowing me? He is my son."

At nine-thirty the next morning a uniformed bailiff banged on the small desk before him and called, "All rise for his honor, Judge William Bailey of the District Court of the State of New York."

A dozen people sat scattered in small clusters throughout the eight rows of rough, wooden benches in the courtroom. In one corner of the room Solomon Gedney relaxed with arms smugly crossed next to his lawyer. Beyond this lawyer huddled a small, terrified-looking boy of five.

In the opposite corner Jacob VanCroft struggled to restrain Belle. "Don't go over to him, Belle. Wait for the hearing."

Angrily, Belle hissed, "Don't talk that to me. He is my son!"

At the bailiff's call, the several murmured conversations stopped. The people all shuffled to their feet. Bright morning sun streamed through five tall windows and splashed across the smooth plank floor.

A small side door opened for the judge. He mounted three steps to his raised seat. After reviewing the court papers, he turned to Belle. "Is that your son?" And he pointed at the boy cowering on the end of the bench.

Belle rose and solemnly nodded. "That is my Peter, my flesh-and-blood boy."

The judge turned to the boy. "Is this woman your mother?"

The boy wildly shook his head, wailed, "No! No! No!" and tried to crawl behind the bench away from both Belle and the judge.

Solomon Gedney sneered and chuckled, arms still crossed, feet still stretched out before him.

Puzzled, the judge turned back to Belle. "How long has it been since you've seen your son?"

"Two years, sir." she answered. Then she added. "But I know him for sure and always. That is my boy."

The judge shrugged. "You understand, I can't release the boy to you unless I am convinced it is really your son. Otherwise the boy will stay with Mr. Gedney.

"He is nobody's son but mine," begged Belle.

Solomon Gedney smiled and stretched confidently.

The judge thought for a moment, studying first Belle and then the trembling boy. "Bring the boy forward," he directed.

Gedney's lawyer dragged the wailing boy before the judge's raised bench. Judge Bailey rose, walked around to the front of his bench and squatted beside the frightened child.

The judge reached out to lay a hand on the boy's shoulder. The boy screamed in terror and flinched away. "Did anyone tell you to say that wasn't your mama?" asked the judge.

The boy stared silently, eyes big as walnuts, mouth trembling.

"Let me see the boy's back," said the judge.

Gedney bounded to his feet. "You got no call to do that, judge. I say he's not her child. She's lying. And you got no call to believe a slave over a property owner and law 'biding *voter* in this county."

The judge's face was set grim and hard. "Bailiff, remove his shirt." Then he turned to the boy. "Son, no one's going to hurt you here."

The child went rigid with fear as the bailiff gently pulled his ragged shirt over his head to reveal a mass of welts and gashes and the crisscross scars of almost constant beatings.

The judge sucked in his breath and turned to glare at Gedney, now leaning forward tensely. Softly he said, "Boy, did that man beat you and tell you to say this wasn't your mama? You answer me, boy, and tell the truth."

In a halting, timid voice reflecting a life of abuse, the boy whispered. "Yes, suh. He did."

"Is your name Peter, and is that woman really your mama?"

The boy's eyes shrank away in panic. "He'll beat me, suh."

"No, he won't," said the judge. "But you have to tell the truth."

The boy's eyes first dropped to the floor and then rose to gaze at Belle. "That's my mama, suh."

The judge stood and motioned for the bailiff to help Peter back into his shirt. Returning to his seat, the judge tapped his gavel. "Peter, you're free and can go with your mother."

Belle rushed forward and dropped to her knees, cradling her son in trembling arms, tears of joy streaming down her face.

Tiny five-year-old shoulders began to heave as the boy melted into his mother's arms. "I sorry, mama. But the man . . ."

"Shhh. Shhh," she cooed. "You're free and everything is fine." Gently Belle rocked her son back and forth on the courtroom floor, humming a sad, sweet lullaby near his ear.

Gedney fidgeted and bit his lip in humiliated and angry silence.

Jacob VanCroft rose. "Your honor. That man cruelly beat this child and should be punished by this court."

The judge glared at Gedney, slowly nodding his head. Then his jaw tightened, he sighed, and rapped his gavel. "This case is closed." He rose without another word and left the courtroom.

Solomon Gedney, a white man, was never charged or punished either for breaking New York law by selling a slave out-of-state, or for beating Peter. Many were outraged. Belle was not one of these. She didn't care what happened to Mr. Gedney. Her son was free.

Isabelle was the first freed slave woman to file a suit in a United States court of law. And she won. But Isabelle was just beginning. In 1841 she changed her name to Sojourner Truth. "Sojourner" because it means traveler, and she had decided to travel and lecture on behalf of slave's and women's rights. And "Truth," because she wanted everyone to always know exactly what she would tell.

Sojourner Truth was the first black woman to go on a lecture tour in a time when it was a rare thing for any woman to do. She was a tireless worker and charismatic speaker for abolition and for women's rights. She met with both

President Lincoln and President Grant in the White House, and was the only black woman to do so. But that is another story.

Questions to Explore

The Declaration of Independence says that all men are created equal. The Revolutionary War was fought to make all Americans free and equal. But do you think the founding fathers meant for *all* men and all *women* in this country to be free and equal?

What evidence can you find in the library to support your belief?

References for Further Reading

- *In the Children's Library*

Krass, Peter. *Sojourner Truth: Anti-slavery Activist.* New York: Chelsea House, 1988.

McKissick, Patricia. *Sojourner Truth: A Voice for Freedom.* Hillside, NJ: Enslow, 1992.

Ortez, Victoria. *Sojourner Truth: A Self-Made Woman.* New York: J. B. Lippincott, 1974.

- *In the Adult Library*

Bernard, Jacqueline. *Journey Toward Freedom.* New York: Feminist Press, 1967.

See your librarian for additional titles.

Property or Person?

A story about Elizabeth Cady Stanton, who began the women's suffrage movement

About This Story:

In the early 1800s American women could not own property or claim wealth; their husbands owned everything. When a woman married, all her possessions became the property of her husband. Women couldn't divorce as easily as men. Women couldn't hold elective office. Women couldn't vote. Women couldn't become the legal guardian of their own children. Women couldn't bring suit or appear as witnesses in a court of law. Women weren't supposed to travel alone. Women weren't allowed to give speeches in public. Women weren't allowed to go to college, and few were allowed more than the most basic education. Women weren't allowed to enter most professions. Teaching, childcare, and domestic work—sewing, laundry, and so on—were the only jobs open to women.

And yet early proponents of women's rights called for only minor adjustments to the laws and customs of the day. They dared request only the smallest possible steps in the direction of women's equality. It was not until the middle of the nineteenth century that an American woman called for major change in how the American legal and social systems treated women. When that first woman did, it created a shock wave that swept across the nation. This is a story about that woman.

For three long days out of New York, a screeching wind tore at the ship's top and mizzen sails, the only ones the captain dared leave up. Angry, black clouds boiled overhead like swirling fingerpaint. Monstrous, gray-green waves rose like mountains from the endless ocean depths and exploded over the bow of the *Montreal* as the sturdy ship lurched, shuddered, and rolled with each new pounding.

Thirty-three-year-old Henry Stanton, who had looked and felt so tall, bold, and dashing standing on the New York pier, now looked and felt like a shriveled, pale green lump. He lay, curled on his side on a narrow berth, hands pressed against his wretched, seasick stomach. Even after three days, his stomach wrenched and heaved with each roll of the ship. A sheen of cold sweat covered his pale face, a moan of agony escaped his lips.

What, Henry decided, made him feel worse was that his new bride, Elizabeth, felt not even a little seasick, and showed scant pity for those who were. The cabin door burst open and Elizabeth rushed in, bracing herself against the top bunk as the ship lurched heavily to starboard, her cheeks flushed bright red from the invigorating wind. Her brown curls and clothes were soaked from rain and lashing salt spray. A trail of puddles down the ship passageway marked her path.

"Henry, you really must come up on deck. It's so exciting!"

Henry crammed his eyes shut and groaned. Elizabeth shrugged. "You're missing the most incredible storm! This is a once-in-a-lifetime chance. Oh, well. Suit yourself."

And she was gone again, off to relish the adventure of a stormy sea.

On the fourth day, May 24, 1840, the North Atlantic magically flattened into a smooth carpet. A full complement of white sails billowed in the fresh breeze overhead.

Henry began to feel almost human again. He even felt strong enough for a moonlit stroll on rubbery legs around the deck.

The light of the quarter moon filtered down through the sails, splashing it's golden reflection like twinkling fairy lights off each gentle wave. This was a honeymoon cruise for Henry and his twenty-five-year-old bride. They paused near the bow, leaning on the railing. Henry, at six feet two inches, towered over Elizabeth, who stood only five three.

Elizabeth's face looked as soft as the moonlight. But, Henry realized, it also looked sad. Elizabeth's face always looked sad—pretty, but sad. Maybe it was her large, round, brown eyes that held the faraway look of deep sadness. Maybe it was the way her mouth turned down at the corners. Whatever it was, her face always held that look of secret sadness—even when she laughed, even when she was flushed with excitement, even when she teased and poked fun at him—all of which she did with great regularity.

Elizabeth hadn't really wanted to marry at all. Her father was a lawyer. Elizabeth had grown up reading his lawbooks and knew all too well the grim legal fate awaiting any woman foolish enough to marry. Long before she reached an age when young men seemed interesting, Elizabeth had decided that marriage looked little better than slavery, and that, if she got married, she would be more property than person.

Then Henry Stanton swept her away with his fiery words and passionate crusades against injustice. Here at last, she thought, was someone who understood. Henry allowed Elizabeth to omit the word "obey" from her wedding vows. She had also wanted to keep her own name (after all, slaves take on the name of their master, don't they?), but she decided that not promising to obey was as much of a social scandal and breech of convention as she dared.

And now they were on a grand honeymoon adventure to an international abolitionist convention in London. Henry was to be one of the American delegates.

A number of their fellow passengers also sailed to the London convention. Dinner and evening conversations were filled with passionate denouncements of every aspect of slavery. Elizabeth listened intently to each word. Her concern had always centered on the lack of legal rights for women in her father's lawbooks.

So Elizabeth was fascinated to hear speaker after speaker use the same words in their ringing calls for abolition that she used when thinking of the need for women's rights; "freedom," "rights," and "human decency." Those delegates expressed the same resentments for the people they were representing that she felt. Only each of these speakers was referring to American blacks not to American women and wives. Elizabeth's forehead wrinkled in concern. Why didn't anyone say that rights were rights, injustice was injustice, and a human being was a human being, without having to add the modifier "black" every time? Did these noble citizens consider injustice to women a lesser evil than injustice to blacks?

For the remainder of the ten-day crossing, the seas were calm, but Elizabeth's mind was troubled. In their rush to correct injustice to American blacks, was the world overlooking the fact that many of the same rights were also denied to American women?

Elizabeth and Henry woke early on the morning of June 12th, a rare brilliantly sunny day in London. After a hurried breakfast, they rushed to Freemasons' Hall for the opening session of the convention. Walking through the maze of narrow, twisting London streets, Elizabeth rehearsed her statements on the issues she felt most important, the points she most wanted to bring up.

Conventions in the 1800s weren't the planned list of presentations and speakers that we see at modern conventions. They more closely resembled open debates on a set topic, with delegate after delegate marching to the podium to argue their views before a final vote.

Shouts of greeting filled the early morning air as delegates jammed the lobby waiting for the three sets of double doors to the main lecture hall to open. At nine o'clock one of the doors creaked open and a tall, formally dressed man with a well-trimmed, pointed beard stepped out and raised his hands for quiet.

In a booming voice he welcomed the delegates and announced the schedule for the day. Elizabeth, unable to see through the forest of taller men and dying of curiosity, climbed onto a high-backed chair to count the number of women delegates.

Henry hissed at her to get down. Elizabeth smiled back, "I haven't finished counting." There was a sizable contingent of women. Surely women's issues and views would be well represented in the day's discussions.

As a final announcement the man said that, of course, women would not be permitted in the main lecture hall or to participate in any discussions, but that they could listen to the proceedings from behind a curtain screening off a back alcove of the main room.

Elizabeth felt a stab of icy cold. Outrage stuck in her throat like a chicken bone, and although she opened and re-opened her mouth, she was unable to voice her words of protest. Henry apologized, shrugged that there was nothing he could do, and told Elizabeth not to worry because it was for a good cause.

Flushed with fury, Elizabeth swept behind the curtain like an angry sea and plopped into a chair. All of her worst fears had been confirmed. Even to these men who had gathered specifically to fight injustice, women were not real people, only something to pile into a hidden corner like so much baggage.

Next to Elizabeth sat a middle-aged Quaker woman, every bit as calm as Elizabeth was agitated. "Thou are not pleased with the arrangements?" she asked in such a quiet voice that she might have been asking if Elizabeth wanted one or two lumps of sugar in her tea.

"I most certainly am not pleased," snapped Elizabeth. "I have half a mind to tear down this curtain and storm the stage!"

The woman smiled behind her plain, gray bonnet. "Thou wishes thou were a man?"

The question reminded Elizabeth of her childhood. "My father always wished I had been a boy. But instead, I always wished that being a girl could be different. That is still my wish."

"We should talk," said the woman extending her hand in greeting. "I am Lucretia Mott. Come. Let us leave and talk elsewhere."

"But the convention . . ." protested Elizabeth.

Lucretia looked sternly at her. "Why be here if we aren't respected and valued as equals? I am an elected delegate to this convention, but I am not allowed to speak or vote."

The two women slipped back out the double doors arm-in-arm just as the bearded man pounded his gavel on a podium for quiet. As they walked, the two women spoke of their dreams for equality. They shared their bitter complaints of injustice, their resentment at not being taken any more seriously than a child, and their loathing at not being allowed access to education and rewarding professions.

Elizabeth and Lucretia walked the same crooked, colorful streets that had thrilled Elizabeth just two hours before. On this walk, though, she didn't even notice them. Elizabeth was completely absorbed into her conversation with this thoughtful, intelligent woman who had so many more years of experience and struggle to share.

Glancing up, Elizabeth noticed they were passing the famed British Museum. "Let's go in," she suggested with characteristic enthusiasm. "I've always wanted to see this museum."

They started up the wide, stone stairs, but paused to finish one point in their discussion. At three o'clock that afternoon, they still sat on the museum steps, never having made it to the top.

"It's clear we can't wait for men to give us the rights and respect that are properly ours," exclaimed Elizabeth. "We have to take them. We have to organize and meet. We as women have to act, whether it's proper and legal or not."

Lucretia rose with her soft, powerful smile. "We will do exactly that, thou and I. I feel certain of it. But first we should get back to Freemasons' Hall. The convention may already be letting out."

Henry paced anxiously in front of the now-empty hall as Elizabeth and Lucretia rounded the corner. "Where have you been?" he exclaimed. "I was worried sick."

At their return to the hall, Elizabeth's resentment and anger returned, flashing in her brown eyes. "In the baggage section, hidden away out of sight in the back."

"I looked behind the curtain. You were not there either during the lunch break or after the day's close."

"I left with Lucretia Mott," answered Elizabeth, gesturing to Lucretia. "Lucretia, this is my husband, Henry Stanton."

"How could you leave? The conference is so uplifting, so positive. So much is happening to promote freedom."

Elizabeth snapped, "I didn't see any freedom happening inside Freemasons' Hall!"

Henry couldn't fathom his wife's bitter reaction. "I know it seems a bit unfair, but look at the good that's being done here."

Elizabeth planted her small feet, hands jammed onto her hips, eyes blazing. "I think it more important to look at the injustice and cruelty that's being done here."

The remainder of the four-day conference passed in strained silence for Elizabeth and Henry. She couldn't understand why he wouldn't champion women's rights with at least as much enthusiasm as he poured into the fight for the rights of American slaves. He couldn't understand why she refused to acknowledge and rejoice in the good being done for the abolition movement.

The next several years sped by for Elizabeth, filled with raising three small children and with setting up and managing new homes for the family—first in Boston and then in Seneca Falls, New York.

In May 1848, Lucretia Mott visited a cousin in Seneca Falls. Elizabeth rushed to see her friend.

"Thou and I have not yet organized our great meeting," said Lucretia, her soft smile twinkling from under a Quaker bonnet.

Elizabeth started to explain about how much time the children took and how busy she had been setting up their new houses. Then she stopped herself. Excuses weren't important. The convention was. "We'll have it here, this summer," she answered.

The women printed notices in area newspapers announcing a two-day convention on July 19th and 20th at Wesleyan Chapel in Seneca Falls, to discuss the civil and legal rights of women.

Elizabeth was to write a resolution describing the goals of their convention to be voted on by the delegates. Her mind constantly whirring with thoughts of what she should say in her resolution, she dove into house and family chores with an enthusiasm and passion she hadn't felt since 1840.

Approvingly noting the change, Henry said, "I think it's wonderful you're getting together with other women. Have you prepared any proposals to present and discuss?"

"Yes," answered Elizabeth without glancing up from editing her final draft. "I wrote a Declaration of Sentiments. It's modeled after the Declaration of Independence and lists our grievances and the rights we both deserve and demand."

Henry chuckled. "Pretty strong words, Elizabeth. Can I read this powerful declaration?"

Nervously Elizabeth slid her document across the table to her husband. He picked it up with a great show of mock seriousness, as he would a child's report. "Well, let's see what the women of America demand."

As Henry's eyes skimmed down the list of demanded rights, his smile first froze, and then faded to a look of shock and dismay. "What is this resolution number nine, Elizabeth?" he demanded. "It's absurd to demand the right to vote. It makes the whole document look ridiculous." He ranted and paced. She would be laughed at, he told her. *He* would be laughed at, for goodness sake. Mentioning women's suffrage was totally unacceptable and unfounded, he concluded, and that resolution would have to be crossed out.

"Women are people," answered Elizabeth. "Women work. Women pay taxes. Women raise our future leaders. It seems to me women deserve a say in the running of this country."

Flushed with anger, Henry wagged his finger in her face. "If you insist on reading that ridiculous proposal, I shall have to leave this town."

"Leave if you wish," said Elizabeth, her own anger beginning to rise.

Henry stormed away muttering that she was making a fool of herself, that no one would come to their silly meeting anyway, and that no other woman would risk angering her husband over a preposterous issue like women voting.

Henry was wrong.

In Albany, New York, twenty-seven-year-old Elouise Rafferty's husband refused to let her travel to Seneca Falls for the convention. So she lied, saying she was going to visit her sister, and, with trembling knees, boarded the train to Seneca Falls anyway.

In Elmira, New York, thiry-five-year-old Monica Hafford heard her husband yell, "If you leave for that convention, don't ever come back!" She let the screen door slam behind her as she marched down the front steps. Praying that her husband didn't really mean it, she mounted the carriage to Seneca Falls.

In Philadelphia, sixty-one-year-old Elizabeth Furman walked proudly down Dorchester Street as her husband yelled out the window that she was a crazy fool to waste her savings on a women's gossip session. For years the seamstress had saved one penny a week out of her wages for "something very special." Every penny of that money was clutched tight in a felt purse and would go toward her train ticket to Seneca Falls.

By foot, by horse, by carriage, and by train, women found a way to Seneca Falls. Meeting other delegates on the road, or outside the Wesleyan Chapel, fear and worry turned to exuberant joy, energy, and hope. With an electric tingle the women realized this meeting would be special. The very air that muggy July morning seemed charged and ready to explode.

Over 300 women crammed into Wesleyan Chapel. Elizabeth and Lucretia were overwhelmed. They had told each other they'd be happy with "twenty or so."

Lucretia welcomed the delegates. Then Elizabeth rose to present her "Declaration of Sentiments."

"We hold these truths to be self-evident," she began, "that all men and women are created equal . . ."

The crowd cheered.

She ended with her list of resolutions calling for the right to own property, the right to keep their own earnings, the right to be legal guardians of their own children, the right to equal pay for equal work, the right to higher education, the right to enter all trades and professions, the right to bring suit, the right to easier divorce, and, finally, she said, "Resolution number nine: We demand the right to be free as man is free, to be represented in the government we are taxed to support as man is represented. We demand our right to vote."

Elizabeth nervously gathered her pages and stood for a moment, waiting for the women to react. After each of the other resolutions Elizabeth had been interrupted by enthusiastic applause. After this last one the room sat in stunned silence, overwhelmed by hearing someone utter those words they hadn't even dared to dream.

Slowly at first, then faster and louder, gaining momentum like a speeding freight train, the applause and cheering rocked the chapel. For five minutes, ten minutes, it could not be stopped. Elizabeth had to take a dozen separate bows. The cheering lasted over half an hour before Lucretia could call for discussion.

Elizabeth Cady Stanton's Declaration of Sentiments passed unanimously in less than an hour and was signed by over 100 delegates.

On that hot July day the women's movement was born, and Elizabeth Cady Stanton was its mother. The struggle for the equality of American women began. It would be a long, costly struggle. Elizabeth was disowned by her father for pressing for the right to vote. She was ridiculed in newspapers and from pulpits.

In spite of this vilification, Elizabeth Cady Stanton led the women's suffrage movement for over forty years. More importantly, she made Americans aware of the basic injustice and inequity of the American system. She set in motion the forces that would eventually create and ratify the Nineteenth Amendment to the Constitution of the United States. Of course, that didn't happen until 1920, eighteen years after Elizabeth's death, and seventy-two years after she first demanded the right. But that's another story.

Questions to Explore

Elizabeth Cady Stanton found that women were not granted the same basic rights as men. Do you think women are treated equally today? What evidence can you find to support your position?

Most women still change their last name to their husband's when they marry. Many still promise to obey their husbands as part of their wedding vows. Do you think the fact that these things haven't changed is important?

Can you find things that have changed for women that you think are significant?

References for Further Reading

- *In the Children's Library*

  Peavy, Linda, and Ursula Smith. *Dreams into Deeds: Nine Women Who Dared.* New York: Charles Scribner's Sons, 1985.

  Gleiter, Jane, and Kathleen Thompson. *Elizabeth Cady Stanton.* Milwaukee, WI: Raintree Children's Books, 1988.

- *In the Adult Library*

  Forster, Margaret. *Significant Sisters: The Grassroots of Active Feminism.* New York: Oxford University Press, 1984.

  Dubois, Ellen, ed. *Elizabeth Cady Stanton and Susan B. Anthony: Correspondence, Writings, Speeches.* New York: Schocken Books, 1981.

See your librarian for additional titles.

Conductor on the Train

A story about Harriet Tubman and her work to free slaves

About This Story:

In the early nineteenth century, runaway slaves were savagely hunted across the South by a small army of slave catchers, each with a pack of hound dogs. Posted rewards of $75 to $100 per runaway were common. Still, thousands of slaves each year risked their lives on a desperate scramble through unknown and unfriendly country to reach the free states of the North, or the real safety of Canada.

Many bolted on their own. Many more were helped along by a courageous network called the "Underground Railroad." This railroad wasn't really a train, and it didn't go along a fixed route. It was made up of a network of people who provided hideouts where runaways could safely rest before heading out for the next house.

Safe houses along the various routes north were called "stations." Guides who led runaways from station to station were called "conductors."

Most conductors were white (often Quakers). If discovered, they risked prison, having their houses burned, even being killed by lynch mobs.

A few conductors were escaped slaves. These were the most hated beings in all the South. One escaped slave who returned south as a conductor freed over 300 slaves during nineteen separate trips up the railroad.

This conductor was often called "Moses," in reference to the biblical figure who led his people out of Egypt to freedom. A $40,000 reward was posted for Moses' capture. But she was never caught. Yes, she. This is a story about her.

It was Saturday, June 8, 1849. You could smell the coming rain still far off in the west. The Maryland afternoon dragged on, oppressively hot, as the slaves toiled and sang in the fields.

There's no rain to wet you,
Oh yes, I want to go home.
There's no sun to burn you,
Oh yes, I want to go home
Oh push along, believers,
Oh yes, I want to go home.

At six o'clock that evening, with the sun still blazing down through the haze, the overseer's horn blew. Quitting time. The slaves shuffled back toward the flimsy row of shacks that was their home.

As gnarled and callused hands stacked hoe and rake in the barn, black faces began to smile. Tomorrow was Sunday. There'd be no hoeing or weeding, no overseer's horn or whip, not for a whole day. But four of the blacks smiled a different kind of smile: the smile of hope mixed with heart-pounding fear.

Clouds piled up thick and black, hiding the sunset. At twilight the rain finally broke across Mr. Edward Brodas' plantation in Dorchester County, on the Eastern Shore of the Chesapeake. But the slaves never called him "Edward Brodas." Mostly they called him, "Master."

As pounding rain turned dust to mud around slave row, some people gathered to talk, some drifted toward sleep, and four waited anxiously. Around eleven o'clock, four figures stole, one by one, each from a different cabin. Each tiptoed out to the twisting pasture oak where Old Cudjoe used to tell them stories when they were children.

"Hatti, is that you?"

" 'Course it's me. You think it's the overseer?"

The overseer, armed with whip and gun ran the slaves and was the most feared white man on any plantation.

"William Henry. Robert. Are you both here, too?"

"Shhh. Keep your voice down, Benji! You don't go callin' out the names, takin' role like the overseer, when you runnin' away."

Twenty-eight-year-old Harriet Tubman, called "Hatti," or occasionally "Minta" by friends and family, rose and tied her sack of mattress ticking around her waist. She breathed in a deep, slow breath. "Corn's just startin' to really shoot up. But I do love the smell of this here cornfield." Then her face hardened. "And I never want to smell it again. Now let's go."

Benji held back, fidgeting under the oak. "Maybe we should wait, Hatti, and see what the mistress does, now that ole Massa Brodas died."

"Sell you down south—just like two of our sisters. That's what she'll do," Harriet snarled. "Now come on."

The life of a slave on a Maryland corn plantation was bad enough. But the threat of being sold, "down south," to a South Carolina, Georgia, Mississippi, or Alabama cotton plantation drove true terror into a slave's hearts. They had heard that slaves were treated with even more cruelty down south, and the work was harder. It seemed a far worse fate than death itself.

Robert eased over beside Benji. "How we gonna know which way we're goin' without the moon? It's a long way to freedom, Hatti. We make one slip we'll be caught for sure."

Harriet Tubman wasn't interested in cold feet at the start of her race to freedom. "I figure I get one of two rights: freedom or death. If I can't have the one, I'll take the other. But I won't live as a slave. Done that twenty-eight years. Won't do it no more."

William Henry, the oldest at thirty-four, tried to sound thoughtful instead of scared. "Maybe we haven't done enough plannin', Hatti. Maybe wait a couple more weeks to get the details down . . ."

Harriet spun around, planted both feet in the rich Maryland mud, and slammed both fists onto the hips of her short, thick body. Powerful arms and shoulders rippled in the dark. Her wide, plain face was set, hard and cold. Her glare was the most fierce they had ever seen. Even in a whisper her voice rang with power.

"We *got* to go tonight. It's Saturday. No fieldwork tomorrow, so no one will miss us till Monday. By then we'll be two nights north, way ahead of the slave catcher's dogs. I only told you 'bout this 'cause you're my brothers and I want you to be free with me. The only way we'll get caught is if we stand here jawing. Now move!"

The four started north single-file, groping through the black-as-ink night with no moon or stars to help them. An occasional streak of lightning silhouetted the four runaways against a tangled web of vines, bramble, and trees of the swampy woods on this Eastern Shore of the Chesapeake Bay. Rain swirled in thick sheets so it always seemed to blow straight into their faces no matter which way they turned their heads.

Feeling her brothers' courage ebbing, Harriet chuckled. "This surely is a perfect night for escapin'. Rain and mud make our tracks that much harder to follow."

For two long hours they tore their way through the woods. The three full-grown men stumbled, crying into tangled prickler vines, and crashed, groaning over roots and into the mud. Their sister walked in the lead, slow, steady, and quiet. "Shhhh back there. Why you boys makin' so much noise?"

"It's pitch black," hissed William Henry. "I can't see a thing."

"Didn't Daddy teach you how to walk through the woods?" Harriet whispered back.

"We were never allowed to spend time with Daddy, chopping logs for that builder like you were—Owww!" And William Henry flopped onto his face again. Benji tripped over him and sprawled into the blackness as well.

As they slowly picked themselves up, rubbing sore elbows and bleeding scrapes along their legs, Robert shielded his eyes from the driving rain and squinted into a grove of towering trees on their left. "Wait!" he commanded. "I've seen these trees and this spot already tonight. We're walking in circles! We haven't gone anywhere."

Benji began to whimper. "We're gonna get caught. I know it. We're gonna get caught and whipped or shot for sure."

Harriet scoffed, "I was first whipped when I was five for not carrying yarn fast enough. On my first day in the kitchen at six, Miss Susan snapped a rawhide strap across me four different times. By the time I was eight I had more whipping scars than sense. Whippin's don't scare me much. Death don't scare me at all. Living as a slave does. Now come on!"

Robert reached out, feeling for his sister in the night. "Hatti, we'll never make it, not in this weather. I'm going back."

"He's right," said William Henry still on his knees. "If we make it back before we're missed, we live to try again another day."

"Ain't no other days, and there ain't no goin' back," hissed Harriet. "You three move or die!"

Mud and rain streaming down their faces, all three men laughed. "What you gonna do, Hatti? Gonna stare us to death?"

Deadly serious again, Robert added, "We only get killed if we stay out here till we're seen."

"You gotta understand," begged Harriet. "This Quaker lady told me 'bout this Underground Railroad to freedom. She gave me a piece of paper that's got the name of a safe house, a station. We get there and we get whisked north on the train to a promised land. See, I know where that safe house is!"

William Henry reached out a hand, "Come on, Hatti. We're going back. We won't make any safe houses in a storm. Freedom's gonna have to wait. I'm sorry."

As she trudged south after her brothers, bitter frustration raged through Harriet. She muttered to herself, "Next time I'll have a gun. There won't be no quittin' and turning back then!"

It rained hard all Sunday to match Harriet's mood. On Monday she was horrified to see a familiar hoe slapped into her hands, to see her own feet march into the cornfield as if nothing out of the ordinary had happened. The corn smelled like bitter defeat.

Mid-afternoon Harriet's heart froze. Her stomach churned and her knees trembled. A wagon rode slow past the field. Three white men with rifles rode in the front. Four black men huddled in back, hands and feet bound by thick ropes, a wild, haunted look in their eyes. They were being sold off south!

All three of Harriet's brothers rode in that wagon. She struggled to breathe. She felt dizzy and faint, and sank to the clay she had just hoed. Her brothers, her family, gone! If only they hadn't turned around Saturday night.

Crack! The overseer's whip snapped across Harriet's back tearing through the thin material of her dress and leaving a stinging welt. "Back to work, you! No sitting down on my shift."

For the rest of the afternoon Harriet savagely ripped at the weeds between the long rows of corn as one word repeated in her mind. "Tonight. Tonight. Tonight!"

The overseer's horn blew as the sun dipped below western treetops. Harriet raced to her cabin. John Tubman, her husband, wasn't there.

"Good," thought Harriet. John was a blacksmith's assistant and had an easy life here. He couldn't be trusted. He'd never risk his comfort for freedom. Harriet had never so much as mentioned her escape plan to her husband.

With trembling fingers she snatched the ticking bag from under the bed. In it she stuffed the meager possessions she would need: a week's food, the few coins they had saved, and John's sharp hunting knife. Kicking off her tattered, worn shoes, she slipped her feet into his fine, new high-top leather boots.

Harriet wiggled her toes and grinned, "Won't he be mad now!"

Tying the bag around her waist, Harriet cautiously eased along the shacks of slave row and past the open backdoor of the main house. Inside, her sister busily chopped vegetables for the Brodas' dinner. Harriet had to tell somebody she was running away so the rest of her family wouldn't think she'd been sold down south or stolen.

Softly she began to sing, the one thing slaves could do without arousing suspicion.

When that old chariot comes,
I'm bound for the promised land.
Friends I'm going to leave you,
I'm bound for the promised land.

Harriet's sister turned, mouth dropped open, and stared in mid-chop. Thwack! A leather strap snapped down across her hands. She jumped and, head down, returned to her chopping.

Harriet stole into the woods, locked her eyes on the North Star, and started north and east, a giddy energy in every step.

The Quaker lady told her to swing wide around the busy harbor town of Cambridge, pick up the Choptank River, and follow it north to it's source. Then break cross-country north by northeast for twenty miles to Camden and seek Ezekiel Hunn's house. He'd direct her from there.

Harriet forced her way through tangled woods, then open marsh, then dense swamp, and then brambled woods again, past the village of Bucktown and north toward the Choptank River. Briars tore at her legs. Thorny vines clawed at her hair and arms. Harriet scarcely noticed and certainly didn't care. She felt as if she soared high above all barriers and worries. She felt free!

Crickets chirped in time with her footsteps, like army drummers to speed her on her way. In the reeds and cattails, bullfrogs sang a marching tune to cheer her as she passed. Night birds added the melody to her sweet freedom song. Her mouth silently formed the words,

When that old chariot comes,
I'm bound for the promised land.
Friends I'm going to leave you,
I'm bound for the promised land.

Why had she waited twenty-eight long years to snatch delicious freedom? Every human deserved a long, satisfying drink of this sweet nectar called freedom.

Then a lone weight dropped on her heart to dim her joy. Her brothers were still in chains, heading south. Her parents were old and might die as slaves without knowing freedom. "I'll come back for them, one and all," Harriet vowed to the swamp around her.

Dawn streaked the eastern sky. Harriet's dress was torn and tattered. Her sack of food was soggy with swamp and creek water. Her arms and legs had been rubbed raw by the tangled miles she had struggled through. Thick mud covered her boots and lower legs.

By noon Harriet reached the wide Choptank River and found a sheltered thicket where she could rest and eat.

"The alarm'll be for me sure. Floppy-eared huntin' dogs'll be whoofin' and sniffin'."

Her heart leapt at the soft snort of a nearby horse. She heard the sharp clomp of hooves over pebbles in the rough road along the river. She heard a voice. "Whoa. Hold up, boys. Let's stop in this clearing for a bite to eat."

Harriet's heart raced. Were they slavecatchers? Did they have dogs prowling the woods? Were they after her? She froze, still as stone, afraid to breathe as these four men dismounted and dragged food sacks out of bulging saddlebags. One by one they dropped into the shade, not more than twenty feet from Harriet.

Slowly, oh, so slowly, one hand inched toward her ticking sack. Inch by inch that hand eased noiselessly inside and felt for John's long hunting knife. She clutched the handle so hard her knuckles turned white as she thought, *If I don't get freedom, I'll die fightin'. But I won't be a slave.*

The men flopped back against tree trunks, eating dried beef and bread, sipping water, and lazily talking.

"We only got notices on four runaways to search for, John?"

"No. Five. New one came up from Dorchester County early this morning. Female. Short. Big scar and dent over her right eye."

Harriet's hand silently lifted to the long scar and dent just over her right eyebrow. Her eyes opened wider. Her heart sped up again. *They are hunters. And lookin' for me!*

"Oh, and the notice said she's supposed to be tough and feisty."

The four men laughed as Harriet glowed with pride and her chest swelled. She thought, *You just come into this here thicket and find out how feisty!*

As the men stretched and remounted their horses, the leader said, "That new one won't be this far north yet. We'll ride down nearer to Cambridge and break out the dogs."

Their hoofbeats scarcely faded into the south before Harriet bolted across the road and plunged into the Choptank River. "Dogs can't follow through water."

For a day and a half she waded, splashed, and paddled up the ever-narrowing Choptank. Harriet tripped over a submerged branch and crashed headlong into the shallow water for the tenth time that day, soaking her food pack. Bounding back to her tired feet, she slapped the water surface. "This is the awfulest railroad in the world! Where's my coach seat so I can put my feet up an' ride in comfort? Where's the engineer to do all the work? Where's the conductor?"

Then she smiled at herself. None of that mattered. This Underground Railroad might lack comforts, but it rode straight to freedom.

By midnight of the second day the Choptank shrank to little more than a muddy trickle. Again Harriet locked her sights on the North Star as her father taught her to do. Wringing out the hem of her dress, she repeated the Quaker lady's directions. "Twenty miles north by northeast to Camden and find Ezekiel Hunn."

As the first deep blues edged into the eastern sky next morning, Harriet saw the lights from clusters of houses up ahead. "Careful girl," she muttered to herself. "Most folks up there just as soon shoot you as help you spit."

She crept closer to these first outskirts of Camden, staying deep in the cover of thick woods. Two ramshackle cabins stood well apart from the other houses leading toward town. Harriet nodded to herself. Only black folks would live in those houses.

Summoning all her courage, Harriet crept to the first cabin and knocked softly. Silence. She knocked again, still too scared to make much noise. She heard the soft shuffle of feet. A voice whispered, "Who dat?" It was the voice of a black person.

"I'm Harriet Tubman. You know Massa Ezekiel Hunn?"

After a long pause the voice through the door whispered, "Who wants to know?"

"I done told you my name," hissed Harriet. "This Quaker lady sent me."

The door unbolted and swung open. "Almost every black in this town knows Ezekiel Hunn. But don't you call him 'massa.' He says he is not massa to anyone. He's a good man. I'll show you his house."

Twenty minutes later, a tall, elderly white man in a black coat said, "Thou lookst tired. Come in and rest while I get thee breakfast."

A sense of peace and gratitude washed over Harriet. She had found the station house. She was on her way up the railroad to the promised land. That land, however, gave escaped slaves a cold and hard welcome. Harriet traded a slave's cabin for a run-down one room tenement flat and a hotel cook's job working twelve hour days.

But Harriet Tubman did not fight her way to freedom just to work in a hotel. Through the Philadelphia Vigilance Committee, a group that ran part of the Underground Railroad, Harriet volunteered to become a conductor, or guide, for groups of slaves struggling north. When the committee said, no, it was too dangerous, Harriet simply demanded to go.

Harriet Tubman guided nineteen groups of slaves from safe house to safe house up the Underground Railroad, leading over 300 slaves to freedom. Both numbers are records. A reward of $40,000 was offered for her capture, dead or alive. Still she continued her trips. During her daring raids, she freed three brothers, two sisters, and both parents, even though they were too old and frail to walk and had to be carried most of the way on stretchers and in carts.

In 1858, Harriet Tubman began to make speeches to overflowing crowds around the North decrying the terrible ills of slavery. When the Civil War started in 1861, she volunteered as both nurse and spy. When slavery ended along with the war, Harriet picked up the cause of women's rights, and was a powerful and popular speaker for the suffragists.

Harriet Tubman died in Auburn, New York, in 1913. A year later a stone tablet in her honor was dedicated by the city. Even the U.S. Postal Service joined the long parade honoring Harriet, releasing a stamp in her honor on the opening day of the first Black History Month. But that's another story.

Questions to Explore

Why did some white people risk their homes, livelihoods, and lives trying to free slaves?

Who are the Quakers?

What do the songs of the slaves say about the people who sang them?

References for Further Reading

- *In the Children's Library*

  Sterling, Dorothy. *The Story of Harriet Tubman: Freedom Train.* New York: Scholastic, 1987.

  Carlson, Judy. *Harriet Tubman: Call to Freedom.* New York: Fawcett Columbine, 1989.

  Smith, Kathie, and Pamela Bradbury. *Harriet Tubman.* New York: Simon & Schuster, 1989.

  Elish, Dan. *Harriet Tubman and the Underground Railroad.* Brookfield, CN: Millbrook Press, 1993.

- *In the Adult Library*

  Petry, Ann. *Harriet Tubman: Conductor on the Underground Train.* New York: Archway, 1955.

See your librarian for additional titles.

Not Our Way

A story about Sarah Winnemucca, a spokesperson for Indian rights

About This Story:

In the late nineteenth century many Native American tribes were caught between a deadly rock and a hard place. On one hand, they were losing the struggle to hold to traditional patterns of life and fight the flood of white settlers from the East. On the other, they didn't want to give in to the pressure to take up white ways, for this meant the loss of tribal identity and tradition.

The United States government forced Indian tribes onto reservations and stole their land to make room for the white settlers. But the Indians were forced onto the worst land in the West, and most tribes couldn't survive on the alien, harsh reservation lands. It seemed all options led to destruction of the Native American heritage and way of life, if not the very people themselves.

But some Native Americans saw other alternatives for their tribes. One Paiute woman found another option for her people, one that used the white man's ways and processes to preserve Indian rights and dignity. She became a principal spokesperson for the Northern Paiute Indians and an important advocate of Indian rights. This is a story about her.

In 1864 Geronimo was still a young man and had not begun his war against the United States. George Armstrong Custer was still a colonel fighting the Civil War. He would not reach Montana's Little Big Horn for twelve more years. The wars between Plains Indians and white settlers were just heating up. The massacre at Wounded Knee was still twenty-six years in the future.

By 1864 Native American tribes had been at war with white immigrants for 200 years. But Indian nations were isolated from each other. Word of what befell the Mohawk and Cherokee tribes in the East never reached the Plains Indians. The continuous disregard by white people for the rights of Plains Indians was not learned of by the tribes living in Nevada and California.

So each tribe met white immigrants with a clean slate and no reason to fear or distrust them. Some tribes soon resisted white invasion and fought. Some struggled to maintain peace. None worked harder for peaceful relations that the Northern Paiute (PI-yute) who lived in the mountains of western Nevada. They saw their first white trappers in the 1820s, saw their first wagon train creep toward California in the 1840s, and saw their first white town in the 1846.

Then the California gold rush of 1849 increased the trickle of immigrants to a flood. Nevada silver strikes brought a second wave. Migrating Paiute bands were slowly pushed out of more and more of their traditional territory. Those few groups who fought, died at the hands of the U.S. Cavalry. All bands of Paiute Indians struggled to create new schemes for survival. In 1864 Winnemucca (Win-nee-MUCK-a), chief of the Northern Paiute, thought of a novel solution.

• • •

"Five minutes! Five minutes to Act Two!"

The stage manager cupped his hands to his mouth as he wormed his way down the crowded backstage hallway. "Five minutes!" Stagehands wheeled racks of costumes out for the tableaus of the second act. Others dragged heavy backdrops and boxes of props.

Some of the Paiute performers lounging on the hallway floor glanced at the small, balding stage manager and his beet-red face and laughed. Some ignored the man all together and continued their excited conversations.

"I said, 'Five minutes!' " he repeated at the top of his lungs. Mopping his face from heat and frustration he muttered, "Do any of these savages understand bloody English?"

"No. Many do not," replied one of the two female performers in the Paiute touring show. "But they are all eager for the second act and will be ready."

The young woman was the twenty-year-old, slender daughter of the Paiute chief, Old Winnemucca. Her face featured the strong, straight nose; wide mouth; and sad, dark eyes typical of her tribe. The sadness of her eyes was more noticeable because she was the only performer not celebrating the happy rush of a successful First Act.

"Sarah, why do you look so sad?" asked her proud, aging father, dressed in elaborate ceremonial costume and tall top hat for the opening scene of Act Two. "Everyone else is having a wonderful time. Our white brothers seem to love us and our show."

Sarah Winnemucca gazed into her father's wrinkled face and clear, bright eyes. "I have said it before, Father, both to you and to my grandfather, Captain Truckee. But never have I felt it more deeply. This . . ." Sarah gestured around the crowded backstage. "We should not be here. This is not our way. This is the white man's way."

The billboard out front of the Metropolitan Theater on San Francisco's Montgomery Street all week had read, "Saturday, October 22, 1864, Winnemucca, Chief of the Paiute, accompanied by his two daughters and eight braves will appear in a series of tableaus, dances, and songs depicting authentic Indian life."

A sellout crowd had gathered as the band of Paiute paraded down Kearny and Montgomery Streets in buckskin and bright feather headdresses, faces and chests streaked with bright vermilion and ocher paint. Chief Winnemucca rode on a splendid pinto pony, brass and gold epaulets on his shoulders, a crown of feathers sprouting from his head.

Only Sarah felt ridiculous as the sidewalk crowd whooped and cheered. Only Sarah felt embarrassed as Old Chief Winnemucca opened the show talking of the friendship between Paiute and white. Only Sarah felt foolish as she and her sister sang and as painted warriors danced and strutted, looking here on this wooden stage nothing at all like Paiute dancing their sacred dances at their camp along the shores of Pyramid Lake.

Winnemucca gently patted his daughter's shoulder. "This show is important for our people, Sarah, and is not just for entertainment—although I think it is going very well, don't you? And it's getting many ovations. Did you see how their hearts warmed to my opening speech?"

Winnemucca caught his runaway enthusiasm and forced himself to become serious. "We are here to save our people, Sarah. We have never been a rich and powerful nation. But we have always lived peaceful and content, in harmony with our land and our animal brothers, and with the whites, when they came. But now we must share some of the best pine nut gathering areas with Nevada silver mines, the best hunting grounds with white cattle ranchers, and the best lakes and streams with white settlements and farms. Food and blankets are scarce for our people. Starvation rides with our camps, circling closer every day.

"To survive we need white man's money to buy food and blankets. These performances should get us money enough to feed our people through the winter. That is why we are here, daughter."

Sarah struggled to find the right words. She didn't want to hurt her father or crush his enthusiasm. She also knew it was not right for a Paiute to feel ridiculous. The Paiute people were proud; no Paiute should have to feel this way.

Winnemucca shook his flowing white hair and raised his hands. "The second act is even better than the first, Sarah. You will see."

He returned to the curtain, leaving Sarah with a deeper sadness and a sense of bitter frustration. "We must find a way to survive that is *our* way, father," she whispered. But no one listened in the rush to get ready for the opening of Act Two, the Council War Dance.

Sarah thought back over the many times she had thought those words, "Not our way," and her resentment at being pushed into the white man's world. The first time had been almost fifteen years ago, when Sarah was only six.

It had been August, 1850. A line of thirty Paiute ponies had walked the winding emigrant trail through shimmering high desert heat toward the Carson River in what is now western Nevada, south and east of Lake Tahoe. The line snaked past broken and abandoned wagons, bleaching like ancient bones in the blistering sun; past discarded boxes, sacks, and bags; and past a steady trail of other discarded junk that marked the arrival of white settlers where once only bands of Paiute had wandered. Hurriedly assembled wagon trains had streamed down this trail all summer racing for the great gold strike in California.

Twenty-nine of the ponies carried a solitary rider. On the other pony rode a thirteen-year-old Paiute boy and his six-year-old sister. The boy called toward the front of the line, "Sarah's crying again."

Captain Truckee, Paiute Indian guide and leader of this small band, sighed, shook his head, and raised his hand for a stop. He turned his horse and trotted back to where the two children sat on their pony. "What's the matter now, Sarah?"

Huge, salty tears streamed out of round eyes and down the little girl's face. Her straight, black hair was tied back with a leather strap. She sobbed, "The white cannibal owls will eat me! And my name is Thocmetony (THOCK-me-TOE-nee), not Sarah."

Captain Truckee raised both his hands to the sky in frustration. Many of the others chuckled at the girl's silly fears. "Our white brothers are our friends. They will not harm anyone. *I* am the one who said they look like owls because of their beards and light colored eyes. But they are not the cannibal owls you've heard of in children's stories." His brown face, wrinkled from years of desert winds and sun, softened. "Sarah is a good name for you, my child. It will help you get along in our white brother's world. Besides, I think it means, 'Shell Flower,' just like your Paiute name, Thocmetony."

Thocmetony momentarily stopped her crying. "It does?"

Captain Truckee reached out a wrinkled, brown hand and tenderly patted the girl's shoulder. "Sarah, there is so much we can learn from following the whites. You have already seen how much better their rifles, that some call 'fire sticks,' are than our bow and arrow. Wait until you see the fabulous clothes they wear, and their houses. In white man towns food is plentiful, and they build houses that float on the water and talk, making even a greater noise than you."

Sarah and most of the others laughed at the silly picture of a talking, floating house. Then her lip began to quiver again. "But look, Grandfather, they even ate their wagons and left the bones here to die."

Captain Truckee tipped back his head and let out a great belly laugh. "That wagon just broke, Sarah. So they had to leave it here. No one eats wagons."

He started to ride back to the head of his band, then stopped. "Sarah, the white man even has a magic thing called 'writing.' One speaks his thoughts onto a rag called 'paper.' Then another white man many miles away and days later looks at the rag and knows the thoughts of the first. I have one of these papers."

Proudly he reached into a pouch and lifted out a folded paper. "I got this from General Fremont in California. I call it my 'rag friend.' When I show it to whites they all smile and give me gifts. Come. You will see that I am right."

With a wave of his hand, Truckee re-started the band toward the white settlement of Genoa, near what is now the California-Nevada border.

"This is not our way," whispered Sarah through her weeping.

Sarah's thirteen-year-old brother, Tom, hissed, "Stop your crying. You embarrass us."

Sarah choked down a sob, and held her breath to lock away her tears. But she couldn't help remembering a vision the medicine man had shared with her during last fall's annual pine nut hunt.

One morning he asked Thocmetony to stay behind as the others streamed out to gather nuts. When they were alone, he asked her to sit by the fire with him and said, "In a vision I have seen that the white man will not destroy all our people. Their guns and diseases will kill many, but not all. What will kill us all is white man's ways. We will need a safe place where we can protect our ways. But I cannot see the way to this safe place. I have tried, but I cannot." He paused, gazing at Thocmetony and added, "Someone must find the way to that place or we will vanish. In my vision that someone was you."

Still confused and unsure, six-year-old Sarah cringed and dug her fingers into her brother's back as they neared the small, dingy town of Genoa along the Carson River. She trembled, eyes closed as the white people gathered outside a dusty honky-tonk saloon to stare at the Indians. When she cautiously peeked at them, the faces she saw were all pasty white and sick looking. Worse, they looked fierce and filled with scorn. Sarah squeezed her eyes shut again.

Then Sarah heard the whites laugh and cheer as Grandfather Truckee talked in the white language. She heard him unfold his rag friend and show it to the whites. Sarah listened to the murmurs of approval. But could not understand the white words she heard.

"What's that Injun got, a letter?"

"It's from General Fremont in Californee. Says this here Injun was a big help during the Bear Flag Rebellion that freed Californee from Mexico. Says whoever reads the letter should thank him and help him."

"Well, I'll be . . ."

Now the whites all cheered, and scrambled to fetch gifts for the Paiute band. Sacks of flour, shirts, dresses were passed out to all. A woman tried to shove a bright calico dress into Sarah's clenched fists. Sarah, eyes still squeezed shut, was too frightened to grasp the cotton dress and let it flutter to the dirt.

Back on the trail leading up over the Sierra Mountains, Captain Truckee dropped back to ride beside Tom and Sarah. "Sarah, you acted very badly in Genoa. Those whites are our friends and brothers. Learn to act and think like them."

With dark, sad eyes the girl said, "My name is Thocmetony, Grandfather."

Now, twenty-eight-year-old Tom squatted next to his sister in the backstage hallway of the San Francisco theatre. "You look a million miles away, Sis."

Sarah jumped at being pulled from her memories. "I was remembering something important."

Then he saw how unhappy she looked. "What's wrong, Sarah? What memory makes you so sad?"

"Do you remember the Coyote stories we enjoyed so much as children?" she asked.

"I love Coyote stories," laughed Tom. "They're funny."

Sarah nodded solemnly. "I remember several stories where Coyote pretended to be something he was not. Once he pretended to be a bird and almost convinced everyone he could fly. He looked and acted ridiculous, and we all laughed."

Tom laughed at the memory. "But why does remembering a funny story make you sad?"

"Because tonight we look more ridiculous than Coyote, pretending to be something we are not."

Tom reached out to hold his sister's hand. "Sarah, we need the money to buy food."

"We need to preserve our ways. We need to live as Paiute."

"What good are our ways without food for our bellies?" scoffed Tom.

"What good are *we* without our ways?" asked Sarah.

Tom huffed and rose. "The whites live better than we do. Maybe we should all live as whites."

"White ways are powerful ways and may be good for whites," answered Sarah. "But they will destroy *us*. We must preserve our own ways."

"You sound like an old worrywart," snapped Tom. "I plan to enjoy the Coyote Dance and the 'Scalping of a Prisoner' tableau!" And he stomped toward the curtain.

"One minute!" shouted the exasperated stage manager. "Places everyone! Someone get these ignorant savages ready! One minute!"

Sarah sat, frozen in confusion. Were her grandfather, father, and brother right? Should they all adopt white ways? Or was the old medicine man right? The medicine man had been right about white man's diseases. Typhus had first struck during the winter and spring when Thocmetony was seven. She lost six aunts and three uncles. Only one of all of Thocmetony's cousins was still alive. Fall gatherings that used to number in the thousands, now found fewer than a hundred in camp.

But then her grandfather had been right about the wonders of the white man's cities. Down the western slopes of the Sierra Mountains and onto the grassy plain beyond, Captain Truckee led his band into the bustling, bulging town of Stockton, California. Even Sarah had to gape and stare at the long rows of tall buildings and stores, at the wide, smooth streets and at the great crowds of whites dashing everywhere, back and forth, up and down. She had been unable to resist feeling the strange, red building material called brick.

Even Sarah squealed in wonder at the sight of three houses stacked on top of one another with stairs climbing to the top two houses, or floors. Even Sarah couldn't keep her eyes off the plumes, frills, bustles, layers, and colors of clothes white women wore. It was as if each one tried to stand out brighter than a rainbow by wearing every color in the world. Even Sarah clapped with glee when a huge floating house called a steamboat paddled up the river and yelled at them with a great blast on its horn.

Who was right? What way should the Paiute follow?

As the theater owner announced the return of the wild savages from Nevada for the second act of their authentic tribal performance, an answer formed from the confusing mist swirling in Sarah's head.

She rushed to her brother's side, her face radiating joy and energy. She felt a great weight had been lifted as she stretched onto her tiptoes and whispered, "I know the way to the safe place the medicine man told me to find. But the 'way' is not a trail, or path through the mountains."

As the curtain rose and gas lamps around the stage brightened, Old Winnemucca strode proudly before the audience. Tom hissed, "Shhh! The show's starting." Then he glanced at his sister. "What 'way'?"

"Now I see that we cannot protect our way of life by hiding from the whites," said Sarah. "The whites will always come to where we are. We cannot protect ourselves by hiding. *But* the white man's ways are powerful enough to protect our ways. We must use the laws and rules of the white man to enforce our rights and defend the ways of the Paiute. I have lived with the whites almost all my life. I know their ways and can use them."

Old Winnemucca bowed to the thunderous applause and tipped his top hat as he introduced the "War Council Dance."

Backstage Sarah finally smiled. "I will not be part of this Coyote pretending, my brother. This will not save our people. I will return to Nevada and study white laws until I find the ones that will protect our ways."

For the next twenty-five years Sarah Winnemucca acted as a primary advocate for the rights of the Paiute and other Indian tribes. She became the voice of the Indian and very skillfully maneuvered the power of the American legal and political system to act on behalf of the tribes she represented. She lobbied governors, senators and congressmen. She met with President Rutherford Hayes.

She negotiated with representatives of major governmental departments. She argued reservation boundaries and treaty rights with the Department of the Army.

And she succeeded far better than any agent for, or representative of, an Indian tribe had before. She secured reservations in the traditional homelands of the Paiute, rather than in Oregon and Arizona deserts as the government wanted. She enlarged reservation boundaries to include lakes and forests the Paiute needed in order to survive. She secured repeated government guarantees protecting the lands and rights of her people.

Fighting alone in a foreign world, brave Sarah Winnemucca successfully demanded that Indians be treated as human beings with dignity and respect. While her people did not fare well in the hands of white Americans through the late nineteenth and early twentieth centuries, they fared far better than other western tribes. But that is another story.

Questions to Explore

What "rights" did Indians want to preserve as whites pushed farther and farther into traditional Indian lands? Where do those "rights" come from? Have all people claimed and demanded similar "rights?" Have all people been given those rights?

What factors led white people to take the lands of the Indians?

How honest has our government been in dealing with Native Americans?

References for Further Reading

- *In the Children's Library*

    Morrow, Mary. *Sarah Winnemucca.* Milwaukee, WI: Raintree, 1990.

- *In the Adult Library*

    Canfield, Gae W. *Sarah Winnemucca of the Northern Paiutes.* Norman, OK: University of Oklahoma Press, 1983.

See your librarian for additional titles.

The Right Dress

A story about Amelia Bloomer and her work for women's rights

About This Story:

The emerging call for women's rights during the nineteenth century in America was a complex and multi-faceted cry. For some, the cornerstone was temperance (or outlawing alcohol), because drinking by men caused most domestic violence and squandered paychecks, depriving women and children of needed support. For some, the place to start was with education for women. Some claimed it was with a demand for equal pay for equal work, and with improved job and career opportunities. For others, the women's vote (suffrage) was the key. Some wanted to attack unfair laws that kept women from owning property or from divorcing unjust husbands, and which gave all a woman's property and income to her husband.

But there were still others who felt that women would never win any of these basic rights as long as they wore the ridiculously confining clothes they were expected to wear during the mid- and late-1800s. This theory held that as long as society demanded women wear clothes that made them physically helpless and unable to move as easily as men, they would never be taken seriously enough to gain any social or political rights.

Amelia Bloomer was not an early advocate of this theory even though she was a champion of women's rights in general. Still, of all the valiant and beneficial contributions she made for the cause of women's rights, it is the fight to allow women to wear practical and comfortable clothing that made her famous, and for which she is best remembered. This is a story about Amelia Bloomer, the fashion that took her name, and the woman who created it.

May was always a pleasant month in the upstate New York town of Seneca Falls. The emerging green of grass and leaf, and the spreading buds, blossoms, and flowers reassured the town that the warmth they felt could no longer be snatched away by a late-season snow. The deep heat of summer that would make people fondly think of falling snow as "invigorating" and "refreshing" was still months away.

May was a time for everyone to venture out. And that's why Amelia Bloomer liked May so much. Her post office was always full of pleasant conversation in May. During the sweltering days of August, and again in the bitter, frozen dark of January and February, folks looked for any excuse to avoid a trip to the post office. But in May, they'd go out of their way to stop in and chat, even if they knew perfectly well there were no letters waiting in their pigeonhole slots along the post office wall.

Amelia had taken the job as deputy postmaster not because she was dedicated to the postal service. Rather, she snatched the position as a practical demonstration of a woman's right to occupy any job she was able to do, and to show that she was perfectly capable of performing the job as well or better than any man. Amelia's real love was her monthly newspaper, the *Lily*, the first paper in the country dedicated to promoting women's causes and issues. However, it *was* mighty convenient for her to be at the post office to collect incoming information for the *Lily*, and to mail outgoing copies of each issue.

It was May, 1851, and the day had bloomed bright as apple blossoms. Amelia Bloomer, a short, pleasant woman, sat on a tall stool behind her counter, her tightly curled, black hair and clear blue eyes shining out at the gathered crowd of strollers. Amelia was thirty-two and in the prime of her energetic and productive life.

As did all respectable women of the day, Amelia wore long underwear trimmed with lace; a stiff petticoat that stood out like a bell; a flannel padded petticoat with a scalloped hem; a second flannel petticoat over that; a plain, white, heavily starched petticoat; a fancy white scalloped and embroidered petticoat; and finally, a huge, heavy skirt that reached to the ground, jokingly called a "street sweeper." All of these layers combined often weighed more than fifteen pounds.

Around her middle Amelia wore a rigid corset of whalebone stays, or slats. Every woman who could afford a corset wore one. It was far more than a fashion. It was the expected dress of all decent women.

Each morning this corset was cinched painfully tight to make Amelia's waist look fashionably tiny, like a wasp waist—or at least considerably smaller than nature had intended or provided. Over the corset and under her dress she wore a camisole to protect her dress from snagging on the whalebone stays.

Unfortunately, nothing protected Amelia, or any other woman, from the rigid stays that gouged painfully into her ribs and sides and pressed against her kidneys and stomach. It was always hard to breathe under a corset, so hard physical exertion was impossible—even though women were generally responsible for housework, cooking, gardening, and child care.

Still, Amelia and virtually every other woman in Seneca Falls had worn this outfit all their adult lives, and they were used to it by now.

It was during an afternoon lull in the social buzz of the post office that the small bell mounted over the front door rang and two women entered. One was a good friend and neighbor, Elizabeth Cady Stanton, one of the founders of the women's suffrage movement. The other woman Amelia did not know.

As the two women entered, Amelia's mouth dropped open, and she stared, her hand frozen halfway through sliding a letter into a top row slot. Elizabeth Stanton nodded as they approached the counter. "Good afternoon, Amelia. Isn't the weather lovely this time of year?"

Amelia held up one hand to stop her words. "Pleasantries and chitchat can wait, Elizabeth. Tell me what you're wearing."

Thirty-five-year-old Elizabeth Stanton smiled broadly. "Ahhh, I thought you'd be interested. Let me introduce my cousin, Elizabeth Miller. What you see is her creation. She should explain."

Twenty-six-year-old Elizabeth Miller smiled sweetly through the long, chestnut ringlets that cascaded down around her face. "Call me Lizzy," she said, extending her hand to Amelia. She paused for a moment gathering her thoughts. "Where to start? Well, like most women, I suppose, my figure's not quite what it ought to be. I'm very flat-chested, so I've always had to cinch my corset tightly to create the proper proportions."

As she said this, Lizzy twirled slightly, better showing her outfit of a short skirt falling a few inches below her knee and over loose-fitting Turkish pants gathered around each ankle. Neither woman wore the customary corset or layers of stiff and heavy petticoats.

"I suppose there are two specific events that inspired what you see us wearing today," continued Elizabeth Miller. "The first occurred in my garden earlier this spring. It was hard for me to breathe as I worked because of painful bruises on my ribs from the tight stays. Worse, I found they jabbed fiercely into my back when I tried to reach up to a fruit tree, and into my front when I tried to bend over to pull weeds and plant seeds. Worse yet, when I did force myself to wince and bend over to do my gardening, my wide skirt covered the very weeds I wanted to pull. By the time I pushed them aside, I had not a free hand left to garden with!

"It seemed ridiculous to me that I should have to wear clothes that would prevent me from doing the very activity I set out to accomplish."

Amelia and Elizabeth Stanton both nodded in understanding. This complaint was a common one, and both women had experienced it many times. "But tell me about your clothes," insisted Amelia.

"Let her finish," said Elizabeth with a delighted chuckle at how excited her postmistress friend had become.

"The second incident happened a week later while I was visiting a friend recuperating at a convalescent rest home," continued Lizzy.

Again Amelia nodded knowingly. Convalescent hospitals had cropped up across New England like weeds. Virtually every woman had either been to one or knew women who had. These hospitals were filled with women recovering from the damage done to their bodies by tight corsets. They came with cracked and broken ribs, with huge and ugly welts, and with damaged internal organs.

These women hid away in convalescent hospitals until they were healthy enough to don a corset and again be presentable in open society. "That day, I became aware for the first time," said Lizzy, "of the special hospital outfits the recovering women wore. They looked like the first comfortable clothes I had ever seen in my life. Each woman wore these loose fitting pants, tied at the ankle with a skirt that stopped a few inches below the knee. It was the first time I had ever seen a woman wear something that acknowledged she had legs. The pants are called 'Turkish' because that's the country they came from."

Lizzy smiled and shrugged. "I went home and made myself a pair that very night."

"And what reaction did you get?" demanded Amelia, more intrigued than ever.

"Both my husband and my father were very supportive. They said I looked happier and more graceful than ever. But then my father is a reformer and has always believed women would never win any rights until they wore practical clothes they could move in."

"And your neighbors?" continued Amelia, now leaning over the post office counter.

Lizzy grimaced. "My New York neighbors were not as receptive. I have been jeered and laughed at by men, and snubbed by women. The women have actually been the most viscous, attacking me and my outfit at every opportunity. I am no longer invited to any social functions or welcomed at meetings. I am even shunned at church, for goodness sakes. Our minister suggested I go elsewhere."

Several other women had entered the post office by this time, each drawing back in angry and indignant horror. The words, "The nerve!" and "They should be ashamed!" forming on their shocked and disgusted faces.

Amelia settled back on her stool, glanced around the post office, and nodded. "I thought as much."

Elizabeth Stanton said loud enough for the whole room to hear, "When Lizzy first showed the fashion to me last week, I, too, thought the outfit outrageous and ridiculous, and that she had surely lost her mind. Then she showed me that *she* could climb stairs without using one hand to hold her skirts. That's very important to me now because I need one arm to hold my baby, and one for a candle. I haven't been able to climb stairs at night without help for months.

"She also showed me that she could freely bend, reach, and work so much more efficiently and quickly." Elizabeth Stanton smiled and gestured to her own outfit like her cousin's. "So, here I am."

Amelia rushed excitedly from behind the counter to more closely inspect these Turkish pants and short skirts. The two women who had been observing the conversation stormed out in an angry huff. "Are they really as comfortable as they appear?" Amelia asked.

Both Elizabeths smiled and nodded. "Even more so."

Amelia slowly circled the two women, examining every aspect of their revolutionary garb. "I must write a glowing article in the next issue of the *Lily*," she declared.

Amelia Bloomer had been a journalist for a decade, writing columns under the pen name "Gloriana" to hide her identity and avoid the verbal and physical harassment other women writers faced. When Amelia began publishing the *Lily* in 1849 as the nation's first periodical published, edited, and distributed by a woman, it had focused only on the issue of temperance. In the two years since, she had steadily expanded the *Lily*'s role to speak for all women's issues. Articles decrying the horrors of corsets and heavy petticoats had already appeared in past issues. But here was not another complaint; here was a solution!

Amelia looked up and beamed. "And I will certainly need a Turkish outfit of my own by tomorrow."

When the next issue of the *Lily* was bound and mailed five days later, its entire front page was devoted to Turkish pants. "Cease groveling and throw off your 'clothes prisons!' " Amelia urged in her lead article. "There is no reason why a woman should enslave herself with clothes to the detriment of her health, comfort, and productivity while man is allowed to adopt a style that enhances freedom of limb and motion."

Reaction was swift and powerful. Like a lightning rod, the *Lily* became the focus of a gathering national storm. Letters poured in from across the nation from women begging for the pattern so they could make their own Turkish outfits. Subscriptions to the *Lily* increased more than tenfold in just two weeks.

But for every supporter, a dozen angry detractors seethed at every corner. Clergymen from every denomination sternly lectured their congregations on the evils of the disgraceful abandon of women wearing pants. Editorials in over twenty papers scoffed that these crazed and envious women must be trying to become men. *Godey's Lady's Book*, the leading women's magazine of the day, called Turkish pants indecent, and a deep embarrassment to American womanhood.

Amelia Bloomer blasted back that forcing women to wear clothing that destroys health and the ability to productively function is like enslaving half the country with a prisoner's ball and chain. "If men find corsets and long, heavy petticoats so appealing," she wrote in the next *Lily*, "let men wear them. I challenge any man to get through *one* day wearing what you expect women to cheerfully wear *every* day!"

When she received no takers, Amelia triumphantly wrote that this proved that the cowardly male population recognized the torturous discomfort of women's clothing and had created the fashion as a plot to keep women passive, unhealthy, and subservient.

Because most people learned of Turkish pants through Amelia Bloomer's articles, the style was often referred to as "Mrs. Bloomer's outfit," or as "the Bloomer outfit." Soon both supporters and detractors simply called them "bloomers," referring both to the pants and to the movement for women's freedom that lay behind this dress reform.

The powerful *New York Tribune* wrote that Bloomerism really meant national revolt. Their editorials fiercely demanded an end to Bloomerism in order to stop the decay of society. Songs and cartoons ridiculing the style abounded.

Elizabeth Miller, the style's creator, never minded that her creation came to be known as "bloomers" instead of "millers." She returned to her home in New York and happily wore her bloomers for the rest of her life.

Elizabeth Cady Stanton, a giant in the fight for women's suffrage, wore bloomers for three years, then abandoned them because they detracted from her ability to promote what she felt were more important issues.

Amelia Bloomer, one of America's first female journalists, the first woman to own, edit, and publish a periodical in this country, and one of the country's great voices fighting the oppression of women, wore bloomers for eight years, reverting to more conventional styles when she and her husband moved to Iowa in 1859.

Sadly, she concluded that bloomers failed to be accepted by society because neither men nor women were ready for the mobility and role choices the costume implied. "The time for its adoption has not yet come," she wrote in the late 1880s. "American women are not sufficiently self-assured and independent to dare to strike out for health and freedom."

Such a time would have to wait well into the next century. But that is another story.

Questions to Explore

Why did women in the mid- and late-1800s wear heavy, restrictive clothes that actually damaged their bodies?

Why did men oppose more practical clothing for women? Why did women?

Do women still wear clothing that damages their bodies? What about high heels and corsets? Can you think of other examples?

Can you find information in the library describing how women's fashions have changed over the last 300 years?

References for Further Reading

- *In the Children's Library*

  Forbes, Malcolm. *Women Who Made A Difference.* New York: Simon & Schuster, 1990.

- *In the Adult Library*

  Autumn, Stevens. *Wild Women.* Palo Alto, CA: Bonari Press, 1992.

See your librarian for additional titles.

Vote to Win

A story about Susan B. Anthony and her fight to secure the right to vote for women

About This Story:

The struggle for women's rights began in earnest in America in the early 1800s. By the last quarter of that century, the fight centered on the right to vote. If that right could be won, activists believed, all others would surely follow.

But how were women to win that right when no woman could vote for it, and when no woman could hold one of the elected or appointed offices that created laws? Women had to ask men to give up their monopoly on political power in this country. As you might imagine, most men found it difficult to voluntarily give up half of the power they had been born to believe would always be theirs.

It took a great deal of effort, struggle, and commitment by many talented women, and by a number of farseeing men to force change onto a system quite willing to continue the status quo. This is a story about a woman who, perhaps more than any other, symbolized the struggle for women's suffrage.

The glow of gas streetlamps glittered across the thin sheen of frost that covered the city of Rochester, New York. Somewhere far above the dreary layer of clouds and fingery wisps of fog, the first glimmers of morning streaked the eastern horizon. But the soothing warmth of dawn felt worlds away down on the streets this morning of October 26, 1872.

A stately band of sixteen women bravely rounded the corner from Broadway onto West Street in the frosty pre-dawn cold. Darkened storefront displays stared back, and early morning walkers and workers openly gawked as this odd parade of dignified, well-dressed women marched by.

Many of the women whispered self-consciously back and forth, covering their deep nervousness behind shared giggles. However several of the women, especially the group's leader, marched boldly down the sidewalk, as if daring anyone to stand in their way.

"Keep together ladies. Less than a block to go," called the leader over her shoulder. Her bright blue eyes glowed with passionate determination. She walked with the straight-backed grace of someone used to being in charge. The fact that her mouth naturally turned down at the corners, had led many in the press to label her, "a sour old spinster out to stir up needless mischief."

But those who knew fifty-two-year-old Susan Brownell Anthony knew her warmth, humor, and deep commitment to the cause of women's rights. Trained as a school teacher, Susan made her first speech for women's rights almost twenty years earlier, in 1853.

She hadn't planned on making a speech at that 1853 teacher's convention. Women weren't supposed to. But after three male speakers in a row decried teachers' low pay and claimed there was no reason for it, Susan bounded to her feet. "It is because women are allowed to teach," she said. "As long as women are considered of lesser intelligence and lesser worth than men, professions open to women will be low paying." The tremendous response she received convinced Susan there was a great need for promotion of women's rights.

"There it is across the street, ladies," Susan called, briskly rubbing her gloved hands together. "Our moment in history awaits there, at the voter registration table in the West Street Barbershop."

Women were not allowed in barbershops in the nineteenth century. So it seemed a natural spot to set up voting booths for elections. The West Street Barbershop was the polling headquarters for the city's eighth ward.

As the stragglers in Susan's group bunched around her, Susan slowly shook her head. "To think, a seemingly innocent conversation in Elizabeth Stanton's home has led here, to challenge the very core of America in a barbershop."

Hannah Anthony Mosher, Susan's sister, fidgeted with her coat collar. Her breath hissed in tight clouds of steam. "Are you sure this is right, Susan? I mean, isn't it illegal?"

Susan B. Anthony gazed sternly at her sister, barely visible in the dull glow of Rochester streetlamps. "Don't you remember the conversation two months ago, Hannah? I was grousing about our lack of vote. Someone, I don't remember who, asked me why I didn't just vote if I wanted to. 'After all,' she said, 'I was a citizen, wasn't I?'

"It was Elizabeth Stanton who recognized the genius of that idea. 'Yes, vote Susan,' she said. 'You're famous. If they let *you* get away with it, then they can't stop any woman. But if they stop you, they will have said that every mother, wife, and daughter in this land is less of a citizen than every freed black man, all of whom can now legally vote. The country would be outraged and finally galvanized into action. Either way we win.'

"Don't you see, Hannah," continued Susan, now raising her voice loud enough for the whole group to hear, "once we walk through that door and register to vote, the only way we can be defeated is by being ignored. And I will not be ignored!"

The women cheered. But Susan sensed little enthusiasm behind the cheering. She knew her followers feared being branded as radicals and snubbed socially. She knew they feared the wrath of husbands who would become laughingstocks for not being able to control their wives.

A little rabble-rousing was in order before they rushed the barbershop. "Ladies, what do we want?" she called in a commanding voice. "We want the right to own our own property! We want equal pay for equal work! We want the right to speak in public. We want the right to hold our own incomes without having them automatically become the property of our husbands. We want the right to be educated! And what do we need in order to get those basic rights?"

Many in the group nodded shyly. Several whispered, "the vote."

"What do we need?" shouted Susan.

Most shrugged and softly answered, "the vote," as they glanced nervously about hoping they weren't making too much of a spectacle of themselves. A few caught Susan's enthusiasm and shouted it out. "THE VOTE!"

"What do we need?" screamed Susan.

"THE VOTE!" cried most of the group. The rest at least smiled bravely and raised a fist in the air.

"To the polling place!" cried Susan and started briskly across the street.

The two barbers, one customer, several men in for a cigar and early morning conversation, and Mr. B. W. Jones, the Registrar of Voters all stared, dumbfounded and open-mouthed, as an army of elegantly attired women burst through their door.

"My name is Susan Anthony. I am a natural born citizen of these United States, and have been a resident in this ward of Rochester for far longer than the required thirty days. Therefore I am here to register to vote for the November 5th election."

All eyes turned to B. W. Jones, who turned beet-red and stammered, "But . . . but you're women."

"That's tellin' her, B. W." scoffed one cigar-puffing man.

Jones cleared his voice. "Ladies, ladies," he said in a singsong voice with a wide, condescending smile, "You know women can't vote. And you shouldn't be caught in a barbershop. What will your husbands think? Now run along home. We don't want an incident here, do we?" His arms folded over a barrel chest.

Susan's steady gaze wilted both his smile and his confidence as she stood erect and unflinching before him. From her purse she flourished a printed copy of the U.S. Constitution and flopped it onto Mr. Jones' registration table. "If you'll bother to read this document, and in particular the Fourteenth Amendment to it, I think you will find that *all* citizens are granted the right to vote. I defy you to point to the place where our Constitution says I cannot."

B. W. Jones recognized a no-win situation when he saw one. He didn't dare argue with this woman who obviously knew more about the Constitution than he did. But he was also being watched by half a dozen men, and didn't dare accept this woman's claim that she had a right to vote. What should he do?

With a nervous laugh he said over his shoulder, "I'll let the boys at City Hall take care of this one. It'll give 'em a laugh and something to do."

With that, he opened the Voter Registration Book and gestured for Susan to sign.

Ten days later Susan Anthony's army returned to the West Street Barbershop as the polls first opened at seven o'clock in the morning. A thin, freezing rain made the walk treacherous and reduced the early morning voters to a trickle.

"Ladies, ladies," explained the election judge. "It was one thing to register. But you know you can't really vote."

"I know no such thing," snapped Susan. "Here is the Constitution. Show me where it says I cannot."

The judge felt the heat of a blush creep under his collar and up his neck.

"Then is there a New York law that forbids me from voting?" continued Susan, turning all the power of her formidable gaze on the election judge.

"No, of course there's no specific state law," barked the flustered judge. A growing crowd of curious men pressed in around the judge's table. "But you don't own property. You're women. You can't vote. Women have never been able to vote."

The crowd of men cheered.

"You're saying," said Susan, "that we can't vote because we don't own property? Do all recently freed black male slaves own property?"

"Certainly not . . ." began the judge.

"But they can all vote," interrupted Susan. "Are you saying that we are lesser citizens than a freed black slave? Are you saying your own wife is worth less, your own mother?"

"I said no such thing!" snapped the red-faced election judge. Then he turned for help to the ring of men behind him. "You argue with her, George. I don't know how to say it."

"Say we can vote," insisted Susan. "It is our right as citizens."

The judge threw up his hands in frustrated surrender. "Fine. Go ahead and vote. But they'll probably dump all the votes from this ward before they'll let yours count."

Leaving the voting booths, most of the women laughed with a giddy sense of triumph. But not Susan. She brooded as they inched their way back up slick West Street. "That was too easy. We weren't arrested or refused. And I fear he's right. Our votes will simply be ignored. We needed to cause a ruckus that would ripple through the whole nation, not just in the eighth ward of Rochester. I fear what we have done here today will simply be ignored and forgotten."

At midnight that Tuesday evening, the mayor of Rochester and his entire staff sat scowling at a stack of sealed ballot boxes in the basement of City Hall. "Don't you dare touch those boxes," the mayor growled at his chief of elections.

The balding chief nervously dabbed a handkerchief across his dripping forehead. "But mayor, it's already midnight. We *must* count the ballots. It's the law."

As the mayor waved his fifth cigar of the night, its long ash tumbled to the floor. "Open those boxes, George, and you'll have to count the votes of sixteen blasted women that are buried somewhere in there. If we toss the boxes, we'll be arrested for tampering with a federal election. I've sent a wire to the governor. No one touches those ballot boxes until *he* says what to do."

At six o'clock in the morning, Chief of Staff Albert Michaels rushed into the oval office where President Ulysses S. Grant sipped an early morning cup of coffee. "Mister President, an urgent wire has come from the governor of New York. We have a problem in Rochester. Some women have voted."

The president groaned and rocked back in his chair. "Can we hush it up, keep it quiet? I don't need this kind of a headache this year."

Laying the New York and Philadelphia papers across the president's desk, Michaels shook his head. " 'Fraid not, sir. The press already got hold of it. Look. Besides one of the women was Susan B. Anthony. She's been lecturing on women's rights for twenty years. She'll never let something like this be hushed."

At the same moment that President Grant grimaced at the two-inch-tall headlines, a stately woman in Rochester with a naturally turned-down mouth squealed with delight reading the same front page: "Ill-Minded Suffragists Steal Vote in Rochester."

"This is wonderful," Susan called to her sister. "Front page in both papers! The press says we've usurped Congress' authority. They say we're female lawlessness at its worst, and that we've broken every law in the land. They want us lynched, or at least locked away for the rest of our lives."

"And that's good?" asked Hannah, her eyes fearfully big.

"We've made the front page around the nation. We win!"

"What we win is prison," moaned Hannah.

"Relax, Hannah. We won't go to prison," said Susan. "But now the nation must admit this gross inequity during our trial. When I testify I'll make sure they do. Then we win."

Of the sixteen women who tried to vote, only one was charged with violating federal voting laws: Susan B. Anthony.

U.S. Senator Roscoe Conkling, President Grant's right-hand man, traveled to Rochester to coordinate the prosecution and make sure both that Anthony was found guilty and that the women's suffrage movement was squashed.

Fair-minded district judge, Nathan Hall, was sent on prolonged vacation. Recently appointed U.S. Supreme Court Justice, Ward Hunt (who owed Conkling a favor) was assigned to try the case. The nation buzzed at a Supreme Court Justice trying a minor circuit court complaint.

The trial was delayed until June 17, 1873, a warm and breezy day in upstate New York with the flags snapping under a sparkling blue sky. As the courthouse bell tolled, a great mass of reporters, supporters, and hecklers jammed into every nook and cranny of the cramped courthouse, and spilled out to fill the entire courthouse square.

Susan arrived looking triumphantly radiant and resplendent in a flowing black satin dress with white lace collar. Grabbing the sleeve of her Quaker lawyer, Henry Sheldon, Susan yelled over the spectator's roar, "Look at the size of this crowd, Henry. We were not ignored. We have won!"

"Not yet you haven't," cautioned her grave lawyer. "This trial has all the markings of being rigged top to bottom. You will very probably lose."

Susan laughed. "Win or lose the case, I'll be able to present my message when I testify. It will be in the official record. And every one of these people will hear it. *That* is when I win."

The trial proceeded swiftly with Senator Conkling beaming confidently from the sidelines, Judge Hunt looking bored and disinterested on the bench, and reporters scribbling furiously in the gallery.

The prosecution presented its case in less than a day. Then all eyes turned to lawyer Sheldon and the expected fireworks of the defense.

Sheldon rose. "Your honor, the defense would like to call the defendant, Susan B. Anthony."

"Denied," barked the judge.

The courtroom erupted in surprised murmurs.

Sheldon gaped at the judge and stammered, "But your honor, every accused has the right to testify in their own behalf."

Judge Hunt slammed his gavel on the wooden bench. The sharp thunderclap echoed through the court. "The defendant is not competent to testify in her own behalf. She is a woman."

Senator Conkling chuckled as Susan trembled with rage.

"*I* will represent the defendant," continued the judge throwing a condescending smile in Susan's direction. "I will summarize her testimony from the pre-trial hearing."

"You most certainly will not!" exploded Susan, blasting to her feet.

The rap of Hunt's gavel sounded like deafening machine gun fire. "The defendant is ordered to sit. Bailiff, if she makes one more sound of any kind, remove her from this courtroom."

Susan sank into her chair, her knuckles white where she gripped the table.

As Susan seethed, Judge Hunt flipped through the transcript of her pre-trial testimony, badly summarizing some parts, skipping many others, and randomly quoting and misquoting single phrases and sentences.

In five minutes it was over. Judge Hunt fished a prepared paper out of his pocket, turned to the jury, and began to read. "You gentlemen have heard all the pertinent evidence in this case. The defendant has clearly voted illegally, and is not protected by the Constitution in this matter . . ."

Sheldon shot to his feet. "I strongly object, your honor. You are dictating a verdict to the jury in direct violation of every principle of our legal system."

Again the gavel slammed onto the bench. The sound exploded across the court. "Be quiet and sit this instant, Mr. Sheldon, or I will have you disbarred."

For a long moment the two men glared at each other. But the power of a Supreme Court Justice was too much for Henry Sheldon to withstand. He lowered his eyes and sank, defeated, into his chair.

Judge Hunt turned back to the jury. "You are therefore ordered to find this defendant guilty on all counts."

Ignoring the growing roar of outrage in the courtroom, Judge Hunt turned to the clerk of the court. "Record that verdict now."

Stunned, the clerk obediently mumbled, "Gentlemen of the jury, hearken to your verdict as the court has recorded it. You say you find the defendant guilty of the offense whereof she stands indicted, and so say you all."

The jury had said no such thing. They had not said anything at all. They sat in open-mouthed and embarrassed silence while these words were crammed into their mouths.

Judge Hunt quickly rapped his gavel. "Gentlemen of the jury, you are dismissed."

Senator Conkling, smiling broadly, clapped the judge on the back as they retired together to the judge's chambers.

Susan Anthony was outraged at being cheated out of her moment in court. She vowed never to pay one penny of the $100 fine Judge Hunt imposed until she was given a chance to speak her mind. She never paid, and no one in the Justice Department dared bring her back into court to make her pay.

But in a very real sense she had won. Susan's name became a household word. For the next thirty years she lectured tirelessly to packed houses on women's rights and women's suffrage.

Susan B. Anthony died in 1906, fourteen years before the Nineteenth Amendment was ratified, specifically granting women the right to vote. Still, while it was being debated and voted on, that amendment was often called "The Susan Anthony Amendment," in honor of the woman who had fought so tirelessly in its behalf.

When it finally passed, the face of American politics was forever changed. The right of women to help guide the policies of their country had been affirmed. The door had been opened for women to begin learning to wield and marshal the power of the substantial women's vote in the name of a variety of causes, candidates, and issues. But those are each other stories.

Questions to Explore

Why weren't women allowed to vote in the United States for so many years?

Were women allowed to vote in other countries before they gained the vote in the United States?

Were women allowed to vote in some states before others? Which states?

References for Further Reading

- *In the Children's Library*

Boynick, David. *Women Who Led the Way: Eight Pioneers for Equal Rights.* New York: Thomas Crowell, 1959.

Clinton, Susan. *The Story of Susan B. Anthony.* Chicago: Childrens Press, 1986.

Jacobs, William. *Mother, Aunt Susan and Me.* New York: Coward, McCann & Geoghegan, 1979.

Smith, Senator Margaret Chase, and H. Paul Jeffers. *Gallant Women.* New York: McGraw-Hill, 1968.

- *In the Adult Library*

Barry, Kathleen. *Susan B. Anthony: A Biography.* New York: New York University Press, 1988.

Dubois, Ellen, ed. *Elizabeth Cady Stanton—Susan B. Anthony Correspondence, Writings and Speeches.* New York: Schocken Books, 1981.

See your librarian for additional titles.

Coffee and a Roast Beef Sandwich

A story about Jane Addams, America's first social worker

About This Story:

Social work was a new concept in the late 1800s. The first social work study program was created at Chicago University in 1892. Those first programs assumed that the needy would travel to some central facility for assistance. Moving out into the community to assist those in need seemed revolutionary. It had never been tried. It had never even been seriously considered.

The notion, however, was propelled into national prominence by the efforts of one woman. She didn't set out to revolutionize the way we as Americans view our responsibility toward our fellow citizens, she only sought to do something worthwhile with her life, but her effect was profound. This is a story about this remarkable woman.

"We'll talk in the dining room. I don't think it's being used right now."

Thirty-year-old Jane Addams had to raise her voice to be heard over the din of mothers and young children bidding loud farewells for the day in the wide hallway. As an afterthought she added over her shoulder, "And welcome to Hull House, Carolyn."

Jane threaded her way through the human obstacle course toward the front of the sturdy old brick mansion in the southside slums of Chicago on this October 1890 morning. Lugging her heavy suitcase, bewildered twenty-five-year-old Carolyn Porter, a recent graduate of Ratcliff College, struggled to keep up with the Hull House Director. "My whole last term I dreamed of living here at Hull House, helping the needy," she said. "It's a miracle that I'm finally here."

"The real miracle is that Hull House, itself, is here," corrected Jane. "When we first proposed it a year and a half ago no one lifted a finger to help. The project was nearly crushed before it started."

Nearly tripping over several children and two men carrying theater props toward a back room, Carolyn said, "I hadn't expected so much . . ."

Jane held up one hand to signal Carolyn to hold her thought, and turned to two elderly women standing just inside the front door and looking very lost. "Good morning, ladies, I'm Jane Addams. How may we help you? . . . Ahh, the dressmaking class. It meets upstairs—second door on the right. Yes, go right on up. No, there's no charge. And welcome to Hull House."

Jane turned her head, "Sorry, Carolyn. You were saying?"

The new college graduate stammered, "Every room is so busy . . . so full. I had expected . . ."

Again Jane raised her hand to stop Carolyn. "Excuse me again, dear." Jane pushed open a richly paneled door that led into a long, bustling kitchen and called,

"Ellen?" When a brown head with a wide, infectious smile popped up from among the row of women turning mounds of lettuce, tomato, bread, and roast beef into sandwiches, Jane said, "When you have a moment, I'd like to talk about your changes to the cafe menu. I'll be in the dining room with a new volunteer."

The door swung shut. Jane turned back to Carolyn. "I'm sorry for the interruptions. The dining room's right over here."

Carolyn followed, shaking her head. "I thought it would be . . . well, quieter, with volunteers going *out* into the neighborhoods from the residence house to perform service."

"As you can see, it's quite the contrary," laughed Jane. "Hull House is an activity center, service center, and helping hand rolled into one. People come to us with their needs, and we create the needed services. We serve a dozen ethnic immigrant ghettos that would otherwise be isolated from each other and from the city. The only things they shared before are poverty and overcrowding."

Jane and Carolyn pushed through mahogany double doors into a chandeliered dining room. Two long tables with over twenty chairs each stretched the length of the room.

The main front door swung open and an expensively tailored, red-haired woman in her early thirties rushed in. "Ahh, Jane, there you are. Wonderful news from City Hall!"

The woman slipped off her coat and closed the door to shut out Chicago's brisk October winds. As she and Jane hugged in greeting, Jane said, "Julia, you must meet our new live-in volunteer, Carolyn Porter. She's from Ratcliff and has volunteered to join our Hull House team. Carolyn, this is Julia Lathrop. She's lived here for five months, runs the Heroes Club, and has been pestering the city to build the first city-financed playground right here in our neighborhood."

Julia blurted out, "The Planning Commission has picked a site, only a block from here!" Then she added with a smug grin, "And this morning the mayor promised me the funding will be approved at next week's board meeting."

"Splendid!" squealed Jane. "Keep after them, Julia. If you'll excuse us, Carolyn and I were just beginning a chat."

"The Heroes Club?" asked Carolyn, dropping her suitcase and settling into one of the richly appointed chairs next to Jane. Carolyn's brown eyes were still wide with surprise at the amount of action at Hull House. Her face was framed by shoulder-length blond hair.

"The Heroes Club is one of a dozen clubs we have formed here at Hull House in the last year," explained Jane. "It's for school-aged boys. We read them stories about heroes and do related activities after school in the hope that they'll find positive role models."

Jane's large, brown eyes, and downturned mouth made her look serious, even when she laughed. Her spine had been curved during a childhood illness so that she carried her shoulders and head at an odd, stiff angle, and walked pigeon-toed. But to most eyes, Jane's plain looks were invisible next to her magnetic energy as she orchestrated Hull House.

"Is that all you do here?" asked Carolyn. "Start clubs?"

"Heavens no," laughed Jane. "Clubs, classes, services, kindergarten, daycare— you saw the mothers just dropping off their children as they head off for their shift in the factories."

Jane shifted in her chair to ease her back. "Hull House was built as a country estate by Charles Hull, but the spreading Chicago slums engulfed the countryside he had moved out of the city to find. As Hull's neighbors sold their land and moved away, tenement shacks sprouted like weeds onto what had been spacious lawns. Saloons and factories replaced groves of trees. Hull sold the house and its lands and moved on. The grounds were sold piece by piece, but the big house still stood."

The dining room door swung open, interrupting Jane. A woman's head poked in. "Excuse me Miss Addams, but we haven't had a single hat donated for our *Snow White* play. What should we do?"

Jane Addams pursed her lips in thought for a second. "The millinery class meets tonight. I believe there are over a dozen students in it now. Have them make the hats."

The door swung shut. Jane turned back to Carolyn. "Where was I? Oh, yes. Ellen and I leased Hull House a year ago as a place where volunteers like you and I could live and provide whatever services and facilities the nearby neighborhoods need. We believe that if we don't actually live in the community we'll never see the real needs of its people."

"And the neighborhood boys need role models and stories?" asked Carolyn.

"Much more than that. Those lucky few children who don't work."

"Work?" exclaimed Carolyn. "Young children?"

Jane nodded. "The families here are poor. Everyone works. Most children go to school part-time and work in the factories. The rest had no place to play after school while waiting for their mothers to get home." Now she smiled and shrugged. "So we started the Heroes Club and along came Julia just in time to run it. We've also started two similar clubs for girls."

The door slid open and short Ellen Starr swept in with a warm smile. Her brown hair was styled fashionably, swept up on top of her head. She wiped both hands on her apron before extending one to Carolyn. "Welcome. You must be Carolyn Porter. I read your letter asking to volunteer here."

Jane asked, "Ellen, please tell me why you've changed the cafe menu."

Turning to Carolyn, Ellen explained, "Many local families are too poor to get a balanced, nutritional diet. So we started a cafe."

"With a scientifically and dietetically correct menu, I might add," insisted Jane.

"Which so far has been a complete flop," added Ellen.

"It wouldn't be our first," agreed Jane.

Carolyn asked, "If they're poor, how can they afford to eat at a cafe?"

Jane answered, "Most Hull House activities are supported by donations from the wealthy."

"But no one eats that scientifically correct menu," said Ellen. "It all tastes delicious, but they don't eat it."

"They should," snapped Jane. "It's what they need."

"But it's not what they *want*," countered Ellen.

"Ah, I see," nodded Jane, eyebrows raised. "What they *want* is coffee and roast beef sandwiches?"

"Just a hunch," shrugged Ellen. "But, we've always said our mission is to provide what our neighborhood really needs, not what we think they need."

As she closed the door, Ellen said over her shoulder, "I'll let you know in two hours if I'm right."

"Have you really had other flops?" asked Carolyn.

"Lots of little ones," laughed Jane. "Usually they happen when we try to do something without truly understanding the needs of the neighborhood."

Jane laughed at the memory of one of her first flops. "I'll tell you one that happened at the Christmas party last year. We bought great bowls of candy for the children and placed them all over the sitting rooms, but most of the children wouldn't touch a one. When we asked why, we found out those same children work sixty hour weeks in the factory that makes and wraps those candies. It was the last thing they wanted to see. They couldn't wait to get out of here and away from those horrid candies."

"This house is much more vital to the life of the community than anyone suggested at Ratcliff," said Carolyn. "How were you ever able to start it?"

"With a dream, lots of faith, and very little support," chuckled Jane. "The dream started when I was seven. I rode one day with my father on some errands that took us through the slum area of Centerville, Illinois, my hometown. Our house was one of the finest and surrounded by other grand homes with spacious, manicured lawns.

"This was my first trip to the overcrowded squalor of the tenement shanties. From our carriage, I watched boys with nothing more to throw than clods of dirt and nothing better to throw them at than piles of dust. I watched a girl whose only doll was a battered broom that she was supposed to be using to sweep a dilapidated porch.

"A picture, a dream, came to me then and has stuck with me ever since. I wanted to live in a big house right in the middle of those flimsy shacks, so that all the neighboring children could use my house as a decent place to play.

"That idea took a more concrete form when I traveled through Europe three years ago. I visited the English Settlement House, Toynbee Hall. It became my model for Hull House. The real struggle was to get support."

The great front door creaked open. Three older women tentatively stepped in, each carrying a small suitcase.

"I'm Jane Addams. How may I help you?" asked Jane, stepping into the entry hall.

Two of the women stood with eyes downcast as they toed the floor. The third glanced nervously about the room. "We work at the necktie factory . . ."

"Ah, yes. With the strike on you probably need a place to stay," said Jane soothingly.

"During the strike we get no paycheck to cover rent. Our landlord threw us out till we can pay again. We heard that you . . . well, you know . . ."

"Yes, we have rooms," smiled Jane. "You'll stay in the Jane Club."

"Jane Club?" asked Carolyn.

Over her shoulder Jane said, "It started last winter when a young woman arrived badly beaten by her husband for losing her wedding ring. She needed a place to stay. Her name was 'Jane.' We converted several rooms into women's dormitories. Striking workers often use them, too."

"We can't pay. But we could work some . . ."

"That won't be necessary," said Jane. "The rooms are yours as long as you need them." She turned down the hall and called, "Dorothy? Three more strikers for the Jane Club." Turning back to the women she said, "Dorothy will show you to your rooms."

"Thank you. Thank you very much, ma'am. We won't forget this."

"You are most welcome. We'll talk later about some of our classes you might want to join."

Turning back to Carolyn, Jane said, "I'm sorry, dear. Now where was I?"

"You were talking about getting support to start Hull House."

"Ah, yes. Ellen and I approached Chicago's high society during an important winter party in February of 1889. We were very naive to think the wealthy would rush to our support with open checkbooks as soon as they heard our plans.

"At the party I slipped into a circle of the most elite women in Chicago, including Mrs. Charles VanSlater. 'What's this I hear, my dear, about you wanting to be poor?' she asked with a tittering laugh. The other ladies all cackled along with her.

" 'Not *be* poor,' I corrected. 'I want to live *with* the poor in a settlement house.' Seeing blank looks all around, I explained, 'It's a house easily accessible, ample in space, hospitable and tolerant in spirit, and situated in the midst of some foreign enclave that might otherwise isolate itself from the rest of the city. It's a place where neighbors can drop in for aid and support.'

" 'And you'll actually *live* in this house in the slums?' asked Mrs. VanSlater, dramatically dragging out the word, 'live.'

"'But why?' blurted a plump woman, 'when we've worked so hard to get away from the poor and create nice neighborhoods for ourselves to enjoy?'

"Mrs. VanSlater scowled at me. 'Rethink your idea, young lady. Intentionally living in the midst of squalor is folly.'

"Across the room, Ellen had cornered Reverend Frank Gunsaulus, minister at the Fourth Presbyterian Church, which was attended by most of the rich and powerful people in Chicago. As she described our plan to open a settlement house in Chicago, he looked mournful.

" 'Why such a discouraging look?' Ellen asked him. 'I thought you of all people would share our enthusiasm.'

"He sighed and shook his head. 'I've seen this many times. Well-to-do young women filled with noble intentions rush to the slums to champion the poor. But the novelty soon wears off, and the wealthy women get bored and wander off to take up some other cause, leaving the poor worse off than ever.'

"He reached out and patted Ellen's arm. 'Leave charity work to the church.'

"Meanwhile, I maneuvered myself into conversation with two of Chicago's most important men, Vice Mayor Walter Stevens and the scholar Thomas Davidson, whose nose was said to be just long enough for him to look down it on the whole world.

"Mr. Stevens asked me, 'Why Chicago?'

" 'Chicago is bursting with poor, ethnic, immigrant neighborhoods,' I answered.

"Mr. Davidson poked his pipe at me. 'What makes you think your new neighbors will trust you and your live-in do-gooders enough to come by?'

" 'If we provide services they really need, they'll come,' I said. 'It works in London.'

"Davidson gazed down his long nose at me and tapped his pipe at the air to emphasize his point. 'Ahh. But that's London. This is Chicago. I fear that all this silly venture will do is get you laughed at and robbed.'

"The consensus was that we wouldn't last three weeks. But here we are a year later bustling with worthwhile programs!"

Ellen Star burst back into the dining room. "It worked! They wanted familiar food, not fancy gourmet dishes they'd never seen. The cafe is packed! Coffee and sandwiches are flowing like Niagara Falls."

"Well done," exclaimed Jane. "So we learn our lesson once again: don't provide a service unless you're sure it's what the people really need."

Carolyn sighed, "I'm not sure I'll ever be able to keep up with this place. There's too much happening. I'm exhausted just hearing about it."

Jane reached out and patted her hand. "True there's lots happening. But there's so much more to do. But first lunch. Anyone for a roast beef sandwich?"

Whenever a neighborhood need arose, the volunteers of Hull House rose to meet it. Word of Hull House successes spread like the wafting scent of fresh baked bread, luring enthusiastic volunteers to Chicago. Soon as many as fifty women lived at Hull House, running classes, programs, support groups, and services for whoever needed them in the neighborhood. Hull House became the center of community life.

By 1910, Hull House included a compound of thirteen buildings covering a whole block. A library, post office, gymnasium, theater, and classrooms were added. Hull House activities involved as many as 2,000 people every week.

By living in, and by being a part of, the community she served, Jane Addams was able to identify the real needs of her neighbors. She got elected to the school board and forced the district to open new schools in poor neighborhoods. She helped create the country's first juvenile court system so that children offenders would not be treated as adults in court.

Jane saw that tenement disease was linked to neighborhood filth. Garbage cans overflowed, and trash was dumped onto the unpaved streets. Jane talked her way into an appointment as a garbage inspector. Then she hounded the garbage collectors until they made pickups as regularly in her slums as in the rich sections of town.

Hull House became the national model of successful social work and community involvement. Hundreds of similar houses sprang up across the country. Social work became a viable and respected profession. In taking care of one neighborhood by becoming a vital part of it, Jane Addams changed the way a whole nation looked at its poor and its responsibliity to all who belonged to each community.

Still, Jane Addams' work extended far beyond Hull House. As a firm believer in justice and freedom, Jane helped to found the American Civil Liberties Union in 1920. Because of her deep belief in peace and nonviolence, she created the Women's International League for Peace and Freedom. In 1931, she became the first woman to win the Nobel Peace Prize.

One reporter wrote, "If she were a man, she'd be a landslide, shoo-in, sure-thing bet to be the next president." But that, of course, would be another story.

Questions to Explore

Do you think it's our responsibility to provide for the poor? If not, whose responsibility is it?

If you do think we have such a responsibility, what would you provide? How?

How would you determine what the people you are trying to help really need?

References for Further Reading

- *In the Children's Library*

  Kent, Deborah. *Jane Adams and Hull House.* Chicago: Childrens Press, 1991.

  Kitridge, Mary. *Jane Addams.* New York: Chelsea House, 1988.

  Wheeler, Leslie. *Jane Addams.* Englewood Cliffs, NJ: Silver Burdett, 1990.

- *In the Adult Library*

  Addams, Jane. *Twenty Years at Hull House.* New York: New American Library, 1960.

  Peavy, Linda, and Ursula Smith. *Dreams into Deeds: Nine Women Who Dared.* New York: Charles Scribner's Sons, 1985.

  Stoddard, Hope. *Famous American Women.* New York: Thomas Crowell, 1970.

See your librarian for additional titles.

Go Ahead and Shoot

A story about Mary Harris ("Mother") Jones and her work as one of America's first labor organizers

About This Story:

By the mid-eighteenth century America ran on coal. Coal powered transportation, heated homes, and fueled factories. Most of that coal came from the rich deposits in West Virginia and western Pennsylvania. Hidden away in the rugged northern Appalachian Mountains, those coal mines were some of the cruelest worksites in America. Working conditions were dismal. Pay was frightfully low. The mining companies owned whole towns surrounding the mines and grossly overcharged miners for rent and food. Most of the miners were new immigrants, ill-equipped to fend for their rights in this new land. They became "wage slaves." They earned salaries, but not enough to change jobs, move, or better their conditions.

A labor organization, The United Mine Workers of America (UMWA), was formed to represent and protect these miners and their families. But at the turn of the century no mine willingly let labor organizers in. Strong-armed thugs were hired to keep miners in line. Those who tried to join the new union were often threatened and beaten.

The process of securing decent pay and work conditions for coal miners more closely resembled a war than modern labor negotiations. Organizing for the UMWA was tough, dangerous work. Two of their most successful organizers were women. This is a story about one of them.

The handcrank wall phone in the mine security foreman's office jangled. The burly security foreman, Mike Kozlowski, tipped back his broad brimmed hat to wipe away the trickle of sweat already forming on his brow.

Not seven o'clock yet and already hot and muggy. The West Virginia heat had settled into this tiny valley like it would never leave. It was August 8, 1903—still at least six weeks before Mike could hope for any real relief from the heat. Mike grumpily snatched the phone from it's cradle. "Kozlowski here."

On the other end of the line he heard the panicked voice of one of his assistants at the south entrance guard shack to the Cripple Creek Coal Mine. "Mike? You better get down here right now."

Kozlowski rubbed the slowly growing ache under his forehead. "Carmine? That you? What's happening?"

"You just get down here fast. And bring guns."

Mike and four guards ran down the narrow road from the Cripple Creek Mine main office to the gate and guard shack at the south entrance. Carmine Bertoli pointed wildly down the road toward the tiny company-owned town of

Cripple Creek, West Virginia. In his other hand he carried a bulky pair of binoculars.

Mike Kozlowski snatched the binoculars from Carmine and looked down the dirt road toward town. His mouth slowly dropped open. "Oh, no. There must be 200 women comin' this way." Then his jaw tightened. "Well they're not gettin' past me. And they're not shuttin' down my mine!"

• • •

Anymore, Carl Tolliver had to struggle to stand in the mornings. His back was so brutally stiff from being bent over in a low-ceilinged mineshaft all day, it took him ten minutes just to straighten out and stand up. Then there was his cough. He could never quite catch his breath. It felt like his lungs weighed fifty pounds each. Everyone knew it was coal dust—they called it "black lung"—and it killed many a miner while still a young man.

Carl shook his head and grunted. He was only twenty-seven. Too young to be a wheezing cripple. But West Virginia coal mines did that to a man.

At quarter to seven in the morning, he stepped out the door of the flimsy shack the Cripple Creek Mine Company rented at an inflated price to Carl and his family. Again he shook his head and grunted. Hot already. At least it would be cool in the mine. Carl wouldn't suffer from heat today like his wife and two children would.

Then Carl Tolliver saw the parade marching solemnly up Cripple Creek Road toward the mine. Women. Lots of women. Carl tingled with excitement. He had heard stories of this happening at other mines. Women marching in to close the mine and force a strike for better pay, better treatment of miner's families, schools for the children, and better working conditions for the men.

"Bridget, come and look," Carl called over his shoulder as he hurried up the street.

• • •

Mike Kozlowski planted himself in front of the south gate like an oak tree, legs spread, repeating rifle gripped tight in both hands. A row of heavily armed guards stood just behind him.

Kozlowski shouted, "That's far enough. This mine is private property. Now you all go back."

Behind him one guard sucked in his breath and moaned, "Oh, no. That one in all black in the front—that's Mother Jones."

The kindly looking old woman the guard called, "Mother Jones," turned her head toward the women marching behind her. "Are we going to listen to him, ladies?" she called.

"NO!" came the shouted reply.

"Are we going to march in and shut down this mine until they pay a decent wage to their workers and take care of worker's families?"

"YES!"

Mother Jones scrambled onto a rock to raise her five foot three inch head above the crowd. Her prim, white hair; sweet, grandmotherly face; wireless spectacles; and plain, black, high-collar dress hid powerful shoulders and a thick, muscular trunk and disguised her booming voice and razor-sharp tongue.

"We will never go back. Because the working men of America will never go back. They march forward." Both her arms now pointed dramatically toward the south gate of Cripple Creek Mine. "And so we will march forward."

A great cheer rumbled up from the growing crowd of miners crowding in beside and behind the women.

With a deep, rattling cough Carl Tolliver whispered, "Who *is* that?" to a stocky, bearded miner cheering next to him.

"That's Mother Jones," answered the man in a tone that said he was surprised that Carl didn't know. "She's a miner's best hope for salvation, and the best storyteller in this state."

"Storyteller?" questioned Carl. "I hoped she was a labor organizer."

The bearded miner laughed. "She's both. I heard her at another mine. She said she was seventy-five one day, and sixty-five the next. Once she claimed to have four children; next day none. She said her husband died working in the mines. But I heard he worked for a bank."

"If she's not a miner's wife," asked Carl. "Why is she here?"

The other miner shrugged. "Just be glad she is, friend." He thoughtfully pulled at his beard and added, "I guess she just hates to see people treated unfairly—hates it enough to stand up and fight. I heard she was helping children forced to work in factories back east before she came out here."

Standing in front of the south gate, Mike Kozlowski called over his shoulder, "If those fool women get within twenty feet, shoot to kill." But he could feel his own uncertainty gnawing at the pit of his stomach. Sweat trickled down his face. In his loudest voice he added, "Bring out the machine gun."

A wooden panel dropped from the wall of the guard shack. The nine gleaming barrels of a crank-operated Gatling gun were shoved forward.

Mike turned back to the approaching women. "I said that's far enough, ladies, and I meant it." But his hands were beginning to tremble. Could he really order his men to mow down unarmed women?

A growing crowd of miners began to chant, "Let them in! Let them in!"

The women pressed forward. Some were miner's wives in their late teens. Some were mothers and grandmothers of miners or of sons who would become miners. Carl Tolliver had squeezed himself up to the front row of the crowd, but now hesitated, staring wide-eyed into the muzzles of the guards' rifles. But the back rows pressed him ever forward. "Let them in! Let them in!"

Only Mother Jones marched steadily, unhesitatingly, confidently forward, straight toward Mike Kozlowski.

The foreman groaned. If he fired, this day would turn very ugly, indeed. If he let them through, though, he'd be fired for sure.

Jubilantly swept up in this protest against their cruel and slave-like treatment, more than 100 hundred miners pressed toward the gate behind the ranks of women, taunting the six guards nervously arrayed behind Mike Kozlowski.

Kozlowski raised his rifle to his shoulder. "Stop now, or we'll fire!" he ordered.

"Booo!" hissed the miners.

"Cowards!" yelled Carl Tolliver.

And Mother Jones kept marching forward.

"Let them in! Let them in!"

A tray of photographic flash powder exploded off to the right.

"Sweet mother of heaven!" growled Kozlowski, "she brought the newspaper!"

Thirty feet now separated the marchers from Mike Kozlowski. Now twenty-five.

"Let them in. Let them in!"

Now twenty feet. Now fifteen.

All eyes were fixed on Mike Kozlowski as he sighted down his rifle at a point right between Mother Jones's eyes, his knuckles turning white as he gripped his rifle tighter and tighter.

At ten feet Mary Harris "Mother" Jones stopped and mockingly rested her hands on her hips. Her voice carried over the suddenly silent crowd, its echo rolling down into the ramshackle town. "Go ahead and shoot—if you're brave enough to shoot an unarmed, seventy-year-old woman and grandmother. Go ahead, if you dare slaughter an innocent grandmother in front of all these people."

Her stern gaze seemed to cut into Mike Kozlowski's resolve like a razor blade. Mother Jones's eyes hardened and narrowed. "But I tell you this. My husband and two of my children died in the mines. And if you dare lay one finger on me, a thousand enraged miners will swarm out of these mountains and tear you limb from limb. Now stand aside. I'm comin' in."

Poof! The photographer's flash powder exploded again.

Mother Jones marched forward, sweeping past Mike Kozlowski with the confidence and certainty of an incoming tide as he stood frozen with indecision. A great cheer erupted and the parade of women and miners surged forward behind her.

The Cripple Creek guards dashed for the safety of their shack and bolted the door. Mike Kozlowski grumbled, "If she was a man, I'd've decked her!"

At the main mine entrance, another hundred miners waited in a wide semicircle, not wanting to miss a moment of a Mother Jones spectacle. The mine owners emerged from their plush office behind the local sheriff, who'd been ordered to drag Mother Jones off the mine property.

The miners jeered and booed.

"Cowards," yelled Carl Tolliver between deep coughs.

Picks and shovels were raised. Threats were hissed. The sheriff wavered, and Mother Jones swept past him like a freight train.

Mother Jones climbed onto a mine car and drew the miners in close about her. "Shame on you," she scolded, her finger wagging around the thick circle of upturned faces. "Shame on you all. You pity yourselves. But you do not pity your brothers. You do not pity your wives and children." Her sharp words pounded the miners like sledgehammers. "If you did pity each other, you'd stop breaking your back every day like dumb work animals and stand up together—brother with brother, father with son. Stand up for yourselves, instead of making an old grandmother come in and do it for you!"

The crowd cheered. A man next to Carl rubbed his whiskered chin. "She scolds us worse than my mother."

"She *is* your mother," whispered Carl. "She's every miner's mother."

Mike Kozlowski and his guards slinked into the owner's office through a back door. "If she was a man, I'd've shot her, boss."

The mine owner glared at the sheriff. "Do, something!" he bellowed.

The sheriff fidgeted, staring at the crowd of 200 angry miners.

Outside, Mother Jones rocked back and forth on her mine car as she hurled her words at the waiting miners. "The guards are not your enemy. The owner is not your enemy. Poverty is your only enemy, the poverty you allow yourselves to live in. Poverty eats away at your heart and eats away at your families. Shame on you for allowing your families to live in desperate poverty!"

Some of the miners shouted in anger. Some wept in sorrow and shame.

"Have you told each other of your lives?" Mother Jones demanded. "Have you showed each other the festering sores on your feet where the sulfur water of the mines has eaten through your shoes? Have you shared how your empty stomachs churn in growing hunger day after day? Have you shared your pain at having to watch your children and wives run ragged and barefoot in the bitter winter snow and ice?"

Carl Tolliver's shoulders began to heave as he sobbed in frustration. Every word Mother Jones said seemed to stir a inferno of rage inside him that he was unable to quench.

"Awaken your minds, my children," she cried. "Awaken your minds and do what you must do to improve your lives. Stand up with your brothers, and act."

Mother Jones stepped down from the car. All around her miners and their wives poured out their tears of frustration and sorrow. Then the cry began. "Strike! Strike!" As it grew, the cry seemed to suck up helpless sorrow like a maelstrom and to spit out anger and fierce determination. "Strike! Strike!"

The power of the cry filled every miner in the yard. "Strike! Strike! Strike!"

Carl Tolliver felt the first ray of hope since he signed on at Cripple Creek five years before. The words charged him with strength. "Strike! Strike!" The words kindled powerful pride in his heart: pride in himself, pride in his fellow miners, pride enough to finally stand up to the owners and hired thugs called guards. "Strike! Strike! Strike!"

· · ·

Mother Jones had worked another miracle and slipped in to organize another mine's workers where no man could have set foot. The Cripple Creek strike lasted six bloody weeks. Eleven miners died during battles between company hired thugs and strikers. The company food store closed and many families nearly starved.

But the UMWA and the miners would not break. After six bitter weeks came the triumph of a better contract: better pay, a community school for the children, safer working conditions. A miner's life at Cripple Creek was still dismal and difficult. But after Mother Jones, it was better. After Mother Jones, the miners felt pride and strength enough to fight on their own for a decent life for themselves and their families. And after they organized, they had the power to continue demanding better contracts, improving their conditions even more.

The United Mine Workers of America was this country's first organized labor union. Mother Jones was one of its first, and most effective organizers. She knew well the dangers she faced at every mine. The other female UMWA organizer, Fanny Sellins, was shot and killed at a Pennsylvania mine confrontation similar to the one described above. Still, there seemed an almost magic flare in the way Mother Jones tore down the blockades at mine after mine.

For over fifteen years Mother Jones lived as a gypsy, traveling through the coal rich Appalachian Mountains from mine to mine, from hotel to jail cell with her one suitcase, the fire in her eyes, boundless energy, and the dream of a decent living and justice for all.

Mother Jones died in 1930. The violent struggle she helped to start for decent treatment of miners would rage on for decades more before miners won the respect and protection she sought. But that is another story.

Questions to Explore

Why did workers in the United States organize into labor unions?

What need did unions address?

Do you think unions are still necessary today? Why or why not?

Do other countries have labor unions? Which ones?

References for Further Reading

- *In the Children's Library*

  Long, Priscilla. *Mother Jones, Woman Organizer.* Boston: Red Sun Press, 1976.

  Peavy, Linda, and Ursula Smith. *Dreams into Deeds: Nine Women Who Dared.* New York: Charles Scribner's Sons, 1985.

- *In the Adult Library*

  Gilbert, Ronnie. *On Mother Jones.* Berkeley, CA: Conari Press, 1993.

See your librarian for additional titles.

2

Stories About Politics

Indian and English

A story about Pocahontas and her efforts to maintain peace between the Powhattan Indians and the English Jamestown Colonists

About This Story:

The race to colonize the New World was really part of a long-standing feud between three European powers: England, France, and Spain. The French established bases in Canada. Spain built St. Augustine in Florida. England rushed to grab the middle section of America. The first English colony on Roanoke Island, Virginia, disappeared after two years. Jamestown was the second attempt by the English. Sanctioned by the King, its mission was to claim land and extract wealth to ship home (especially gold) more than to establish a self-sufficient, thriving colony.

The voyage was not well planned. People with many of the wrong kinds of talents were taken, and there were few with the skills necessary to flourish in a complete wilderness. The people of Jamestown struggled bitterly to survive. Captain John Smith, elected leader of the colony for two years, claimed their very survival should be credited not to any of the colonists, but to an Indian girl, Pocahontas.

A romanticized version of the story of Pocahontas and John Smith has become popular in America. Certainly they developed a friendship, and, yes, she did save his life. But in truth, there was no romance between John Smith and Pocahontas. She was only eleven when they met. He was twenty-six. What is true, though, is that she was a strong, intelligent girl who repeatedly saved the British colony from starvation and destruction. This is a story about her.

On a bright, late-November morning in what would be called Virginia in another hundred years, the sun rose through bare tree branches to banish the fuzzy crystals of frost that spread through the woods each night. An eleven-year-old girl hiked down a winding path toward the river. Her arms swung loose and free, her steps filled with the bounce and exuberance of youth. She had tied her straight, black hair back from her face with a beaded leather strap. Her dark eyes flitted through the quiet woods searching for birds or lingering flowers. Golden sunbeams splashed across the path, vines, and trees before her. Mist from evaporating frost hung in light wisps in the air.

Her name was Pocahontas (Poe-ka-HON-tas), daughter of Powhattan (Pow-HAT-tan), chief of more than thirty tribes, king of a great nation along both sides of the Chesapeake Bay. Pocahontas skipped and sang, first in the dialect of her native Powhattan nation, next in the halting English she was trying to learn. She stumbled over the words and laughed at herself.

Through the trees ahead she could hear the river, and she could hear hammers, saws, and shouts—the enchanting sounds of the Jamestown colonists. "Enchanting" because they were different than any sounds Pocahontas had ever heard. "Enchanting" because the tools and weapons that made those sounds were unknown in all the lands of the Powhattans.

Crossing a marshy clearing that teamed with mosquitoes in the summer, Pocahontas reached the tall wall of thick tree trunks pounded side by side into the ground and laced together. The barricade stretched three-fourths of the way around Jamestown now. Smoke puffed from each hut's chimney inside. Five men strained to raise a new tree trunk into the fort wall as she approached.

"Hello, George. Hello, Charles," she called.

The five stopped and smiled at seeing this bright and familiar face. "Ahh, here comes little Pocahontas."

"Come to help, have you, little princess?" The English loved to tease Pocahontas.

Pocahontas studied the wall and shook her head. "These trees will not grow like this," she told them.

The men laughed, loud and long.

George Percy, a weak and skinny man who had whined about mosquitoes all summer, said, "Let me see if you remember the cartwheel I showed you last week."

"I remember," she replied with the brash confidence of an eleven-year-old, and turned two perfect cartwheels through the dirt.

They laughed and applauded. "Very good, little Pocahontas!"

William Farmer, a barrel-chested strongman, knelt beside her. "Ready for a new word today?"

"Oh, yes!" squealed Pocahontas.

"All right," he continued. "Let's see . . . Ah! 'Parliament.' "

"Par-lee-ment," repeated Pocahontas.

"Very good! Parliament is where English laws are made."

George Percy added, "It's where English chiefs meet to make decisions," when he saw a confused look on her face.

Pocahontas's face brightened. "It is like our council of werowances (WEAR-o-wance), who are our tribal chiefs."

With a final laugh the men returned to their construction and Pocahontas skipped into the compound with a grateful smile. In her village five men would not stop their work to play with a young girl. They would not indulge her curiosity. These English were nice.

The English had appeared one day, half a year before, as if by magic, with their tall ships and loud voices. Pocahontas was fascinated. She was awed. Who wouldn't be? The English muskets, pikes, axes, and cannon shone in sunlight and roared louder than thunder. The Powhattan people called it magic. English clothes seemed comical and impractical. Their beads and bells made such pretty tinkling noises and sparkled in her hand. Their small, musty houses and scratchy, colorful beards made her laugh.

But through the summer and fall of 1607, Pocahontas also watched the English die, go hungry, and waste their energy on petty fights over nothing more than pride. Soon she realized they had no real magic at all. The sun has magic power. People do not. If her father had realized this that first summer, he would have killed them all.

Almost all Powhattan people feared and hated the English, and would only visit Jamestown when a werowance (chieftain) ordered them to go. Powhattan, himself, was harsh and swift to act. He wanted to kill them all that first summer. But his medicine men counseled caution saying the English brought great and terrible evil and should not be attacked while they could still use it.

But more than anything, the metal tools, cannons, and muskets of the English filled Powhattan with longing. He feared that English magic might be too powerful for his people in battle, but he also craved the power of their magic weapons for himself.

Skipping through the rows of Jamestown houses, Pocahontas stuck her head through the door of one of the largest huts. Inside, a lone man sat writing in a journal. He glanced up as her shadow blocked his writing light.

"Ahh, Pocahontas! I knew you were here. I heard the men laughing. Anymore, there is no laughter in Jamestown unless you grace us with a visit."

Pocahontas scrunched up her face in concentration. "I do not know many of those words. But I think you are glad to see me."

"Always," smiled Captain John Smith. "Please, sit down."

John sighed and threw down his quill pen. "Powhattan bowmen killed another of our men this week. We've less than five days full rations. We are a desperate camp, Pocahontas."

"Things maybe go better," said Pocahontas, "if you stop planting trees where they will not grow, and gathered food instead."

Smith threw back his head and laughed. "I never looked at walls that way before."

Pocahontas saw Captain John Smith as an eagle in a camp of sparrows: proud, independent, powerful, fearless. He was short with thick, powerful arms, hair as fair as corn silk, eyes that sparkled deep blue like lakes, and an easy smile that stuck out from under a long curling mustache.

John rubbed his face with his hands. "The problem is I can't send out gathering parties with those bowmen out there. We're trapped in this fort."

Powhattan had directed a lesser werowance to set braves lying in the marsh grass near the fort. When an Englishman came within range, arrows would fly. Several English workers on the fort or in the fields would fall. A warning bell would clang. Men ran for metal coats and muskets. Cannons roared and huge holes were ripped in the marsh grass. During the summer and fall of 1607 Powhattan's bowmen killed many English. The English killed mostly marsh grass.

"Cut down grass far away from fort," instructed Pocahontas.

"Of course!" exclaimed Smith. "Splendid idea. All this time I've been posting more and more guards."

At first John Smith and Pocahontas had communicated with signs and gestures. Soon they added words for everything they could touch or point at. Later they added words for actions and ideas.

John clenched and unclenched his hands in frustration. "Why does your father hate us so? Why is he bent on killing us or seeing us starve?"

Pocahontas thought for a long moment. "He is afraid your weapons have magic and he wants it."

"Then why does he let you visit so regularly?"

Again Pocahontas thought. "He does not like me to come. But he does not mind if he thinks I am trying to find secrets about your weapons."

"Are you?" asked John.

"I do not think there are any secrets. You know about metal. We do not. Powhattans know how to live in the forest. You do not."

John smiled and nodded. "For someone so young, you are very wise, Pocahontas." Then he turned serious again. "How will we survive the winter?"

He asked it more to the air than to the girl before him. But she answered anyway. "I know of two tribes, the Quiyoughcohanock (Key-yough-CO-han-ock) and the Paspahegh (PASS-pah-hay). You can reach them by traveling downstream on the river where it is safer. They are more friendly and have much food. They will trade."

John Smith's blue eyes sparkled bright as a summer sky. "Two tribes? Really? Bless you, Pocahontas! You've saved us again."

"I should go now," she said.

"Pocahontas," he said as she reached the door. "Thank you. We will all be forever grateful."

As Pocahontas passed the tree wall she thought, *I am not even allowed to sit in council meetings for my Powhattan nation. Here the leader asks my advice and help. Maybe I am more important to the English than I am to my own people.* The thought made her feel important and special.

Then in early December, with ice creeping into quiet pools and swamps, John Smith was captured. He and three men sailed upriver with ice clinging to their mast and rudder in search of friendlier tribes and better ground for a permanent village.

The party split in half. John Smith and one man hiked inland. Powhattan's braves slit the throats of the other two before they could leave the shore.

A half mile inland a well-aimed arrow drilled into the back of John's companion and pierced his heart. He crumpled dead before he could utter a sound.

John Smith was alone and surrounded by 200 armed warriors. Because Pocahontas had told everyone John Smith was a great chief of the whites, these braves dared not kill him as they had the others of his small hunting party. But also they did not kill him because he showed no fear. He turned on them as if he were the hunter and they were the prey. Outnumbered 200 to 1, John Smith bluffed, acting as if he had the advantage because he held a pistol in his hand. The Indians thought maybe the pistol held more powerful magic than anyone had guessed.

They decided to negotiate right there in that clearing. All 200 warriors put down their bows and clubs and motioned for John Smith to do the same. He refused. Instead he grabbed a prisoner and held the pistol to his head. The Powhattans took up their weapons again. But John Smith marched toward the river and his boat, keeping his prisoner held tight to him and always between himself and the Indians.

Inch by inch Smith wove his way through a maze of warriors, shouting fierce threats, and acting as if he planned to kill them all. He seemed so sure of himself, so unafraid, that no one dared block his path. Two hundred warriors stood rooted in indecision on the ice and mud as one short white man snarled and swaggered his way through and around their trap.

Then the ice broke under his foot. John and his prisoner tumbled into a swampy bog. The water was nearly frozen. Neither man could breathe in the numbing cold. They struggled for shore. But the mud slopes were too slippery. John had to reach for a helping hand or freeze. A warrior snatched his pistol away. The chief of the whites was captured.

Word raced from village to village, from tribe to tribe. Every person rejoiced when they heard the powerful chief of the whites had been captured! Now Powhattan glowed, knowing he, at last, had the chance to show who was the greater chief!

Rather than deal with him straight away, Powhattan had John Smith paraded from village to village to see if his bravery would falter or if he would give up some secret. Pocahontas begged to travel with him as interpreter. Her father refused to let her leave Werowocomoco (Wear-o-WO-co-mo-co), his home village, where he planned to finally bring John Smith.

In two separate villages, lesser werowances wanted to kill John Smith because he would show neither respect nor fear. But his ability to speak the language saved him. In both villages he convinced the people that frightening and terrible things would happen if he was killed. The medicine men had said he brought evil magic, so everyone believed him.

Pocahontas hid her happiness. She had saved John Smith's life by teaching him to speak. The thought filled her with a new pride in herself and her powers. She, a young girl, had influenced mighty werowances.

Powhattan was impressed and angered by John Smith's boldness. How dare a captured invader not show fear? What did he know that the chief of the powerful Powhattan nation did not?

After two weeks of parading his captured prize from village to village, Powhattan grew tired of waiting for him to crack. It was time to deal with him directly. John Smith was marched to Werowocomoco.

Four hundred warriors painted for battle greeted him with silent scowls and fierce glares. John Smith did not tremble as he should, but marched straight through them as if they had come to wish him well.

Powhattan had him placed in the great longhouse that could easily hold 500. The warriors surrounded him, dancing the terrible dance showing how Powhattan prisoners are cut into pieces one piece at a time. The dancers acted enraged to signify that they would enjoy hacking John Smith slowly into small pieces. They leapt and screamed and swooshed heavy clubs through the air.

Carefully watching through a small slit in the longhouse wall, Powhattan was confused and furious when John Smith smiled and clapped his hands instead of begging for mercy.

Pocahontas smiled to herself. She knew what her father did not. John Smith could not understand the meaning of the dance, and thought it was only a lively entertainment performed in his honor, as were English dances. Her father did not know the English as she did, because he had not taken the time to learn as she had. The great chief of the Powhattan nation was confused and perplexed while she was not. Again her knowledge made her feel strong.

Finally Powhattan entered the hall and a great feast was served. Pocahontas sat between her father and John Smith, now confident that she could persuade her father to spare John's life, and convinced that she must teach the people about her English so that they would understand their ways as she did. Pocahontas was not a mischievous child. She cared about the English and she cared about peace. She was determined to use her powers and knowledge to show her people not to fear the English, so that they could live in harmony.

After the platters of food were removed Powhattan asked, "Why have you come to my lands?"

John smiled and answered with a casual shrug that they really weren't staying. They were driven off-course and were only waiting for more supplies before they moved on to their real destination. The lie, he hoped, would make Powhattan see him as less of a threat than he really was.

When part of John Smith's answer wasn't clear, Pocahontas acted as translator, helping him find the right words to express his thoughts.

Powhattan scowled at John's answer and turned away. After a short discussion with several medicine men Powhattan asked, "Why do you always carry muskets and cannon if you are peaceful visitors? Why not lay down your weapons and extend the arms of friendship?"

John Smith answered that English weapons were only a concern for enemies. If Powhattan came in friendship, he shouldn't worry if the English carried their weapons or not.

Powhattan demanded, "If you are peaceful visitors in my land, why have you not sent proper gifts to me, the king, as is our custom?"

The Powhattan had no such custom. Powhattan hoped the lie would force John Smith into offering muskets and metal swords.

John Smith smiled and said that he had not been aware of the custom.

Powhattan pressed harder, saying, "Now you are aware. You are also aware that I have treated you with great kindness. Still you have offended all Powhattan by not offering proper gifts."

Powhattan smiled smugly and crossed his arms at trapping John Smith into offering whatever gifts Powhattan would chose. But John Smith answered, "There is only one king, Edward I of England, and I will not give gifts to any other."

Powhattan flew into a rage, and said no one could live in his lands without showing proper respect. He bared his teeth, scowling at John Smith, and ordered a huge stone to be rolled into the middle of the longhouse. Her father looked so angry that Pocahontas dared not speak.

Twenty warriors sprang forward and seized John, dragging him backward toward the rock as they whooped and cried fierce threats. A dozen pinned his arms and legs, forcing his head onto the stone. Others swung spiked clubs high over their heads. The clubs whistled ominously through the smoky air.

For a long moment even Pocahontas was frozen in fear. She had helped the English in secret for months, and been secretly pleased at each of her successes. She had come to know and care for these strange foreigners, but she had never admitted her feelings to anyone. Powhattans were supposed to hate the English.

Secret help would not save John Smith now. Did she dare act now, in the open and against the wishes of her father? Part of her believed Powhattan would not kill John Smith, because then he would never obtain English weapons or learn their magic. Part of her believed he would, because his pride and honor were being challenged. Part of her feared that her father would lash out at her in anger if she spoke or moved.

Clubs spun. Warriors chanted and shouted. Powhattan sneered and crossed his arms to show disdain, as if John was less worthy than an insect. Drums pounded. All stared, eagerly waiting for the first blow to crush his skull.

Pocahontas dared not wait another second. She dared not think of what father might do. She sprang forward, shielding John Smith's head with her arms. By this act she claimed him for her own. This claim was her right as a Powhattan woman and princess, and put him under her protection, as one protects a younger brother. It may seem odd for an eleven-year-old girl to claim and protect a twenty-six-year-old man. But it was all Pocahontas could think of to save John Smith's life.

Powhattan smiled and jumped down from his raised chair to help lift John back to his feet. It may well be that Powhattan planned all along to force his daughter to claim John Smith. It may be that he knew what she would do, for as soon as she acted, Powhattan said that John Smith must now be adopted into the family. Unsure of what was happening, but grateful to be alive, John Smith agreed.

Heart still pounding, Pocahontas sighed with relief and hope. Her father was not furious with her. Maybe English and Powhattan could live side by side in peace.

With songs and dances there in the longhouse, Powhattan adopted John Smith as a son. Then Powhattan instructed his new son, saying, "Now that you are my son, you must return to Jamestown and offer proper gifts to ensure no bad blood between family members. Because you are new to the Powhattan family I will tell you what is proper: two cannon and one great millstone for grinding corn. You must give these things to me and then all will go well in our family."

Pocahontas's joy was crushed, realizing it had all been a ploy by Powhattan to get English weapons with which he could attack Jamestown. She was sure John Smith saw it too, and would refuse. Bitter war would continue. To her surprise John smiled, bowed, and agreed.

Returning to Jamestown with five warriors chosen to carry the gifts back to Powhattan, John Smith offered the two biggest cannons in the fort. Each weighed over 4,000 pounds. The grinding stone he offered weighed far more.

The warriors could neither lift nor budge any of the gifts and had to return empty-handed. John Smith declared that because his gifts had been refused by Powhattan's representatives, he was no longer obligated to give anything at all. John Smith had escaped alive, and had given up nothing.

Powhattan was enraged and stayed in a fierce mood for a month vowing to kill every Englishman. The war continued.

Yet no matter how fierce the feuding grew, Pocahontas's role never changed. She was council and aid to the English, and a bridge between the two peoples. John Smith returned to England in 1609, and Pocahontas eventually married an

Englishman, John Rolfe, and lived with the English. But her role as a mediator between her two peoples didn't change.

Though the peace and harmony she sought were never realized, Pocahontas never abandoned her fight to achieve these goals. Rather than being remembered as the girl who saved John Smith on a winter's eve late in 1607, Pocahontas should be remembered as an intelligent, energetic woman who believed her people were wrong in wanting to destroy the English, and that peaceful co-existence was possible if the two peoples knew and understood each other. She should be remembered as a woman brave enough to act in accordance with those convictions. It is unfortunate that 100 years later there was no English princess who would care half so much for the lives and welfare of the Powhattan people. But that is another story.

Questions to Explore

Why were the English in such a rush to establish colonies in America?

Why did they pick Virginia?

Using the resources in the library can you track the expansion of England, France, and Spain from Europe throughout the world?

References for Further Reading

- *In the Children's Library*

  Carpenter, Frances. *Pocahontas and Her World.* New York: Alfred Knopf, 1957.

  Fritz, Jean. *The Double Life of Pocahontas.* New York: Puffin Books, 1983.

- *In the Adult Library*

  Woodward, Grace. *Pocahontas.* Norman, OK: University of Oklahoma Press, 1969.

See your librarian for additional titles.

Presidential Tracks

A story about Belva Lockwood, the first woman to run for president of the United States

About This Story:

Women had not yet won the right to vote in America in the late 1800s. No women held elective political office. Near the end of the nineteenth century this inequity began to change. As with all social change, it began slowly and on many fronts, with long years of tireless struggle by many brave women, and with positive results few and far between.

Women had to learn how to compete successfully in the political environment of the late 1800s. Campaign meetings and rallies often seemed wild and woolly, rough and tumble affairs by our modern standards. One of the people who worked hardest to secure women's suffrage (the right to vote) was also one of the first to try to battle her way through the elective campaigning process, and the first woman ever to run for president of the United States. This is a story about her.

The train's whistle carried over miles of rolling Ohio and Indiana farmland. It was October, 1884, and brilliant fall colors splashed across the landscape where clusters of maple and elm trees stood at the edges of freshly harvested fields.

The train chugged along at forty miles an hour toward Terre Haute, Indiana, still three hours away. Again the shrill whistle stretched out across the miles.

Marietta Stow reached up to hold her hat as the train rolled through a sharp turn and accidentally bumped Elizabeth Cady Stanton, who was sitting next to her on the narrow coach seat.

"Sorry," she apologized, straightening up against the red upholstered seat. Then she turned to Belva Lockwood, sitting across from her and already decked out in her long, black velvet dress for the rally that night in Terre Haute. "Why do we have to ride coach, Belva? Why can't we ride first class if we have to spend so much time on these awful trains?"

The whistle screeched again.

"Oh, and that awful whistle will drive me positively batty long before election day!"

Fifty-four-year-old Belva Lockwood smiled thinly from her cramped seat and gazed out the smudged window. "We ride coach, Marietta, because our Equal Rights Party is small and barely has the funds for us to ride at all."

Belva's chestnut hair was pulled up into a topknot bun. The expression on her square-jawed face changed from kind to cold and back, usually with traces of both.

The four women were crammed knee to knee in the cramped coach seats. Marietta and Elizabeth sat on one side. Belva and Susan B. Anthony sat on the other. Elizabeth Stanton and Susan Anthony were leaders of the national women's suffrage movement. The train ride was a much-needed opportunity for Elizabeth and Susan to discuss Belva's campaign for president of the United States as the nominee of the Equal Rights Party.

Both Susan and Elizabeth showed signs of the discomfort they felt as this meeting began. Susan spoke first, trying to look as supportive as possible.

"No one is saying you haven't done great service for women's rights over the years, Belva. But . . . why muddy up our fight by running for president? The right to vote must always be our paramount concern, and I'm afraid your candidacy will hurt more than help. Have faith with the path we're on for a little longer and women will get the right to vote."

Belva had hoped for enthusiastic support from the two famous women and struggled for a moment to form her answer to this unexpected attack. One thing was certain, though. She was not going to back down. Belva had never backed away from a fight, and never would.

"When I was a girl . . . Oh, this was back in 1837 or '38, I dreamed of moving mountains, and thought faith alone could do it. I even tried to walk on water by faith alone and nearly drowned. I've learned that faith doesn't get the job done without action to back it up.

"The words, 'we the people' in the Constitution don't mean men only. We women are people, too. There are over twelve million female property owners in the country. Don't they deserve to have a say for what will be done with their tax dollars? Well, it's time we relied on more than faith. I want to be the wedge that forces the door to elective office open to women. Only when women hold office will men listen."

Now Elizabeth Stanton leaned forward to take a turn. Before she could begin, two men careened down the aisle grabbing at the rows of seats for support on the swaying train. Suddenly one pointed at Belva. "Aren't you that woman running for president?"

Belva nodded politely. "And I assume I can count on your vote, Mr. . . .?"

"You should be ashamed of yerself, you immoral hussy," he sneered.

Shaking his head, the other man added, "It ain't right for a woman to go around talking in public like a man."

"There, you see?" admonished Elizabeth as the men lurched on down the aisle. "We must focus each election on the issues: the women's vote and equality of education, pay, and property rights. Your actions have shifted the debate to whether a woman is worthy to hold office, rather than the necessity for a woman to be able to vote."

Belva answered, "We may not yet be allowed to vote. But there is nothing that says we can't be voted *for*. Women won't get the vote until a woman is in an office of power to give it to them."

Susan Anthony leaned back and sighed. "Then you're really serious about running for president with Marietta as your vice president? I mean, you're really going to campaign? Judging by what we just saw, it could get very nasty."

Belva's eyes lit up. "Susan, before I was seven I could walk a fence rail, ride a horse bareback, and bring in and milk the cows. I'm not afraid of snakes, spiders, dirt, or hard work. And I'm not afraid of the opinions of a few men stuck deep in ancient ruts, unable to see what's good for the country."

A woman leaned across the aisle. "I think it's wonderful that you're running, Mrs. Lockwood. It makes me proud to be a woman. You'd get my vote—if I could vote. But my husband will vote for you, or he'll hear about it every day for a year!"

"There, you see?" Belva smugly smiled, crossing her arms.

Susan clutched Belva's arm, her eyes narrowed. "But all the papers are writing about *you* and not women's suffrage. One paper described your party as a 'disgusting band of eccentric zealots.' The Boston paper called you 'an immodest minx.' "

"And the Scranton paper called me a 'starry-eyed Goddess of reform.' So what? The point is, if I can get votes, then, and only then, will congress-*men* have to take us seriously."

"And if you *don't* get votes, you'll look a fool, and so will we," sighed Elizabeth.

The train whistle rattled through the car. Marietta groaned and covered her ears. Susan continued, "I've read in four papers that the real purpose of your campaign is to drum up business for your law practice . . ."

Belva laughed, a great horsey laugh. "I could certainly use the business. Most people in Washington don't know what to do with a female lawyer yet."

"Is it true? Is that why you're running?" pressed Susan. "It would be an awful shame for the whole women's movement to be derailed just to satisfy one member's greed." The hard looks in her and Elizabeth's eyes showed that they feared this was exactly what Belva's real purpose was.

"Shame on you, Susan B. Anthony," scolded Belva. "You think I would use the women's movement for my own gain that way? I fought my own way into law school in '57, and it was a long and fearsome fight—all because I was a woman. Then I had to fight for the right to receive a diploma once I completed the course work. I had to fight to be permitted to take the bar exam. I passed easily and then had to fight to be admitted to the courts in Washington. But I did fight, and now I am the first female lawyer in Washington, D.C."

By now Belva's voice had risen as if she were delivering a campaign speech. Everyone in the car stared and listened. "Because I was a woman I had to fight tooth and nail every step along a path that men walk without any obstacles at all. I had to fight for the same reason every woman in every profession has to fight: because men will never *give* anything of value to women. We must *take* it. And the place to start is at the top! That is why I'm in this campaign, Susan. And I should think you'd rejoice and support my effort!"

Most men in the train car laughed and booed. Some women applauded and shouted, "Here, here!" and "Hooray for Belva!" Their husbands growled at them to hush up.

Elizabeth asked, "Couldn't we compromise? Find a sympathetic man and throw all our support to him?"

"Ha!" snapped Belva. "Might as well ask a field mouse to find a sympathetic snake."

"At least stop riding that silly three-wheeled cycle," snapped Susan. "It makes people think you are immodest and gives them a reason to laugh at you, and, through you, at our entire movement."

"But Susan," laughed Belva, with an impish twinkle in her eye, "have you ever ridden one? They're wonderfully fun!" Then she turned serious. "Before you decide if my candidacy hurts or helps our cause, watch one rally. Come tonight in Terre Haute and see the support I get."

Susan B. Anthony and Elizabeth Cady Stanton both sighed and nodded their agreement.

The train pulled into the Terre Haute station just past five o'clock with a series of ear-piercing whistle blasts. Equal Rights Party organizers swarmed over the platform. Placards and hand-painted signs on tall sticks waved in the stiff afternoon breeze like a forest of Kansas wheat. Red, white, and blue banners and streamers fluttered everywhere.

Three hundred loyal supporters, mostly women, noisily cheered and waved as the train hissed to a stop, spraying a thick cloud of steam over the crowd. A ten piece marching band, wearing ill-fitting rented uniforms, launched bravely into a slightly off-key rendition of "The Battle Hymn of the Republic."

Inside the last coach car, Marietta Stow jammed her face to the window and reported on the scene to the other three. Belva stretched in the aisle, straightened her black velvet dress, and pinned a large corsage of white roses to her bodice.

"Only 300 people, and no reporters?" asked Elizabeth. "Is this your idea of a *strong* rally?"

Stretching to ease her aching back after the long ride, Belva glared at Elizabeth Stanton. "This is just the welcome and the beginning of our hour-long parade. The rally is set for six thirty at the town hall. And yes, there will be reporters."

Belva turned for the door of the coach, carefully pasted her friendliest smile across her face, and called over her shoulder, "Come along, Marietta. It's show time."

Belva took one last deep breath and burst onto the platform, all big waves and smiles. The crowd cheered. Placards waved. The party photographer clicked his camera, his pan of flash powder exploding with a loud "pop!"

Someone thrust a cone-shaped megaphone into Belva's hands. She raised it to her still-smiling lips. "Welcome, Terre Haute, to the party of equality, to the party of justice, to the party of the future. In November we march to the White House. Today we march to the town hall!"

Supporters cheered. Hecklers booed and jeered. Several men angrily flipped cigar butts onto the platform near Belva. One supporter swung his "Vote for Belva!" placard at a heckler, knocking the man to the sidewalk. A fistfight broke out. Someone threw a cabbage at Belva. It missed and splattered against the train.

"Forward to the town hall," cried Belva.

The parade began. The band stepped out smartly, followed by Belva and Marietta waving as hard as their arms could stand. Then came the placards, organizers, supporters, and hecklers. Susan Anthony and Elizabeth Stanton followed off to one side, leaning quietly on parasols, slowly shaking their heads.

"Not once did she mention the issues," moaned Elizabeth.

The parade marched up one street and down the next, gathering supporters and hecklers like a magnet gathering iron filings. The crowd swelled. Pushing and shoving broke out. The tuba player and a trombone player were pelted with tomatoes and stopped playing to wipe the goo off their clothes and instruments.

"Keep moving, no matter what," yelled Belva over the roar of the crowd to her running mate. "If you stop, you're an easy target."

The sun set in a wash of orange light. Torches were lit to illuminate the parade as it neared the rally site. "Great crowd," beamed Belva. "Lots of spunk, like me."

Susan Anthony rolled her eyes. Elizabeth hissed into Belva's ear, "The issues. Talk about the issues!"

The wide double doors of the Terre Haute town hall were flung open and the crowd poured in. As was the custom of that period, there were no seats. The crowd milled about in front of a raised wooden stage. Gas lanterns blazed around the walls. Cigar smoke drifted in thick clouds toward the ceiling.

Hecklers jeered and tossed vegetables at the speakers. Supporters paraded through the room yelling songs. Reporters crowded around Belva shouting questions. She ignored the ones she didn't like, pretending not to hear them over the din. Her biggest smile was still spread across her face.

"Victoria is Empress of India and Queen of England," she cried through her megaphone. "Catherine is Czar of Russia. Do American women deserve any less?"

"NO!" screamed the crowd.

"Go back to the kitchen!" screamed the hecklers.

"Is it true you're running for president just to get publicity for your law practice?" shouted a reporter.

Belva smiled, ignored the question, and screamed into her megaphone. "Women in this country have fewer rights, and less representation than did America's founding fathers when they revolted against King George. Women deserve equal pay! Women deserve equal education!"

"BOOO!" screamed a large group of men under a thick cloud of cigar smoke. Belva supporters spun around waving "Vote for Belva!" placards in their faces. Shoving and pushing broke out. A volley of vegetables flew toward the platform striking three reporters and the president of the Indiana Chapter of the Equal Rights Party.

"Women deserve equal property rights," continued Belva. "Women deserve the vote! Women *demand* the vote!"

Marietta was broadsided by a tomato. Four men tumbled to the floor in a fistfight. The roar in the room was so loud people were unable to hear their neighbors shout in their ear. The double doors burst open and fifty young men from the local Mother Hubbard political club burst in.

"Oh dear. Not them," moaned Elizabeth Stanton.

Political clubs commonly wore outlandish costumes as they paraded through the streets to gain publicity for their candidate. Men in the clubs supporting Belva usually wore long, loose dresses, called "Mother Hubbards," and billowing bonnets with long raised bills. Because of these costumes, all male supporters of Belva Lockwood were labeled, "Mother Hubbards."

They burst into the meeting hall clanging bells, banging pots, and caterwauling songs. They each carried a broom to symbolize "a clean sweep" for Belva.

Everyone laughed and cheered or booed. People marched, and shoved, and yelled. The Mother Hubbards noisily stomped back and forth pretending to sweep the floor clean of anti-Belva voices. Hecklers booed and snatched at their brooms. No one could hear the speeches. The band began to play again as it marched out the doors to return their rented uniforms. With a great cheer the overflowing crowd followed, bursting noisily into the quiet Terre Haute evening.

"That crowd was awful," gasped Susan Anthony, her ears still ringing as the din faded into the night.

"I thought it was a wonderful crowd," corrected Belva.

"What?" exclaimed Elizabeth. "They didn't listen. They yelled, fought, and threw things."

Belva nodded in agreement. "True. But more importantly, they were here, almost 2,000 of them and more than thirty reporters. As long as they turn out, we cannot be ignored."

On Wednesday, November 3, 1884, Belva Lockwood and Marietta Stow sat in Belva's office as news of election returns were telegraphed into Washington from all over the country. Belva studied the handwritten sheet of election returns an Equal Rights Party member had just dropped off. Marietta studied the large portraits of George and Martha Washington hanging on one wall.

Belva sadly shook her head. "A decent showing in Indiana. As expected, we're holding our own in California. But New York is bad, and so are Maryland, Pennsylvania, and Illinois. We're not going to get the strong showing we'd hoped for."

Then she brightened. "We won't come close to winning. But I think we'll do better than anyone thought we would. We showed the world that women can run a tough campaign as well as any man. We cracked open the door, Marietta. And that is the first step."

Receiving only 6,000 votes nationwide out of ten million cast, Belva Lockwood never ran for office again. Instead she tirelessly lobbied and lectured for the rights of women and minorities, and for world peace. She won major court cases for blacks and for the Cherokee Nation, and was appointed by the State Department to represent the United States at four international conferences.

Belva Lockwood died in May, 1917. Two months before her death, the first woman to win a major elected position, Jeanette Rankin of Montana, was sworn into the House of Representatives. That same year, the House also started debate on the constitutional amendment granting women the right to vote. One year later it passed the House. In 1919 the Senate passed the same measure and sent it to the states for ratification. Belva's dreams became reality.

But beyond these dreams, Belva Lockwood should be remembered as the first woman lawyer allowed to present cases in front of the U.S. Supreme Court, and as one of the first women lawyers to practice in Washington, D.C. But above all, she proved a woman could run for the highest office in this country. That is a race we are still waiting for a woman to win. But that is another story.

Questions to Explore

Belva Lockwood ran for president of the United States. Have other women run for this position? Why haven't we heard of them?

Has a major political party ever nominated a woman for president? Vice president? Senator? Governor?

What women have been elected to high office in your state?

What have been the contributions of women elected to high office?

References for Further Reading

- *In the Children's Library*

  Brown, Drollene. *Belva Lockwood Wins Her Case*. Niles, IL: Albert Whitman & Company, 1987.

- *In the Adult Library*

  Dunnahoo, Terry. *Before the Supreme Court: The Story of Belva Ann Lockwood*. Boston: Houghton Mifflin, 1974.

See your librarian for additional titles.

Convention Halls and Cowtown Saloons

A story about Frances Willard and Carrie Nation and their separate work to promote temperance

About This Story:

Shortly after the Civil War a growing concern spread across America. Men drank too much alcohol. In what was then the American West (Indiana, Illinois, Iowa, Kansas, Missouri), liquor was linked to crime and violence, especially violence against women. In the East, liquor was viewed as a sign of moral decay and the result of unnatural pressures of the growing urban and industrial centers. A call for temperance, or the outlawing of alcohol, arose.

The Temperance Movement started in the West but spread quickly east. It began as a single-issue women's movement. But slowly in the late 1800s one brilliant woman linked temperance with other mainstream issues of the day and made temperance synonymous with a belief in family, order, and moral values. This woman worked through grand conference halls and the corridors of power in the nation's great cities. This one woman, more than any other single factor, created the political consensus needed to finally pass the Eighteenth Amendment to the U.S. Constitution creating Prohibition. She was a political mastermind.

At the same time, a second woman, working with all her might for the same cause, brought temperance into the headlines. This woman worked virtually alone in small, dusty towns of the rugged Wild West of frontier Kansas.

Neither woman approved of the other's tactics, and even though they worked for the same goal, they never met. Still the two of them are both important parts of the story of the drive toward Prohibition. This is a story about those two women.

At six o'clock in the morning on June 5, 1896, Frances Willard rose from her bed in a V.I.P. suite in New York City's Astoria Hotel. She ordered coffee and a simple breakfast and settled in with three staff members to coordinate convention plans.

Some of the southern and West Coast delegates were wavering, not as committed as Frances would like. She had scheduled meetings with these two groups: one at eight A.M. and one at nine. At nine forty-five she would meet with her own delegates and volunteers for a pep rally, and to place them strategically around the convention floor. By ten minutes after ten, she would have to be on the convention floor itself. This would be quite a day.

• • •

82

Also at six o'clock that same morning, in Medicine Lodge, Kansas, Carrie Nation rose from her simple slat bed and crossed the bare, wood floor of her small frame house to gaze at the stacks of rocks, bottles, bats, and hatchets she had lined up in the dirt next to her front door. If she was lucky, she'd use them all today.

She'd leave at nine o'clock for Kiowa, allow two and a half hours for the ride, and leave the afternoon free for whatever might happen. She rubbed her hands together in anticipation. This would be quite a day.

• • •

Between nine and ten in the morning a great crowd of fashionably dressed women gathered in the Astoria's grand ballroom, coming from every state in the nation. The tasteful placard next to the ballroom's entrance announced the opening session of the 1896 Convention of the National Council of Women. Twenty gold chandeliers draped in glass teardrops hung from the ceiling. The round tables were set with the finest satin and lace.

At ten fifteen, fifty-nine-year-old Frances Willard glided gracefully in from her last meeting. An excited buzz rippled through the crowd. Graciously she accepted every hand extended to her. She greeted every face that turned her way with a warm and genuine smile. Slowly she meandered through the crowd toward the raised speaker's stage along one long wall of the ballroom.

An aide and lieutenant in Frances's well-oiled political machine joined Mrs. Willard and walked at her elbow, whispering a summary report. "I've stationed loud supporters in each of the state delegations where we are the weakest. There are a dozen senators and congressmen here. I gave each of them the usual cigar and boutonniere with your compliments."

Frances nodded. "Excellent, my dear. We've planned for this convention for a long time. If the votes swing our way—and I believe they will—this great convention will adopt our resolutions and temperance will be a central plank of every women's and family organization in the country."

• • •

Fifteen hundred miles away, giant sunflowers stood like wilting soldiers along a winding stream. Dustdevils danced across a dirt road. Heat shimmered up off the Kansas prairie, fuzzing out the letters on the signpost reading, "Kiowa, Kansas, 2 miles." Flat Kansas prairie stretched out as far as the eye could see, an ocean of yellow grains clinging to life in the parched summer heat.

This prairie looked every bit as "rough and tumble" as the reputations of Kansas residents William "Billy the Kid" Bonney, the James and Younger brothers, the Dalton Gang, and Bat Masterson. Yet the woman hunched over the reins in the lead buggy winding its way toward Kiowa looked even tougher. Over six feet tall, she had powerful shoulders and thick, muscular arms. Her mouth lay wide and flat in a square face, set as if daring anyone to cross her. Behind thin, wire-rimmed glasses, her eyes flashed.

Fifty-year-old Carrie Nation turned in her seat and called back to the second dust-choked buggy, "I feel the strength of a giant today. Before this sun sets I will surely give the devil his due!"

Carrie's black alpaca dress was buttoned tight up to her throat, her lace "war bonnet" pulled down tight around her ears. Her horse strained at each gentle rise to haul the weight of the rocks, bricks, bats, throwing bottles, and hatchets in the buggy.

At noon, on the main street of Kiowa, Carrie Nation reined her horse to a stop in front of a popular south-central Kansas watering hole. The gaudy sign, with "Lewis's Bar" painted on it, squeaked back and forth in the midday breeze from its mount between the swinging bar door and long, plate glass windows.

Bible and hymnal in hand, Carrie jumped to the dirt street as two similarly clad women, whose black dresses had turned light gray with road dust, emerged from the other buggy.

"Gather 'round ladies. It's time to pray for the souls of our dear Kansas men."

The few strollers stopped to watch in wonder and amusement as the three women dropped to their knees in the dusty road facing Lewis's Bar. In an impassioned voice Carrie Nation began to pray and sing.

• • •

In New York, the crowd at the 1896 National Convention of Women cheered and applauded as Frances Willard was introduced. Graciously, Frances rose, politely nodded to the audience and ascended the podium like a queen.

An aide rushed to her side whispering frantically in her ear. "A wire just came in from Topeka. Carrie Nation is at it again in some tiny town called Kiowa."

Frances faltered. Her eyes flickered toward the ceiling and then closed as she groaned. "That wild woman's hatchet-wielding, terrorizing tactics will set our movement backwards faster than you and I can push it forward."

She recovered and sighed. "Nothing to be done about it now. All we can do is continue to build an unstoppable national consensus behind the temperance movement."

Frances finished her march to the podium listening to the enthusiastic cheers of the crowd. Gathering herself with a couple of deep breaths, Frances Willard seemed to take on a great presence. With no movies, television, or radio, and with vaudeville considered far too risqué for respectable folk, speeches were the main form of public entertainment. And Frances Willard was a world-class entertainer.

"Women of this convention, citizens of this country," she boomed in a melodic voice that made each listener feel she spoke only to them. "In every corner of this land the voice of American womanhood is swelling. Our pride in womanhood is growing. Women came to college and humanized it, came into literature and hallowed it, came into the business world and ennobled it."

The crowd cheered. Frances waited politely. "As the president of this great body of women for five years, and as the president of the Women's Christian Temperance Union for over fifteen, I tell you each and every one, we are now faced with a mighty task and with an equally mighty opportunity."

Again the crowd interrupted with cheers that echoed off the gilded ballroom walls.

Frances raised her hands in an impassioned plea. "It is time for us each to redouble our efforts to bring every citizen behind the banner of temperance in the name of Home Protection." Her voice picked up a note of irritation. "We may disagree with the tactics and efforts of *some*. But let us disagree with gentleness. Then our ultimate victory will be an even greater Christian triumph."

The crowd roared that they would triple, quadruple their efforts if Frances Willard asked.

• • •

Young Bruce Dennis burst through the swinging doors of Lewis's Bar. "Hey everybody, come and look! There's women praying in the street outside."

Lanky Ted Lewis froze in the middle of polishing one of his carefully stacked bar glasses. His floppy handlebar mustache drooped below his chin. His eyes opened wide in fear. His voice dried up to a dusty whisper. "Is one of 'em carrying a hatchet?"

Twenty-year-old Bruce peered back over the swinging doors. "No, just Bibles, Mr. Lewis."

"Is one of 'em wearin' head to toe black?"

"All three of 'em are, Mr. Lewis."

The color drained from Ted Lewis' face faster than whiskey from a bottle in the hands of a dozen thirsty trail hands after a long cattle drive. Ted felt his knees begin to wobble. "Quick! Hide the bottles!"

But it was too late. A voice like the sound of doom itself bellowed from the street. "Christian women arise! Forward to save the boys of Kansas. Smash!"

A salvo of rocks exploded through the bar windows. Armed to the teeth with the buggy's arsenal, Carrie's vigilantes attacked.

The swinging doors crumpled to a pile of kindling under fierce hatchet blows. The men inside scattered for cover. Two squeezed into the broom closet. Ted Lewis, clutching three bottles of his best brandy, cowered behind the bar.

The next rock salvo shattered Ted's elegant beveled bar mirror, the pride of all Kiowa. With machine gun rapidity, Carrie launched a barrage of rocks and bottles that swept the counter clean of glasses and liquor bottles. "Destroy that devil's brew that destroys the souls of men!" she cried. Whiskey ran in streams along the wooden floor.

"The hatchets ladies!" cried Carrie, now worked into a frenzy. At the top of her voice she began to wail hymns as one of her ladies attacked the bar itself, wood chips flying. Carrie turned on the tables splintering several with her mighty arms. She easily hoisted one heavy oak table and heaved it through a side window that had so far escaped destruction. The air was filled with wood chips, exploding glass, the wrenching sounds of destruction, the smell of running liquor, and the caterwauling of Carrie's hymns.

Her eyes gone wild, Carrie kicked a cuspidor over the potbellied stove back by the broom closet. Then she attacked the stove itself for good measure, rending great gashes and dents into it with her hatchet.

Carrie spotted Ted Lewis fearfully poking his head out from behind the bar. Dropping her hatchet and raising both clenched fists, Carrie began a dancing shuffle across the glass-strewn floor. "I dare you to come out and mix it up, you son of the devil!"

Ted Lewis seemed to turn to stone, unable even to shake his head.

In a rage, Carrie wrenched the massive brass cash register off its stand and heaved it out the door. It smashed through the wooden sidewalk and settled with a resounding "thud" and a cloud of dust in the street.

In awe and wonder, Bruce Dennis whispered, "Three men can barely lift that thing, and she just heaved it out the door."

Carrie's two helpers turned to the gas lamps, ripping them from the walls. A small fire started in one corner and spread in thin blue flames along the rivers of whiskey.

Carrie attacked the pool table. With the cry, "These are for Satan himself!" she fired the fifteen numbered balls like a professional pitcher at anything that moved or wasn't already shattered. Then Carrie's hatchet splintered the table itself.

In less than five minutes it was over. The women regrouped at the bar door. Carrie dropped two copies of her temperance newsletter, *The Smasher's Mail*, on the floor. "You owe me 10 cents for these, Mr. Lewis."

Turning to her compatriots, and taking a deep, satisfied breath, Carrie asked, "Ready ladies?"

They marched out to the sidewalk leaving an awe-inspiring scene of total destruction behind them. Over her shoulder, Carrie called, "God be with you, one and all."

The great ring of onlookers in the street gawked in amazement as the three liquor and sweat soaked figures emerged from the growing smoke of the bar.

"What are you lookin' at?" snarled Carrie. "Either stand aside or arrest us. Where *is* the sheriff? I dare him to arrest me!" She snatched two gleaming hatchets from her buggy and swirled them high over her head. "I raise my hatchets to save the souls of Kansas. Go ahead and shoot me down if you dare!"

"Sheriff, do your duty," begged Ted Lewis, still clutching his three bottles of brandy in the shattered doorway.

The sheriff quietly shook his head and shrugged. "It's a shame about your bar, Ted. But you know perfectly well bars are illegal in Kansas. Oh, sure, we pretty well ignore that law. But how can I arrest her for tearin' up something that doesn't officially exist?"

Snapping the reins as she started for home, Carrie muttered, "Nuts. Didn't even get arrested this time . . ."

• • •

In New York, Frances came to the resounding finale of her speech. "We must all unify behind Home Protection, protection of our children our sisters and mothers, our values, our way of life. Home Protection is not a luxury, it is necessity.

"For Home Protection we need education for women and young children, we need garbage pickup and central water service and utilities, and we need strong temperance laws to prevent so many of the hardships our women must now endure. One and all, pick up the cry, 'Home Protection and Temperance!' Carry it out into the streets, into your lives, 'Home Protection and Temperance!' Thank you very much."

The ballroom crowd surged to its feet chanting, "Home Protection and Temperance! Home Protection and Temperance!" Frances Willard was mobbed by supporters before she could reach the stairs of the stage.

• • •

With Kansas stars twinkling high above, Carrie Nation settled sullenly back onto her small bed that night. "Shoot, I didn't get arrested, whipped, shot, or nothing. Not as much of a day as I hoped."

• • •

Around midnight, Frances Willard wearily bid farewell to the last of the well-wishers in her hotel suite. The convention had backed every one of Frances' proposals by landslide votes. Legislators and congressmen alike had left pledging their support.

Home Protection was now the rallying cry of the two largest women's organizations in the country. A constitutional amendment to enforce temperance was its central plank. Frances's dream was so close to becoming national reality she could taste it.

Frances turned to an aide, busily clearing away glasses and cleaning ashtrays. "Have you heard if Carrie Nation did much damage today?"

The aide smiled. "As I understand it we were lucky. She wrecked a bar, but it wasn't picked up by any of the major papers. I don't think she did much damage to our cause today."

Frances smiled and settled back into a deep, soft chair. "It was really quite a day."

• • •

When Frances Willard died in February, 1898, over 30,000 mourners a day waited in long lines in bitter Chicago snow to file past her coffin. The national press called her the, "Queen of Temperance." She was eulogized by three U.S. Senators. All Chicago flags flew at half-mast. The *New York Independent* wrote that, "no woman's name is better known in the English-speaking world than Frances Willard, save only the great Queen of England, herself." The president lamented that the foremost woman in American public life had died. When the Eighteenth Amendment creating national Prohibition was finally ratified, it was said that the memory of Frances Willard drove it through both Congress and the various state legislatures. Yet by the end of the twentieth century it is hard to find anyone who recognizes her name.

• • •

When Carrie Nation died in 1911, only one doctor and one nurse were in attendance. No reporters or well-wishers crowded around Evergreen Hospital in Leavenworth, Kansas, to be present when she died. Carrie was buried in a grave in Arkansas that remained unmarked for twelve years.

Yet Carrie's raw energy and dramatic flare would not die. Her valiant struggle grew to join the other Kansas greats of western lore. She became a Kansas legend of passion, commitment, and unrelenting destruction.

In 1923, a headstone was erected at her grave that read, "She did what she could." Her longtime home in Medicine Lodge, Kansas, was acquired as a public monument. Statues and plaques in her honor have sprung up all over Kansas. By the late twentieth century, virtually every American has heard the name of Carrie Nation.

• • •

Two very different women. Two very different strategies. But each of these women did what they could, and what they thought right, to reach their one common, uniting goal. That goal, national temperance, flickered briefly to life with the passage of the Eighteenth Amendment in 1920, and then died a violent death amongst the speakeasys and machine-gun-toting mobsters of the early 1930s. But that's another story.

Questions to Explore

What is temperance?

Should alcohol be outlawed in the United States today? Why or why not?

What was the result when alcohol was outlawed by the Eighteenth Amendment? How and why did it fail?

Why do you think more women were active in the temperance movement than men? What evidence can you find to support your view?

References for Further Reading

- *In the Children's Library*

Madison, Arnold. *Carrie Nation.* Chicago: Nelson, 1977.

Mason, Miriam. *Frances Willard, Girl Crusader.* New York: Bobbs-Merrill, 1961.

- *In the Adult Library*

Bordine, Ruth. *Frances Willard: A Biography.* Chapel Hill, NC: The University of North Carolina Press, 1986.

Taylor, Robert. *Vessel of Wrath: The Life and Times of Carrie Nation.* New York: The New American Library, 1966.

———. *Women and Temperance.* New Brunswick, NJ: Rutgers University Press, 1990.

See your librarian for additional titles.

Save the Fire

A story about Queen Liliuokalani, the last queen in America

About This Story:

Did you know that kings and queens once lived in, and ruled over what is now part of the United States? The crushing forces that eroded, and then toppled that monarchy, are the same forces that steamrolled across the native cultures and peoples of much of continental North America, profit and greed. In the end, the Hawaiian monarchy was overthrown to save 3 cents per pound on sugar exports. While the names, conquests, and stories of mighty Hawaiian kings, like Kamehameha and Kalakaua, have become famous, a story of even greater bravery involves the end of this centuries-old monarchy and the queen who fought to save it. This is a story of the courage of the last Queen of Hawaii.

Glossary of Hawaiian words:

Aloha (ah-LO-ha).   A general greeting. Means both hello and good-bye.

Alii (ah-LEE-ee).   Hawaiian nobility.

Conch shell.   A large spiral ocean shell that produces a loud sound like a trumpet.

Haole (HOW-lay).   White foreigners, principally Americans.

Lanai (lah-NIGH).   Wide, usually shaded, outdoor sitting porch.

Mumu (MOO-moo).   Loose-fitting dress that hangs from the shoulders.

Pali (PAH-lee).   High mountain cliffs.

Pele (PAY-lay).   Goddess of fire. Pele appears as an old woman and lives in volcanoes.

Trade winds.   Brisk afternoon winds that blow across the islands and break the heat.

She said it so softly and suddenly that no one was sure they heard correctly.

"We are *dying*," she repeated to their stunned faces.

All four people on the *lanai* with Queen Liliuokalani froze in surprise and fear. Her voice sounded soft and soothing like the afternoon trade winds, in sharp contrast to her word's terrible meaning.

"Are you ill, my queen?" asked Lihuli, the oldest and wisest of the queen's advisors.

89

"Not me," answered the fifty-seven-year-old queen, who had reigned for less than a year, since her brother's death. "What is dying is the fire that makes us Hawaiians."

Through a long moment of silence, Lihuli and the three other aids traded nervous glances, waiting for the queen to explain her words. Instead she rose from her polished chair of bent cane and walked toward the railing of the second floor *lanai* of Westminster House, the residence of the Queen of Hawaii. It was July, 1895, and the trade winds blew warm and fragrant, ruffling the queen's loose *mumu.*

The bustling city of Honolulu spread out below Westminster House, which rested on the slope of the extinct volcano called Punch Bowl Crater. The fiery red of sunset reflected on Honolulu harbor. Always a favorite place of the Hawaiian Kings, Honolulu had become a sprawling beehive of *haole* houses, factories, and warehouses because of it's deep natural harbor. The American navy liked Honolulu, too, because of the protected, deep-water bay just to the west of town, Pearl Harbor.

Finally Lihuli, a white-haired sage who had counseled the kings of Hawaii for fifty years, politely cleared his throat and spoke. "Exactly *who* is dying, my queen?"

Liliuokalani turned to face her trusted servants. She was tall, stately, and slender for an Hawaiian. Her short, curly hair clung tight around her kind Hawaiian face. Her words came measured and thoughtful; her voice soft and lyrical.

"When Pele, the Goddess of Fire, left the volcanoes here on Oahu to breathe her fiery majesty into the volcanoes of the big island, all that remained here were empty shells of rock. The life and fire had died."

She searched the four familiar faces before her in the red glow of sunset before continuing. "In the same way, I see the fire that breathes pride into our people withering, about to flicker out. All that will be left are the shells of our bodies. Our Hawaiian spirit will be gone."

"It is the *haoles'* fault, my queen," cried fierce Kimo, a slight, wiry man of thirty with sparkling black eyes and a wide smile that could sweeten lemons.

Liliuokalani reached out a hand to stop him. "No. It is our fault. Whatever they have done, we let them do. I asked you here this afternoon to tell you what I have done to retake control of our land and our people."

"We must go to war!" cried Kimo, his clenched fists raised, his eyes blazing. "King Kamehameha the First lead 1,000 warriors rushing from outrigger canoes to defeat armies on three islands. Hawaiians are fierce fighters. We will raise as many to follow you."

"And the *haoles* will call in 10,000 of their navy and marines," interrupted the queen. "They will march into battle with canons, machine guns, and rifles. And then, dear Kimo, your army will die."

"Then you will not fight?" asked Lihuli.

"I most certainly *will* fight!" cried Liliuokalani. "But this is a different kind of enemy. We thought enemies arrived with spears, not smiles and trinket gifts. We thought enemies fought with clubs and swords, not with 'partnerships,' 'land purchases,' and 'job offers.' "

"But how can we fight the *haoles*?" wailed Wahinalea, a personal attendant, wringing her old, wrinkled hands.

Kimo rose, his powerful arms imploring Liliuokalani. "I beg you, my queen. Give me the word, and I will raise an army to sweep every *haole* from this land!"

"Both of you, stop!" commanded Liliuokalani. "I could not bear to be the cause of the death of even one of my precious people. There are too few of us left already. But we have moaned and wrung our hands far too long. Only new ways can defeat this new enemy."

The queen stood gazing at the sunset. Lihuli sat deep in thought. Kimo paced and planned for war. Wahinalea sat, helplessly wringing her hands. And Waimaha quietly grieved to see her queen so tormented.

Liliuokalani began, "I remember once four years ago talking with my brother, King Kalakaua, before he died. We sat on this very *lanai* enjoying the cool trade winds.

" 'I do not recognize my own country,' grumbled Kalakaua. 'I look past the palms and valleys to the *pali*, and the land looks like my Hawaii. But the people, the way of doing things, of acting, the very way of life is not Hawaiian any more.'

" 'The *haoles*,' I answered. 'When they first arrived seventy years ago our parents welcomed them with open arms. Now each day they grow stronger, while we grow fewer and weaker. More Americans arrive. More Americans are born. Every day *haole* diseases kill more and more Hawaiians. Fewer of us are born each year. We are disappearing in our own land.'

"King Kalakaua waved his hand to show that I had missed his point. 'It is much more than just the number of Americans . . .'

" 'Yes,' I agreed. 'Their religion, their institutions have replaced our own. Our very culture is ridiculed and laughed at in our own land. Our ceremonies are ignored. Our chants and *hulas* are forgotten. Worst, our youth have turned to America. Hawaiian blood flows in their veins. But their hearts and minds have turned to *haole* jobs, *haole* clothes, *haole* values, *haole* lives.'

" 'Exactly!' exclaimed my brother. 'But how did it happen?'

"The great King Kalakaua hung his head and clasped his hands between his knees. His broad shoulders seemed to wither and shrink. His voice was barely a whisper. 'I am the king. I see my Hawaii dying, and yet I cannot stop it. There is no enemy for me to strike down and defeat.' "

The queen's eyes lit with the fire of Pele's volcanic fire. Her mouth smiled. Her face began to glow. "Now I am the queen, and *I* do know the enemy: the *haole* legislature, president, and courts that block my every move. Our way to fight has become clear to me. The *haoles* hide behind their constitution. I will manipulate their paper laws to restore the power of Hawaiians over these islands."

She paused, glanced around the *lanai* to be sure no others listened. "Today I fired the entire president. The *haoles*' constitution says I can. I called them together, thanked them for their service, and ordered them to get out. At first they chuckled, thinking it was a joke. Then they screamed and threatened.

"I told them to be careful with what they said to their queen. I might consider it a threat to the monarchy and have them arrested. When I called in five powerful Hawaiian guards, they meekly left like scolded children."

With triumph ringing in her voice Liliuokalani concluded, "Tomorrow I will appoint a new president of noble Hawaiians. I have already picked the names. I will rewrite the constitution with the help of this new president. Then I will hold new elections for the legislature—elections Hawaiians will win."

Quiet Waimaha said, "You are all alone now, my queen, the last of the *alii*, nobility by birth. How can one fight so many *haoles*?"

"We will *all* fight!" cried Kimo.

"No," Liliuokalani commanded. "Too many Hawaiians have already died. I could never do something which would cost the lives of any of our people. I will stand tall and strong against the *haole* legislature, president, and courts. This fight is for much more than the monarchy. I must save our people's pride and the fire that makes them true Hawaiians. All Hawaiians must see their queen stand unafraid against the *haoles* as a proud and powerful Hawaiian."

. . .

Hidden in the deep shadows that night, Kimo paced under the cover of a giant banyan tree, the Meeting Tree, practicing his words of inspiration. The giant banyan's branches had sent shoots into the ground in a wide circle around the base of the tree, creating a tent-like space, seemingly under the very roots of the tree.

"With fancy written words and pockets full of money, white Americans, the *haoles*, want to steal our islands of Hawaii. But I do not believe even Queen Liliuokalani can stop them alone anymore. She needs our help and our strength. She is a true queen and would never ask. But I know she needs it."

Kimo heard a soft rustling as a group of men slipped in under the Meeting Tree.

"Who comes to this place?" whispered Kimo.

"Kuhiko," came the whispered answer. Kimo could just make out the thick arms, sturdy legs, and great round belly of his lifelong friend. "*Aloha*, Kimo, I'd know you anywhere. You are too skinny for an Hawaiian." Kuhiko and the men behind him chuckled.

"I have the guns," said Kimo. "They are hidden. When I give the call, bring all the men you can trust."

"Must we kill the *haoles*?" asked Kuhiko. "Too often all killing leads to is more killing."

Even in the dark they could sense Kimo's fierce determination. "Yes, we must! At least all the *haoles* in the legislature." Then he softened and added, "We'll start there, and then we'll see."

Kuhiko solemnly nodded. "When?"

"Soon. The queen has a plan. She has fired the *haole* president. If that works, fine. If not, I will call."

Kuhiko started to leave, then stopped. "How did we get to this . . . this war with guns?"

Kimo answered, "It started almost thirty years ago, the year I was born. The *haoles* forced a vote and passed a constitution. The king allowed it, I think, just to humor the *haoles*, because he thought votes meant nothing. Constitutions meant nothing in a land where king's word is law. But there were already more *haoles* than Hawaiians, and most Hawaiians didn't vote. The *haole* constitution won."

"I remember that silliness," chuckled Kuhiko. "We don't need to vote. The king speaks for us."

Kimo held out his hands to quiet his friend. "But that vote created a constitution and a legislature, president, and courts. The constitution said that only males with money and property could vote. That meant that almost all voters from then on would be *haole*. The constitution said that everyone must obey the written laws of the legislature. Worse, through votes and legislative appointments, the president and courts are all run by *haoles*. There are no Hawaiians in our own government."

Again Kuhiko interrupted his friend with laughter. "What are these things to a king? The king's word is law!"

"Not to *haoles*," hissed Kimo. "They ignore the king and listen to courts and written laws and the legislature. And the *haoles* have the American navy and marines. Over the years they held more votes. But only those with money and property could vote. So the *haoles* always won and stole more and more power away from the king."

"So now we fight," sighed Kuhiko.

"If the queen's plan fails, yes!" hissed Kimo.

• • •

Eight weeks later Liliuokalani and her four assistants gathered again on the Westminster House second-floor *lanai*. The queen said, "Howls of protest rang from the legislature when I fired my *haole* president."

"Secretly we laughed and cheered," interrupted Kimo.

"The people were proud of you," agreed Lihuli.

Liliuokalani continued, "I named a new president of noble Hawaiians. But the constitution says the legislature must approve the president ministers. They would not approve any of my choices. I appointed another slate. Again they refused. Last month the legislature tried to appoint a president of all *haoles*. I refused to let them serve."

Her voice rang like thunder with the proud strength of the great kings. "Then I rewrote the constitution myself without the help of a president and included a provision that all Hawaiians have the vote." Slowly the fierceness in her words changed to frustration. "This week the legislature claimed that the existing constitution says they must approve any changes to it. The courts agreed with them. The legislature has refused to even vote on my new constitution."

Wise Lihuli said, "Now the *haole* court says you are violating the constitution by not picking a president."

"All that is left to us is war!" cried Kimo.

"They're plotting to steal your throne, my queen," Lihuli continued.

Kimo hissed, "They circle like rats in the shadows."

"Why?" asked the queen. "Do they hate us so?"

"I do not think the *haoles* love or hate," answered Lihuli. "They see only money. The United States enacted a tariff of 3 cents per pound on imported sugar. The *haole* growers and shippers here must pay that 3 cents. If they overthrow your monarchy and become part of the United States, they won't have to pay it anymore."

The queen's eyes smoldered with anger. "They would destroy our way of life for 3 cents?"

"I think," Lihuli answered, "these *haoles* would do anything for 3 cents a pound."

"We will not be destroyed for 3 cents a pound!" vowed Kimo. "We will fight!"

"No, Kimo, fighting means death." Liliuokalani's shoulders drooped as she said it. "It is the precious spark in our Hawaiian people that must never die. I will continue to fight this war of legal maneuvers. If I fight well, if I stand firm and unafraid against the *haoles*, the fire in every Hawaiian heart will survive. That is the way it must be."

But Kimo's eyes blazed with his own plan.

• • •

Late that night the repeated call of conch shells drifted up Manoa Valley. Kimo would have preferred less moon. The light would make it harder to hide their movements. But they could not wait. It had to be tonight.

"Shhh!" hissed Kimo, hearing a rustling under the banyan. "How many do you bring?"

"Twelve."

Kimo sucked in his breath. "Only twelve? We are too few! Too few. But we cannot wait. We must act tonight. A great American war ship steamed into Pearl Harbor today. If we wait, I know they will use their navy to stop us. Come, I will lead you to where I hid the guns."

Creeping through fragrant shadows with his friend Kuhiko, Kimo whispered, "Now there is whispered talk of arresting the queen. Still she will not budge, and demands that Hawaiians rule our islands. She stands like a solid rock holding back the waves. But without help, even a rock breaks."

Silently the line of thirty Hawaiians followed Kimo through the tropical night. By the *haole* calendar it was Sunday, October 12, 1895.

"Stay to the shadows," whispered Kimo. "There is enough moonlight for even *haoles* to see."

A warm breeze drifted down Manoa Valley carrying the fragrant smells of a thousand tropical flowers and the fresh scent of the afternoon rains which had fallen on the *pali*, or steep mountain cliffs, high above.

"I buried the guns in the garden behind Iolani Palace," Kimo whispered to Kuhiko as they slithered from shadow to shadow among the thick vines and towering palm trees. For such a big man, Kuhiko moved as swiftly and silently as a cat. In the distance they heard the soft conch shell calls of other groups sifting toward the palace.

Kimo pushed through a thick hedge into a manicured garden. "The guns are buried behind that gardener's shed," he whispered. "Dig quietly. Once we have the guns, we attack at dawn. Then we rush in and capture the palace and legislature room inside."

Kuhiko grunted his agreement. Behind him, a line of thirty brave Hawaiians filed into the silent Iolani Palace gardens.

Outside the shed the steady, soft sound of shovels ripping through the moist earth made Kimo glance nervously around. "Shhh! Dig quietly."

A solid, "Thunk!" announced that the shovels had reached metal.

"The guns," concluded Kimo. "Come, it is almost dawn. We attack now."

. . .

Tears flowed down Liliuokalani's face on the morning of Monday, October 13, 1895, as she stood on her second floor *lanai* with armed marines behind her. On the wide lawns below, four companies of heavily armed U.S. Marines led a scraggling line of barefoot Hawaiians off to prison in the early morning rays of a warm, tropical sun.

Word of the revolt had leaked to the legislature. The marines were ready. The Hawaiians were captured before they crossed the gardens.

By noon, Justice Dole (pineapple grower and Hawaiian Court Justice), Misters Castle and Cook (heads of the legislature), and John Stevens (American Minister to Hawaii) arrived with a platoon of marines to arrest the queen for attempting to overthrow the constitution.

By three o'clock, Dole and Cook delivered an ultimatum to Liliuokalani: abdicate and abolish the monarchy, or all Hawaiians captured during the revolt would be shot.

Before the afternoon trade winds faded and the sun set, huge and red over the western sea, it was finished. To save the lives of her people, Liliuokalani allowed the Hawaiian monarchy to be dissolved. Liliuokalani, the last queen of Hawaii spent the rest of her life as a prisoner under house arrest in Honolulu. Within a month the Hawaiian legislature petitioned to become part of the United States. Within six months the request was granted. The country of Hawaii ceased to exist and the sugar growers saved their 3 cents a pound.

It is easy to overlook the courage and bravery of Queen Liliuokalani in the midst of the tragic loss of her kingdom. Even though her brother and uncle before her had been unable to oppose the steady takeover by American *haoles*, she dared to stand firm and fight for her people and her country even at the cost of her own freedom.

Though Liliuokalani is better remembered as the author of the song, "Aloha Oi," she should be remembered as a strong, intelligent, and brave leader who guided her people through very difficult days with a spirit and dignity that can still be felt in the valiant spirit of the Hawaiian people today. But that is another story.

Questions to Explore

What kinds of roles have monarchs played in history?

What is the most important job of a king, queen, or chieftain of a nation of people? How does a king or queen accomplish this?

How have the roles of monarchs changed?

Can you find stories of successful kings and queens in the library? Can you find stories of unsuccessful ones?

References for Further Reading

- *In the Children's Library*

  Malone, Mary. *Liliuokalani, Queen of Hawaii*. Champaign, IL: Garrard, 1975.

  Wilson, Hazel. *The Last Queen of Hawaii*. New York: Alfred Knopf, 1963.

- *In the Adult Library*

  Allen, Helen. *The Betrayal of Liliuokalani*. Honolulu, HI: Mutual, 1982.

See your librarian for additional titles.

Alone I Stand

A story about Jeanette Rankin, America's first congresswoman

About This Story:

For our country's first 130 years all elected officials were men. It wasn't that women were specifically excluded from office. But women hadn't been given the right to vote, so none were ever nominated or elected. In the late nineteenth century, this injustice began to be corrected—slowly and grudgingly. Stories of many courageous women are written in the long and bitter struggle for women's suffrage and for women's representation in major elected bodies. Slowly but surely, barrier after barrier to women's full participation in the elective governmental system was crushed.

Almost no barrier loomed bigger, or was protected more fiercely, than the U.S. Congress. At the beginning of the twentieth century, there had never been a woman in congress. Most men assumed there never would be. This is a story of the woman who tore down that particular barrier.

Speaker of the House Champ Clark of Missouri pounded his gavel on the podium of the House of Representatives Chamber in the United States Congress building as the murmur in the gallery began to grow. "War . . . war . . . war!"

"Quiet in the gallery. The vote of this House of Representatives has not been completed. Congresswoman Rankin of Montana, how do you vote?"

It was the afternoon of April 6, 1917, a warm and beautiful spring day in Washington, D.C. The very air seemed filled with new life and with joy. Each breath seemed to bring a bounce to the step and a whistle to the lips.

But Congresswoman Jeanette Rankin felt none of this springtime joy. This vote weighed very heavy on her heart and mind.

The slow southern drawl of the speaker was edged with irritation. "Congresswoman Rankin. We're all waiting for your vote."

All Europe was at war. Freedom everywhere hung in the balance. President Woodrow Wilson himself had said it earlier this day. Only America could make the world safe for democracy. We had to go to war with Germany. It seemed the whole country was ready and willing to go fight.

But only Congress could send the country to war. This morning the Senate had voted overwhelmingly in favor of war. Now the House had to vote. Name by name the Speaker called the roll. "Aye," after resounding "Aye!" echoed through the chamber to the cheers of gallery onlookers.

As thirty-seven-year-old Jeanette Rankin rose from her seat, she felt that the eyes of the whole nation were on her. Her auburn hair was pulled back in a bun. Her straight, plain face seemed a part of the Montana prairie from which she had come. Her eyes, as always, sparkled with fire, but today reflected a distant sadness.

Jeanette Rankin was the first woman ever elected to Congress, one lone woman in a sea of 434 men. This was the first month of her first term and her first important vote. It was up to her to prove that a woman could effectively help run the country and open the door for other congresswomen. How should she vote?

The House chamber hushed. A thousand eyes all stared at Jeanette Rankin. Her mind still wrestled the issue, tumbling over and over. How would she vote?

It felt as if a scale in her mind teetered back and forth. On one side of the scale were the words of President Wilson and the veiled threats from other congressmen that she would never be respected as a legislator if she didn't show the courage to vote for war. In addtion, there were the pleas of her dear brother, Wellington, to vote "yes" in order to maintain her popularity and ensure her reelection and letters from women all over the country begging her to vote "yes" and show the world that women can be just as firm and tough-minded as men.

On the other side of the scale sat only her own lonely conscious, her deep belief that war can never create a lasting solution, that there is always a better way. Could this one belief possibly be enough to balance so many reasons to vote "yes"? And yet it felt to Jeanette that the scale teetered, perfectly balanced, waiting for some final argument to drift down on one side or the other and forever tip the balance.

The sharp clap of Speaker Clark's gavel echoed through the quiet chamber. His voice dripped with sarcasm. "Congresswoman Rankin, I know you're new in this house, and this is your first vote. Maybe you'd like one of the *male* members to show you how to vote."

A deep chuckle rumbled through the House floor and viewing gallery. Jeanette's cheeks flushed with anger and nervousness. How should she vote?

Jeanette felt she was completely alone in her indecision. Congress's head-long rush to declare war had the momentum of a speeding freight train. How could one woman stand alone, hold up her arms, and halt it in its tracks? It was a very difficult moment for a new congresswoman trying to use her vote wisely and justly.

But this was not the first difficult moment through which Jeanette Rankin had stood alone, nor the first time her face had turned red with anger.

She thought back to a summer afternoon seven years earlier when she had been talking to her brother, Wellington, at the family home in Helena, Montana.

• • •

"The legislators laughed at us again," she hissed. "This is 1910 for goodness sake. It's modern times! And our state legislature has had the women's voting bill for eight years and they won't do anything with it."

"Why should they?" asked Wellington. "None of their voting constituents want the bill."

Jeanette's eyes flashed. "Don't you start on me, too! I was laughed out of five legislator's offices this morning."

"All I'm saying," said Wellington, holding up his hands to ward off his sister's attack, "is that they'll never pass the bill and submit it to a popular vote unless you make them think it's in their own best interest to do so. Till then you'll never be more than a bad joke to them."

"But how can we do that?" asked Jeanette.

"Not 'we,' dear sister, *you,*" answered Wellington. "If you think it's important, *you* do it."

Three weeks later, Jeanette Rankin stood all alone in front of the assembled Montana legislature, the first woman ever to address that body.

"Would you like some tea, Mrs. Rankin?" asked the Speaker.

"No," she answered. "I came to speak."

"Some new breakthrough in the kitchen, I presume?" asked one snickering legislator puffing on a fat cigar.

Jeanette's eyes flashed and her cheeks flushed bright red. She gripped the podium hard to keep from trembling.

"Gentlemen," she began, "I must talk to you today about the most important pillar of democracy, the vote. Half of the settlers of the Montana territory were women. Women felled trees, plowed fields, and built houses right alongside men. Women tended the sick, nourished the young, and made our state grow every bit as much as men.

"We shared in the struggle to create the state of Montana. Now we must share in the vote."

With each word, Jeanette Rankin's voice grew stronger. The faces before her grew thoughtful and serious.

"Gentlemen, your wives, mothers, and daughters will continue to shape and build this state. They are devoted to Montana and her welfare every bit as much as any man. The women of Montana will not use their vote frivolously. They will work to strengthen this state."

Suddenly Wellington's words echoed in her mind. "Make them think it's in their own best interest."

In a rush she added, "And gentlemen, if *you* give women the vote, they will surely remember your names on election day."

All over the room eyebrows raised, heads nodded approvingly. Jeanette Rankin was applauded as she stepped from the podium.

In 1913 the Montana legislature passed Jeanette Rankin's Women's Voting Rights Bill. Jeanette was thrilled. Triumphantly waving a copy of the Helena newspaper she cried, "I won!"

"Not yet," cautioned Wellington. "The voters must still approve it."

Jeanette scoffed, "All Montana women will vote for it. How can it lose?"

"Women can't vote until *after* this bill passes," reminded her brother. "It's sure to lose unless someone convinces Montana's men to vote for it."

"Who and how?" asked Jeanette.

Wellington slowly smiled and shook his head. "Who else, my dear sister? Who else but you?"

Jeanette Rankin packed her bags and crisscrossed the state speaking to men's clubs, groups, and labor unions. She spent her days on horseback or in rickety wagons on dusty prairie trails. She spent her evenings talking.

She talked about the value of women, and about the share of the state's work they performed. She talked about justice, fairness, and rights. She was answered by bored stares, snickering, billowing cigar smoke, and polite dismissals.

She was failing. Then Wellington's words came to her again. "Make them see it's in their own best interest."

By the next evening's speech to the men's club of Great Falls, she had added a new closing wrinkle. "Gentlemen—and I assume you are all learned and convincing gentlemen—if your wife has the vote, all you need do is convince her your view is correct and she will vote as you do and *double your own voting power*. I am certain *you* gentlemen can convince your wives to vote as you want."

Eyebrows raised. Heads nodded approvingly. Cigars were waved about thoughtfully. A murmur of excited voices rolled across the meeting room. It was a brilliant tactic. Jeanette Rankin had again found the key to victory.

Jeanette celebrated the election night victory of her Women's Voting Right Bill at home in Helena with her brother, Wellington. Late that evening Wellington reached behind the couch and retrieved a large, rolled banner. "Here is something I want you to see, Jeanette."

He unfurled the banner and held it up so his sister could see the words. Her eyes widened. Her mouth dropped open. "Wellington, is this some sort of joke?"

His eyes sparkled with confidence. "Not at all. And you know you could win."

"But . . . but how could I?"

Wellington let the banner flutter to the floor at Jeanette's feet. In bold blue letters on a red background it read, "Jeanette Rankin for Congress."

Again she protested. "There has never been a woman in Congress—never!"

He shrugged. "Then it's about time you changed that, isn't it?"

"But Wellington, if I did win, I'd be all alone back there in Washington."

"Not alone," corrected Wellington. "You'd have your beliefs, your principles, and the trust of every person in Montana. You'll be great!"

• • •

The sharp crack of Speaker Clark's gavel snapped Jeanette back to the present. Champ Clark leered down from his podium. "I hate to rush a gentlelady like yourself, Congresswoman Rankin, but I had hoped to complete this vote in time for dinner." His voice raised to a shout. "Now, how do you vote?"

For a moment Jeanette struggled with her indecision. Then it seemed as though a single feather landed on one side of her mental scale, tipping it toward a decision. With a deep sigh she suddenly felt at peace and sure of herself. She had always stood by her beliefs and principles, and they had never let her down. She would not abandon them now.

In a clear strong voice Congresswoman Rankin answered, "Mister Speaker, it is clear we must aid our friends and allies in Europe. But war is not the answer. In the words of the very wise Chief Joseph of the Nez Percé Indians, 'I will fight no more forever.' If we take the time to look for it, we will always find a better solution than war. Alone I may stand, but stand I must. I vote, 'No.' "

Boos and catcalls broke out from the gallery. Congressmen shook their heads in disgust and muttered that women weren't fit to run the country. Someone yelled, "Go back to the kitchen where you belong!" Someone else screamed, "Coward!" Others, jeered and called her a traitor.

The words stung Jeanette. She felt overwhelmed by the anger of this Congressional crowd. Her resolution wavered. Then she remembered Wellington's now-familiar advice. "I just need to find a way to make them see that peace is in their best interest. If I don't find it today, I'll find it tomorrow. I just have to find a way to make peace popular."

For the rest of her life, Jeanette Rankin worked for peace. At age ninety, she received the Hall of Fame Susan B. Anthony Award. President John Kennedy said of America's first congresswoman, "She was one of the most fearless people in American history." Though her vote wasn't enough to keep America out of both World War I and World War II, Jeanette Rankin lead a constant struggle in Congress to find a better way, to convince others that peace was in their own best interest. But that fight is, of course, another story.

Questions to Explore

Do wars ever really solve problems between countries? Can you find examples when wars did solve problems? When they did not?

Which takes more courage: going against your personal principles to protect your reputation or cause or following your values, regardless of the consequences?

References for Further Reading

- *In the Children's Library*

  Block, Judy Rachel. *The First Woman in Congress: Jeanette Rankin*. New York: Contemporary Perspectives, 1978.

- *In the Adult Library*

  Alonso, Harriet. *The Women's Peace Union and the Outlawry of War*. Knoxville, TN: University of Tennessee Press, 1989.

See your librarian for additional titles.

Madam President

A story about Edith Wilson, the first lady who in 1919 stepped in for the ailing president

About This Story:

The first lady, the wife of the president of the United States, was supposed to sparkle, adding beauty and grace to the White House like a crystal ornament. The first lady's duties were entertaining in the White House and organizing charity events. But she certainly was not supposed to dabble in government affairs, in policy matters, or in political decisions. That was for the president and his all-male staff.

At least that's what folks in Washington thought about first ladies, until one first lady effectively ran the government of the United States for several months, opening the door for future first ladies to assume more substanial roles. She did not set out to seize political power. She had no ambition to hold the reins of government in her hands. Yet for several months she alone exercised the real power of the presidency. This is a story about that businesswoman turned first lady.

The mayor of Wichita, Kansas, and the county democratic party leaders paced, nervous and excited, across the train platform in neatly pressed formal topcoats. This would be a special day for them. Red, white, and blue balloons, streamers, and banners fluttered everywhere. A huge crowd fanned out from the station in a deep semicircle. "Hooray for Wilson," and "Peace in our time!" and "The League of Nations is the answer!" placards rose on thin wooden poles.

It was a steamy afternoon on September 18, 1919, and the mayor impatiently dabbed the sweat from his balding forehead and snapped his fingers at an aide. "Is everything ready? Everything double-checked?"

"Yes, sir," nodded the young aide, thumbing through the pages on his bulging clipboard.

"Well, where is he? When's his train due?" growled the mayor.

The aide checked his pocket watch, fastened on a silver chain. "Another forty-five minutes, Chief."

They heard the first faint echo of a train whistle drifting over the prairie from the west. The aide rechecked his watch and smiled. "Sounds like the president is running a few minutes ahead of schedule."

• • •

On board the *Presidential Special* a black-coated conductor stepped into a plush sitting car behind the public cars crammed with reporters. He faced a lone, seated woman. "You called for me, ma'am?"

"How soon will we reach Wichita?" asked forty-seven-year-old Edith Wilson.

The conductor fished a watch out of a vest pocket and clicked it open. "Ohhh . . . 'nother forty minutes, ma'am."

"Don't stop in Wichita," said Mrs. Wilson. Her voice was cool and calm, but with an icy edge that said she didn't want any trouble from this conductor.

"Don't stop, ma'am?" His voice rose toward a nervous squeak as he repeated the words, hoping he had misunderstood.

"That's correct," she said, smiling graciously, as if she were asking for nothing more serious than lemon for her tea. "Proceed directly to Washington as fast as possible."

The conductor stared. His mouth opened and closed twice before he could stammer, "But . . . but the speaking tour. We still have a dozen stops scheduled."

The woman before him sat motionless, like nobility, he thought. Her tailored suit was immaculate. Her handsome face was framed by short, stylish, brown hair.

"Skip them all and proceed directly to Washington."

The conductor pulled a stained handkerchief from a back pocket and wiped it across his mouth. Nervously he cleared his throat. "But there are other trains on the tracks."

"Have them move aside for the president's train."

He sensed deep urgency in her voice, a readiness to explode into anger. "We run that many trains onto side lines, ma'am, lots of folks gonna' scream bloody murder."

She sat, gazing through him, as if what he had said didn't warrant a reply. His eyes dropped to the carpeted floor of the train car. Again he nervously cleared his throat and tugged at the hem of his jacket. "What I mean is, ma'am . . . well, that is, to do all *that*, I ought to have the word straight from President Wilson, himself, ma'am."

Her penetrating eyes narrowed slightly. "Do you know who I am?"

"Oh, yes, ma'am. You're Mrs. Edith Wilson, the first lady, ma'am."

Her gaze sharpened, but her voice remained calm and pleasant. "Are you saying you refuse to act on my word?"

The conductor cringed as he felt the trap close around him. "Oh, no, ma'am. But, you see, ma'am, I've been running this train for five presidents now. And, well, it's just that first ladies don't usually get involved in . . . well . . . decisions."

Edith rose from her seat. She was a tall woman, and now wearing high heels, she towered above the conductor. "As of today, I do. As of today, I speak for President Wilson. Do you understand?"

As she said these words, Edith Wilson thought, "Heaven help me. How many times in the next few months will I have to speak for my husband? How will I convince anyone else to believe me if I can't convince the conductor on our own train?"

"Yes, ma'am . . . It's just . . ."

Edith cut him off. "Then do it. I thank you for coming by." She turned to a table behind her and picked up some papers, signaling the end of the conversation.

Resistance collapsed. "Yes, ma'am. I'll take care of everything, ma'am." He started for the door, but paused. "The president *is* all right, isn't he, ma'am?"

Edith smiled and seemed to relax. "He's fine. He's resting in with Dr. Grayson."

The conductor turned and hastened toward the engine. Edith blew out a long, slow breath. "I certainly hope it gets easier."

• • •

The crowd on the Wichita platform stood, open-mouthed, as the *Presidential Special* roared through on the main line at sixty miles an hour, whistle blaring. In fifteen seconds it was gone, leaving Wichita balloons, streamers, placards, and mouths to droop in the searing afternoon heat. The mayor's carefully rehearsed welcome speech remained forever unspoken.

• • •

Edith reached the private sleeping car, two cars back, just as Dr. Grayson tiptoed out and silently eased the door shut.

"How is he, doctor?"

He patted her hand. "He's fine, Edith. He just needs a good rest."

She grabbed his wrist and squeezed it hard. "Doctor, I am the first lady of this nation. I have responsibilities. The press is already screaming to know why we bypassed Wichita. I need to know the truth."

Grayson sank into an overstuffed chair, rubbing his hands through thick, gray hair at his temples. "He's sixty-four, Edith. This sort of thing isn't uncommon at that age—especially for someone under as much stress as he's had to bear trying to convince the Senate to ratify the Treaty of Versailles."

"What is it, doctor?" she demanded.

Grayson sighed. "All right. The president's had a stroke. His left side seems completely paralyzed. Fortunately, I don't think his brain has been affected at all. But he's still suffering blinding headaches. He's sleeping now. I'll stay with him."

Left alone, Edith sank into the same overstuffed chair. Shock turned to deep sorrow for her stricken husband, a great idealist with so much still to do, and now physically unable to do it.

She forcibly banished sorrow from her mind. "There's no time for silly self-indulgence now," she told herself.

With sadness set aside, Edith found what remained was a fierce determination to make sure her husband had a chance to complete his noble goals for world peace. If the senate Republicans discovered President Wilson was desperately sick and weakened, they'd grow bold enough to block ratification of the Treaty of Versailles, which must be passed to create the League of Nations. Woodrow Wilson, her husband, would feel like a failure if his own country killed his personal vision for world peace. "That," Edith told herself, "I cannot allow to happen."

But how? What could a president's wife do to keep her husband's dream alive until he was well enough to carry on himself? The idea settled slowly over her as the *Presidential Special* raced over rhythmically clicking tracks. She could do little outside the White House, but she could hide the president's illness and let no knowledge of it leak to the outside world.

Edith Wilson vowed that the nation would never know how sick the president really was until he had recovered enough to resume his normal duties. The press wouldn't know. The Senate wouldn't know. The president wouldn't know. Most of the White House staff wouldn't know. Even Vice President Marshall wouldn't be told unless the president's condition worsened. If the vice president knew, he'd have to assume responsibility. Then everyone would know Wilson was ill. No, Vice President Marshall must never know unless Edith feared the president might die.

Edith sagged against the chair cushions wondering if her scheme were illegal. *No, not quite*, she thought. *I'll never sign anything or create policy on my own. My husband will be able to advise me; I'll simply act as a shield for him, deflecting problems, questions, and issues to those staff and president members who would be involved anyway.* She stared out the window, wondering if she had any hope of running the White House and the country without arousing undue suspicion, without being challenged, without being flattened by the powerful political machinery of Washington.

Edith's face clouded. She would have to constantly lie and deceive the American people. Wouldn't that, at least, be unethical? Then she realized it didn't matter. She had no choice. This was Woodrow's only chance of success and that was all that really mattered.

Idly twirling her plain, gold wedding band as she thought and planned, she smiled. It suddenly seemed comical that two such private people as Woodrow and she would have placed themselves in this public fishbowl.

They met in March, 1915, only three months after President Wilson's first wife died. They tried to keep their whirlwind White House romance a secret, but how could the president keep such secrets?

He wrote to her every day, saying that with every dreary letter he was forced to write to some foreign head of state, he thought only of writing words of love to her. He learned that orchids were her favorite flower and had one delivered to her house every day. He sneaked her into the White House every chance he got, but you just couldn't keep something like that hidden from nosy reporters.

Edith remembered the thrill she felt when Woodrow asked her to stay one night and help draft his protest to the German government after their submarines sank the famed cruise ship, *Lusitania*, in May, 1915, killing all 128 Americans on board. She was overwhelmed, debating in the oval office whether one version of the letter sounded too strong, or if another did not rebuke the Germans quite enough, scribbling words that would become the official voice of the United States of America. Woodrow smiled and said that she was intelligent, thoughtful, efficient, and a darn good writer.

In December of that same year, the world whined in protest when only fifty close friends were allowed to attend their private wedding at Edith's mother's house. Only fifty guests were invited, but more than 1,000 presents flooded the White House from every state and nation, including a gold nugget from California that Woodrow had made into the wedding ring Edith now twirled as the *Presidential Special* sped east through the night.

Who would have to know? Dr. Grayson would, of course, and a team of medical specialists. Some of the White House staff would have to know. Could she keep the seriousness of her husband's illness from the president? From the president's aides and staff? She decided to make herself the sole access between the president and the rest of the world. No one, and nothing, would get to the president unless she approved. She would create an iron band of secrecy around the president.

Her first orders were to seal the White House. The Pennsylvania Avenue gates were closed. Marine guards carefully screened all who tried to enter. The press howled in protest at being locked outside and demanded to know what lay behind this increased secrecy. They were told only that everything was fine, and that the president was functioning normally.

Dr. Grayson and a team of specialists huddled in the president's room. Dr. Walter Dercum, neurologist, and head of the team, described for Edith the tightrope she would have to walk.

"To recover, the president needs rest and to be kept totally free of stress. When you bring a problem to him, any problem, it will be like turning a knife in an open wound. Yet he also needs mental stimulation and motivation to recover. He must be involved in the affairs of government, but not so much that he is stressed."

"How will I know how much is too much?" asked Edith.

Dr. Dercum awkwardly shrugged. "You just have to feel your way."

Edith dictated a memo to all staff, departments, and president members requiring that all problems, concerns, and requests be submitted to the president in writing. Every afternoon, Edith and a handpicked team of staff members carefully screened the enormous stack of documents this order produced, as well as all briefings on national and international developments. Some of the problems were delegated to president members to handle as they saw fit. Some issues they decided on their own, trying as best they could to hold true to President Wilson's wishes, policies, and interests. A select few concerns were set aside for Edith to take to the president during their evenings together.

The burden of running the government of the United States lay squarely on Edith Wilson's shoulders, who had been a quiet, competent businesswoman all her life, and who never entertained any dream of political power. It was a crushing burden, made doubly difficult because she could not act openly. She was only the first lady and had no official power.

It was a grueling schedule. She spent her mornings issuing staff orders, receiving foreign dignitaries, and meeting with president officials and congressmen. She was required to explain constantly that the president, "was fine, but ill and resting for a few days on doctor's orders. He was so sorry to miss this meeting, but would be back on his feet and in touch soon."

September dragged into October. Woodrow slowly but steadily recovered. October drifted toward November. Edith was constantly battling concerned government bureaucrats and elected politicians to persuade them to accept her word as that of the president. Constantly she had to battle angered White House staffers and aides now shut out from the president. Many accused Edith of trying to illegally grab the power of the presidency. Several quit in protest.

Edith had to quash repeated rumors of the president's demise. First people claimed he had gone insane and was chained in the White House basement. Next they said that he had actually died.

Edith laughed a well-rehearsed laugh each time a rumor was mentioned and said the president also found them personally amusing. But, she added sternly, the president feels such rumors are destructive to the strength of the country, and so should not be spread or tolerated by loyal Americans. She insisted at every inquiry that the president *had* been sick—nothing major, just persistent, was recovering nicely, and would be up and around in no time.

Edith had to endure vicious attacks from Republican Senators claiming that a first lady had no business meddling in the affairs of government. At news conferences they labeled her, "the iron queen," "the presidentress," and "America's first woman president." Edith never responded publicly, but steadfastly kept working toward her husband's goals.

"It's working!" Edith's weariness showed through the exuberance of her words. "If the Senate had known the truth of the president's condition in September, they'd have thrown him out of office in a minute. We've held the world at bay and kept the government running for two months. The president's recovering nicely. If we can hold out a little longer, I think this will have worked."

"*We* can hold out," the secretary responded. "But can you?"

In the afternoon, Edith and her small circle of trusted staff members met to review the day's mail, memos, and reports. Over dinner she met with Dr. Grayson and showed him the items she needed to discuss with her husband. They would weigh the urgency of each item against the president's slowly improving medical reports, and make a final decision on what the he would actually see that day.

Then came the evenings, Edith's one time of peace and joy. She sat at Woodrow's bedside. They talked. She held his hand. She sat quietly and watched him if he dozed. If he felt alert, they discussed news, events, and the chosen policy items. She jotted handwritten notes on his comments and the decisions to be enacted in the morning. But for Edith what mattered was that they were alone and together. Evenings spent with her husband gave Edith strength to endure the days.

By mid-December Woodrow Wilson could sit up in bed and work for an hour or two each day. Senators and eager press were ushered in; treated to the charming, confident Wilson smile; and reassured that there had never been any serious problems.

By January, 1920, Wilson was being rolled up and down the White House halls in a wheelchair to wave at reporters and greet dignitaries. But always in the background, steadfastly managing the president and the country, lurked Edith Wilson. For three months she ran the government of the United States. For six months more she acted as the chief assistant to the president.

When Woodrow Wilson left office a year later, after Warren Harding won the 1920 election, Edith and Woodrow retired to a charming house in northwest Washington, D.C., and to the privacy they both relished. Woodrow died in 1924. Edith Wilson lived quietly in that house all the rest of her life. She died in 1961 at the age of eighty-eight, with little national notice or attention.

Yet it must be said that no first lady ever matched the courage, wisdom, intelligence, and devotion of Edith Wilson or rose to meet the demands of her office as well. It is also true that during the last quarter of 1919, Edith Wilson came closer to the Presidency of the United States than any woman will until one is finally elected to the office. But that is another story.

Questions to Explore

Do you think it's all right for the president's family and staff to hide a serious illness from the public? If you do, for how long, and for how serious an illness?

Have any U.S. presidents suffered through major illnesses while in office? Which ones? How was the country run while they were ill?

References for Further Reading

- *In the Children's Library*

  Giblin, James. *Edith Wilson: The Woman Who Ran the United States*. New York: Viking Children's Books, 1992.

  Lindsay, Rae. *The President's First Ladies*. New York: Franklin Watts, 1989.

- *In the Adult Library*

  Anthony, Carl. *First Ladies*. New York: William Morrow, 1990.

  Wilson, Edith. *My Memoirs*. New York: Bobbs-Merrill, 1938.

See your librarian for additional titles.

Only Eleanor

A story about Eleanor Roosevelt, one of America's most influential first ladies

About This Story:

There have been more than forty wives of presidents, or first ladies, in the history of America. But up through the late twentieth century, we've only had one who held her own regular press conferences for women reporters, maintained her own career, toured on regular inspection trips for the president, and went on to important appointed government service after she and her husband left the White House. This is a story about that first lady.

In late June, the days never seem to end on Campobello Island off the northern tip of Maine. Just when you're sure that the sun will finally set, it hangs on, struggling to ride just above the horizon for an extra hour or two.

The salty island air is crisp and clean, the sun warm—but never uncomfortably hot—and the water is always cold. Some people, like Franklin Roosevelt, called these coastal waters invigorating and refreshing. Most, like his wife Eleanor, called it bitter cold.

In the summer of 1921, thirty-seven-year-old Eleanor and the Roosevelts' five children traveled to Campobello a few days before Franklin to "open up the cottage." The "cottage" was the Roosevelts' thirty-room sprawling summer house with massive fireplaces for heat, wicker furniture, wolf and caribou skin rugs scattered on the floor, tall bay windows everywhere, and a glorious rocky coast on two sides for endless hours of watching crashing waves, rolling fog, birds, and falling summer rain.

Franklin stayed in New York for a final few days of political meetings. Though he and his presidential running mate, James Cox of Ohio, had lost the 1920 presidential election to Republicans Harding and Coolidge, Franklin was still flooded with requests, offers, proposals, and political schemes.

By early July, Franklin left his few remaining New York affairs to his longtime assistant, Louis Howe, and joyfully fled to Campobello Island. The Roosevelts settled into their normal summer routine: Franklin's invigorating swims in the bay, family picnics, walks through the woods, sailing, explorations along the craggy coast, games in the wide parlor, and whole afternoons and evenings curled up by the fire with a book.

The Roosevelts were rich, and life seemed to flow easily for them. Both Franklin and Eleanor came from families entrenched in the "American aristocracy." The Roosevelts were at the heart of the "in-crowd," the "haves," or, in the slang of the 1920s, the "swells."

Eleanor loved to sit at the wide bay windows of the cottage and watch Franklin walk down to the bay for his morning swim. Franklin was tall and lithe. He was a natural athlete and glided easy and surefooted over rocks, as if he knew they wouldn't dare stub his toe or snag his foot. Eleanor always felt like a giraffe lurching, sprawling, stumbling her way down to the shore.

Eleanor was amazed they were married at all. He was the easy-smiling, quick-to-laugh, glib-talking, fun-loving, perfect-in-every-way epitome of the rich and famous good life, and seemed at ease everywhere. Eleanor, who grew up the only ugly duckling in a family of handsome people, felt out of place in almost every setting. She had no chin, buckteeth, and lips that were too big for her mouth. Her spine curved and everyone complained that she was far too serious. As a child she'd needed leg braces. Even in flat shoes she still couldn't enter a room with even a hint of grace or elegance.

On a morning in the middle of July, 1921, Eleanor watched Franklin stride toward the bay just as he had on every previous summer morning. He stopped, shading his eyes, to scan the horizon for signs of incoming clouds. Then he studied the chop and swell of the bay's gray-green water to get a feel for its flow and rhythm. Finally, he turned toward the house, smiled his famous vote-winning smile, waved, and turned back to gracefully disappear into the icy water of the bay.

When Franklin rose from the gentle waves twenty minutes later, Eleanor noticed he moved more stiffly than usual. Certainly the cold water always chilled his muscles and stiffened his joints, but it normally took only a minute or two for his limbs to regain their loose and agile flow. The stiffness this day seemed far more exaggerated. Franklin swayed and slowly plodded over the rocks.

Complaining of a nasty chill and throbbing pain in his legs, Franklin limped in for a nap, something the energetic thirty-nine-year-old man never did. Within two hours, Franklin could move neither arms nor legs. Within two days, specialists rushed to the island and confirmed their fears: Franklin Roosevelt was paralyzed with polio.

Survival was questionable. Recovery would be partial at best. Franklin's political career seemed over. Who would vote for a cripple? Eleanor brought her husband home on a stretcher for a two month stay in a New York hospital.

Franklin's mother was elated. Now Franklin would have to return to the family home in Hyde Park and live out his days as a country gentleman securely tied to her apron strings. The thought of shedding the political spotlight for a quiet country life appealed to Eleanor. The thought of living with her controlling, critical mother-in-law did not.

In the midst of her late summer uncertainty, Louis Howe, Franklin's secretary stopped by the Roosevelt's New York townhouse to visit Eleanor. In the beginning she hadn't liked Louis. He was a gnome-like man, small and wrinkled. His clothes always looked as if they'd been slept in, even though they had just come from the cleaners. Worse, his jackets were constantly sprinkled with flecks of cigarette ash because he chain-smoked. He smelled so strongly of stale smoke that it made Eleanor cough and her eyes water.

But over the years they had grown close. Eleanor could appreciate Louis as "the other ugly duckling." His rumpled appearance was soon overlooked, and finally valued by his employer's wife, desperately searching for someone even less glamorous and elegant than she. Besides, Louis Howe was as loyally dedicated to Franklin as a lap dog.

This morning in early September, Louis's face was etched with concern as he barged into Eleanor's study and, excusing himself for intruding, pulled a chair up close to her seat by the windows. "Eleanor, we have to get Franklin back into politics. He looks awful."

She laughed wistfully. "I thought everyone agreed his political career is over."

Louis's determination was unflappable. "He is still the greatest man I have ever known. He's still Franklin Roosevelt. By gad, legs or no legs, Franklin will be president!"

"President," laughed Eleanor. "Aren't you setting your sights a bit high, Louis?"

"Not right away, mind you," he answered. "First we get him back involved with New York State politics. If he isn't actively involved in politics, he'll wither up like a crinkled, old cornstalk."

"Easy to say," said Eleanor. "But with Franklin still flat on his back, how do you propose to do it? Wheel him up and down the street so he can shake hands from his bed?"

"I have a better plan," said Louis, his small, black eyes gazing hard at Eleanor. "*You* get into politics and bring politics here to Franklin until he's able to get out on his own."

"*Me?* In politics?" she guffawed. "Surely you jest. I'm too shy to make a speech. I have no self-confidence. I lumber into rooms like a cow. Remember Louis?" Her voice began to rise, edging toward anger as she finished. "I'm the one who hates being in the public spotlight."

"It's your duty," he answered quietly, eyes downcast. "For Franklin, you have to."

Eleanor sat silent for a long moment, bathed in the morning sun that sifted through the New York skyline and found its way through her windows. "Do you realize you're asking me to do the very thing I fear and loathe most in all the world?" she demanded.

"It's your duty to Franklin."

Eleanor shifted nervously in her chair, sighed deeply and rubbed her forehead with one hand. "When I was a little girl, Louis, visitors at our house would tell my parents, 'What beautiful boys you have . . . Oh, and here's little Eleanor, too.'

"I was called 'odd,' 'that funny girl,' 'poor Eleanor.' My own mother even called me 'granny.' People patted her shoulder and spoke in hushed tones, describing me as a burden. My grandmother was quick to tell anyone that I was the family ugly duckling. Then she'd add that she didn't think there was a swan stuffed inside my misshapen body.

"I grew up convinced I was the least attractive, least desirable girl in all of New York. Mother reminded me daily of my buckteeth, weak chin, and misshapen body. Never once did she mention that I have attractive eyes, or beautiful hair.

"I grew up afraid to meet anyone, afraid to talk, terrified to draw any attention to myself, because all the attention I got was negative. Louis, I grew up afraid of water, boats, snakes, the dark, dogs, horses, and strangers; I was afraid of being with others and afraid of being alone. Yet I would gladly face all these fears together rather than speak in public. That is my single greatest fear."

She waved her hand for emphasis as she spoke. "I am a very shy and private person, Louis. And now you ask me to get into politics? The answer is No!"

Louis rose, pacing across the thick carpet as he lit a new cigarette. "Franklin is destined for greatness. But while he recovers from this disease, he must not fade from the public eye. The political world has a very short memory, Eleanor. In order to keep him involved and vital, the political leaders of New York must parade regularly through this house. For that to happen, you must be active in New York politics while Franklin cannot be." Louis stopped his pacing and faced Eleanor pleadingly. "It's the only way. Please. It is your duty as Franklin's wife."

Again Eleanor sat still and silent for a long moment. When she finally raised her face to Louis, pride, sadness, and a small bit of enthusiasm were mixed in her beautiful green eyes. "All right, Louis. It seems it is time for me to stand up to my fears. I'll do it."

Louis quickly scheduled her to speak to the Women's Division of the State Democratic Party. Eleanor was so nervous, she could scarcely hold the pages of her typed speech. She excused herself several times from the head table at the luncheon to pace anxiously back and forth in the ladies washroom. When she finally rose to speak, her voice nervously rose higher and higher, becoming shrill and squeaky. She couldn't wait to dash from that crowded room back to her own townhouse where she could slam the door, shutting out the world, and locking herself away from the public eye.

"I was awful!" she wailed.

"You'll get better," comforted Louis.

"I'm terrible as a public speaker," she protested.

"I'll teach you some voice exercises to make it easier," he answered.

Within a month, Eleanor Roosevelt was firmly entrenched in both the State Democratic Committee and the Woman's Trade Union. She was in demand as a speaker across the state. Even after Louis claimed she had become an acceptable speaker, Eleanor still hated the shrill, nasal sound of her voice and the terror she felt before every speech.

More importantly, political dinner parties and strategy meetings became a regular part of the evening fare in the Roosevelt home. Now able to sit in a wheelchair, Franklin took a keen and active role in every gathering.

Louis Howe beamed with pleasure, both at the color in Franklin's cheeks and the gleam in his eyes, and at how well Eleanor progressed as a public figure.

"I'm afraid this is a fear I will never overcome," she confessed.

"To everyone else you appear poised and self-confident," Louis answered.

Eleanor laughed, "Anything but! And worse, with Franklin in a wheelchair, I've had to confront so many other lifelong fears."

Louis pulled back and looked quizzically at Eleanor. "Really? Such as?"

Eleanor counted them off on her fingers as she answered. "I'm terrified of automobiles and driving. But someone needs to do it, so I just got my first driver's license. You know I'm deathly afraid of water, swimming, and boating. But I don't want my children to inherit these fears. With Franklin out of commission, I have just signed up at the YWCA for a swimming and boating class."

Deeply impressed, Louis nodded his head. "Bravo! No wife could ever have done more for her husband and family than you have."

Franklin Roosevelt stormed back into politics, first as governor of New York, and then as president of the United States from 1933 until his death in 1945. Rather than retreat as a quiet, "behind-the-scenes" first lady concerned only with entertaining and charity events, Eleanor dove in headfirst to support her wheel-chair-bound husband. She became her husband's roving eyes and ears, driving or flying off across the country at a moment's notice, studying conditions, listening, speaking, and always returning to give the president detailed reports.

In only one year as first lady, Eleanor Roosevelt presided at White House teas for 22,353 people, received 16,650 White House guests, answered 84,000 letters, and held formal dinners for 5,485 guests. She also flew over 40,000 miles a year and logged another 20,000 miles behind the wheel of her car.

Eleanor also pursued an active career of her own. She went on planned lecture tours, had her own radio show, and wrote for newspapers and magazines. She became the first first lady to regularly hold her own press conferences. Every company in the late 1930s felt the squeeze of the depression, and Eleanor feared female reporters might be the first released by major newspapers unless they had exclusive access to important stories. So Eleanor opened her press conferences to only female reporters. Editors screamed and complained, but all held onto their women writers.

After Franklin died, President Harry Truman appointed Eleanor Roosevelt as U.S. Representative to the General Assembly of the United Nations, the first woman to ever serve on that delegation and the first ex-first lady ever assigned to an important government post. There, she served as Chair of the United Nations Human Rights Commission until 1953. But that is another story.

Questions to Explore

Eleanor Roosevelt was very involved in running the government as first lady. Can you name other first ladies who have been active in creating governmental policies?

Can you find good arguments for why these non-elected officials should or should not be so involved?

References for Further Reading

- *In the Children's Library*

    Jacobs, William. *Eleanor Roosevelt: A Life of Happiness and Tears.* New York: Coward-McCann, 1983.

    McConnell, Jane, and Burt McConnell. *Our First Ladies.* New York: Thomas Crowell, 1969.

    Stoddard, Hope. *Famous American Women.* New York: Thomas Crowell, 1970.

    Whitney, Sharon. *Eleanor Roosevelt.* New York: Franklin Watts, 1982.

- *In the Adult Library*

    Smith, Senator Margaret Chase, and H. Paul Jeffers. *Gallant Women.* New York: McGraw-Hill, 1968.

    Roosevelt, Anna Eleanor. *The Autobiography of Eleanor Roosevelt.* New York: Harper & Row, 1961.

See your librarian for additional titles.

3

Stories About Sports

Stroke, Breathe, Kick, Glide

A story about Gertrude Ederle, the first woman to swim the English Channel

About This Story:

The English Channel separating France and England has always been treacherous. It's waters are cold and choppy. Its currents run strong and dangerous. Storms with howling winds brew up fast.

Even so, long-distance swimmers have been drawn to the Channel as the ultimate test of swimming endurance. But no one completed the more than twenty mile swim between England and France until 1875. By 1925 only five men had made the crossing successfully, though many had tried and failed.

Then a petite American woman tried. She was not the first woman to attempt the feat, but she was the first woman to swim the English Channel, an historic accomplishment. This is a story about that young woman.

Nineteen-year-old Gertrude Ederle fidgeted nervously in the back seat of a shiny, red roadster. Despite her broad shoulders and powerful arms she looked petite and delicate. She wished with all her heart that she could get this silly parade over with and get back home where it was quiet.

Gertrude had almost gotten used to having a frenzied pack of reporters nipping at her heels, each yelling questions for which she could never think of good answers. Almost used to it, but not quite. Worse, the trays of magnesium flash powder made her jump and gasp every time they went off, with their great blast of light and sharp "Pop!" It seemed a forest of pencils and notepads waved and scribbled everywhere she turned.

"Miss Ederle, what was your scariest moment?"

"I wasn't scared."

"Miss Ederle, were you surprised you set a world record?"

"No."

"Miss Ederle, did you ever think you weren't going to make it?"

"No."

"Miss Ederle, how does it feel to be a national celebrity?"

"The same."

"You're not much of a talker, Miss Ederle."

"No. I'm a swimmer."

"Smile for us, Miss Ederle. You're so pretty when you smile."

"Oh, brother . . ."

Pop! Another tray of flash powder exploded. Gertrude jumped, nearly tumbling out of the roadster and onto the pavement of Broadway.

"Miss Ederle, what will you swim next?"

Gertrude ignored the question as two burly New York City policemen forced their way through the crowd. "It's time, Miss Ederle. There's a good crowd all the way up Broadway. We'll slowly cruise behind the bands to let everyone have a good look at you. You'll have eight police motorcycles escorting you in front, three in back. Only four will have sirens on, so the noise shouldn't be too bad."

The other officer, a red-headed Irishman, leaned in front of his partner to interrupt. "Don't you worry your pretty head about all that technical junk, missy. You sit back and enjoy the ride. Just remember to smile and wave a lot. Oh, here, the commissioner thought you might want to wave these."

He handed her two small American flags on thin wooden poles. Then he turned toward the row of uniformed motorcycle police in front of the roadster. "Move out, lads! Let's get this show on the road!"

Motorcycles roared to life as shiny black police boots stomped down on kick starters. The two marching bands shuffled into formation. Gertrude's driver started the roadster and shifted into first. The mayor of New York, Joseph McKee, riding in the back of another convertible, pulled up next to Gertrude's car. "Welcome home, Miss Ederle!" he called over the noise with a wide politician's smile. "I'll be riding just in front of you in the parade."

On the sidewalk next to Gertrude's car, Dan Smallings, a New York radio reporter spoke into his broadcast microphone. "On this clear and warm morning of September 2nd, 1926, history is once again in the making in our great city of New York. Engines are revved, sirens wail, as New York welcomes home its very own nineteen-year-old swimming sensation, Gertrude Ederle, the sweetheart of all New York, with the first tickertape parade ever given to a woman after she swam thirty-one miles across the English Channel in record time of fourteen hours and thirty-one minutes."

Gertrude's older sister, Margaret, leaned back from the front seat. "Relax, Trudy. It's not like you have to do anything." Then she added, "This is so exciting! Millions of people all here to see my little sister." She squeezed Trudy's hand. "I'm so proud of you."

Gertrude winced as another flash tray exploded and wiped her short brown hair out of her eyes. "I still can't believe they all want to talk to *me* and take *my* picture. No one did a month ago."

"A month ago you weren't the first woman in the world to swim the English Channel, and hadn't beaten the old men's record by two hours," answered her sister.

The roadster fell into line behind the mayor's car and inched it's way up Broadway. The first showerings of tickertape and confetti floated down from the skyscrapers towering above. Holding out a hand to catch the paper flakes that would fall blizzard-thick for the next forty blocks, Gertrude gazed out over a vast sea of cheering admirers.

It seemed Gertrude had spent this summer gazing over vast seas. The sea as it sloshed up onto the shores of France four weeks before also looked endlessly vast. There had been a small sea of curious people that morning, too.

• • •

August 6, 1926, dawned cool and windy on France's Normandy coast. But at least it was clear. The crowd began to gather an hour before sunup, the headlights of their motorcars bouncing wildly over the dirt roads and grassy fields as they drove toward the shore of Cape Gris Nez.

In the cramped hotel room she used as a training headquarters, Gertrude didn't feel nervous or apprehensive. She felt impatient and anxious to get in the water and get on with the swimming.

Gertrude's least favorite part of long swims in frigid water was the greasing she had to endure to keep out the cold. Margaret was there to help. First a one-eighth-inch thick layer of lanolin was spread evenly over Gertrude from head to toe, then a thicker layer of heavy grease. Only then could Gertrude slip into her bright red bathing dress with matching red skullcap and goggles. Then Margaret slathered the final layer of heavy grease over the top, again head to toe.

The eager crowd of reporters divided themselves between the beach and one of the two tugboats that would escort Gertrude on her swim.

Microphones were shoved into her face as she walked to the shore and stretched. Pencils waved and tapped the edges of notebooks for attention. It was just before seven o'clock in the morning.

"Miss Ederle, only five people have made this swim, and all of those were powerful men. You're so small. How can you hope to swim the distance?"

Shyly, Gertrude shrugged. Margaret spoke up, "She's in great shape and she has more endurance and persistence than any man."

The reporters chuckled in disbelief. Given this moment to gather her thoughts, Gertrude said, "I want to make this swim to destroy the myth that women are frail and can't perform high-endurance athletics."

With a final stretch, Gertrude stepped into the water at exactly nine minutes after seven. Trays of flash powder exploded all around her. "It's almost like fireworks for a send-off," she thought.

When the chilly water reached waist deep, Gertrude dove forward and began her strong, steady crawl stroke.

Margaret and her father were rowed out to the escort tugs, bobbing 200 yards off shore.

Stroke, breathe, kick, glide; stroke, kick, glide. Stroke, breathe, kick, glide; stroke, kick, glide. At first Gertrude counted the strokes. When she reached twenty-four, a thought flashed through her mind, "Only 70,000 to go."

She stopped counting and concentrated on the rhythm. Stroke, breathe, kick, glide; stroke, kick, glide.

As Gertrude reached the escort boats, her swimming coach, William Burgess, the only Englishman in the exclusive group of five to have swum the English Channel, leaned over the side and yelled, "You're doing thirty strokes a minute, Miss Ederle. Too fast. Slow down and save your strength."

Stroke, breathe, kick, glide; stroke, kick, glide. Gertrude felt incredibly powerful, invincible. Thirty strokes a minute suited her just fine. She just might speed up to thirty-two.

On the press tugboat, cameras and flash trays dangled over the side. Pencils scribbled busily.

Stroke, breathe, kick, glide; stroke, kick, glide.

On the official escort tug, Gertrude's coach, father, and sister huddled over the charts, compass and tide tables. Mr. Ederle turned on the shortwave radio to test their reception by anxious listening stations in London and New York.

William Burgess slammed his pencil down onto the wide nautical chart, as if he had hoped this thousandth recalculation of the tides and currents Gertrude would face might say something more encouraging than had the first 999.

"Conditions are bloody awful this year!" He angrily crossed his thick arms and scowled as if nature had played this cruel trick on purpose. "The year I swam it, Channel currents and tides lined up, so I could ride the current the whole last seven miles. But this year . . ." Burgess angrily tapped a finger on the charts and tide tables. "Today is as good as any day this summer. Still, the better she swims and the sooner she nears Dover, the *worse* the current will be for her during the last four or five miles. No matter what she does, she'll have to swim straight into the tide."

"Does Trudy know that?" asked Margaret.

Burgess shrugged. "Why make her worry about the last four miles before she swims the first twenty?"

"How far will she have to swim?" asked Mr. Ederle, his face tightening with worry.

Burgess pointed back to the charts. "It's twenty-one miles straight across. But with these currents and tides dragging her about, I figure she'll actually have to swim just over twenty-six."

Gazing at the steady strokes of his daughter twenty feet off the port side of their tug, Mr. Ederle nervously rubbed his forehead. "Twenty six miles. That's a long way even for Gertrude."

Searching for some shred of optimistic news, Margaret said, "At least the water's calm today."

"Just wait until the afternoon winds kick up," replied Burgess, squashing Margaret's last ray of real hope.

Mr. Ederle put his arm around Margaret's shoulder. "Don't fret. She's got spunk and determination. If any woman can make it, Gertrude can."

Stroke, breathe, kick, glide; stroke, kick, glide. Stroke, breathe, kick, glide; stroke, kick, glide. Time and place ceased to hold any meaning for Gertrude. There was only the endless salt water, the seamless flow of her arms, the slow, steady kick of her feet, and the clockwork rolling of her head: left to breathe, down to glide and exhale. Thirty times a minute, roll left to breathe, down to glide and exhale.

• • •

Gertrude's head slowly rolled left and right as she rode down Broadway with the same steady cadence she used on the swim. Left: wave and breathe. Right: smile, wave, and hold. Left: wave and breathe. Right: smile and AHHH! "Pop!" A flash pan exploded next to the car. A photographer yelled, "Thanks, Miss Ederle."

Two bands blared in front of her. Sirens droned in an endless rising and falling screech. A crowd that stretched on beyond sight yelled, cheered, and waved from all sides. The combined noise blended and dulled as it crashed over and over into her ears.

Just like the waves.

• • •

Three-foot swells began to buffet Gertrude about noon. Often her head rolled left to breathe and found itself still well under the surface of a wave crest. Sometimes her head rolled down to glide and found itself looking down to the water surface as she popped out of a wave and over a trough.

Gertrude's progress slowed to a crawl. Most of her effort was wasted riding up and down with the waves instead propelling her forward. It was hard to hold her rhythm. Each stroke began to feel like an individual effort.

At twelve thirty Mr. Ederle flipped on the radio to announce that Gertrude had crossed mid-channel, well ahead of the world record pace. The news flashed to radio stations and electronic billboards in Times Square. Cars honked their horns. Pedestrians stopped and cheered.

On board the tug the captain signaled with a great blast of the horn. Everyone applauded and shouted encouragement to Gertrude—everyone except William Burgess. He slumped in a deckchair with a sour look. "The winds have kicked up early. It's gonna get brutal this afternoon. And I don't like the look of those clouds."

Stroke, breathe, kick, glide; stroke, kick, glide. Gertrude couldn't remember walking on dry land anymore. It felt like the whole world had always been water.

The bow lookout yelled back, "Jellyfish!" and pointed off to port.

"Not this, too!" muttered Burgess and slammed his hand onto the table, making his pencil and compass bounce. "Captain, ten points to port. Ease in closer to Miss Ederle. Deck hands, ready with the nets!"

He grabbed a bullhorn and leaned over the rail. "Miss Ederle, we've spotted jellyfish ahead. Tread water until we come alongside. Then swim slower until I give you an 'all clear.' Don't worry. We'll keep them off you."

"They're just jellyfish," snickered Margaret.

Burgess snarled at her. "If one of those jellyfish is a stinger and touches your sister, it's poison will cramp her up and she'll be out of the water in less than half a mile."

Both tugboats fell deathly silent. All eyes searched the gray-green water. Gertrude shifted to a leisurely breaststroke while they inched forward.

Someone would shout, "There's one!" A loose mesh net on the end of a long wooden pole scooped into the water like a pelican beak diving after its prey. The jellyfish was flung across the boat to plop back into the ocean on the other side.

"All clear!" called the lookout.

"All clear Miss Ederle," called her coach.

Gertrude shifted gears back to her powerful crawl. Stroke, breathe, kick, glide; stroke, kick, glide.

By four o'clock the sun disappeared behind heavy, black clouds. The wind had risen to a steady moan, whipping the sea into an endless field of choppy whitecaps. Both tugs rolled and pitched. Any loose equipment crashed across the decks.

At first Margaret thought it was only a headache. But soon, feeling pale and green, she realized she was seasick, and collapsed, groaning to the deck, her head leaning through the starboard rail. She would be useless to her sister in these final desperate hours.

Stroke, breathe, kick, glide; stroke, kick, glide.

"Land ho!" cried the lookout. Half the shipboard crowd rushed to the rails to gaze west, northwest at the white cliffs of Dover. The other half yanked on pocket watch chains to check the time.

"Gracious. It's only five twenty!" cried Mr. Ederle. "She's way ahead of the record. She's only ten and a half hours out!"

"Aye, but she looks frightfully tired to me," said Burgess with a slow shake of his head.

"Of course she's tired," snapped Mr. Ederle. "She's been swimming in rough, cold water for ten and a half hours! How much farther does she have to go?"

Burgess scowled and pointed at the chalk-white cliffs faintly rising out of the distant sea. "It's only four or so miles to those cliffs. But she'll never make it."

"I'm tired of your British pessimism!" snapped Mr. Ederle. "She's got plenty of strength left for four miles, and she's got more than enough steel-willed Yankee determination to make these four miles even if she didn't have the strength."

"Look at the sea, man," wailed Burgess. "The currents have turned on her. I told you they would. Now besides that cursed wind in her face, and this dangerous chop, she's got a two knot current driving straight into her. I don't care who she is. Fighting that combination, the cliffs might as well be twenty miles away."

Mr. Ederle stared in helpless frustration at the churning sea, and then at his struggling daughter.

The captain blew a long blast on his horn to celebrate the sighting of land. As if that note were a signal to the heavens, the wind increased from a moan to a howl. The clouds seethed and rain fell, hard and cold.

Stroke, breathe, kick, glide; stroke, kick, glide. Gertrude sensed a new feeling to the water flowing around her. She raised her head, treading water for a moment. Rain. Fresh water tasted strange after so many hours of washing saltwater through her mouth.

No. There was something else. As soon as she stopped kicking, she could feel herself drifting backwards, farther out to sea. She was swimming into a tidal current, a strong one. She was already very tired. All her normal swimming speed and power would be eaten up by this current. She would have to draw on all of her reserves to make any progress. Gertrude reached deep inside and found a new source of determination and strength.

Gertrude threw herself back toward the beach, digging hard into the ebbing water with every stroke. Her hands clawed at the waves searching for handholds to pull herself toward the distant shore. Her back arched like a sprinter trying to force her way through the sea.

Wind tore the top off every wave. Flying spray mixed with rain. Visibility dropped to a matter of yards.

Burgess raced into the wheelhouse, where the captain struggled with the tug's wheel to stay on course and hold his position next to Gertrude. "What's our speed?" Burgess demanded.

Sadly, the captain shook his bearded head. "Through the water, a good two knots. But not an inch closer to shore."

"We're standing still?" exclaimed Burgess.

The captain shrugged. "Forward one, back two. We won't make shore till the tide turns."

Burgess dropped back to deck level and grabbed his megaphone. "Miss Ederle, I want you to stop."

"No!"

Stroke, breathe, kick; stroke, breathe, kick. Gertrude knew there could be no gliding now. Her pace was well up over thirty strokes a minute, not a safe pace for someone who'd already been in the water eleven hours.

"You can't fight this current. Weather's getting worse. Give up."

"No!"

"For your own safety, I order you . . ."

"No!"

Mr. Ederle grabbed Burgess' shoulder and spun him around. Ederle's eyes were cold and hard. "It's my daughter's swim. She stays in the water 'till she says it's time to quit."

Nervously Burgess nodded and paced across the deck. Then he snatched the charts and spread them out over a rain-soaked table. "Turn sixty degrees to starboard," he yelled. "Come to due north!"

Turning to Ederle he said, "She can't swim straight into that current. But she might be able to slice diagonally across it, like tacking in a sailboat."

"How many miles will that add?" demanded Ederle.

Burgess rubbed his tired face and shrugged. "Maybe five. But . . ."

"Five miles?" exclaimed Ederle. "That means she'll swim over thirty!"

"It's that or give up here. This storm'll just get worse."

Inch by inch the distant cliffs drifted by as the wind howled and rain pounded down. The sun sank toward the western horizon, lost behind thick clouds. It grew dark.

Stroke, breathe, kick; stroke, breathe, kick. There was no getting tired any more. There was no feeling at all. There was only swimming.

A long caravan of cars, trucks, and buses streamed out of Dover, heading north to meet the swimmer. Huge bonfires were lit along the beach to light her way.

Gertrude's ears, ringing from their long pounding by the waves and salt-water registered a new sound far up ahead: big and crashing, slow and rhythmic. Both tugs throttled back, dropping away from her.

Gertrude sluggishly wondered why. She paused and raised her head in the dark. A sea of fires, lanterns, and lights sparkled only a hundred yards ahead of her. To Gertrude they looked like a sea of stars or fairy lights.

Then it hit her. The shore! The new sound was waves breaking on a beach. She had reached England.

Weary arms mechanically plunged ahead in their unstoppable cadence. Stroke, breathe, kick. A cheering crowd waded into the sea to greet her. Gertrude's feet brushed sand. She stood in waist-deep water and waded ashore.

"Fourteen hours, thirty-one minutes. A new record!" yelled a reporter as Gertrude reached the beach.

• • •

"Too bad it's over," said Margaret as the New York air slowly cleared from falling streamers and paper flakes. Behind their roadster, the crowd drifted back to daily routines. Ahead of them footsore bands loaded onto buses. New York's first tickertape parade in honor of a woman had ended.

Besides being the first woman to swim the English Channel and breaking the previous men's record by over two hours, Gertrude Ederle broke virtually every women's swimming speed record over the next six years. President Calvin Coolidge called her, "America's best girl." She was elected to both the International Swimming Hall of Fame and the Women's Sports Hall of Fame.

Ironically, after the constant pounding of the waves during her Channel swim, Gertrude Ederle became completely deaf by the time she turned thirty. She spent the rest of her life teaching deaf children how to swim. But that is another story.

Questions to Explore

What do you think would be the scariest part of a very long ocean swim? What would be the hardest parts?

How many women's swimming records are there? Who holds them now?

References for Further Reading

- *In the Children's Library*

While she's listed in many record books, very little has been written about this remarkable swimmer.

- *In the Adult Library*

New York Times, Saturday, August 7, 1926, pages A1 and A3. Numerous articles on Gertrude Ederle's historic swim.

See your librarian for additional titles.

Bat-Her Up!

A Story about Maria Pepe, the first female Little League player, and Margaret Gisolo, the first woman to play American Legion baseball

About This Story:

Two and one-half million children play Little League Baseball every year. Half a million more play American Legion ball. Today one out of every fifty players is a girl. That may not sound like very many, but there used to be none.

Two girls changed all that. They weren't trying to revolutionize the sport. They each simply wanted to play ball. Each was certainly good enough to earn their spot on the team, but they were girls poking into an all-boy domain. And they were not wanted by the men who ran the sport of baseball. So before they could raise a cloud of dust sliding into a stolen base, they swirled the blinding dust of legal, civic, and moral controversy. These women believed they had a right to play the game they loved, so they fought for that right. This is a story about those two girls.

A fierce May sun beat down onto the ball field, so that the fans on the third baseline had to squint and shade their eyes. Still none of them thought of leaving or of shifting to the seats along the first baseline, where the worn wooden bleachers of Stevens Park Little League Field were even more crowded.

The air was charged with electricity. Instead of lounging back to relax and settle into another season of Little League ball, the crowd leaned forward expectantly, soaking in every nuance of the warm-ups.

The one-square-mile town of Hoboken, New Jersey, that had until now been famous only as the hometown of singer Frank Sinatra, and the location of the Marlon Brando movie, "On the Waterfront," was about to stake another claim to history. Even the smoky factories and refineries of Bayonne and the dense, urban sprawl of Newark looked a bit more glamorous this Saturday afternoon.

Down on the field, coach Carmen Rongo clapped his hands to gather his Hoboken Young Democrats team before the game. As fifteen small heads wearing the team caps, red with the letters "Y D" on the front, packed into a tight huddle, Carmen muttered to his assistant, "This crowd is bigger than at the playoffs last year."

He leaned into the huddle with his keyed-up, anxious players. Some tapped fists into gloves. Some nervously licked their lips. Some looked scared and probably wished they were someplace else right now. Carmen glanced around the circle of faces and knew he saw the same sight 150,000 other coaches would see this year: fifteen ordinary American kids excited and nervous at the start of a ballgame.

"First game, new season. Let's look sharp out there like I know you can. We're the home team, so we're in the field first. You know the line-up. Now concentrate and play your best. Let's go!"

With a well-rehearsed collective, "Go team!" the huddle broke. Six Young Democrats shuffled toward the bench with Coach Rongo. Nine sprinted onto the field.

The crowd hushed and leaned forward, straining to see. Starting from the shaded first baseline stands and rippling around to the right, cheers erupted. Yes! One of the players dashing onto the infield had a brown ponytail swinging from under her red cap. The girl was going to play! She was about to become the first girl in the world to play a Little League baseball game.

"Play ball!" cried Howard Metsger, full-time cab driver and part-time Little League ump. Twelve-year-old Maria Pepe took the mound pounding the game ball into her glove. The crowd went wild. The girl was the starting pitcher!

An eighty-four-year-old man in the top row tapped the shoulder of the nervous looking man next to him. Beyond him sat a woman, looking more relaxed, but no less excited. "What's all the fuss about?"

The middle-aged, chunky, Italian man wiped his sweaty palms on his pant legs. "A girl's playing."

"So?" asked the old man, beginning to smile. A bushy white mustache spread out over a face full of wrinkles. "Is she any good?"

"She's a darn sight better'n most of those boys," his benchmate snapped, wiping the nervous sweat from his upper lip and forehead.

"Relax Patsy," cautioned a woman next to him. "Maria will do just fine."

On the mound, tall, dimpled Maria Pepe leaned forward to get the catcher's sign, her green eyes flashing a silent warning to the pudgy C. C. Casalino Hardware batter.

Behind her the infield launched supportive chatter. "No batter. No batter. You got him. Fire it in there. No batter!"

In the Casalino dugout, most boys laughed, figuring it would be a batting heyday for them, and hooted, "They can't even put a real pitcher on the mound!"

"So there's a girl pitching who's a good ball player," pressed the old man. "What's the fuss?"

Annoyed, Patsy turned to the old man. "Look, mister, this is the first . . ."

Patsy Pepe froze mid-sentence as his daughter started her wind-up and fired. "Ball one."

Patsy grimaced. The crowd groaned.

"Look, mister. I told you. A girl's playing. This is the first time a girl ever played baseball."

The old man's smirk spread into a full belly laugh. "Is that so? Let me tell . . ."

Patsy held up one hand for silence as Maria fired her second pitch. "Ball two."

Patsy stomped in frustration. His head drooped forward. Then he straightened, sucked in a great breath, and closed his eyes in silent prayer. "Come on, baby. You can do it. I know you can. Throw strikes, baby."

Chatter rolled across the infield like a ritual chant. "Make him be a hitter." "C'mon, pitcher, fire it in there!" "No batter." "No batter"

"Strike!" called Howard Metsger. The crowd cheered.

The old man leaned closer to Patsy. "I can see you're a tad nervous with your daughter playin' her first game."

"A *little?*" interrupted Patsy. "I haven't been able to sleep since I gave her the okay to sign up. Don't get me wrong. I know she's plenty good, and the coach said he'd play her because he needed a good pitcher. The Hoboken League president said he figured no one would raise a fuss, so go ahead. Still I wasn't sure: a girl playing a boy's game. Then the papers got hold of it. And just look." Patsy gestured around the packed stands.

The old man shook his head. "How soon we forget. This is no 'first.' I'll tell you about the real first."

"Strike two!" called the ump.

Patsy yelled, "Way to go, baby!" and clapped his hands.

"I'll tell you when the 'first' was. It was in the summer of 1928."

"Get out o' here," scoffed Patsy. "There was no Little League in '28."

"No. But there was American Legion Junior baseball."

Patsy's head snapped toward the old man. His eyes widened. "I played American Legion ball."

"Strike three! Yer out!" cried Howard Metsger, pumping his right arm.

Patsy snapped back and sprang to his feet. The crowd exploded in cheers. "Way to go, baby! Knock 'em dead!"

Now the C. C. Casalino players realized they'd have to take this pitcher seriously. Jeers started from their bench. "Smash it out, Arnold. The pitcher throws like an old lady! She's got a rubber arm."

A broad shouldered, powerful twelve-year-old stepped into the batter's box and glared at Maria.

"Fire it in. No batter. No batter. You can do it, Maria!"

"So what happened in '28 in Legion ball?" demanded Patsy out of the side of his mouth, so he could keep his eyes on his daughter.

The old man's blue eyes twinkled as he leaned closer. "American Legion ball started in 1925 to promote physical conditioning, good sportsmanship, and citizenship. Blansford was a tiny coal mining town."

"Never heard of it," said Patsy as Maria tried a curve that drifted outside for ball two to the tough Casalino twelve-year-old.

"In western Indiana," said the old man. "It's too small for anyone to have heard of. The '27 Blansford American Legion team didn't win very many games. American Legion tournament lasts for nine games, you know."

"I know. I played Legion ball," interrupted Patsy.

"Strike one!" called Metsger. Patsy exhaled in relief.

"Your daughter's got a nice fastball," observed the old man. "Anyway, the '28 coach, Charlie Griesman, wanted to do better. He grabbed all the best kids in town.

"Almost tops on his list was Margaret Gisolo. Her dad, Angelo Gisolo owned the general store in Blansford. Margaret was a five-foot-two, wiry, fast, fifteen-year-old. She starred for the elementary school team. She played in all the local 'pick-up' games. The Gisolos helped pay for the home field so it could be located across the street from their store. It was the only way Margaret could get some of her chores done between games."

Patsy Pepe gasped as, "crack!" the Casalino boy swung and connected. The crowd gasped and rose to their feet as the ball rocketed down the third baseline. For four long seconds, no one moved, spoke, or breathed. They stared, first at the ball sailing for the left field corner, then at the ump; then back at the ball, then at the ump.

"Foul ball!" cried Metsger.

The crowd roared and sank back to the wooden benches. Patsy dropped his head into his hands, his heart pounding.

His wife patted his leg. "It's all right, Patsy. She's doing fine."

Patsy asked, "So what happened to this Margaret Grisola? How come I never heard of her?"

"*Gisolo*," said the old man. He sucked in a deep breath. "So the '28 tournament started and Margaret was playing second base and no one in town thought much about it, except that she was a better player than any of the boys who might have played in her place.

"Her father wasn't even nervous that first game against Clinton—another tiny town five miles away. He knew Margaret could play and he knew she loved the game."

"Ball three!" called the ump.

Patsy groaned, "Oh, no. Full count . . . So how'd Margaret do? What happened?"

The old man smiled. "At the end of nine innings the game was tied seven to seven. Margaret had turned two doubleplays at second, she played error-free ball, and she went three for four at the plate including two doubles and a pair of runs batted in."

Patsy nodded, impressed. "That's pretty good."

"*But*, the game was still tied, and headed for extra innings. In the twelfth inning, Blansford got a runner to second with two outs. Margaret stepped up. The Clinton players had long since stopped teasing her because she was playing better than they were. She slammed a screamer into the left field corner. The boy on second scooted around to the plate. Blansford won!"

The crowd cheered. Patsy's wife nudged him. "Aren't you going to cheer? Your daughter just got another strikeout."

Patsy shook his head to get back from 1928. "What?! That bruiser? She struck him out? I missed it!" Patsy screamed. "Way to go, baby. Give 'em your good stuff!"

"The point is," continued the old man, "trouble started when the papers got hold of the story. Local papers wrote that Clinton was beaten by a girl. The Clinton coach felt backed into a corner and protested the game, claiming the rules stated only boys could play.

"Legion local officials referred this political hot potato to the state office. There, director Robert Bushee said that the line in the rules, 'any boy is eligible to play,' didn't say anything about excluding girls. But he thought he ought to check with the national office anyway.

"By this time Blansford won a second game, 11 to 1 over Hornsby, another small town. Margaret went three for five with four runs batted in, and played one heck of a game at second.

"The papers went wild. The Gary, Indiana, paper headline read, 'Small Town BIG Star Is a Girl!' Buffalo said, 'Blansford Is One Girl Too Many for Opponents.' *The New York Times* covered it. Margaret made the *Movietone News*, for heavens sake! Blansford won eight of their nine games and won the state championship. Margaret was voted their MVP."

The crowd sprang to its feet. Patsy leapt onto his bench to see better. The third Casalino player popped a fly ball high over the infield. Maria drifted off the mound toward first, waved off the other infielders, and made the catch. Three up, and three down—it was a perfect inning. The crowd roared as the Young Democrats jogged toward the bench. Several nearby parents reached over to congratulate Maria's parents.

As C. C. Casalino players grabbed gloves and raced into position, Patsy turned to the old man. "If your story's true, how come girls haven't been playing American Legion ball all along?"

"That was '28," said the old man. "Before the 1929 season, the American Legion national office inserted a new sentence into the rules: 'This competition is open only to boys.' Margaret couldn't play again. She cried so hard the next spring, she got sick."

"They can't do that," cried Patsy. "It's discrimination."

"In '29 they could," said the old man. "The question is, 'What will they do here in '73?' "

As an eleven-year-old boy stepped up as the first batter for the Young Democrats, Patsy turned and studied the old man. "How do you know all this?"

The wrinkles around twinkling blue eyes lifted into a broad smile. A thin right hand reached out to shake. "Let me introduce myself. I'm Angelo Gisolo. Margaret is my daughter. So I know how you feel today."

Even though the Hoboken Young Democrats lost that first game of the 1973 season, Maria Pepe pitched three scoreless innings and got one hit, a solid double to left-center. Reaction from the Little League headquarters in Williamsport, Pennsylvania, came fast and lethal, and was no more enlightened than that of the 1928 American Legion. They revoked the entire Hoboken Little League Charter, knocking twelve teams and 180 kids out of baseball. As hoped by the national office, local parents reacted bitterly, blaming Maria and her parents for ruining baseball.

Pressure mounted from friends, teammates, angry parents, and disgruntled city officials. Maria reluctantly agreed to resign from Little League.

Maria's story might have dead-ended just as Margaret Gisolo's had, except that by 1973, the National Organization for Women (NOW) had been created. The New Jersey NOW chapter filed a grievance on Maria's behalf with the New Jersey Civil Rights Commission and won. The Commission ruled that Little League teams had to allow Maria and other girls to register and play.

But the Little League headquarters wasn't about to take this kind of progress lying down. They threatened to revoke all New Jersey league charters unless all 2,000 New Jersey teams suspended registration indefinitely.

NOW filed suit in federal court. Little League defended itself saying, "Baseball was a boys game. To admit girls would cripple it," and "Baseball promotes physical strength and courage. These aren't traits we ask of women."

NOW and Maria won. Fighting to the last gasp, Little League appealed. But before the case could be heard by the Supreme Court, President Ford signed legislation changing Little League's Congressional Charter to read "young people," instead of "boys."

Girls could sign up and play Little League. Maria won on paper, and girls everywhere won because of her. But by this time, Maria Pepe was too old for Little League, and the older leagues still had "boys only" rules. She never played organized baseball again.

Not until 1989 did a girl, Victoria Brucker—a slugger for the San Pedro, California, team—reach the Little League World Series. The bitter questions we are left with are: how good could the '29 Blansford and '73 Young Democrats have been if everyone with talent had been allowed to play? How many other Margaret Gisolos and Maria Pepes never got the chance to play? Have we ignored some of our best baseball talent just because they happen to be female and we've held onto the unfounded belief that girls couldn't and shouldn't play? But that's another story.

Questions to Explore

The arguments used to prevent girls playing in Little League baseball included: it would ruin the game; baseball is a contact sport, so girls shouldn't play; girls are fragile and might be injured; girls aren't as physically developed as boys and so would be at a disadvantage; baseball teaches male virtues and skills (physical strength and courage); and letting girls play baseball would take time away from their developing other, more feminine, talents. Do you believe any of these arguments?

Can you find any information in the library to support your point of view?

References for Further Reading

- *In the Children's Library*

  Rivera, Geraldo. *A Special Kind of Courage: Profiles of Young Americans.* New York: Simon & Schuster, 1976.

- *In the Adult Library*

  Howell, Reet, ed. *Her Story in Sports: A Historical Anthology of Women in Sports. West Point, NY: Leisure Press, 1982.*

See your librarian for additional titles.

4

Stories About Science and Exploration

A Woman Led the Way

A story about Sacajawea, the woman who guided the Lewis and Clark expedition

About This Story:

In 1802, President Thomas Jefferson purchased a vast tract of land lying north and west of the Mississippi River from the French, doubling the size of the young United States of America. It was popularly called "the Louisiana Purchase." Jefferson bought it sight unseen.

In 1803, Jefferson chose an army captain experienced in Indian fighting on the western frontier, William Clark, to head an expedition to survey and explore this new wilderness he had brought into the United States. Clark chose a close friend, Captain Meriwether Lewis, as the expedition's co-leader. In 1804 their thirty-one man party, the "Corps of Discovery," set off down the Ohio River to begin their journey.

This is a story about the clever Shoshone woman who, time and time again, saved their expedition.

Deep in the craggy passes of the Continental Divide, high in the Bitterroot Mountains, nights already dropped below freezing even though it was still August, 1805. Food and game were scarce here high above timberline.

As the expedition struggled higher and higher into the mountains, rivers on which they had sailed and paddled for the last thousand miles narrowed into streams. Streams dwindled to trickles. The bulky boats, which had been their chief means of travel, now were nothing more than heavy baggage. The expedition inched forward on foot.

This U.S. Army "Corps of Discovery" sent by President Jefferson to chart the great wilderness of the Louisiana Purchase north and west of the Mississippi River, was led by thirty-three-year-old William Clark, and twenty-nine-year-old Meriwether Lewis. Both wore long, white feathers in black hats. Their thirty-one men wore blue coats with white or yellow shirts underneath instead of the rough-sewn, leather clothes worn by most trappers. Their white pants were tucked into black boots that nearly reached the knees. Their wide-brimmed, black hats were rounded at the top, and they carried, and saluted, the flag of the new American nation.

Late on the afternoon of August 14, Lewis and Clark sat huddled in their canvas tent. On the cot between them lay a large parchment map of North America. The eastern portion was crowded with markings. West of the Mississippi River the map was blank except for one thin, black line that traced their route to this dangerous mountain spot.

Captain Clark ran his hands through thick, flame-red hair and then tapped the middle of the blank map. "Every Indian tribe said we'd find mountains out here. But no one said they'd be this . . ." He waved his hands searching for the right word. "This . . . big . . . this tall, this difficult."

Meriwether Lewis sucked on the pipe clamped between his teeth. "Only three months out of our winter camp and we already teeter on the brink of failure and starvation."

"Already?" laughed Clark. "If it hadn't been for Sacajawea (Sack-ah-jah-WEE-ah), we'd have starved a fortnight ago."

"We need horses," said Lewis in a low, urgent tone. "We'll never survive without horses. We have to abandon our boats and cross the mountains on horseback."

"The Shoshone," nodded Clark. Almost wistfully he added, "The peaceful, horseraising, mountain tribe." Then he slammed one fist into his other palm. "But where are they? We're in the mountains where they live, but we can't find them. We've had scouting parties out every day for over a week."

"The Frenchman is due back this afternoon," answered Lewis. "Maybe he's had some luck."

"I don't trust that braggart, Charbonneau," hissed Will Clark, turning fierce.

"No one does," laughed Lewis. "But he does know a lot about this territory. And we *had* to take him on as guide in order to get Sacajawea."

The tent flap opened and a slender, black-haired Indian girl of eighteen entered, eyes downcast as was proper for an Indian squaw and servant. She wore clothes and shoes sewn from deerskin, decorated with beads. In one hand she carried a steaming pot.

Clark breathed deeply. "Ahhh."

Lewis's eyebrows shot up. "You found more fresh food! You're amazing, Sacajawea."

A sly smile crossed her lips. "Just mountain artichoke and *wapato* with fennel," she said, as if apologizing. "I know where look."

"What's *wapato*?" asked Clark. "It smells delicious."

"Wild potato," said Lewis. "No dried fish and beef jerky tonight!"

Around his first bite, Captain Clark mumbled, "Your English is getting very good."

The girl smiled. "Drouillard, he teach."

Born in the Shoshone tribe, Sacajawea had been stolen by Blackfeet at ten, sold to Mandan Indians as a slave, and later bought by the French-Canadian trapper, Toussaint Charbonneau. He called her "wife." He really meant "slave," or "servant."

Officially Sacajawea was on the expedition as Charbonneau the guide's wife. Unofficially, Lewis and Clark had been so impressed with Sacajawea's knowledge and intellect when they interviewed Charbonneau, they hired him just to get her to join the expedition. Now she lingered near the tent's entrance as if she wanted to say something.

"What is it Sacajawea?" asked Lewis.

Eyes averted, hands at her sides, she said in a soft voice, "Let go me."

"What was that?" asked Clark. "You want us to set you free? To us you are free. It's the Frenchman, Charbonneau, who owns you and claims to be your husband."

Sacajawea shook her head. Her face darkened as she blushed again and nervously fidgeted with her fingers as she sought the correct English words.

"Me horse go."

Lewis shrugged. "Get Drouillard in here."

Clark poked his head out the tent flap. "Drouillard!"

A tall Pennsylvania sergeant with bushy black hair stepped into the tent. He had been assigned to the expedition as an interpreter because of his understanding of many eastern and Plains native languages and his ability to sign. "You called, sir?"

"Find out what she's saying," instructed Clark, continuing to shovel stew into his mouth.

Peppered with halting Mandan Indian, Sacajawea signed something to Drouillard. He nodded and signed back to her, using an occasional English or Mandan word for clarification. Excitedly she signed back.

Drouillard turned to the expedition leaders. "She says you should let her negotiate with the Shoshone for horses."

Lewis laughed. "*Negotiate* with them? We can't even find them."

Sacajawea tapped Drouillard's arm and signed rapidly to him.

"She says the Shoshone are shy people. They don't like to be found by outsiders."

She tugged at his sleeve and added something.

"Never?" he asked.

She answered. "Yes. They do it never."

"Very good," laughed Drouillard. "You're catching on to English."

He turned back to Lewis and Clark. "She says that Shoshone never trade horses with outsiders."

"Never?" exclaimed Lewis.

"That's what I said, sir. But you heard her repeat it. Never."

Lewis clamped his pipe between his teeth. It helped him think.

Captain Clark said, "So she is suggesting that this official U.S. Army expedition, created by the president, himself, should let an Indian—an Indian *woman*—be our official negotiator?" He shook his head. "I think not."

"Why not?" asked Lewis, pointing his pipe stem at his co-leader. "She *is* Shoshone and she can't do any worse than we are."

"You know I've recognized Sacajawea's abilities since we first met. She is an excellent guide and interpreter. She's brave, clever, and cool-headed." Clark declared. "But we are an army unit. Letting her negotiate for us violates a dozen army regulations. *You* negotiate. Let her interpret."

"What we need is horses," answered Lewis. "And the Shoshone won't negotiate with outsiders."

A loud commotion in the camp interrupted their conversation. The tent flap flew open and Sgt. Gass, a burly Irishman with a perpetual grin, poked his head inside. "Beggin' yer pardon, Captains. But the Frenchie's returned and would like ta' see ya."

A short, thick French-Canadian with a bright red nose brushed past Gass and plopped himself down in front of the two men with a grin that was almost too wide. He spoke awkward English through a thick French accent.

"I, Toussiant Charbonneau, have returned!"

He glanced at Sacajawea standing demurely in a corner. "Hey, squaw! Your husban' ez back. Bring me food."

He looked older than his fifty years, though still rugged and sturdy. He wore a plaid wool shirt under his elk coat.

Lewis said, "We were just talking to your wife, and . . ."

"She ez just a squaw. She knows nothing," spat out Charbonneau. "You talk to me."

Clark held out a hand to stop his friend. Then he turned to his French-Canadian interpreter. "You made contact with the Shoshone?"

"Oui."

"Tell me what you found."

Charbonneau shrugged and smiled extra wide. "Shoshone are out there. I see signs. But they no talk. They no show themselves." His eyes lit with pleasure at how clever he had been. "Ahh, but I set a trap. I capture one Shoshone. I call out, 'Here ez your Shoshone boy! You come talk with me, or I kill him!' " Charbonneau laughed at the memory.

Clark exploded, "You what? You killed a Shoshone boy?"

"No, *mon Capitaine*. I just shake him hard and call, 'You bring me horses!' But Shoshone are stupid people. They no come. I throw boy down and leave him in the dirt."

"You fool," hissed Clark. "You may have ruined what little chance we had to create friendly relations with an important tribe!"

Charbonneau shrugged and smiled. "No, *mon Capitaine*. I am the best. I will get you horses."

"Get out of my sight," yelled Clark.

The trapper shrugged and stomped out of the tent to eat his supper.

The sun gave up trying to warm the mountains and set behind craggy western peaks. Lewis and Clark both wrapped blankets around themselves in their tent. Most of their expedition crouched around small campfires.

Puffing on his pipe, Lewis asked, "Why not let Sacajawea try?"

William Clark sat frowning at the map still unfurled on his cot. "Back East, we're at war with half the tribes we've met. Sacajawea will probably do an excellent job. She always does, but if anything went wrong and word got out that we'd let an Indian commit us to an agreement . . ." He shook his head and chuckled. "Well, no thank you!"

"She's Shoshone," pressed Lewis. "She's one of them."

"Exactly," Clark replied. "Who's to say she wouldn't turn against us?"

Meriwether Lewis angrily threw off his blanket. "We're starving here like fools with your army pride. I say give her a chance."

Clark blew out a long slow breath, a frown still plastered on his face. "All right. I give up. Call her in." Under his breath he muttered, "I'll be the laughing-stock of the entire army."

The tent flap was soon thrown open to reveal the first stars beginning to appear. Charbonneau entered followed quietly by Sacajawea.

With a sneer he plopped down onto the cot. "*I* am guide. The squaw knows nothing. You praise her for digging up roots. Phooey! I know the plants! You should always come to *me*. Now what do you want of my wife?"

Clark rose, grabbed the Frenchman by his plaid shirt, and dragged him to his feet. "If you say one more word, I'll throw you in leg irons till we're back in Washington. Get out of my sight. I called for Sacajawea."

Muttering, "Phooey! Americans are as crazy as Shoshone," Charbonneau stormed off.

"Please sit down," said Clark to Sacajawea as soon as her husband had left. "It better I stand."

Lewis sucked thoughtfully on his pipe. "Sacajawea, we have decided to gratefully accept your offer to negotiate with the Shoshone for us."

Clark caught the flicker of joy that flashed across her downcast eyes. "I get horses," was all she said.

"Start out in the morning," continued Lewis. "We'll come with you. Just let us know what you need."

Backing toward the entrance, she said, "Shoshone good people. Just shy people. I get horses."

With frost lingering in the air next morning, Lewis and Clark found Sacajawea waiting for them at the edge of camp. Two heavy sacks were tied together in a loop over her shoulder.

"What's in the sacks?" asked Clark. "Lunch?"

Lewis pried one open and smelled. "It's sugar," he said.

"Two bags of sugar?" demanded Clark. "We're almost out of sugar and have none to spare. Put it back right now!"

Sacajawea stubbornly remained on the trail. "You want talk, yes?"

"No, I don't want to discuss it. I want you to put the sugar back," replied Clark.

She shook her head in frustration that they didn't understand. "I mean not that."

"Drouillard!" called Lewis.

After a flurry of quick signs and exchanged words Drouillard nodded. "She says that only unwelcome guests arrive at a Shoshone home without a gift. If you want to talk to the Shoshone chief about horses, you have to offer a gift first."

"Ahhh, I see," nodded Lewis.

"Does it have to be the sugar?" pressed Clark.

Drouillard started to sign the question. But Sacajawea already nodded. "Yes, good gift."

The four of them climbed the winding trail through a narrow canyon and into a broad valley, Sacajawea first, Drouillard second, Lewis and Clark last. Sacajawea began to sing, her clear notes rising toward the distant peaks.

"She says it's a greeting song, to let them know who we are," said Drouillard.

"Ahh, I see," added Lewis as he puffed.

Sacajawea dropped both sacks in a small clearing and backed toward Lewis and Clark, still singing. As if out of nowhere, three men rose along the far side. One spoke. Sacajawea answered. Another spoke. Again Sacajawea answered.

"What's going on?" Clark whispered to Drouillard.

"Sorry sir," he shrugged. "They're talking too fast for me to make out many words."

With a final nod, Sacajawea turned and walked past Lewis and Clark, starting down the trail.

"Well?" demanded Clark, racing after her.

"What happened?" asked Lewis.

"Tonight. Before dark. We come chief's tent."

As a party of six prepared to again climb the trail toward the Shoshone camp late that afternoon, Clark grabbed Drouillard and whispered. "Stay close to me and tell me exactly what she says." Then he shook his head and groaned, "I can't believe I'm letting an Indian woman negotiate for the U.S. Army."

But instead of following Lewis and Clark toward the Shoshone chief's tent, Sacajawea again turned for the expedition's supply packs. "Would someone please tell me where she's going," muttered Clark.

"What do you think you're doing?" he demanded as she rummaged through their meager food stores setting aside a bag with half their sugar, another with a third of their corn, and a third stuffed with beans.

"Sacajawea," commanded Captain Clark, "we can't spare that much food."

For the first time in all their months together, she looked straight into William Clark's face. "We need horses more," was all she said as she hoisted the sacks and headed for the trail.

"Help carry those sacks, men," called Lewis. Privately to Clark he added, "She does seem sure of what she's doing."

A special tent had been erected for these talks at the edge of the Shoshone village. Inside this tent five Shoshone leaders listened patiently as Sacajawea made a long speech and passed around samples of the corn and sugar for them to try.

"What's going on?" hissed Clark to Drouillard.

"They seem to like the sugar just fine. But I think they're more impressed with the sacks of corn and beans."

The Shoshone chief, a proud, stern man in his mid-twenties named Cameahwait (Ka-ME-ah-wait) rose and smiled at the white men. He gestured and acted in a very friendly way, making a great long speech holding each of the gifts and smiling.

"Has he mentioned horses?" whispered Clark.

"Not yet," answered Drouillard. "But I think Sacajawea just said the Great White Father will send someone to show the Shoshone how to grow their own beans, corn, and squash."

"What?" hissed Clark. "I can't promise that. Tell her I'll *ask*. But I have to get authorization . . ."

"I don't think it's proper to interrupt the negotiations, sir," whispered Drouillard.

Suddenly, Sacajawea turned to Drouillard and spoke hurriedly, using a combination of sign and Mandan. Drouillard nodded and rose to leave. Clark grabbed his sleeve. "Where are you going?" he whispered.

"She said to bring some of the store of extra rifles, sir."

"What?" wailed Clark. He sprang forward next to his new negotiator. "Sacajawea, we can't give away U.S. government rifles."

She turned and again looked him right in the eye. "We need horses more." Then she added in her best English. "I say guns gift of friendship from you to protect Shoshone buffalo hunters from fierce Blackfeet."

"I see," muttered Clark, sinking back into his seat.

"They're nodding," whispered Lewis. "I think she's making progress."

Two days later the expedition departed north from the Shoshone camp, their supplies now tied to the backs of more than twenty horses and one mule.

Lewis and Clark were still amazed at the ease with which Sacajawea had bartered for the much needed horses that neither of them had been able to secure.

"How did you know what gifts to offer Cameahwait?" asked Clark.

An impish smile danced across Sacajawea's face. Still, she held her eyes down and answered, "Before I stolen, I was chief's daughter. Cameahwait is my brother."

Lewis and Clark reached the Pacific Ocean at the mouth of the Columbia River on December 3, 1805 and returned down the Missouri to St. Louis, reaching their starting point on September 23, 1806. Over the 4,000 miles of that trip, Sacajawea sewed 368 pairs of moccasins, and made over twenty elkskin coats. When their compass was smashed in a river, Sacajawea navigated through mountains and valleys to keep them on course. Sacajawea was with them as guide, interpreter, navigator, advisor, food gatherer, cook, and seamstress every step of that grueling journey. She accomplished all of this, and also gave birth to a child, Meeko, on the journey, and carried and cared for him all across the American west and northwest.

To honor this brave and resourceful Native American woman, a river, a mountain, and a mountain pass have been named for her. Monuments to her stand in four states, from Oregon to the Dakotas. The information she helped Lewis and Clark bring back to a westward-bound United States helped make possible the pioneer trails that settled the American West. But that is another story.

Questions to Explore

If you set off to explore a vast new territory and didn't know anything about it, what would you need to take?

What skills would you want in the people you took with you?

What have other explorers taken in the past?

References for Further Reading

- *In the Children's Library*

  Seymour, Flora. *Sacajawea: American Pathfinder.* New York: Macmillan, 1991.

  Ross, Nancy Wilson. *Heroines of the Early West.* New York: Random House, 1960.

- *In the Adult Library*

  Bryant, Martha. *Sacajawea: A Native American Heroine.* Billings, MT: Council for Indian Education, 1989.

See your librarian for additional titles.

A Cup of Science

A story about Fannie Farmer, who was America's first scientific cook

About This Story:

Our modern understanding of nutrition is fairly exact and complete: get enough of each essential daily vitamin and mineral; eat protein, complex carbohydrates, and lots of vegetables and whole grains; reduce fat and salt intake; and get enough—but not too many—calories. Virtually every one of these concepts and terms is a product of twentieth century science. A hundred years ago, people had no real sense of what nutritional value they received or needed from the specific foods they ate. They ate what they could grow, what could be hunted, and what could be found or purchased.

Open any cookbook and you'll find recipes measured in cups, ounces, teaspoons, and tablespoons. The book doesn't mean to measure ingredients with the cups and spoons you use at the table. It refers to special sets of standardized utensils used only for measuring. Yet one hundred years ago there were no standard measures for cooking. Cooking then was an imprecise art at best.

Then it all turned around. Cooking became an exacting science whose purpose was to precisely create and re-create flavor and nutrition. Much of this change can be credited to one woman. This is a story about her.

Boston can be bitterly cold in the winter. A bone-chilling damp rides on the fog and wind and even in still air creeps down your neck to rob any warmth you tucked inside your coat. On any gray and cheerless February day the mere thought of an icy walk across Boston can send shivers down the spine, even while still curled up in front of a toasty fire. In the damp and gloomy winter of 1879 it was especially true for a young woman of twenty-two with one paralyzed leg to slow her pace.

"I'll be fine, mama," insisted shy, red-headed Fannie for the twentieth time that morning as she limped toward the front door of their modest house at the edge of Boston.

"I just wish you didn't have to take a position so far across town," sighed Mrs. Farmer, wiping her hands on a dishtowel.

"We both know I was lucky to get a position at all," answered Fannie, buttoning her long coat and fishing through the pockets for her gloves.

"If only you could have gone to college like your sisters, or if you didn't have to work at all . . ." Deep concern was etched across Mrs. Farmer's forehead.

"Mother," snapped Fannie. "We have been over this a hundred times. The polio paralyzed my leg, not my life. The leg has meant I couldn't be accepted to college. But I have to do something with myself. Besides, business is down at father's printshop and we need the extra money."

"Of course you're right, dear," agreed Mrs. Farmer, adjusting the collar on her daughter's coat. "It's just such a bitter day. And it will take you forever to walk clear to South Street."

Fannie smiled and shook her head. "Mother, I have gone out almost every day for six years with this bad leg. I'll be fine."

Fannie stepped through the front door and gasped as the icy air struck her face. Her mother called after her, "Remember to use the recipe cards when you cook for the Lancocks . . . and remember to clean up any mess you make . . . and . . ."

"Good-bye, mother," said Fannie to interrupt her mother's litany of reminders. "I'll be fine, and I'll be home for supper."

An hour later, shivering as the damp crept down to her bones, and as her bad leg began to ache, Fannie reached the manicured two-story brick house at 728 South Street. Fresh white trim had been painted around each window and the door.

Fannie knocked on the brass knocker and waited nervously on the front step. She heard hurried footsteps inside and the door was opened by a stately, but stern-looking woman whose dark hair was pulled into a tight bun. The woman towered a good eight inches over Fannie's five-foot stature, and she stared at Fannie with the arched eyebrows and icy aloofness of an aristocrat.

Fannie curtsied as best she could on her bad leg. "I'm Fannie Farmer, ma'am, your new 'mother's helper.' "

The eyebrows relaxed. The head nodded. The mouth smiled thinly. "Ahh, yes. I am Abigail Lancock. Do come in."

Mrs. Lancock stepped back from the door with a regal grace. Fannie stepped awkwardly over the threshold and tried to fluff her brilliant red hair, now matted to her forehead by the swirling fog.

Mrs. Lancock glided across the entry parlor, speaking over her shoulder as she went, and pointing at various doors with her left hand. Her tone reminded Fannie of the dreaded schoolmaster at the high school. "You'll work mostly with the children in the nursery. It's through there. This second door leads to the kitchen. You'll find it well stocked with whatever you need. If there are no other questions, prepare dinner for one o'clock. Ring for us when it's ready. Good morning, and welcome to the household."

With that, the door to Mrs. Lancock's private study swung shut behind her with a solid "thud." Fannie stood open-mouthed and speechless in the entry. To the closed door Fannie softly replied, "Yes ma'am. And it's a pleasure to meet you, too, ma'am."

At eleven o'clock Fannie began her exploration of the spacious kitchen. Mrs. Lancock had not exaggerated. Every kitchen device Fannie had ever heard of was neatly laid out on shelves and in cupboards.

Fannie pulled out the large envelope in which she had carried the recipe cards her mother had given her. She slowly thumbed through the stack, reading the titles, looking for one she felt confident enough to make for her first Lancock dinner.

"Ah, chicken pie with cherry sauce. Perfect! I made this once with mother."

She read the ingredients for the crust. "What's this?" she exclaimed. "A 'lump' of butter? How much is that? Two 'fists' of flour? Whose fist? A cup of water? Which cup? The Lancocks have a dozen—all different sizes." Fannie groaned, "this *can't* be the best crust recipe in the lot."

She flipped quickly through the cards and found five recipes for pie crust. One called for butter the size of an egg (a large egg, or a small egg?). A second wanted two lumps the size of a walnut. A third just listed a medium-sized lump. One needed a dash of salt, another a pinch, a third called for a bit of salt.

"How much is that?" wailed Fannie. "And which is more, a 'dash,' a 'bit,' or a 'pinch'?"

The kitchen clock ticked loudly toward eleven thirty. She'd have to start the pie right now if she was to have dinner ready at one. But how much of which ingredients should she use?

She'd have to guess. Fannie closed her eyes and said a silent prayer. Then she plunged into the crust for her first chicken pot pie with a final grumble. "What good is a recipe if it doesn't tell you how much of everything to use?"

At five minutes past one, she rang the bell and served generous portions of steaming chicken pot pie. As was the fashion of the time, she ladled a sweet cherry sauce over the top. Then Fannie retreated to the kitchen, and paced nervously across the polished wooden floor, waiting for Mrs. Lancock's verdict.

Forty minutes later, Fannie was summoned to clear the dishes. Mrs. Lancock paused at the dining room door. "Your crust needs to be more flaky, my dear. Watch your proportions more carefully next time."

Fannie stomped back into the kitchen. "Watch my proportions," she muttered. "I'd like to watch my proportions. But *how* with these recipes?"

By week's end Fannie was thoroughly disgusted with the current state of cooking instructions. She told her mother, "If I see one more recipe that tells me to use a 'medium hot oven—hot, but not too hot' I'll scream! Oh, and every recipe says to 'cook until done,' or else, 'cook until done just right.' Of course you want to cook it till it's done! But how long is that?"

Her mother patted Fannie's arm, "You'll get a feel for it, dear. You just have to watch things as you go."

"Seems to me, the whole point of a recipe card is to tell you what to do when you don't have 'a feel for it,'" answered Fannie.

That Saturday afternoon, Fannie attended a lecture by the famous female intellectual, Catherine Beecher, sister of author, Harriet Beecher Stowe. Catherine Beecher proposed that, just as men of the late 1800s were using scientific principals and thinking to improve the working world, so must women use this same approach to improve the functioning of the home. She talked to a packed lecture hall of the need to "professionalizing the home" and of "home science" and "home economics."

The crowd of mostly women nodded and applauded enthusiastically. But to Fannie, the words were magic. It was as if Catherine Beecher were talking directly to her. It felt like this famous woman had come to Boston just to tell Fannie what she must do.

When Catherine finished her remarks, the audience had a chance to ask questions and make comments. Fannie leapt to her feet. Others who had simply raised a polite hand, stared in amazement as Fannie bolted out of her chair.

It wasn't that she really wanted to say something, or even that she knew what she would say. It felt more like she *had* to reply to Catherine's wonderful words.

"Home science should begin with cooking," Fannie said in a voice so loud it caused her cheeks to flush in embarrassment.

After a pause for murmurs to dart around the room, Catherine said, "Please continue, Miss . . ."

"Fannie Farmer, ma'am. Cooking is at best a guesswork art. How can we 'professionalize our homes' until cooking becomes scientific? A lump of this, a dash of that, a fist of something else. Cooking will never be exact or scientific until we have measurements that mean the same thing to everyone. Recipes should come out the same every time. But the way they are now written, they never do."

The crowd applauded and heads nodded everywhere. It seemed everyone had their own cooking disasters to whisper to the person next to them.

Catherine Beecher tapped on the lectern to regain control. "Well, Miss Farmer, it seems you have struck a chord with this group. Exact measurement is an important part of modern improvement. This would be a valuable task for someone to undertake."

In the excited rush of the moment, and before she had time to consider what she was saying, Fannie blurted, "I will!"

The crowd applauded appreciatively. Fannie flushed beet-red and sank into her seat, wondering what she had just gotten herself into.

Walking home, Fannie floated on an excited rush from the lecture. Her mind whirled with new, enticing concepts: "Home science," "professionalize the home," "exact, standardized measurements for cooking recipes."

"But how?" wondered Fannie aloud. "What common measurements can every woman use?" Then, in the spirit of Catherine's lecture, she corrected herself. "No. What *scientific* measures can we use to make recipes exact?"

But Fannie hadn't finished high school. What did she know of science? Where could she find out? She detoured to the imposing Boston Public Library. Across the marbled floor she stopped at the reference desk. A kindly woman behind the desk, about the same age as Mrs. Lancock, but with a face made of warm pudding, rather than icy stone, smiled as Fannie approached.

"May I help you, dear?"

Fannie struggled for the right words. "How do scientists . . . measure something?"

"Carefully and accurately, we hope," teased the librarian, her eyes twinkling over her glasses.

Fannie held out her hands as if to erase her last words and start over. "No, ma'am, I mean what do they use?"

"Ah. You mean like balance scales and beakers?"

"No," sighed Fannie, "I need to know what *measurements* they use."

"Ahhh," nodded the librarian, "you want the scientific *units* of measure."

Fannie shrugged and nodded. "I guess so."

"And what are you going to measure?" asked the librarian.

Confused, Fannie shrugged. "Butter, flour, milk, salt . . ."

"I see," interrupted the librarian. "Small volumes of solids and liquids. But probably not gases."

"Gases?" repeated Fannie. "I don't think there are gases in any of my recipes."

"I see," nodded the librarian, adjusting her glasses and folding her arms. "You want to make accurate, scientific measurements for some recipe. Interesting. Then I suppose you would want to use pounds, pints, and ounces."

"I know pounds and pints. But are ounces for solids or for liquids?" asked Fannie.

"Both. A liquid ounce is 1/16th part of a pint. A solid ounce is 1/16th part of a pound. You can buy those measures at a variety of local chemistry shops."

With an excited grin Fannie curtsied, thanked the librarian and hurried back across the marbled floor.

By ten o'clock Monday morning, Fannie settled into the Lancock kitchen with several one-ounce and one-pint beakers, and with a chemist's balance scale and weights varying from one ounce to one pound.

"Now what do I need to measure?" she asked out loud as she pulled out the recipe card she had chosen for today. It was a meat and potato pie with plum sauce. She chose it because it had lots of ingredients and because it had a crust.

"She wants flaky crust? I'll give her flaky crust," muttered Fannie as she lined up each of her ingredients. She read from the recipe, "2 walnut-sized lumps of butter."

Fannie formed the two lumps as accurately as she could. Then she scooped one up with a wooden spatula and pressed it into a one-ounce beaker. She scraped all the excess into a second one-ounce beaker. The first beaker was full and mounded, the second just over half full.

She was about to write, "1 walnut-sized lump equals 1 1/2 ounces," when she stopped. "Wait. To be exact, measurements can't be mounded like this. Everyone would mound them differently. Measurements must be flat and level."

With a knife she sliced the mounded butter from the top of the first beaker and pressed it into the second.

"Ahh, a walnut-sized lump is almost exactly two ounces. So two lumps is four ounces."

She crossed out "2 walnut-sized lumps" and wrote in "4 ounces" on the recipe card.

Then she crossed her arms with a satisfied smile. It was her first scientific measurement.

The next ingredient was flour: "3 fists." As her mother had shown her to do, Fannie lifted three fistfuls of flour from the flour bin and plopped it into a bowl. Now to measure. She scooped a clean one-ounce beaker full from this flour bowl, carefully leveled the top with a knife, and dumped this ounce of flour into a second bowl. "One."

Fannie repeated the process. "Two." And again. "Three." And again, and again, and again. "Four. Five. Six." The bowl was still several ounces from empty.

Fannie sighed. "Measuring flour by ounces is too slow. I need something bigger."

She tried her pint beaker. Three fists of flour more than filled the beaker. But it was too hard to guess the fraction of a pint represented by the leftover flour. "Nuts! A pint is too big."

Then her eyes widened. She'd just have to create a *new* standard measure between an ounce and a pint. She looked around for what to use, and pulled down eight of the Lancock's china cups.

"Halfway between one ounce and sixteen ounces is eight ounces," Fannie told herself. She poured water, ounce by ounce, into each cup until she found one that was exactly eight ounces.

Staring at the cup, Fannie struggled to think of a scientific name for this new measure. Finally the obvious struck her. She called it a "cup," and wrote "1 cup equals 8 ounces," on a note card.

Growing more and more excited, Fannie turned to the next ingredient: "a good pinch of salt." Between thumb and forefinger she gathered as "good a pinch of salt as she could," and dropped it into a one-ounce beaker.

"Nuts, again!" muttered Fannie. "It's just a little bit in the bottom. An ounce is too big."

She thought about it, then smiled. She needed another new measure, something smaller than an ounce. She searched the kitchen and wound up with a stack of spoons on the table in front of her, including large serving spoons, soup spoons, regular place spoons for the table, and tiny teaspoons.

She found that a good, thick pinch of salt almost exactly filled one of the small Lancock teaspoons, and that six of these spoonfuls almost exactly filled a one-ounce beaker. She nodded with satisfaction and wrote, "1 teaspoon equals 1/6th of an ounce." Then she crossed out "pinch," and wrote in "1 teaspoon" on her recipe card.

By eleven o'clock, Fannie had converted the entire recipe to her new standard measures. At one, she stood admiring the golden-brown, flaky crust that had formed over her meat pie as it baked. Then she broke through the crust with a large spoon to serve generous portions onto each plate, and ladled on the thick plum sauce.

As she cleared the dirty dinner dishes at quarter to two, Mrs. Lancock poked her head back into the dining room. "Your crust was much improved, Fannie. Make it that way every time."

Fannie smiled. "I sure will, Mrs. Lancock. I'll make it *exactly* that way, every time."

Fannie Farmer not only created the set of standard recipe measures we all now use, she was a tireless advocate for nutritional cooking. She said that, "knowledge of the principles of diet will soon be an essential part of one's education." To that end she started her own cooking school in Boston, and wrote the world-famous series of "Fannie Farmer Cookbooks," which, in their various reprints and revisions, have sold over six million copies. Perhaps her greatest passion was saved for the time she spent devising healthy and nutritional diets for the sick. Her goal was to create tasty and nutritional hospital fare. But that is another story.

Questions to Explore

When you and your family cook does each recipe always turn out exactly the same? Why not?

Why do you think no one had developed exact measurements for cooking recipes before the late 1800s?

Can you find cookbooks dating back to the early 1900s? to the mid-1800s? Can you find mention of "cups" and "teaspoons" before 1900?

References for Further Reading

- *In the Children's Library*

    Vare, Ethlie Ann, and Greg Ptacek. *Women Inventors and Their Discoveries.* Minneapolis, MN: The Oliver Press, 1993.

- *In the Adult Library*

    Shapiro, Laura. *Perfection Salad: Women and Cooking at the Turn of the Century.* New York: Farrar, Straus & Giroux, 1986.

See your librarian for additional titles.

Bring Your Notebook

A story about Margaret Mead, America's first woman anthropologist

About This Story:

Anthropology, the study of human social relationships and culture, is one of the most recent scientific fields. Unheard of even in the late 1800s, anthropology is a true twentieth century science. Early anthropologists had a double burden. Not only were they trying to learn about other cultures, they also had to learn how to learn about other cultures; that is, how to effectively conduct their science.

One of the people who did most to define the field and its methods of fieldwork wasn't even supposed to go out into the field. This scientist was a rookie both to anthropology and to fieldwork. Worse, she was a "she," a female scientist—rare in all science, and unheard of in the strenuous, dangerous area of anthropological field research. This is a story about her.

"Be quiet!" she hissed at the voices. But they wouldn't stop. There were so many voices inside her head, and they had grown loud and frightening as mile after mile of clear turquoise South Pacific water slid under the bow of the tiny Navy launch. "I mean it!" Margaret barked.

"Mean *what*, madam?" called Ensign O'Rourke over the roar of the small ship's motor.

Twenty-four-year-old Margaret Mead blushed at having been heard and shook her tired, seasick head. "Nothing, Ensign . . . nothing."

"Ahh, well, Right-o." Ensign O'Rourke oozed chipperness and smiles. He acted as if pounding over the ocean in this miniature bathtub of a boat was actually fun. It made Margaret feel all the worse.

"That's the island, Ta'u, up ahead," he beamed, white teeth flashing under a bushy red mustache. "Just off to port. That's 'left' to you landlubbers."

Wearily Margaret gazed at the distant speck shimmering on the horizon. "That dot is an island?"

O'Rourke stepped back from the bridge area to sit beside her. "Small island really. Eleven miles long by eight miles wide." He towered over the seasick scientist. Not that O'Rourke was particularly tall. But at just over five feet tall and less than one hundred pounds, Margaret Mead made everyone look big.

"Seas are calm. Light, regular swells. Ship's riding easy. The U.S. Navy'll have you at the dock in two hours." Unable to contain his enthusiasm, he sprang back to his feet. "You should really stroll out on deck. Fresh salt air, tropical breeze, endless horizon!" He sucked in a great breath as if trying to savor all nature's splendor in one gulp. "Does the body a world of good! Helps you get your sealegs." He disappeared back through the hatchway door.

Left alone in the small cabin Margaret groaned, first because her stomach flip-flopped as the boat slammed through a slightly larger wave, and second because the voices started screaming at her again. She raised both hands to her mouse-brown page boy and shoved her fists against her temples. " 'Be quiet!' I said."

But the voices screeched on. The loudest was that of Franz Boas, Margaret's arrogant faculty advisor at Columbia University in New York City. Margaret could see him so clearly: sitting on the couch in his university office, legs crossed at the knee, cigarette holder haughtily waving away each of her arguments, with a droopy white mustache, and dark eyes mocking her each time he spoke.

"I can't possibly allow you to conduct the field research for your dissertation on some unknown island in the American Samoas a thousand miles from civilization," he said smugly. "This *is* 1924, and you may think it quite normal to call around the country by telephone or telegraph. But from some forsaken South Pacific island it could take you weeks to get a message out. Besides, anthropology is still a new science. You don't know what to expect, or what you'll need."

Margaret argued that the work was important and that no one was studying the indigenous cultures of the South Pacific. He scoffed. "My point precisely. You have no experience, and you'd have no support. You don't even know the language well enough to communicate in an emergency. Besides, you're a woman. How could you protect yourself? The area is infested with snakes, wild animals, disease-carrying insects, and fierce natives. What if something happened, or you develop some tropical illness? You wouldn't possibly know what to do."

She begged. He sneered. "Study teenage Navajo Indian girls. You'll be safe and can get help when you need it."

She countered that *everyone* was studying Indian tribes. She told him the joke circulating through anthropology circles: What is the composition of a typical Navajo six person family? Answer: Two parents, one grandmother, two children, and an anthropologist.

Boas didn't laugh. "I deny your request to spend nine months living with four native villages on a tiny island speck. It's too risky for the university to back. You'll assess cultural influences on adolescent development by studying Navajo teenage girls, or you won't study it at all."

Five months later, though, Margaret sat on this thinly veiled excuse for a torture device the navy called an "Inter-Island Shuttle" feeling every bit as green as an anthropologist as the constant pitching of the boat made her body feel. When Margaret glanced in the cabin mirror, what stared back was a face drained of color; a wide, straight mouth with lips a little too big; and a nose three sizes too large for her head. Others described it as an open, pleasant, inquisitive face. All Margaret saw in it were doubts and uncertainties.

Then she had to stop looking and close her eyes as the boat rolled through another large wave and her stomach wrenched inside her. But nothing stopped the nagging voices. Now she could hear her mother.

"Margaret, dear, this anthropology is such a new field. You don't have established procedures and methods for field study and data collection. How will you ensure that your study goes well when there's no one to consult with? Besides, you've never spent a single night on your own. Are you really up to months of strenuous field research? Do you even know exactly how you'll do your study?" Then she smiled in a condescending way. "Do the Indian study, dear. You'll be happier."

After three weeks on a steamer rolling across the Pacific, and now two days on this horrid little launch, Margaret had to admit, she was miserable. But more than the sea, Margaret's real misery came from those voices and how they reminded her of her own nagging uncertainty in her abilities.

Margaret could hear her father as he slowly blew out a round puff of smoke from his pipe. "Fascinating new field, anthropology. A true science of the twentieth century. Newest field of study in the world. Only a handful of working anthropologists. Only four of you grad students studying with Boas at Columbia. Are you certain you're ready to venture this far into the field? Of course, I'll go along with whatever you say. But, are you certain?"

She heard the voice of her friends. "Margaret, darling, you don't know how to *do* field studies." They dropped the "r," and drew out the word "daaa-ling" as was so fashionable in New York in the early 1920s. "Why cut yourself off from the world for so many months, darling? It all sounds very half-baked and foolish to me. Stay here in New York and study until you're really prepared."

And then the voices started to pepper her all at once.

Franz Boas: "You're not adequately trained for such a project."

Her mother: "But dear, you don't even know the language."

Her father: "Be very certain before you leap."

Other anthropologists: "Stay home, have children, and study them. Don't traipse off to a remote island where a woman doesn't belong and try to do a man's work."

Her husband: "I thought you'd come to France with me while I do my research. Why would you want to squat in some infested, steaming jungle with a bunch of savages?"

Her friends: "Don't rush off until you know what to do once you get there."

From the stew of voices in her mind, a thought seemed to bubble up to the top, feeling like a cool breeze to blow away the discomfort of a sweltering afternoon. *You could stay on the boat and go back. Go back where it's safe and study more. Study in the city with telephones and restaurants and doctors. You could turn around right now and go back.*

Because the university refused, Margaret's father had put up the money for her trip. He wouldn't mind if she gave up and went home.

But then another small voice whispered in her ear. "Someone must learn about this culture before it's too late, before it disappears into the twentieth century world of western ways. This research is critically important. Study now, or whatever is unique and valuable in the culture of this island will be gone forever." This was a voice filled with urgency and need.

Margaret answered that voice out loud, "But they all are right. I don't really know what to do!"

Then a picture of Grandma Mead flashed across her mind and Margaret smiled.

O'Rourke poked his head back down from the open bridge area. "Ah, I see you're smiling. Finally getting used to the sea, eh? Care to bound up and have a look-see at your new island home? You can see Ta'u better now."

Weakly Margaret waved that she'd prefer to remain where she was.

Margaret struggled to remember. *Why did I smile? Oh, yes, Grandma Mead.*

Through all her growing up years, through all the moves to new houses and new neighborhoods, through all her mother's own research that kept her locked away in her study day and night, Grandma Mead had been the one constant in Margaret's life. Margaret had been schooled at home. Grandma Mead was her teacher. In each new neighborhood, Grandma Mead was her first friend.

Margaret suddenly realized that when Grandma Mead had taught her to read, write, and think, she had taught her exactly how to conduct this research she was about to begin. Again smiling, Margaret could hear Grandma Mead's crisp voice.

"Margaret! Come quickly, and bring your notebook."

Tumbling down the narrow stairs from the third-floor, attic room that eleven-year-old Margaret had claimed as her domain, she snatched up a thick leather notebook and pen. Grandma Mead waited on the second-floor landing, pointing out a window onto an expansive lawn that sloped to a meandering stream.

"Look! Your two sisters are outside. Now observe and record how they interact here in the country. Is it different than in the city? What do they play with? How much space do they use?"

For almost three years, much of Margaret's schooling had been to observe her two younger sisters and carefully record what she saw. Then Grandma Mead would review and discuss Margaret's notebook. What did the younger sisters share? With whom did they share? When did they share? What new words did they learn? Why and how did they learn them? And on, and on.

Grandma Mead did not believe children should sit still for long and often interrupted a biology lesson saying, "Oh, pooh! Enough of sitting and chalk-boards. Go out and find me some of these plants we're talking about. Show me what they look like."

Grandma Mead also believed too much reading was bad for children's developing eyes. Margaret had to sneak books into bed at night to get in all the reading she wanted. But observations of people and the world were the heart of Margaret's early education.

"Margaret! Pricilla's found an anthill. Come quickly and bring your notebook."

"Margaret! The girls are fighting by the creek. Come quick and observe. Bring your notebook!"

And always Grandma Mead demanded that Margaret do much more than just write down what she saw. "Think with your mind about what comes in through your eyes, child. What's happening? Why is it happening? What's behind it? What does it mean? How does it fit into an overall pattern?"

In three years, Margaret stuffed four notebooks full of her observations of her sisters.

And that is exactly what she'd do here at Ta'u! Observe at close range, and assess her observations. What did they mean? What did others think they meant?

What were the trends and patterns? How did individual events fit into, or reshape, those patterns?

Margaret felt stronger and calmer than at any time since she had embarked on her voyage.

The boat's engine slowed. Margaret rose to find Ta'u Island had grown up all around them, lush, green, thick, and steamy. The boat glided through a small bay, drifting toward a rickety, wooden pier. Palms crisscrossed the thin strip of sandy beach. Dense forest hid the rest of the island behind a solid green blanket sprinkled with brilliantly colored flowers of every shade. The air hung wet and thick like a sauna.

Margaret stepped onto the wooden pier carrying one bag of clothes, a typewriter, and two boxes of paper, ribbon, drawing paper, and notebooks. With the boat engine off, the rich sounds of a tropical forest flooded into her ears. Staring back at her from the shade of wide mango trees at the end of the pier were eighty pairs of solemn, inquisitive eyes set in handsome brown Samoan faces. No one spoke. No one stepped forward to greet this white-skinned woman wrapped in a traditional Samoan sarong. They stood and stared.

Margaret gulped and tried to force a smile onto her face. "Ta-lo-fa," she called. It was the standard Samoan greeting and literally means, "love to you."

Some giggled at her strange accent and mispronunciation. Many smiled and nodded. Two burly men marched forward to help carry boxes. Margaret Mead had arrived at Ta'u.

Margaret set up cot and typewriter on the back porch of Pharmacist's Mate Edward Holt's bungalow. He ran the Navy's one-man supply depot on the island, was the only other English-speaking person on Ta'u, and had the only building with walls. This provided Margaret privacy when she typed up her notes and analyzed her observations.

Samoan houses had no walls, just a thatched roof held up by poles. Margaret decided the only reason they needed roofs at all was to protect them from the rain that showered, drizzled, sprinkled, or poured down four or five times each day.

Margaret's specific mission on Ta'u was to study teenage girls and see if they experienced the same rebelliousness and turmoil characteristic of teenagers in America. That is, she wanted to see if the stresses that drove teenage behavior were part of all humans, or if they came from the society in which the teen lived.

Her plan was to live as one of the native teenagers and observe them as closely as she could. Was it the correct plan? Margaret had no idea. Anthropology was still so new a field of study that there were no recognized methods of field research. So she did what she knew how to do, observe and fill up notebooks as Granny Mead had taught her.

Margaret dressed in a sarong as they dressed. She walked barefoot with the other teen-aged girls. She adopted a Samoan name, "Makelita." She ate with the young women, wove baskets with them, swam with them, bathed with them, carried torches for night fishing with them, danced, wove mats, worked in the sugarcane fields, and laughed and joked with them.

All the while she listened, watched, and wrote in her notebooks. Each night she tried to assess what she had seen that day. What did these girls think? How did they relate to each other, to boys, to their parents? What were their concerns and fears?

Margaret mapped every house on the island and completed a census of where every girl lived: how many brothers and sisters she had, the family's wealth and status, what role each girl played within the family, and what chores and responsibilites were hers.

She interviewed each girl and virtually every adult about the girls and their life. The girls loved to talk. The adults expected to be paid for information. Within the first month Margaret's interviews cost her 100 envelopes, 200 sheets of paper, dozens of cigarettes, and countless matches, onions, and sewing needles.

Nine months after she arrived, Margaret stood waiting to leave Ta'u as a Navy Inter-Island Shuttle idled up to the same rickety pier. Margaret carried one bag of clothes, one typewriter, and seven boxes of notes, drawings, and observations. Staring back at her from the shade of wide mango trees at the end of the pier were eighty pairs of solemn, inquisitive eyes set in handsome brown Samoan faces. No one spoke.

As a navy ensign lugged Margaret's boxes onto the tiny launch, Margaret was flooded with emotion. She was leaving home and going home. She was leaving family and going to family. She was ending her study, and yet just beginning the study. Joy and sorrow surged within her in equal measures.

She raised one hand and waved. "Talofa." Eighty faces smiled and eighty hands waved back. Margaret turned and stepped into the launch. Instantly her stomach fluttered and her heart sank. She had to spend two days in this bathtub-sized torture chamber and three weeks on an ocean steamer.

The color drained from Margaret's face. A pale-green tinge crept across her cheeks as a smiling ensign helped her on board. "The seas are calm. Only light, even swells. Stroll the deck and get your sealegs. The navy'll deliver you to Pago Pago in no time."

Margaret Mead returned to New York and compiled her volumes of notes into a book, *Coming of Age in Samoa*. It was a bestseller then, and is still the most widely read book on anthropology in the world. In it Margaret Mead showed that Samoan teens suffer none of the problems and conflicts of American teens. Teen turmoils are not necessarily an inherent part of being human, but are part of our specific culture.

More importantly, twenty-four-year-old Margaret Mead brushed aside her own self-doubts, and the "You can't do it's," all around her to dive, as best she could, into her chosen field of work. In so doing, she created the very method of field study that became the standard for all of anthropology. Her system of event analysis showed how to study each individual event and interpret it within the framework of an entire culture.

Margaret Mead studied the cultures of half a dozen other Pacific islands, wrote twenty-seven books and countless articles on her studies, and became the best-known and most-respected anthropologist in the world. But did she ever get over being seasick? That is another story.

Questions to Explore

Is observation a good way to study something? What have you learned by observation? Name something you cannot learn about by observation.

Which fields of science learn through observation?

Where would you find out how observation is used in various science fields?

References for Further Reading

- *In the Children's Library*

Peavy, Linda, and Ursula Smith. *Dreams Into Deeds: Nine Women Who Dared.* New York: Charles Scribner's Sons, 1985.

Saunders, Susan. *Margaret Mead: The World Was Her Family.* New York: Viking Kestrel, 1987.

Stoddard, Hope. *Famous American Women.* New York: Thomas Crowell, 1970.

Ziesk, Erda. *Margaret Mead.* New York: Chelsea House, 1990.

- *In the Adult Library*

Kostmen, Samuel. *Twentieth Century Women of Achievement.* New York, Richard Rosen Press, 1976.

Mead, Margaret. *Coming of Age in Samoa, a Psychological Study of Primitive Youth for Western Civilization.* New York: William Morrow, 1928.

Mead, Margaret. *Sex and Temperment in Three Primitive Societies.* New York: William Morrow, 1935.

See your librarian for additional titles.

Wings of Courage

A story about Jacqueline Cochran and her rival, Amelia Earhart, two of America's first female aviators

About This Story:

When Americans think of women and flying, they almost always think of Amelia Earhart. True, Amelia was labeled "the first lady of aviation." And it is true that she was the first woman to fly solo across the Atlantic, across the Pacific from Honolulu to the mainland, and to fly nonstop across the continental United States both ways.

But she was not the only woman setting flying records in the middle 1930s. Neither, by far, was she the first. This is a story about another of America's talented flying women, one who had to fly for many years deep in the shadow of Amelia Earhart.

The sun had just dipped, like a sizzling-red, brick into the Pacific Ocean. The tarmac of the Los Angeles airport radiated heat like an oven as this sweltering day in May, 1938, finally edged toward its end.

But for some people, the day was just beginning. A man with a blue "Official Judge" ribbon pinned to his short-sleeve shirt pocket and a bulging clipboard swinging in his left hand, strode down the line of single engine planes.

The engine of the first plane roared to life. Gusts of prop wash swirled the judge's tie into his face. He had to cover his clipboard with both hands to keep the pages from tearing loose. He spun his back into the gale force winds created by the propeller of the high-powered racing plane, and jogged to the next plane in line, a specially modified Seversky pursuit plane.

He waved at the pilot to get her attention and then cupped his hands and clipboard to his mouth to be heard over the roar. "You'll be the eighth in line for take-off on runway 2-7 left, Miss Cochran. Winds are light, west-southwest at ten knots. Skies are clear."

Then he chuckled and added, "A lot different from last year, isn't it?"

Twenty-eight-year-old Jacqueline Cochran was just sweeping her long, blond hair from her face so she could put on her flight helmet and goggles. She smiled her glamour-girl smile and nodded in agreement. "The fog was *frightful* last year."

The official started down the line to the next plane. Then he hesitated and called up, "Good luck, Miss Cochran. We're all rooting for you." With a final wave he turned for the next plane.

Before settling down into her cramped cockpit, Jackie paused to look along the line of race planes stretched out ahead of and behind her. "There must be a hundred in the race this year," she said to herself. A crowd of nearly 10,000 spectators spread out behind the restraining ropes at the edge of the runway.

Search lights swept across the sky. A huge "1938 Bendix Transcontinental Air Race" banner fluttered from the hanger that served as race headquarters.

With a final stretch of her arms and neck, Jackie sank into her seat and sighed, "Eighteen hundred miles to Cleveland before I can stand up again."

Instinctively her hands darted over the controls as she started her pre-flight check. But her mind wandered from the step-by-step routine.

"How do I feel?" she wondered. "Excited? Certainly excited. It's take-off time for my third go at being the first woman to win a major air race. But there's something else. What is it?"

Her hands checked fuel, oil, vacuum pressure. Her mind answered, "Sad."

"Yes," she admitted. "I feel sad. Why sad?" Then Jackie nodded her head. "Amelia. Amelia's gone. We lost the best we had." Then Jackie pounded her knee with a fist. "I didn't want to win this way."

Jackie Cochran had dreamed of beating Amelia Earhart. Squeezed into her cockpit on the Los Angeles runway, Jackie could remember the exact moment in 1932 when that burning dream had been born. It started just after she touched down from her certification flight to get a pilot's license. The images of that long-ago flight flashed through her mind as she waited her turn to taxi out for take-off.

It had happened in late May of 1932. Amelia was already a flying legend. Jackie had just finished two weeks of flying lessons at a small Long Island airstrip and was making her check-out flight for a pilot's license.

Grime and grease were buried deep under her fingernails and crept toward her elbows as she finished inspecting the engine and scrambled onto the wing of an old Fleet Trainer. "Husky" Jacobs, a New York State Pilot's Licensing Inspector climbed up behind her, clipboard wedged under his arm.

Jackie was only twenty-two as she stood on the wing, tucked her flowing, blond hair under a leather cap, and turned to wave to the small crowd of onlookers. There were other women pilots by 1932. But, if she was successful on this test flight, she would be the first to earn a license at this Long Island airfield. The event seemed worth covering in the local paper, and worth watching for a number of New Yorkers.

Jackie adjusted her goggles and slid into the pilot's seat of the open cockpit, single engine plane. Husky squeezed down behind and listened as Jackie talked her way through a pre-flight check. The Fleet's eight cylinder engine roared to life with a great cough of black smoke, and, as Jackie maneuvered the stick with both hands, started to roll toward the runway.

A minute later Jackie was in the air, the throb of her plane's engine drowning out all other sounds. In three minutes, she was soaring high over Long Island Sound, the small whitecaps disappearing into a smooth sheet of blue as she climbed over 10,000 feet.

This was only Jacqueline's tenth time behind the controls of an airplane. The thrill and joy of flight still surged through her. She pulled back hard on the stick, listening to the engine strain as she nosed steeply toward 12,000 feet.

Then her goggles went black. Thick goo splattered over the windshield and sprayed into the cockpit. Oil! A seal or gasket had blown. The engine was leaking oil like a strainer. Oil splattered into her face faster than she could wipe it away.

And then the engine froze and quit. The propeller stopped. The gush of oil slowed to a dribble.

Now the soft whoosh of wind was the only sound Jackie heard. She clutched the stick so tightly her knuckles turned white. "Don't panic. Don't panic," she repeated to herself.

She leveled the plane and used the pedals to bank it into a slow, wide turn back toward the southeast. Long Island was a thin, dark line beyond what seemed like endless miles of ocean.

11,000 feet. 10,000 feet. Her eyes stared at the altimeter needle lazily spinning lower as her powerless plane glided leisurely toward land, but dropping much faster toward the waiting sea.

8,000 feet, 6,000. Half her altitude gone and Long Island seemed no closer than before. Jackie had to fight the controls and the gusty crosswinds to keep the nose level and headed toward the distant airfield.

4,000 feet, 2,000 feet. 1,000 feet. Finally beach, grass, and trees rushed up under the plane.

500 feet, 400. Still no sign of the field. 300. 200. Trees and houses below looked near enough to touch. And then, there it was, the airstrip, just off to her right. Jackie eased the Fleet in line with the runway, pulled up on the nose, and just clipped one tree as she glided in for a two-bounce landing.

The crowd ran over, cheering, as Jackie pulled off oil-smeared goggles and helmet and rose to wave. Husky stumbled to the ground, trembling hard, face drained of all color. "Lady, you just got your license. That's one of the best dead-stick landings I've ever seen."

The crowd cheered. Reporters reached for cameras. Jacqueline smiled, waved an oil-black hand, and posed.

A man ran from the hanger office shouting, "She did it! She did it! Amelia Earhart's crossed the Atlantic solo! It's on the radio."

As one, the crowd turned and raced for the hanger. Jackie was left alone posed on her wing, hand still waving in the air, smile frozen on her face. With a four-inch headline about Amelia Earhart, the paper had no room to mention the heroics of a local girl who'd earned her license in such a dramatic way.

Jackie walked alone toward her car not with bitterness, but with a fierce determination. All her life Jackie had started things with nothing and worked her way up. Flying was going to be no different.

"I may not get any headlines today," she said to the empty runway. "But someday I'll beat Amelia Earhart to some great first and then the headlines will be mine!"

That was when Jackie Cochran knew she had to beat Amelia Earhart.

The crackle of radio static brought Jackie's mind back into her cockpit. "Seversky 739er. This is L.A. control, over."

Jackie blinked and looked around her. She still sat on the Los Angeles tarmac waiting for her start in the 1938 Bendix Air Race. Jackie lifted the microphone on her radio set and pressed "transmit." "This is Seversky 739er. Got you loud and clear."

"Roger 739er. Move to 2-7 left and hold for take-off clearance."

Jackie fired up her oversized engine. First puffs of blue-gray smoke and then flame erupted from her exhaust ports. After a short warm-up, all needles read normal. She released the brake, wheeled her plane hard to the left, and slowly rolled toward runway 2-7 left. "I copy, Control. On my way."

A line of small blue lights lining the runway stretched ahead of Jackie as far as she could see. Beyond lay the great expanse of the Pacific Ocean.

"The Pacific," muttered Jackie, and grunted.

"The Pacific stole Amelia and cheated me. For five years I scrambled to become a good enough flyer to out-fly Amelia Earhart. And then last May she tried to fly around the world and had to cross the Pacific."

Jackie scowled, "It's not fair! Amelia's father was a lawyer. They had money. She was *given* flying lessons whenever she wanted them.

"I never owned a pair of shoes until I earned the money to buy my first pair when I was nine. I was seven before I wore anything other than a used flour sack. Her family gives her airplanes. I was already working to earn my keep when I was ten. I had to work a whole year to save the money for flying lessons. And still, by last year I was ready to take her on. It's not fair; the Pacific Ocean cheated me out of that chance!"

Jackie made a quick check of the cockpit: oxygen mask, radio, water bottle with a long straw so she could drink without taking off her mask, pocket full of lollipops to keep her mouth from getting too dry, maps balanced on her knees and tied to her ankle with a string so she could easily pull them back if they flipped off during "bumpy" weather. She was ready.

Through a hiss of static, the tower cleared Jackie for take-off. She jammed the throttles to their stops, waited for her plane to vibrate good and hard, and popped off the brake. Sluggishly at first, but then faster and faster, Jackie's Seversky thundered down runway 2-7 left with its oversized load of 1,000 gallons of fuel and clawed its way up into the Los Angeles sky.

Jackie made a sweeping turn to the right as she climbed and headed due east—east past the Grand Canyon, then turn 15 degrees north and head for Cleveland.

"This year is *my* year," Jackie told herself as she settled into the flight with the monotonous drone of her engine and the constant vibration of her cramped space. "This year has got to be different than last year."

"Last year . . ." Crossing the Mojave Desert, Jackie let her mind drift back one year to the 1937 Bendix Air Race. In May, Amelia Earhart again grabbed front page headlines by announcing her plans for an around-the-world flight. Jackie's second try at the Bendix was less than a month away. Unless she actually won the race, she knew no one would notice as reporters fell over themselves to cover Amelia.

With the fierce solemnity of a vow, Jackie said, "If I have to win the Bendix to show that there are two 'first ladies of flying,' then that is exactly what I'll do."

May rolled into June. Daily reports of Amelia's progress splashed across the papers and radios of the world. Amelia took off from Miami. She logged in at San Juan, Puerto Rico, Caripito, Venezuela, and then Paramaribo in Dutch Guinea.

World maps were taped onto living room and kitchen walls all across the country with pins to mark Amelia's latest fuel stop. Countries and cities no one had ever heard of became household words, as the nation buzzed over it's "Queen of Flight." Natal, Brazil, Khartoum in the Sudan, Asaab on the Red Sea, and

Karachi, Pakistan, were all eagerly pinned and discussed over a million dinner tables as families studied newspaper photos of the smiling Amelia waving from each landing strip.

Through that long month of June, 1937, Jackie Cochran gritted her teeth, practiced, and tuned her Seversky.

On the evening of July 1, 1937, the Bendix Transcontinental Air Race began. The morning *Los Angeles Times* headline announced that today Amelia would attempt the most difficult leg of her entire journey. From New Guinea she would fly nearly 2,500 miles in one hop to Howland Island, a tiny speck in the Pacific Ocean near the equator. Buried in section two was an announcement of the Bendix Air Race.

As Jackie sat in her plane that night in 1937 waiting for take-off clearance, her attention was not on the crowd, the other planes, or even on Amelia's long flight over the Pacific. Her gaze was glued to a wide fog bank drifting up from the Palos Verdes Peninsula south of the airport.

Two planes before Jackie's take-off, the thick fog rolled across the west end of the runway. The first plane hesitated, revving its engine at the end of the 6,000 foot strip of concrete. Then its motor idled down. The plane taxied back toward the hangers, opting to give up the race rather than risk a blind take-off into fog.

With a great roar, the plane next to Jackie sped down runway 2-7 right. Its tail wheel eased up off the pavement just as the plane disappeared into the fog. A second later the yellow flash of a fireball glowed through the fog, and a thunderclap explosion shook Jackie's Seversky and rang in her ears.

Jackie stared dumbly at the growing fog bank. That pilot had been a friend of hers. Now he was dead in a fireball crash. What had happened there in the fog 2,000 feet before her? Had he veered off the runway or hit something on it? What would happen if she, too, attempted to take-off into that fog?

A man from the company that owned her plane and paid for her flying ran toward her, waving his arms, shouting for Jackie to scrub the flight. Hesitating, unsure of what to do, Jackie's eyes fell on the ripped-out headline from that morning's paper. Amelia. Amelia wouldn't turn back over the Pacific, and so neither would Jackie. As soon as ground crews signaled that 2-7 left was still clear, she rammed the throttles to their stops.

Her Seversky sluggishly lumbered down the runway with more than double its normal supply of fuel. Slowly the speedometer crept toward 40 mph, then toward 50.

And then she was in the nothingness of the fog. She could see nothing in front, beside, or below the plane except fog. Time seemed to disappear. It felt like she wasn't moving at all, because the fog never changed. She felt that she was suspended in space and time, as if she had been sitting in this seat, in this fog for a hundred years.

But a small voice deep inside Jackie's head ticked off the seconds. That voice reminded her that she was hurtling down a runway and still needed to gain twenty more miles an hour ground speed before she could lift into the air. That small voice told her she was rapidly running out of runway.

With agonizing slowness, the speedometer wiggled higher. Ten miles an hour to go, now five, now two. Take-off speed. Jackie pulled back on the stick. Motor whining, her Seversky struggled into the air.

Whack! Her radio antenna, hanging from the plane's tail, hit a runway fencepost and broke off. She had used the entire runway and cleared the fence at its west end by only inches. She would have to fly the race without a radio, but she had made it into the air and into the Bendix!

Twenty grueling hours later, Jacqueline Cochran dropped into her approach at Cleveland, Ohio. She couldn't tell if she had won. She'd had problems with electrical storms over Arizona, and a clogged fuel line over Kansas. But through it all she had flown a good race.

Jackie lined up on the runway and felt the glorious bump and squeal as her tires hit the pavement, bit in, and started to roll. Angling toward the airport tower, she scanned for the normal crowd. The field before her was deserted. Only one small group of men were there, huddled around a radio on the judge's table at the foot of the tower.

Jackie killed the engine, popped the canopy, and struggled to smile as she rose, painfully stretching joints that had sat frozen in one position far too long. Bewildered, she climbed onto her wing and slid to the ground. Before she could open her mouth to ask where everyone was, and what was going on, one of the men turned to her, his eyes filled with tears. "Amelia's lost at sea. No contact since dawn. Her last radio transmission said only, 'We are circling but cannot see the island . . . cannot hear you.' Nothing since then. Everyone's gone home to listen. Isn't it terrible?"

As an afterthought, he glanced at his log-in sheets and added, "Oh, congratulations. You came in third."

Jackie didn't hear. Her mind had already raced off to a cloud-speckled Pacific Ocean. She could feel Amelia's mounting terror as the gas gauge edged toward "empty." She could imagine the helplessness of being lost over a thousand square miles of empty ocean. Jackie's heart ached for the lost flyer. "Not Amelia. Not like this . . ."

Jackie gasped as radio static yanked her mind out of last year's race and into her cramped 1938 race cockpit. "Cleveland Control calling Seversky 739er. Over."

"Third place . . ." muttered Jackie. "No third place finish this year!"

She shook her head in frustration. With Amelia lost over the Pacific last year, Jackie would never get to out-fly her, no matter how many firsts Jackie piled up. How can you out-fly a memory? "Go ahead Cleveland Control. This is Seversky 739er."

As she dropped into her approach to the Cleveland airport, Jackie wondered what was waiting for her this year, another empty field? A "good job" handshake given to those who didn't win?

She lined up on the Cleveland runway. But instead of focusing on the rows of runway lights, all Jackie could do was stare at the crowd. Over 200,000 people jammed into every nook and open space around the runway. She was landing into a sea of people.

Her wheels squealed as their rubber slammed into the runway. A puff of smoke drifted back from each tire as it skidded along the pavement, trying to grab hold. Her motor whined as she reversed the engine to push her to a stop.

Crowds of cheering spectators streamed onto the runway as Jackie slowed to taxi speed. They ran alongside of her plane, whistling and shouting, as she taxied toward the terminal. The judge's escort car, its lights flashing, eased through the mob, and escorted Jackie to the winner's platform. A sea of jubilant faces surrounded her.

Cleveland's four-inch headline next day read, "Woman Wins Bendix: Jackie Cochran First Female Winner."

By 1940, Jackie Cochran had broken five speed records. She became a top test pilot, testing new engine designs, new fuels, instruments, propellers, and spark plugs.

As an honorary Captain in the British Air Force, Jackie led a corps of volunteer women pilots who flew for the British Air Transport Service during the early years of World War II. She was then chosen to lead the U.S. WASP (Women Air Force Service Pilots) Program.

As jet aircraft were being tested in the 1950s, Jackie was the first woman to fly faster than the speed of sound. She was the first woman to land a jet on an aircraft carrier, and the first woman to fly mach 2 (twice the speed of sound). But sweetest of all, when she was the first woman to be inducted into the Society of Experimental Test Pilots (in 1971), she was introduced as, "The First Lady of Flying."

Still, though, when we think of the stirring achievements, adventures, and risks taken by early women pilots, few think of the first American woman to fly a plane, Blanche Scott who flew less than a year after the Wright Brothers, or of Jacqueline Cochran whose distinguished flying career spanned four decades. We think of Amelia Earhart, who captured the American imagination, and then was lost trying to set another world record. But throughout the twentieth century, we have had a rich heritage of women flyers, each of whom added her own legacy to American aviation. But that is another story.

Questions to Explore

How many early women flyers have you heard of?

Who was the first American woman to fly an airplane? Who was the first to fly in combat? The first to fly a commercial airliner? The first to fly across an ocean?

How have women pilots helped the United States in times of war?

Where can you look to find information on these women?

References for Further Reading

- *In the Children's Library*

  Bennett, Wayne, ed. *Four Women of Courage*. Champaign, IL: Garrard, 1975.

  Boynick, David. *Women Who Led the Way: Eight Pioneers for Equal Rights*. New York: Thomas Crowell, 1959.

  Chadwick, Roxanne. *Amelia Earhart: Aviation Pioneer*. Minneapolis, MN: Lerner, 1987.

- *In the Adult Library*

  Cochran, Jacqueline. *The Stars at Noon*. Boston: Little, Brown, 1954.

  Earhart, Amelia. *For the Fun of It*. Chicago, IL: Academy Press, 1977.

  Lovell, Mary. *The Sound of Wings*. New York: St. Martin's Press, 1989.

See your librarian for additional titles.

The Sounds of Spring

A story about Rachel Carson, one of America's first and most influential ecologists

About This Story:

We now commonly recognize the words, "ecology," and "ecosystem," and have a good sense for what they mean. Just forty years ago, however, those concepts, and all others relating to environmental protection, were unheard of. The ideas of the food web, web of life, and the interconnection of all life on earth had never been a part of Western thinking.

Then along came pesticides, products of the explosion of chemical technology in the twentieth century. Suddenly chemists created complex chemical chains to kill harmful or economically damaging pests. DDT, the most common of these pesticides, was heralded by industry and government as a great boon to crop yields.

But this "miracle of chemistry," soon became the center of a great national controversy. Some people realized that pesticides destroyed far more than the target insects. Others believed that the increased food production achieved using DDT outweighed those negative side effects. On the one side, people asked, "Improved crop yields at what price to the environment?" People on the other side asked, "Environmental protection and preservation at what price to needed food production?" The national scale tipped in favor of crop yields until one woman, Rachel Carson, jumped into the fight. This is a story about her.

Turbulent, January clouds scudded low across a lead-gray sky, tumbling as if in a clothes dryer. On the land below, a light, Arctic wind whistled in off a churning ocean of whitecaps to sting the ears and nose, and to stir the early morning fog. As you'd expect on such a bitter winter morning, the long stretch of rock and beach at West Southport, Maine, just off the edge of Sheepscot Bay was almost deserted—almost.

Two middle-aged women, coats clutched tight around their necks, wandered slowly along the sand on this January 1958 morning, just out of reach of the regular rush of the surf racing up the beach with first a crashing roar and then a soft, dying "Whooosh."

Gulls glided back and forth across the shore, occasionally dropping down to hover over the women, hoping for a handout. The younger of the two women had a sharp nose, a plain, straightforward face, and curling red hair tumbling over her shoulders. Her name was Rachel Carson. She held a crumpled letter tight in her fist.

Rachel stopped beside a large tide pool trapped between two rock outcroppings. She breathed in the pungent salt air. "Oh, how I do love it here," she sighed. "Especially now when the ebb tide falls early in the morning. I can walk among the pools, and my whole world is filled with the sound of water, the smell of salt, and the softness of fog. I am more at peace here than anywhere else on earth."

The other woman, a taller and stylish woman named Dorothy Seif, stepped back, crossed her arms, and eyed her friend quizzically. "You don't look all that peaceful, Rachel."

Rachel's eyes opened in surprise. "How can you say that, Dorothy? For the first time in my life, I am free from the pressures of job and family cares. I can spend my time in this rich, low-tide world. I am more at peace than I have ever been."

Dorothy shook her salt-and-pepper hair and pointed at the letter. "Then why are you slowly grinding that letter to pulp?"

Rachel followed her friend's gaze to her own clenched fist. For a long moment Rachel stared at the letter, gathering her thoughts. "Dorothy, this is 1958. I am fifty-one years old. For nearly thirty years I've dreamed of being in this place at a time when I could enjoy it. And that time has to be now. And then I received this letter . . ."

The fog thickened, blurring even the nearest trees, and making each long wave seem to materialize out of a fuzzy gray nothingness.

"I've worked all my life, and accomplished a lot. I've done research and technical writing in Washington. I've studied and taught. I've lead extensive field studies diving off Florida. I've been a slave to my typewriter through the writing and rewriting of three books about the ocean. I've won awards and honors for my writing." Rachel's voice slowly rose with excitement. "And all along, I have dreamed of spending my time here in this natural wonderland. And now I have it; each day I live that dream."

Rachel sighed, and the energy drained out of her voice as it shrank back to a low and quiet register. "And then I got this letter." She waved the crumpled pages at her friend.

Dorothy's face tightened in deep concern. She reached out for her friend's arm. "What could possibly be in one letter to so thoroughly rattle this dream world of yours?"

Rachel's eyes burned with anger and frustration. "I'll read it to you." She smoothed the three handwritten sheets against her leg and held them up. "It's from Olga Huckins, a friend living in western Massachusetts. She writes . . ." Rachel adjusted the letter farther away from her face and squinted to read without her glasses.

" 'Dear Rachel, First congratulations on your new book, *The Edge of the Sea*. I thought nothing could eclipse your second volume, *The Sea Around Us*, but I think I like this third one . . .' Blah, blah, blah. She goes on . . . and on . . . Ah, here it is.

" 'Our township government resolved to use that new chemical insecticide, DDT, to spray the local woods and kill mosquitoes. They've been promoting the spraying by saying that 1958 will be the first summer in history when we enjoy the outdoors without the torment of mosquitoes.

" 'Three days ago a plane sprayed white clouds of this supposedly safe DDT over the woods near our house. This "harmless" shower killed seven songbirds in our yard outright before the white mist had completely settled into the trees. We picked up three more dead bodies next morning. The next day, five more lay scattered around our birdbath. I emptied it and scrubbed it thoroughly. But you can never kill DDT. I'm afraid I just poured the DDT from the birdbath to the ground where it will kill something else.

" 'Please, dear Rachel, do something to stop the killing.' "

This time Rachel folded the letter neatly and jammed it into a pocket. The two women walked for a moment in silence. Then Dorothy shook her head and shrugged. "She wants you to save a few birds in western Massachusetts? That doesn't seem so hard for a scientist of your stature. A couple of phone calls to some local planner . . ."

"It's so much more than just those birds at that one spot," sighed Rachel. "If it were only a few birds, I'd be off in a flash. But DDT and the other pesticides affect the whole natural system. I've seen preliminary studies on the effects of these chemical killers. And it's not just western Massachusetts. It's everywhere. The U.S. Department of Agriculture—our government for heaven's sakes—recommends that all farmers use herbicides and pesticides as the best way to get 'maximum yields' from crops. And it's not just the federal government. It's the massive chemical industry. It's the farmers. It's local and state governments."

Rachel slowly let out her breath and shook her head. "It's too much, too much for one person to take on. It's too much for me."

In gloomy silence they turned back toward Rachel's house, tide pools and lapping waves forgotten. "Will other birds die?" asked Dorothy.

"The birds are only the tip of the iceberg," answered Rachel. "A very visible tip, mind you, but still only the tip. What will happen when these killer chemicals get into our surface and ground water systems? Into the food chains? When will they start to poison *people*? I wonder if there will be any natural environment left when we finally notice the damage. Will there be any birds at all, or will we have to get used to hearing eerie, silent springs some year?"

After dinner that night, Rachel, Dorothy, and a former research colleague of Rachel's, Shirley Briggs, sat in the living room of Rachel's rambling Maine house. While the bubbly and sparkling Shirley Briggs laughed and talked her way through first one elaborate story and then another, Rachel stared moodily into the white embers of the fire.

In between stories, Dorothy asked, "It's that letter that's got you feeling so glum tonight, isn't it? Are you going to help?"

Rachel Carson seemed frozen in indecision for a moment. Then she slapped both hands on her knees as if shaking herself out of a trance and smiled with the peace of having finally made a decision. "Nope. Let someone else pick up this banner and carry it into battle. I've finished my fights."

"But who is that 'someone'?" pressed Dorothy.

Through her ever-present smile Shirley added, "*You're* the one who wrote the books that made the sea seem real and important. *You're* the one who made all America understand and care about the complex life in the sea. If *you* don't make us care about what DDT does to life on land, who else will?"

Rachel paced back and forth in front of the fire. "Pesticides aren't the real enemy here. Oh, they kill birds, fish, and insects. But the real enemies are the giant businesses and governmental agencies who created these killers and sprayed them into our environment."

With a shrug Shirley replied, "You'll show them. You always do."

"You don't understand," snapped Rachel with a growing scowl. "This enemy has lots of money and lots of power, and they're not interested in hearing anyone tell them they're destroying America." She sank back into her seat. "I just don't know if I have enough energy left for this fight. Besides, I'm supposed to be here, *enjoying* nature for a change, not out on a campaign to save it."

Dorothy Seif studied her friend's face before asking, "Will you really be able to enjoy your coastal paradise if you don't enter this fight?"

Sadly Rachel shook her head. "You're right, of course. I'll feel no peace at all if I stay silent." Then she stomped her foot. "Damn! Why now?"

She rose and started for the stairs. "I best head for bed early. I'll be off for Massachusetts in the morning. You two enjoy the fire as late as you like."

• • •

Four years later, in the spring of 1962, Rachel Carson lay weakly in bed as her adopted son, Roger, bounded in and blurted, "I was just down by the creek. The frogs are starting to sing. Why aren't you up yet?"

Rachel smiled thinly. "I guess I'm still tired."

"But it's the beginning of spring and it's beautiful!" protested Roger. Then his face turned serious and he asked, "Is it your ulcer again?"

She shook her head.

"Your arthritis? The flu again?" he continued, counting off her recent illnesses on his fingers.

"No," Rachel finally answered, "this time the doctor says it's cancer."

There was a long pause before Roger softly answered, "Oh . . ." Then Roger struggled for a way to change the subject to something less frightening. "Well, is your book finished?"

Rachel first pointed to, and then shook her fist at, the mounded mess on her desk next to the bay windows facing out over marsh and bay. "Not yet, Roger. But I better finish soon or I'll never finish at all."

"Why does one book take so long?" he asked, curling up his nose at the thought of spending four years on one story. "I write my school stories in one day."

"DDT is complicated, Roger. It stays locked in the soil for years. Worms that eat it are unaffected. But robins that eat those worms die. I've had to consult over 200 scientists from all over the world. Just look at those stacks of letters and reports I've gotten back and have had to study!"

"That first stack is going to tip over if it gets any higher," warned Roger.

Rachel rose stiffly and faced her wide bedroom windows. "My purest joy is there, just across the road and a quick scamper down the rocks to the shore. Yet I can't let myself walk over to it until I finish this book. I desperately want to spend these last days enjoying the natural world. But I'm stuck here at my typewriter trying to defend and save it."

"What's your book called?" asked her son.

"*Silent Spring*," she answered.

Again Roger scrunched up his face. "But spring's not silent. It's noisy! Frogs, birds, crickets, bees, insects—heck, everybody's making noise."

Rachel pointed to a neat stack of typewritten pages. "Read the first chapter of my book."

Twelve-year-old Roger curled up with the pages over breakfast. He read of the vast natural beauty of a fictitious valley and town before a white powder was sprayed from the sky, before this "shadow of death" fell upon the town. After, only silence lay over the fields, woods, and marshes.

Roger shuddered. "Yuck. I sure wouldn't want to live there."

"No," answered Rachel, "you wouldn't, and if I write my book well, maybe you never will."

Rachel Carson died in the spring of 1964, one year after the release of *Silent Spring*. She was showered with virtually every environmental- and conservation-related award in America, and heralded by every conservation group from the National Wildlife Federation to the National Geographic Society. She was the first woman awarded the Audubon Society's medal for achievement in conservation. President Carter posthumously awarded her the Presidential Medal of Freedom, the government's highest civilian award.

Rachel and her book, *Silent Spring,* were the wake-up call to America. She dramatically and powerfully exposed the dangers of pesticides, especially DDT, and forced our nation to understand what those dangers really meant in the long-term. Her work formed the foundation upon which was launched a long and arduous, but successful, campaign to ban DDT and other similar pesticides. The struggle lasted fifteen years. But it might never have been taken up, much less won, without Rachel Carson.

Rachel Carson thought of herself as a simple, unimaginative person who marveled at the magnificence of the natural world. To the rest of us she was one of America's first woman naturalists, and perhaps the most powerful writer the American conservation movement has ever produced. Her books introduced the concepts of "ecosystem," "food web," and the connectedness of all elements of the environment. In so doing, she became a founder of the modern environmental movement. But that's another story.

Questions to Explore

Do we still use pesticides or herbicides today? Where and for what? Can you find listings in the library of how much pesticide we still use every year?

Have you ever used chemical pesticides? What were you trying to kill—ants, rats, mosquitoes, flies, snails, slugs?

Are the pesticides we use today safe for the environment? Are they safer than those used in the 1950s and 1960s?

What nonchemical alternatives to pesticides can you find in the library? How effective are these methods? What are their effects on the environment compared to pesticides?

References for Further Reading

- *In the Children's Library*

  Latham, Jean Lee. *Rachel Carson Who Loved the Sea.* Champaign, IL: Garrard, 1973.

  Peavy, Linda, and Ursula Smith. *Dreams into Deeds: Nine Women Who Dared.* New York: Charles Scribner's Sons, 1985.

  Sterling, Philip. *The Life of Rachel Carson.* New York: Thomas Crowell, 1970.

- *In the Adult Library*

  Bonta, Marcia Myers. *Women in the Field: America's Pioneering Women Naturalists.* College Station, TX: Texas A&M University Press, 1988.

  Carson, Rachel. *Silent Spring.* Boston: Houghton-Mifflin, 1962.

  Any of Rachel Carson's three other books.

See your librarian for additional titles.

Monkey Business

A story about Jane Goodall, the first female naturalist to conduct field research

About This Story:

Until the last forty years, all animal research was carried out in a laboratory or zoo, where conditions could be controlled, and where the animal being studied could be isolated. By the middle of this century, however, it became clear that this was a fine way to study worms and spiders, but didn't work at all for more complex species. Many animals act differently in captivity than they do in the wild. Biologists began to realize that Western science had precious little information about natural animal behavior.

However, the other option, observing animals in their natural habitats, is inherently strenuous, demanding, and taxing, and is fraught with risks and dangers. So many factors in the wild are out of the control of the researcher. Animals can be hard to get close to, can act unexpectedly, and can even pose a danger to the researcher. The researcher must face additional challenges, such as living in the wild, conducting research in foreign countries, and working no matter what the weather. Anything might happen to disrupt the study and invalidate its results. As a result, many scientists still shy away from large field studies. This was especially true forty years ago, when there was so little experience to draw on, and when there were no guidelines or models of good field studies to follow.

This is a story of one of the most productive, successful studies of animal behavior ever undertaken in an animal's natural habitat. It was also the first such study ever conducted by Western researchers, a study conducted entirely by one lone woman.

T he air shimmered hot and dry. The thick trees and ferns seemed to beg for a hint of breeze. Jane Goodall sat brooding on the large flat rock resting on top of a rock outcropping. She had dubbed these rocks "the peak" on her very first day in the Gombe Jungle of Africa because they perched at the very end of one of the jungle's long ridge lines, facing out over the slopes and valleys below.

Thinking back to that first day more than five long months ago made Jane scowl fiercely. *Then* she had scrambled eagerly up this steep, slippery slope, binoculars swinging from one shoulder; mud, dirt, and grass ground into her khaki pants and shirt from repeated stumbles and slides during her giddy assent. *Then* she had looked with wonder and delight at each new sight, had found joy in each new jungle sound.

But that was then. *Now*, after five months of careful, patient work, Jane Goodall felt like a complete failure. Sure, she had learned to recognize and follow the winding trails of wild pigs instead of forcing her way through the tough grasses and underbrush. Yes, she had become as surefooted as a baboon, climbing the smooth, exposed roots up the rugged hills. She had learned the patterns and rhythms of the jungle. But none of that mattered. She had failed to get within 500 yards of even one chimpanzee.

Jane tucked her knees up under her chin and wrapped her arms tightly around her legs. She was on her own here in the African jungle. This field research project was her "chance-of-a-lifetime." And she was failing.

She let her eyes wander down the now-familiar steep slopes, ridges, and dense valleys that made up Gombe National Park in Tanzania. Jane's curling ponytail flopped over her shoulders. She was a slender woman of twenty-six, and had a soft, compassionate face. But her look, her skin, and her muscles had been hardened by the long days of strenuous scrambling up and down these slopes.

Jane had been sent into the jungle five months before, in the spring of 1960, by Dr. Louis Leakey, the famed anthropologist who was scouring a gorge at the edge of the Serengeti Plain, searching for signs of the earliest human life. Leakey believed that next to the earliest hominids on the primate family tree lay chimpanzees, our closest evolutionary relative. He thought that if we knew how chimps acted in the wild, we might gain some insights into early human behavior. But modern farms, roads, hunters, and human diseases daily cut deeper and deeper into chimpanzee habitat. Leakey needed a brave volunteer to live with the chimps and catalog their lives and behaviors.

And then along came British-born Jane Goodall, professional secretary and typist, visiting a friend who had moved to Kenya.

Jane shifted on the rock and remembered the fateful meeting in December, 1958, when Leakey offered her this opportunity. She'd sat in Leakey's jumbled office in Nairobi, Kenya. The famed scientist paced across the room as he spoke. "An in-depth, observational study in an animal's natural habitat has never been attempted before."

Jane hesitated, unsure how to respond. So Leakey added, "Never!" for emphasis.

Jane Goodall felt overwhelmed. She loved animals. She loved watching them, always had. But she was a typist and had never set foot in a jungle. Still, she yearned for this challenge and opportunity. "I've always loved the book, *Dr. Doolittle*," she said, not sure what else she had to offer. "Like him, I've wanted to talk with the animals. Living with chimps sounds about as close as I could ever come."

Leakey turned to her and frowned. "But this may be a *long* study."

She nodded. "Yes, I know. I've been studying and watching animals all my life. I can be patient."

"Maybe a year . . . on your own in the jungle."

"A year?" Jane hadn't thought in those terms. Then, not wanting to sound daunted, she added, "I . . . I understand."

He resumed his pacing. "Maybe longer."

Jane began to squirm in her chair. "Longer?"

"Maybe three or four years."

Jane gulped. "Three or four . . . *years*?"

"Maybe more."

Jane began to fidget as Leakey carefully studied her under his bushy eyebrows. "More than three years? For just one study?"

Leakey nodded. "And you'll be in *their* habitat . . . all the time."

Wide-eyed, Jane nodded.

"Alone."

Jane grimaced before she weakly nodded. She was beginning to wonder if he were trying to talk her into the study, or out of it.

Leakey continued. "You'll be completely cut off from support, from civilization, from everything you've ever known."

In a small, squeaky voice Jane asked, "Why do you want *me* to do such an important study? I'm not a biologist. I don't know the jungle. I'm a secretary, for goodness sake."

Leakey stopped his slow pacing and smiled. "You bring three essential qualities to the study that I have been seeking for a long time: a strong desire for knowledge, a deep understanding of animals in general, and an enthusiasm for the work. I would not send you if I didn't think you were the right person for the job, and if I didn't have every confidence in your success."

Shifting again on her flat rock perch, Jane shook her head and grunted. " 'Deep understanding of animals.' Right. Five months and my understanding hasn't gotten me close to even one chimp."

She had often sat face to face with the jungle's silver monkeys and blue monkeys, with red colobus monkeys, and with baboons. Why did the chimps still dash away? She often heard their hooting calls. She called it a "pant-hoot," because the series of sharp hoots was always punctuated by loud, deep breaths.

The first time Jane heard the sound and knew it was a chimpanzee, she was thrilled beyond words. Now the pant-hoots tormented her. They meant chimps were nearby, hidden in the jungle foliage.

She also frequently heard the echoing sound of excited chimps drumming on tree trunks, rapidly slapping the wood with their feet. She had even seen chimps through her binoculars feeding in distant trees. But as soon as she crept within 500 yards, the chimps melted back into the jungle, disappearing from sight.

She slapped the rock in frustration. Her mission was to study and document chimpanzee behavior before human encroachment on their natural habitat altered that behavior forever. Already, in 1960, the number of chimps in this Gombe National Preserve was rapidly dwindling to under 10,000.

"Where are the chimps?" she cried out to the circling birds above. "What must I do to get near them?"

The echo of her voice slowly faded, absorbed into the jungles own constant sounds. Jane shook her head and muttered, "Why am I wasting my time in this jungle? I feel like a fool." She chuckled at herself and added, "What must the natives think of a white person who comes to the jungle just to study chimps and can't find even one in half a year?"

With a long sigh, Jane raised her binoculars to her eyes and wearily scanned the slopes and craggy ridges around her. Then her gaze drifted to the far-off mountains, whose green sides looked as smooth as carpet at this distance.

Jane snapped her head around as she heard a light rustling behind her, and the binoculars dropped from her hands. At first she couldn't tell where the noise had come from. Then she heard it again.

Jane's eyes nearly popped right out of her head. Her shoulders straightened and a chill crawled down her back. Her mouth sagged open and her breath came in squeaky, excited gasps.

Less than fifty feet away across the narrow clearing leading up the ridge line, quietly watching her, stood two male chimps! The larger, nearly five feet tall and weighing over 100 pounds, leaned forward on his knuckles studying her, his eyebrows furrowed with concentration.

The smaller squatted, one forearm wrapped around his bent legs, the other softly fingering one corner of his lower lip as if lost deep in thought. His eyes were locked on her face as if trying to decide what should be done with this odd-looking intruder. Both chimp faces were astonishingly expressive and filled with personality.

Jane felt light-headed with elation at this first direct contact and overwhelmed by the enormity of this breakthrough. She was flustered and a bit embarrassed by the intensity and intelligence of the chimps' gaze. She felt vindicated, joyful, and triumphant, as if this moment proved that all her time and struggles had been worthwhile. Considering the size and raw power of these apes, she also felt a twinge of fear.

Caught in this emotional flood, Jane was too stunned to move, overwhelmed by the wonder of the moment. She tried to breathe regularly and softly so as not to frighten the chimps. She tried to get her brain to click into scientific gear and make objective observations. But her mind was too preoccupied with one glorious thought to function in a rational way. "Chimps at last! They're magnificent!"

After a long minute of silent staring, the two chimps turned to look at each other. The smaller seemed to shrug and then ambled off into the underbrush. The larger turned back to Jane and then slowly wandered off himself.

Jane sat still frozen, eyes glued to the now-empty patch of grass where the chimps had been, pulse racing, heart pounding, breath coming in rapid gasps. "They weren't afraid of me," she whispered.

Jane rose and walked across the clearing. No sign remained of the chimps. She decided to wait quietly on the peak and see if they'd return.

She settled back on flat rock. Would they come again? Would they bring others? She waited, her mind whirring with excitement. Fifteen minutes dragged by. Thirty minutes. One hour. Two hours.

Was that it? Was that one tiny taste all she'd get? Her spirits began to sag and she thought of heading back down the slope to camp.

Then she heard a soft rustling. She looked up to see a group of chimps cautiously edge out of the underbrush and start down the clearing toward her. Two large males led the family group of fifteen chimps. Females either carried or closely herded the children and babies. Several chimps stepped out of line to stare momentarily at Jane with a surprised and slightly frightened look. Then they'd hoot and dash back in line, having reached the limits of their bravery. Within a minute, the whole family had passed around Jane and were noisily attacking ripe fruit in a group of fig trees partway down the slope.

Jane was elated. The first stuffed doll she had ever loved as a girl had been a baby chimp. Twenty-three years later fifteen real ones had just scampered right past her, staring at her through dark, brilliant eyes. This lifelong dream had casually wandered out of the jungle as if this sort of thing happened every day.

Jane was so excited she could barely stand. Her knees were wobbly and she felt faint. It took her several minutes to recover, and then several more to decide that she should follow the chimps down to the fig trees. It meant she'd risk scaring the chimps away. But at least she'd find out how close they'd let her come.

Before Jane could scramble down from the peak, a second, larger group of chimpanzees broke from the underbrush and passed through the clearing toward the fig trees below. Again, many paused to stare, or glare, and hoot at her before rushing back into line. Were the hoots a warning or friendly greetings to a now-accepted jungle neighbor? Jane couldn't tell and, at the time, was too overjoyed to care.

Five groups of chimps marched past Jane that afternoon on their way to the sweet fruits of the fig trees. She never left the flat rock she called the "peak." But she knew an important corner had been turned and she could finally begin the study she had been sent to do. In her diary she wrote, "Without a doubt, this was the proudest moment I have ever known."

The more Jane learned, the more questions she raised, demanding further research and observation. There was always more to do, more to learn, and never a neat, clean ending point for her research. Jane stayed on, first for one year and then for a second.

But a second year melted into a third while she mapped the life history of new chimps. Expecting to live with the Gombe chimps for a few years, Jane Goodall has now lived among them for thirty-four years. The detailed mosaic she has revealed of chimp life has shocked many scientists and thrilled others. She discovered that chimps are not strict vegetarians; they're omnivores and sometimes do kill and eat meat. She was the first human to see, or even uncover direct evidence of, another species' ability to build and use tools, an ability previously thought to be uniquely human.

Jane Goodall discovered a rich and complex social structure among chimps. She was amazed by their intelligence and ability to learn. She was delighted by their playfulness, moved by their compassion. She was awestruck by their bonds of friendship and family. She was amazed by their range and expressiveness of emotion: joy, sadness, pleasure, fear, anger, and love.

Contrary to the previous beliefs of humans, Jane found that chimps think, make plans, show unique personalities, use tools, strategize, work in harmony and concert, form close-knit family units, spend a great deal of time and energy raising and teaching their young, and take time to play and enjoy each other. She found a surprising world of chimpanzees that didn't look all that different from an ideal world of people.

Jane Goodall was the first human to ever attempt this kind of in-depth study of another species in its natural habitat. It has been a brave and risky undertaking: one which has produced an untold wealth of information for humankind, as well as worldwide recognition and honors for Jane. Moreover, Jane's methods, and her study, have become a standard model for the study of the countless species with whom we share this world. But those are all other stories.

Questions to Explore

Could you study four-year-old boys in a laboratory and expect to gain an accurate understanding of how they think and act in the real world? What might you be able to learn in a lab?

Where else would you have to go to understand four-year-old boys? What extra problems might you find in this new location?

Can you find reports of studies on human behavior? Where?

Where would you look to find reports on animal behavior?

References for Further Reading

- *In the Children's Library*

Fromer, Julie. *Jane Goodall: Living with the Chimps.* Frederick, MD: Twenty-First Century Books, 1992.

Senn, J. A. *Jane Goodall.* Woodbridge, CN: Blackbuck Press, 1993.

- *In the Adult Library*

Goodall, Jane. *Through a Window: My 30 Years with the Chimps of Gombe.* Boston: Houghton Mifflin, 1990.

Montgomery, Sy. *Walking with the Great Apes.* Boston: Houghton Mifflin, 1991.

See your librarian for additional titles.

5

Stories About Education

T-E-A-C-H-E-R

A story about Annie Sullivan, who taught the deaf and blind Helen Keller

About This Story:

Unfortunately, education has always been under-supported and under-funded in America, even for children with no special needs. And in the early nineteenth century, special education programs for disabled children were virtually nonexistent. Slowly, programs for the blind were begun in Boston and Washington, D.C. Schools for the deaf grew in many urban centers.

But what could be done for those who were both deaf and blind? There seemed to be no way to communicate with these people, much less teach them. The common belief was that nothing could be done for these individuals. And for the most part, nothing was done. This common misconception was laid to rest largely by one gifted woman, who was, herself, both blind and deaf. This is a story about the woman who reached her and taught her.

The train gave a blast of its whistle as it lurched around a sharp bend and started up a grade toward the bridge spanning the Alabama River. The piercing noise shattered Annie's sleep, bringing her upright with a surprised gasp, "Ohhh!"

She groaned and stretched against the stiff seat. Two endless days on these trains were driving Annie crazy. It had been March 1, 1887, when she'd first boarded. It felt like it must be 1910 by now.

Her eyes ached from coal dust and soot, and from the constant jiggling motion of the train. She longed to soak herself in a long, hot bath. She wanted to sleep without the noise and the lurching, jarring motion of the train awakening her every few minutes.

But most of all, twenty-three-year-old Annie Sullivan wanted a chance to rethink whether she should have accepted the grim-sounding job she was travelling to undertake. It was to be her very first job, and she was beginning to wonder if she could succeed. She could teach a deaf person to "hear" by creating visual cues and language signs. A blind person was able to hear and speak, and could be taught to "see" by talking them through the world around them. Annie sighed. "But what do I do for someone who knows neither sight nor sound? How can I teach such a person to understand language and words?"

Annie planted both feet on the wooden car floor and tried to wedge herself against the window. Again, she edged toward sleep as the warm sun poured through the window and splashed onto her face.

One eye opened angrily and squinted toward the sun. It was too warm, especially for early March. When she'd boarded the train in Boston, snow had covered the ground. Here in Alabama, the sun's heat was giving her a headache.

Annie groaned and shifted away from the bright patch of sun. For what seemed like the hundredth time on this trip, she drifted to sleep.

Then Annie heard voices, strange voices, voices Annie hadn't memorized. At first they were muffled, off in the distance. Then they grew louder, more distinct. The door to her sparse, tiny room opened and the voices entered.

Annie sat up and rubbed her eyes. First she squinted, then opened her eyes as wide as she could. Then she squinted again, struggling to focus. Vague, gray blobs drifted before her, like fuzzy ghosts floating across her room.

The blob voices sounded hollow, distant. "This room, too?" "Yes. All the rooms on this side." "Is that included in your report?"

And then the blobs faded back through the door. They were leaving. Frantically squinting and staring, young Annie saw that one of the blobs seemed to glow in the light, looking far more like an angel than a ghost.

Angel blobs. Maybe they were really angel blobs come to save her, to lead her to someplace better. And now they were leaving the ward. They were leaving her behind. Annie screamed and dove forward, groping toward the shapes. "I want to go to school! Please let me go to school."

With a start, Annie threw open her eyes and found herself on the train. It had been a dream, a nightmare. No, not a dream, it was a memory. Annie turned and saw two people staggering from seat to seat as the train rocked past Alabama farmland, working their way toward the next car. Their voices must have triggered Annie's memory.

Now fully awake, Annie could still see those long-ago blobs. When she was thirteen that was all she ever saw. Her world was a vague gray fuzz called Tewksbury, the Massachusetts State Poorhouse. Annie Sullivan had been abandoned to the poorhouse as a ten-year-old by her father one and a half years after her mother died of tuberculosis.

When Annie was three, a disease had weakened her eyes, beginning a steady downhill slide toward blindness. By the time she was seven all faces looked alike. Trees looked like shimmering walls. By the time she was eight, Annie couldn't see to tell her parents apart.

The steady loss of her vision left Annie trapped in a formless, alien world all alone. She was desperately lonely, scared, and angry. But she lived in a family of immigrant Irish dirt farmers with barely enough time to scratch out food for the family, and none left over for comfort and special care.

So what Annie showed them was anger. She lashed out, hard and often, at every fuzzy blob in a world that refused to let her see it. When her father dumped her in the poorhouse office, Annie heard him tell the administrator, "She's a mean, nasty brat, that one. It's no wonder they stopped the Civil War the year Annie Sullivan was born. She's got more than enough fight in her for both sides."

On the train, Annie rubbed her aching eyes again. But she didn't mind the ache or the blurriness—as if the world were seen through a glass of water. Thanks to a miracle operation when she was sixteen, she could see again. No more gray blobs for Annie. The world and all its colors were back! At least, they were back well enough to read, and that's what counted most.

Annie dug in her purse for the letter that had started her on this venture. It came from Mr. Anagnos, director of Boston's Perkins School for the Blind.

Those formless blobs to whom a desperate thirteen-year-old Annie had pleaded for schooling had sent her to this same Perkins School for the Blind. At Perkins they knew how to teach blind children, and Annie soaked it up like an dry sponge. She quickly learned braille and then devoured books. She studied math, history, and science. She received corrective surgery on her eyes, and she graduated.

Now here she was at twenty-three and on her way to a job—a real job for little Annie Sullivan, the blind girl her father called a worthless brat. She settled back as best she could with a stiff back against a stiffer seat, and reread the letter for the fifteenth time on this journey.

In it Mr. Anagnos described a six-year-old Alabama girl, struck both blind and deaf by illness when she was eighteen months old. Now at almost seven, Helen Keller was described as a true terror. He said all tests indicated that the girl was intelligent, and that this would be a rare opportunity for Annie to use her education and to test her talents. But, he warned, the girl was spoiled rotten and always got her way, because her parents felt too sorry for her to provide any constructive discipline, and she was obstinate and often threw screaming fits.

Annie neatly folded the letter and sighed. Not exactly an ideal first student. But the description of the almost-seven-year-old, fit-throwing terror struck a chord in Annie. Out loud she said, "Pooh, she's just scared and lonely. I would be too if I were blind and deaf and nobody cared enough to help me. She just needs love and discipline—lots of both—and so do her parents. This won't be a position I can walk into softly."

At two thirty that afternoon, the train steamed into Tuscumbia, Alabama, with a great hissing blast and the grating squeal of brakes. Annie Sullivan was the only person to get off the train.

A lone couple standing by a buggy stared hopefully in Annie's direction. "Miss Sullivan?" asked the gentleman with a slight bow.

As Annie nodded, the woman rushed forward. "Thank God you have arrived at last to help our poor, poor Helen. Her tantrums get worse every day, and we feel so helpless and so sorry for her."

Then she realized what an outburst she was making and nervously laughed. "Oh, why just listen to me carry on. I do apologize. I am Mrs. Keller. This is my husband, Captain Keller."

Polite handshakes were exchanged. Then Annie turned to Mrs. Keller. "Please do not ever again let me hear you refer to Helen as 'poor,' or let me catch you feeling sorry for her. Neither will do Helen one bit of good."

Mrs. Keller defensively raised a hand to her throat, she was so taken aback. "Oh, dear. I fear, Miss Sullivan, there may be some misunderstanding here. Our daughter is both completely blind and completely deaf. So, of course, neither can she speak. Now don't you think one who is deaf, blind, and dumb is to be pitied?"

"No," answered Annie. "I think she is to be loved, helped, and taught, but never pitied, and never felt sorry for."

Excusing herself to check on her luggage, Annie stepped around a corner and exhaled gustily, reaching out to the wall for support. Her heart was pounding. Those had been the boldest words she had ever uttered. She had been nearly too frightened to say them to these strangers who were to be her employers. She certainly hadn't walked in softly. Of course, the real test was still to come. Could Annie control and teach a wild, unruly six-year-old terror?

The three of them rode to the Keller home in awkward silence.

Annie stepped down from the buggy to see a small, sad-looking girl sitting alert and pensive on the wide front steps. Instantly the helplessness and frustration of blindness flooded back to Annie. The girl tensed, and her back stiffened as she felt the vibration of new, unfamiliar footsteps.

Feeling to the bottom step with one foot, the girl rushed at Annie. As Annie's arm slid lightly around a small, six-year-old shoulder, the girl's hands and fingers flew over Annie's face, arms, and dress and groped into her handbag, trying frantically to learn about and explore this new being.

Annie gently removed the hand from the bag where it did not belong. Instantly, the girl screamed in rage and kicked out hard at Annie.

Annie reached out and took the girl's hand. The girl screamed like a wild animal and pulled her hand back. Again Annie reached for the hand. Again the girl pulled it back. Patiently, Annie again reached for the hand of the frightened, lonely child. This time Helen hesitated. Annie quickly tapped out "H-E-L-L-O" in her palm using the finger alphabet she learned at Perkins School.

A confused look crossed Helen's face. She held her hand rigid for a moment. Again Annie tapped the message into the girl's palm. "H-E-L-L-O."

Helen screamed; lashed out with her other fist, clubbing Annie in the side; and ran into the house and up the stairs to her room.

Mrs. Keller shrugged and sighed. "Now do you see how hard everything is for our po—"

Annie Sullivan spun round, eyes narrowed, one finger raised in warning.

"It's not as if she can hear us . . ." said Mrs. Keller defensively. Then she sighed. "All right, I shall not say, 'poor.' But what else can you say about someone who is sealed off from the world, with whom no one can communicate?"

"You say she cannot be communicated with, but that is not true. Helen's problem is that she has not yet been taught how to communicate." said Annie. "But she has already taken her first step forward. I just showed her how we'll communicate."

"What you did with your fingers in her palm?" asked Captain Keller. "Is that what you mean?"

"Finger language," answered Annie, nodding.

"Well it didn't seem to work," said Mrs. Keller, on the verge of tears. "It made her scream, cry, and run up to her room."

Annie forced a nervous smile. "Actually, I thought it went rather well."

For weeks Annie struggled to instill basic discipline and control in Helen. She spent long afternoons getting Helen to eat with a fork and spoon instead of with her fingers. Helen reached for the food on her plate. Annie pulled her hand back. Helen became instantly enraged, screaming and kicking. Annie pushed a fork into Helen's hand. Helen flung it away and reached for her food. Annie pulled back her hand. Helen screamed and kicked again. They spent one whole afternoon fighting, because Annie insisted that Helen fold her napkin. Within a week, though, Helen ate with fork and spoon, and only from her own plate.

● Getting Helen to wash her hands and comb her hair consumed several days of struggle and tantrum. Always Annie spelled the nouns and action verbs for what they were doing into Helen's palm. Helen soon understood that this was a way to communicate, and began to mimic a number of the words Annie spelled.

But Annie knew Helen only understood the finger taps as actions to gain a desired end, but could not yet associate a specific word with its appropriate object. That is, she acted like a clever monkey, aping Annie's finger motions, but Helen still did not understand the concept of language and words.

After weeks of work, Helen still used the same tapping pattern for "thirsty," "milk," "mug," and "drink." To Helen, that one sign really meant, "Please put some milk into my mug. I am thirsty and want to drink." To her, it was all one single idea.

In growing frustration, Annie searched for a way to show Helen the concept of language and words. True, she had made wonderful progress with turning Helen into a clean, disciplined child. But language was the key to Helen's real growth. For long weeks that key eluded Helen.

One day Annie and Helen walked through the garden and passed a water-pump. Annie had Helen hold her mug under the pump's steady stream of water. As water overflowed down Helen's hand and arm, Annie spelled "W-A-T-E-R" into Helen's free hand. This is what Annie always did, have Helen feel something and then spell it with finger taps. But as the water flowed across Helen's fingers and wrist, her reaction to this finger spelling was different.

For a moment, Helen stood transfixed. A new light came over her face. Annie took the mug from her hand and let water splash straight into Helen's hand. "W-A-T-E-R." Excitedly Helen pointed at the pump. Annie supplied the word, "W-A-T-E-R-P-U-M-P." She pointed back at the stream of cool, fresh water. "W-A-T-E-R."

Helen dropped to her knees and pointed to the ground. Annie tapped, "G-R-O-U-N-D." Helen pointed to the trellis arching over the pump. "T-R-E-L-L-I-S."

One word, one object. Helen's mind seemed to whir with this incredible new concept: words, nouns, language. Helen snatched a handful of grass. "G-R-A-S-S." She turned back to the pump and felt for its flow of cool, fresh liquid. "W-A-T-E-R."

Helen hesitated. With trembling finger she pointed at herself. "H-E-L-E-N." Then she pointed at Annie. Annie spelled "T-E-A-C-H-E-R." Helen repeated both pointings. "H-E-L-E-N." "T-E-A-C-H-E-R."

By the end of the day, Helen had added several hundred new nouns and the first action verbs to her fledgling vocabulary.

In that one exuberant burst, the world of language opened to a young girl with neither sight nor hearing. Helen Keller said many years later of that day, "I was born again that day. I had been like a ghost floating in a no-world. . . . Somehow in that moment the mystery of language became clear to me."

Annie and Helen were together for almost fifty years, until Annie died in 1936. By then Helen Keller had become a famous lecturer, author, and advocate for the blind. What made all that possible was the steadfast love, devotion, and courage of her teacher. Annie Sullivan taught Helen to view herself as a person. She taught her to be self-reliant. She taught her to play, to laugh, and to stick to a task until finished. Annie taught Helen Keller how to be an active, productive part of the world.

Annie Sullivan's teaching was very deliberate and apparent, its results were spectacularly obvious. But each one of us has been similarly taught by some dedicated teacher. It is unfortunate that most of us neither recognize, nor truly appreciate those teachers who have so enriched our lives. But that is another story.

Questions to Explore

Think about how you would describe the color red to someone who had never seen it?

How would you communicate a thought, or some abstract concept, to someone who could neither hear nor see? Do you think they would think of things in the same way you do?

What language would you use?

Where could you learn of languages used by people who are blind, or deaf and blind?

References for Further Reading

- *In the Children's Library*

Bennett, Wayne, ed. *Four Women of Courage*. Champaign, IL: Garrard, 1975.

Malone, Mary. *Annie Sullivan*. New York: G. P. Putnam's Sons, 1971.

Smith, Margaret Chase, and H. Paul Jeffers. *Gallant Women*. New York: McGraw-Hill, 1968.

Stoddard, Hope. *Famous American Women*. New York: Thomas Crowell, 1970.

- *In the Adult Library*

Keller, Helen. *Teacher: Anne Sullivan Macy: A Tribute by the Foster Child of Her Mind*. New York: Doubleday, 1955.

See your librarian for additional titles.

Ask Not; Get Not

A story about Mary Bethune and her efforts to ensure education for blacks in America

About This Story:

After the end of the Civil War, blacks in the South were technically free. But few had made any real economic or social gains. Opportunities were almost nonexistent. Blacks were still held to the bottom rung of every social and economic ladder. Most survived as sharecroppers on white-owned land.

Schools for white students didn't admit blacks, and few schools existed for blacks. Most were unable to afford either the time or money to go. Black people in the South were surrounded by a very bitter white population that controlled virtually all the land and all the money. Blacks were undereducated (or uneducated), overworked, underpaid, and often cheated by an economic and legal system they could not understand or use.

The beginning of the twentieth century looked very bleak for most black people in America—most. Some, though, seemed endowed with an extra dose of faith, optimism, and energy. These people made the most of their limited opportunities and accomplished miracles, expanding the possibilities for others. This is a story of one such black woman.

The fronds on a row of tall palm trees hung limp in the blistering heat that hugged the dirt roads of Daytona Beach, Florida, in September, 1904. Even birds crowded into scarce patches of shade as waves of humid heat shimmered up over the beach and the lazy ocean waves rolling in from the east.

John Williams mopped his brow again and slowly shook his graying head as he watched a heavyset black woman of about thirty march through the dust toward him, thick arms swinging hard. He was sure she'd collapse from heatstroke walking that fast. But she smiled, sang, and carried on as if she were out for a comfortable stroll on the first nice day of spring. A young boy trotted beside her, struggling to keep up.

Again John shook his head and pursed his lips. "Um, umm. That woman is sure enough somethin'."

"Good morning," she called with a wave as she stepped through the weeds and sand of what once had been the front lawn. The boy stopped, and whined that the stickers hurt his bare feet.

"It's all right, Bret," she soothed. "Mama will carry you to the porch."

As she approached the rundown pillbox house where John Williams waited, leaning against the chipped and peeling front door, she repeated her greeting,

"Good morning to ya. I presume you are John Williams, the real estate agent for this property. I'm Mary Bethune. Susie Warren sent me."

John nodded a faint "hello." "I figured it was you. No one else would stir in this awful heat."

"Is it hot?" Mary asked, glancing around as if for the first time. "I hadn't noticed. Guess I was absorbed in my planning."

"It's real hot, Mama. Too hot for walkin'," added the boy, thrilled to find an adult who agreed with his assessment of the day.

Mary Bethune smiled. She had a sturdy face with sharp hazel eyes and a wide mouth. Her solid body moved powerfully and low to the ground, as if she'd already finished a lifetime of backbreaking physical labor.

"You can play in the shade while I look at the house, Bret." As she set the squirming five-year-old bundle of boy back in the dirt, Mary turned her head to John. "Is it all right if my boy plays under that oak?"

John shrugged his consent and then pointed with his thumb to the tiny four-room house behind him. "As you can see, it ain't much. But if you want it, this dump's for rent."

Mary Bethune took in a deep, satisfied breath as she stepped past the door. She mentally surveyed the house around her: four tiny rooms, not enough windows, poor cross-ventilation, buckled floor, and all the dirt, grime, and bugs to be expected in a house that had sat empty for over a year.

Again she nodded and smiled. "I think it will do just fine."

"This dump?" exclaimed John. "If you don't mind my asking, just what will it do fine for?"

"A school," answered Mary.

"School? This place is barely a house. How can you make it into a school?"

"It will be a fine school," reassured Mary, stepping from room to room. Then she turned back to face John Williams, passion and intensity etched her face. "More than 'fine,' Mr. Williams, this school will be a miracle for poor black girls who would otherwise get no education at all."

John shrugged and mopped his face. "Suit yourself. Rent's eleven dollars a month. I need one month's rent up front."

"I don't have eleven dollars," said Mary.

John pulled at his chin for a moment. "Tell ya what. Five fifty now. You pay me the other half before the end of the month."

Without a hint of embarrassment or apology Mary answered, "I don't have five fifty either."

John slapped his thigh and kicked at the doorframe. "This is crazy, lady. How you expect to rent a place if you got no money?"

Again Mary spoke plainly. "I taught at a mission school in Palatka. I came down here three days ago because I had a dream about starting a school here for the needy children of the Florida East Coast Railroad workers. Susie Warren has let me stay with her until I can get my school set up. The school *will* pay for itself."

"You got a husband?" asked John. "Let him pay the rent."

"Albertus teaches in Georgia. His school has less money than the Palatka Mission School. We don't get to see him very often any more."

John began to fidget with his pocket watch. "Then do you at least have a job? Some income to tide you over?"

Mary nodded. "Of course I do. The school."

"*What* school?"

"*This* school you're standing in. We open in one week."

John exploded, "One week? You gotta be crazy, lady. It'll take you a hard month just to fix this place up, let alone turn it into a school. How you gonna do that and still pay me in one week?"

Mary Bethune patted John's arm to calm his nerves. "I have a week and I have a motto. 'Ask not, get not.' I have to do a lot of gettin', so I plan to do a lot of askin'."

John shook his head in slow admiration. "Lady, you are definitely somethin' else."

"Besides," she added, breaking into her great, broad smile, "I don't see any real problems here. This will be child's play compared to what I've already done."

Mary Bethune carefully spread her dark, full-length skirt and settled onto the steps of the small front porch. "Sit down, Mr. Williams, and I'll tell you why getting this school open will be easy."

Both hands jammed in his pockets, John toed at the floor by the front door. "Listen, lady. I'm sure it's a wonderful story. But I gotta get *something* toward the rent."

Her steady, firm gaze melted his resolve, and he sank onto the porch. "All right, let's hear the story."

"Mr. Williams, I was born in 1875, the fifteenth of my parents seventeen children. We were sharecroppers in South Carolina. *That* was a hard life, trying to squeeze a subsistence cotton crop out of a too-small patch of overworked and near-dead land. When I was six, our mule died. Us children took turns, two at a time, taking the mule's place, pulling that heavy plow through the long rows. There were only eight of us children left at home then, so no one got off. Two pulling, one pushing that plow whereever it needed to go.

"Even as small children, our only 'play' was to do all the work that needed doing on a farm. I could pick 250 pounds of cotton a day. That's a fair haul for a full grown adult. I was eight.

"But none of that compares with how hard I had to work to go to school. Mama took in wash for extra money. I'd help her carry the loaded baskets back to the big houses of the white folks. Then I'd play out back with the white children while Mama put everything away.

"One day I found them looking at picture books. It struck me that besides the pictures, the black squiggles on the page somehow stood for words, and that these white children knew how to tell what those squiggles were—they called 'em 'letters.' Everyone called it, 'reading.' What hit me was the realization that every white person I knew could read, and none of the blacks could. Right then I knew I had to read.

" 'What's an 'A'?' I asked.

" 'You can't read!' they all snapped.

" 'I know I can't,' I said. 'That's why I want to know what an 'A' is.'

" 'Reading is only for white people. All you can do is look at pictures.' And they shut their books so I couldn't see them.

"I stomped all the way home, vowing that one day I'd outread every one of them, and laugh right back in their faces. I was seven then. It took me three years of constant begging before my parents allowed me to go to school. It was a huge commitment for the family. Schooling cost money, something we didn't have, and I'd be the first in our family to ever set foot inside a school. Instead of letting me out of some chores to concentrate on my studies, Papa made me work extra hard to help pay for my schooling.

"Still, I proudly skipped the mile and a half into Mayesville every morning to go to school. The white children I passed laughed and spat at me. 'Go back to the field and be a mule. At least there you'd be useful.' "

Mary shook her head and chuckled at the memory. "For four years I was up two hours before sunrise and didn't finish chores and study till almost midnight. Then I was awarded a scholarship and took the train up to North Carolina to a full-time academy."

"Mama, it's terrible hot," whined Bret. "Can we go swimmin'?"

"We can go, darlin'," Mary answered, rising to her feet. "But your mama's got a powerful lot of work to do in one week." She turned back to John Williams. "I have one week to start the fall semester on time. I may not have money, but I have more than enough faith, and plenty of energy to back it up. If you let me have this place, the school will open and you will get your eleven dollars every month."

John stared back at this unflappable woman, his head slowly bobbing up and down like a sandpiper. "Lady, I believe you. Pay me when you can. You are sure enough somethin' else!"

With a handshake, the deal was struck. And the whirlwind that was Mary Bethune was unleashed.

She spoke to church congregations, asking for students and donations. She begged at stores for old boxes to use as desks and chairs. She found a large barrel in the dump and sawed it in half to make her own seat. She scoured the dump for logs, and burned them to get charred splinters to use as pencils. She mashed elderberries for ink. She begged paper from wrappings thrown out by stores and housewives.

On the third of October, 1904, clouds and a sweet, cool breeze blew in to break the heat. At eight o'clock that morning, Mary Bethune stood proudly on the tidy front porch of the Daytona Literary and Industrial School for Training Negro Girls and rang the large bell she had gotten from a farmer who no longer kept cows. The sound rang like the sweet notes of freedom in Mary's ears.

Five girls showed up: Anne, Celeste, Lena, pig-tailed Lucille, and Ruth, all ages eight to twelve. Their parents paid fifty cents a week tuition. Mary's son, Bret, was the only boy.

As the children piled into the classroom, Mary pointed at the boxes neatly arranged in rows. "Find one you like and sit down. This will be your very own desk for as long as you are with us."

The girls, many of whom had little or nothing they could call their own, carefully inspected the desks before settling onto one of the boxes with a look of pride.

Once their excited giggles were quieted, Mary took her barrel seat at the front of the room. Five shining faces glowed back at her. Today we'll start with what's most important of all."

On a large piece of paper, Mary drew a capital "A." "This is an 'A.' Memorize it. Never forget it. And never let anyone tell you you don't know, or that you're not smart enough to know. Know this 'A,' and you are already beginning to read!"

Because of endless faith backed by boundless energy, the school survived and grew. Within two years, enrollment was up from the original five to over 250, most of whom were full-time, live-in students. Most of these children came from desperately poor families and money was always scarce. Often Mary Bethune would serve breakfast to her children, not knowing where the money to buy dinner groceries would come from.

In 1906, Mary needed a bigger site for the school. John Williams took her out to look at available property. Late in the day they passed a large parcel at the swampy end of a dump.

"This one," declared Mary.

"*This* one?" exclaimed John. Then he shrugged and nodded his head. "All right. If you want it, it must be right."

A passerby stopped to watch Mary and John smiling at this soggy mound of garbage. He asked what she saw in the trash to make her smile.

"I see no trash," answered Mary. "I see a fine college where black girls will receive the finest education in America and march out to change the world. Can't you see it, too?"

The man stood and blinked for a moment before he said, "You know. I think maybe I can." He made a ten dollar cash donation on the spot.

"This lady is sure enough somethin' else!" chuckled John.

Bethune-Cookman College opened in 1923. Mary was its president until 1942, when she was appointed to the Department of Education by Franklin Roosevelt. Nineteen years after her death in 1955, on what would have been her ninety-ninth birthday, more than 20,000 people from all over the United States gathered in Washington, D.C. to celebrate the unveiling of the Mary McLeod Bethune Memorial, the first monument to either a black person or to a woman to be raised on public land in the nation's capital.

Mary Bethune received more honors and awards for her tireless efforts to educate black people than she could count. What gave her far more satisfaction was that many students over her years of teaching affectionately called her, "Mother," and that these students spread out across America brimming with knowledge and confidence and the desire to improve the lives of all blacks and women. But that is another story.

Questions to Explore

If you wanted to help a race of people who were being held to the very bottom of the social and economic ladder, which would you work on first: job opportunities, education, wealth, or political opportunity?

Where have others started? What has worked in the past? Research people who have taken different approaches to changing the socioeconomic opportunities of minorities.

References for Further Reading

- *In the Children's Library*

  Halasa, Malu. *Mary McLeod Bethune, Educator*. New York: Chelsea House, 1989.

  Kostman, Samuel. *Twentieth Century Women of Achievement*. New York: Richards Rosen Press, 1976.

  McKissack, Patricia. *Mary McLeod Bethune, A Great American Educator*. Chicago: Childrens Press, 1985.

- *In the Adult Library*

  Meltzer, Milton. *Mary McLeod Bethune, Voice of Black Hope*. New York: Viking, 1987.

See your librarian for additional titles.

6

Stories About Medicine

Out of Darkness

A story of Dorothea Dix and her work for the mentally ill in America

About This Story:

Through the early nineteenth century the treatment a mentally ill person received depended on how wealthy their family happened to be. Patients from rich families were placed in clean, well-run sanitariums. The latest medical technologies and theories (few of which have been proven to be valid treatments) were carefully prescribed.

However, poor people who were mentally ill were treated worse than criminals. No one wanted to help them, because these patients couldn't pay. But the public also didn't want the mentally ill running loose where they might be a nuisance or damage something. They were labeled "crazy," "insane," "deranged," and "possessed." Regardless of the extent of their illnesses, they were locked away in cages, crates, cells, and dungeons in the worst conditions imaginable. They were chained in filth and given only the barest minimum of food. Many died from malnutrition and disease. But these people were unwanted by society, and once out of sight, they were promptly forgotten by the public.

Forgotten, that is, until one woman took it on as her life's work to make the American people and government responsible for all our mentally ill. In five years this one woman did more for the mentally ill in this country than the collective efforts of families, doctors, clergy, and concerned citizens during the previous fifty years. This is a story about that remarkable woman.

Red clay dust swirled into the scorched air behind the stagecoach. Once bright red with yellow wheels, the coach was now dull brick-red as it thundered over the rolling hills of southern Georgia.

The driver, who'd started the day with brown pants and hat, a yellow shirt, and an oversized blue bandanna tied over his nose, mouth, and neck, was now coated head to toe with the same shade of dull brick-red. Dust swirled through the coach, coating each of the six passengers, causing them to cough, tinging them all with that same Georgia red.

It was August, 1844, and far too hot and humid to even think of closing the stagecoach's windows. Even with windows open, sweat trickled down each passenger's face and neck leaving thin tracks of mud through the layer of dust.

The sound of two rifle shots cracked through the coach. The driver yelled, "Whoa! Whoa there." And then, "Don't shoot, mister."

Horses whinnied. The stage lurched to a stop. A harsh voice off to the left yelled something the passengers couldn't understand.

Forty-two-year-old Dorothea Dix leaned her head out the window, blinking in the harsh sunlight. A tall, slender woman, Dorothea wore what had begun the day as her usual crisp, gray dress with white collar and cuffs.

"What's the matter, driver? What's happening?" Her voice was low, melodic, and quite distinctive.

The mounted gunman's head snapped toward the coach. "You. Lady. Say something else."

"What? Oh, my goodness. It's a highwayman." Dorothea turned back to her fellow passengers. "We're being held up."

The gunman's rifle slowly drooped to his saddle. "That voice. I know that voice. " He straightened in a flash of recognition. "You're the one who saved my mother. You made them take care of my mother in Pennsylvania last year."

He tipped his hat toward the coach and turned to the driver. "Drive on! I won't take money from anyone in . . . in . . . What was your name, ma'am?"

"Dorothea Dix," answered Dorothea, too taken aback to think of anything more clever.

"That's it! In Miss Dix's company."

The other passengers stared in awe. Dorothea settled back into her seat with a, "Well, I declare."

An eight-year-old girl's mouth dropped open on the opposite seat. "I've heard of you." Excitedly she turned to the woman next to her. "Mommy, that's that Dorothea Dix woman!"

"Clara, hush now," hissed the woman in low, warning tones behind the polite smile planted on her face for Dorothea's benefit.

But the girl was too excited to heed the warning. "Really Mommy, she *is*. You're Dorothea Dix, aren't you?"

Dorothea nodded with a hint of an amused smile.

"You're the woman who pokes around jails for crazy people."

"Clara!" blurted her mother, embarrassment deepening the dust's red glow on her cheek.

Dorothea nodded. "That's right. My work is to improve conditions for the mentally ill in America."

The girl leaned closer to her mother, but whispered loud enough for all to hear. "See, Mommy? That's *her*. Daddy says she must be crazy herself. Remember? He says she's just an old busybody with nothing useful to do."

"Clara! You hush this instant!"

The girl stiffened, then ducked her head and muttered, "Well, that's what he said."

The mother smiled apologetically.

Dorothea laughed. "I've been called much worse and more times than I can count. It seems anyone who tries to help the needy these days is."

The dust-covered stagedriver, still shaking from staring down the muzzle of a rifle, opened the door and poked his head into the coach, chomping hard on a great wad of chewing tobacco.

"Everyone all right?" He turned to Dorothea and pulled off his hat. His words were hard to understand around that great plug of tobacco filling his mouth.

"Seems I owe you a couple o' thanks, ma'am—one fer saving my coach and my cash box, the other fer savin' my uncle. His side of the family moved north to Massachusetts near forty years ago when he was just a wild and crazy boy. There was supposed to be some doctor in Boston who could help him." The driver shook his head and spat tobacco juice into the road. "By the time he was twenty, they said his mind was hopeless and he was chained in a dungeon in the East Cambridge jail."

"East Cambridge?" gasped Dorothea. "What an awful place." Her body shuddered at the memory.

A small man in a bowler sitting next to the little girl thoughtfully tapped one knuckle to his chin. "East Cambridge jail. Seems I remember the fuss about that place. About three years ago, wasn't it?"

Dorothea nodded, with a hint of sadness in her bright blue eyes. Even on this miserable journey she looked elegant and pretty. "Yes, I first went there and reported conditions in '41."

The driver grinned, showing a row of dust covered and badly stained teeth. He jerked one thumb toward Dorothea. "Yeah. And got 'em to put my uncle in a hospital room with heat and a real bed, instead of being chained in a metal cage in the basement." He climbed back to his seat on top of the stage and, "Heeeeyaw!" started the horses back on their way to Valdosta.

A lanky man in a black suit next to Dorothea tipped his hat down over his eyes and folded his arms across his chest as if trying to sleep. From under his brim he said, "I heard that was all a hoax. Just a publicity stunt by bored do-gooders with nothing better to work on."

Eight-year-old Clara nodded in an exaggerated way. "That's exactly what my Daddy says."

"Clara!" hissed her mother.

Dorothea turned in the cramped coach as best she could. Her blue eyes blazed. "A hoax, sir? I saw that place with my own eyes. You might call it an abomination, a horror, a shameful blight on man's soul. But, sir, it was no hoax."

The man with the bowler asked, "Why'd you go there in the first place? You spend your life searching out misery?"

"I am a teacher by profession," answered Dorothea. "I opened my first school when I was fourteen." She laughed at the memory. "I wore one of my grandmother's dresses and tied my hair back in a bun to look older so parents would trust me with their children. For the next eighteen years I ran two schools and wrote textbooks. A severe case of tuberculosis forced me to retire. It has left me with only one lung and fragile health."

The coach rolled into a tall forest, and all six passengers sighed with relief. The air cooled, and the dust lessened.

"I was living in Cambridge and attended Dr. William Channing's Unitarian Church. Volunteers from that church led Bible readings for the women in Cambridge Jail. One rainy Saturday, in late March of '41 as I recall, young John Nichols, who led the program visited me at my boarding house. He said they needed someone to run the women's Sunday program the next day and did I know anyone? I volunteered."

All five passengers listened raptly as Dorothea recounted her visit inside the ancient stone prison. After describing the jail and her Bible service, she said,

"I had heard in Dr. Channing's church that some mentally ill patients were housed in that jail, even though they had committed no crime. I asked the burly jailer if I could see them.

"He laughed and asked, 'You want to see the crazies?' He continued to laugh and shake his head as he walked me toward the exit.

"Again I asked him. Again he refused. Finally I begged him.

"He stopped and glared at me. 'They're possessed, you know. They're unnatural, evil. They shouldn't be seen by decent folk.'

"With growing fear I asked again.

"He shrugged. 'This way.'

"He led me back past the jail cells—cold but tolerable. He led me past the gallows where the condemned were hanged and to a separate stone building. Near the front door he unlocked and opened a massive trapdoor, and lowered his torch to light the stone stairs leading down. 'Down here, lady.'

"There were no windows or permanent lanterns in that awful cellar. The people locked in that dungeon lived in a forever midnight-black world except for the two times each day when food was delivered. Neither was there any ventilation, and the stench was overpowering as I closely followed the jailer and his lantern down the stairs.

"One by one he lit a series of torches along the stone walls, throwing pale yellow light across each rusty, iron cell door. 'We used to keep condemned prisoners down here too,' said the jailer. 'But they complained about the crazies' screaming. So we had to move them up topside.'

"He had to raise his voice to be heard as the moans, cackles, and screams of the patients locked inside rose with the growing light.

"I said, 'Let me into the cells.'

"He shook his head. 'I'd rather not, ma'am.'

"I insisted. He shrugged and unlocked the nearest door. It took all his strength to force the rusted hinges to move. Metal screeched in protest as he grunted and pulled back the door.

"I asked, 'How long since this door was opened?'

" 'Days, weeks. Who knows?' he answered. 'No need to go in much. We shove food and water in through that slot in the bottom.'

"Appalled and frightened, I took his lantern and stepped through the door."

Eight-year-old Clara's mouth hung open. Her eyes had widened to twice their normal size as she stared at Dorothea. Her mother and the man in the bowler leaned forward, hanging on every word. Even the man who had been pretending to sleep sat ramrod straight, eyes wide open.

"The dirt floor of that cell was half covered in mud, half in ice," continued Dorothea. "It was bitter cold. I could plainly see my breath, even in the dim torchlight. On the floor of that cell sat two rough wooden cages. In each huddled an emaciated woman, clothes turned to rags, hair wild and matted from months without combing, faces and bare arms coated thick with mud and filth. Their eyes stared straight through me, haunting and animal-like. A thick, metal band around the waist of each woman was connected to a heavy chain bolted to the stone wall next to the cage.

"I covered my mouth to stifle a scream of shock and horror, and stumbled back out of the cell. The jailer chuckled. 'I warned you, ma'am.'

"My mind reeled with questions and protests of outrage. 'Are they all like this?' I asked.

"The jailer scratched his thick chin for a moment and shrugged. 'Some better; some worse.'

" 'At least give them some light and heat,' I begged.

" 'Can't do that, ma'am,' he said. 'If we gave them braziers for heat, they'd hurt themselves or tip them over and start fires. Besides, they're daft. They don't feel the cold anyway.'

" 'But why the chains and cages?' I demanded.

"He jerked his thumb toward the cell I had seen as he shrugged. 'They used to claw and scratch at the walls and each other. This way's better. Easier, anyway, for the keepers. And this way they don't cause no trouble.'

"I was so overwhelmed by the sights, smells, and sounds of that awful place that I couldn't find words to express my outrage. Lamely I said, 'But they'll never get well down here.'

"The jailer actually laughed. 'Lady, they're insane, they're crazy. They don't get well. They just stay down here out of everyone's way till they die.'

"Then he took my arm and led me toward the stairs, saying he had other duties and I would have to leave."

After a long silence broken only by the steady clomping of horse's hooves and by an occasional "Heeeeyaw!" from the driver, the man in the bowler cocked his head slightly. "And so you just happened to stumble into the one jail that mistreated mentally ill patients?"

"Oh, no. They're almost all like that," answered Dorothea. "I spent eighteen months touring prisons, poorhouses, and jails in Massachusetts. After I reported my findings to the Massachusetts Legislature, I moved on to Rhode Island."

The black-suited man laughed and again tipped his hat low over his eyes. "So what do you do," he asked, "barge in and yell at everyone to clean up the place?"

Dorothea said, "No. I observe. Then I prepare reports and release them to legislators, clergy, newspapers, and concerned citizen groups. Then I meet with legislators to draft and promote new laws to provide for the mentally ill. Sometimes, as in New York and New Jersey, it takes a very great deal of persuading to get anything done. Sometimes, as in Pennsylvania last year, the government is more receptive and change comes easier."

A light suddenly lit in Clara's eyes. "The gunman said you helped his mother in Pennsylvania. Was she chained up in a dungeon?"

Dorothea smiled down at the girl. "If I helped her, she probably was."

Clara leaned close to her mother and whispered, "Miss Dix doesn't sound even one bit crazy to me, Mama."

Her mother patted her knee and nodded, "Nor to me, Clara. Nor to me."

Dorothea Dix toured prisons, jails, and poorhouses in over fifteen states. In each, she used her observations and reports to persuade, cajole, beg, and pressure legislators to act to properly house, treat, and care for all mentally ill patients. She also lobbied Congress for several years to create similar programs at a national level. She was personally responsible for the construction of four hospitals for the mentally ill, including one in New Jersey that she actually designed.

Single-handedly, and in the face of public ridicule and scorn, Dorothea made this nation face what so many tried to conveniently sweep under the rug and forget. She made us take responsibility for our fellow citizens.

But that's far from all that Dorothea Dix accomplished. By profession she was a teacher. She opened her first school in Boston when she was fourteen, teaching over a dozen children full-time and studying long into the nights to stay ahead of her charges. Within three years, she'd opened a second school for poor children who couldn't pay for an education. During her eighteen-year teaching career, Dorothea wrote over a dozen textbooks and many stories for her students.

When the Civil War broke out, Dorothea Dix's reputation and experience as a champion of mentally ill patients led to her appointment as Superintendent of the new U.S. Army Nursing Corps. Throughout the war she selected, trained, and supervised all army nurses in all army hospitals, and did much to establish standards for sanitation, food, and patient care. But that is another story.

Questions to Explore

What is our responsibility to those who cannot take care of themselves? The mentally ill? Children? Animals?

What have other countries and other civilizations done to help their dependent populations?

References for Further Reading:

- *In the Children's Library*

Bennett, Wayne, ed. *Four Women of Courage.* Champaign, IL: Garrard, 1975.

Malone, Mary. *Dorothea Dix: Hospital Founder.* New York: Chelsea Junior, 1991.

Schleichert, Elizabeth. *The Life of Dorothea Dix.* Frederick, MD: Twenty-First Century Books, 1992.

Stoddard, Hope. *Famous American Women.* New York: Thomas Crowell, 1970.

- *In the Adult Library*

Colman, Penny. *Breaking the Chains: The Crusade of Dorothea Lynde Dix.* White Hall, VA: Shoe Tree Press, 1992.

Schlaifer, Charles, and Lucy Freeman. *Heart's Work.* New York: Paragon House, 1991.

See your librarian for additional titles.

The Joke's on Them

A story about Elizabeth Blackwell, America's first female doctor

About This Story:

In the mid-nineteenth century being a doctor wasn't as prestigious as it is today. Doctors weren't paid well. Medical school lasted only two sixteen-week terms. Often medical school students were those who couldn't get into more prestigious fields, such as business or law.

Still there were no American women doctors or women nurses in 1845. The only role open to women was as unlicensed midwives. It wasn't that women didn't want to be doctors, but medical schools refused to admit women. And most doctors in private practice refused to train women and prepare them for medical school.

Then in 1847, one woman won the long fight and entered the medical profession through her own hard work and the help of one progressive Quaker doctor in Philadelphia. She slipped past the last great hurdle, acceptance into medical school, as part of a joke. It was then that her determination and perseverance opened the door for other women to follow her into the medical profession. This is a story about that woman.

An air of triumphant joy radiated from the trim, young woman and filled the whole train car. Just passing through that coach-class sitting car toward the dining room two cars ahead, people felt their step quicken, their shoulders straighten, and a smile creep across their lips. The crisp morning air this November 6, 1847, and the bare, western New York scenery seemed grander out the windows of this car than from any other windows.

It wasn't that twenty-six-year-old Elizabeth Blackwell did or said anything to actively transmit her jubilation to her fellow passengers. She sat calmly in her window seat. Elizabeth had always been able to hide her emotions behind an outward calm. But her pale, green eyes shone with the sparkle of a hard-fought victory. Her smooth, pale face glowed with success. She seemed much taller than her actual five one. On any day Elizabeth was pretty. Today she was radiant—even after six hours on the noisy train from Philadelphia to Genoa, New York.

Again Elizabeth smiled for the thousandth time on this trip. "Genoa College wants me! I'm going to be a medical student!"

Such sweet triumph to have proved them all wrong! She could picture each of the twenty doctors she had begged to study with who had each turned her down flat, her own family, and twenty-nine colleges that had laughed in her face. Their voices that had weighed so heavily these past two years now seemed comical in her ears.

"I'm glad you have a goal, dear. But . . . doctor? Wouldn't you rather be a midwife? There's something medical a woman can do."

"Try nursing. I hear nursing is beginning to open up to women."

"Women aren't suited for medical practice. They simply don't have the mental or emotional capacity for it."

"There are no women doctors and never will be. If you insist on being one, disguise yourself as a man."

"Maybe a European school would admit a woman, dear. They're more progressive than the schools here in America."

"Female doctor? Impossible. Forget it. No one would go to a female doctor."

"It would be a waste of this college's time and resources to admit a woman. First, a woman would never be able to complete the studies, and second, women don't have the physical constitution to handle the rigors of medical practice."

Elizabeth couldn't hold back the laugh of delight that escaped her self-imposed calm. Triumphantly she raised the letter in her clenched fist. This glorious piece of paper proved them all wrong. She didn't need to open it and read. She had memorized every word of this acceptance letter from the Genoa College School of Medicine.

A woman *could* be a doctor. A woman *could* study medicine. Genoa College had proved it. They accepted her. They wanted Elizabeth Blackwell to be one of their students.

There was no way Elizabeth could possibly know it was all a joke.

• • •

In mid-October of that same year, with glorious fall colors ablaze across the campus, a desperate meeting had been held in the office of Dr. Charles Lee, Dean of the School of Medicine at Genoa College. Five men crowded into the room, all doctors and senior faculty. Cigar smoke rose in thick columns toward the ceiling. Dark paneled walls soaked up the light and made the room appear dim even with sunbeams streaming through large double windows.

"Gentlemen, we have a problem," announced the dean, holding up a three-page letter. "A woman has applied to be one of our medical students."

A ripple of laughter circled the room.

"Saying 'no' doesn't sound like such a problem, Dean," said one professor.

"It's preposterous. She can't be admitted. Don't even bother to reply," scoffed another.

"She's not the first to try to get in," sneered a third. "It won't be any harder to keep her out than the others."

"But here's the problem," continued the dean rattling the letter. "This is a glowing letter of recommendation for Miss Elizabeth Blackwell penned personally to me by Dr. Joseph Warrington of Philadelphia. Apparently she studied with him over the past year."

Eyebrows raised. Heads nodded. A murmur mixed with the drifting cigar smoke. Dr. Warrington was a nationally prominent physician who had generously supported the medical school at Genoa College. While it was true that, as a Quaker, some of his views were too liberal for mainstream doctors to swallow (like allowing a woman to study under him), still, Joseph Warrington was not someone to be ignored.

"But you can't let her in!" wailed one of the professors.

"Of course I can't," snapped Dean Lee. "But how can I refuse without offending Dr. Warrington? That is my problem."

Again murmurs circled the smoky room.

"Well, gentlemen," demanded Dean Lee, rising to his feet, "any ideas on a way out of this pickle?"

An awkward silence followed while several thankfully puffed on cigars to give them something to do. The youngest member of the staff, Dr. Stephen Kingsly, pulled thoughtfully on his mutton-chop sideburns. "Let the students decide."

Puffing stopped. All eyes and ears turned to Kingsly to make sure they had heard correctly. He shrugged, "The college charter says we are a democratic institution. Let the students vote on whether they want her in or not. Put it in their hands."

"They'll certainly vote against it," laughed one professor.

The dean beamed. "And I'll be bound by their decision. Then I'll *have* to turn her down. But it won't be my fault. Brilliant idea, Kingsly. We're saved!"

Two days later, all 129 students of the medical school assembled in the dining commons as rain slashed at the windows. Crackling fires in massive, stone fireplaces at each end of the room kept everyone bright and cheerful.

Theodore Stratton, the senior class president, pounded his gavel for order from a raised platform next to the bank of vaulted windows. The rowdy assemblage below snickered, hooted, wrestled, and dove across furniture before slowly quieting. The medical profession of the mid-nineteenth century was not held in high regard. Medical schools often housed young men who hadn't been able to get into schools for more prestigious fields, such as business or law. The students of the Genoa College School of Medicine were mostly rural farm boys out for a lark far more than a serious education.

Stratton pounded his gavel one final time and nodded to Dean Lee, who raised his hands to quell a new round of hoots and catcalls. "Gentlemen, the faculty of this college have been presented with a most profound request. This is a matter of such great importance, that we cannot in good conscious decide it alone."

He opened a leather satchel and dramatically flourished Elizabeth's letter of application. Looking as stern as possible, Dean Lee read it to the students. He had to shout to be heard over laughter, hoots, and caterwauling as he read much of the letter. Again he raised his hands. Stratton pounded his gavel.

"Gentlemen, we leave it for you to decide. Do you think a woman deserves to be given the benefit of a medical education? Do you think women are fit to be doctors? Do you want a woman in your midst as a fellow student? Discuss it and vote. Your word will be final. I will await your decision in my office."

Momentarily awed by this trust and authority, 129 young men sat stunned and silent. Dean Lee took advantage of the lull for a hasty exit. Other faculty congratulated him in the hall on a superb presentation. Chuckling to themselves at their cleverness, they retired to the dean's office to await official announcement of the negative vote.

Pandemonium ripped loose across the dining commons.

"Women doctors? How about male mothers!"

Each hollered comment was acknowledged with shouts of laughter.

"What would we call her? Doctress?"

"I bet she's six feet tall, wears a mustache, and can whip the lot of us in arm wrestling."

"Just think. One hundred twenty-nine of us and one lady."

"She can't be a 'lady!' No lady'd want in here with us."

Stratton pounded his gavel. "Gentlemen! Gentlemen!"

A half dozen students had not participated in the outburst. Scattered across the room, they quietly studied what this vote meant.

One of these, Steven Smith, rose to speak. "If we admit this . . . lady, we'll have to act like gentlemen around here."

Laughter stopped. Smith was right. But was that good or bad?

"Wait a second, we're not allowing females in here!" shouted several.

"No women doctors!" shouted others.

Another of the quiet ones rose. "Surely the dean knew that's how we'd feel. Why did he let us vote? Why didn't he reject her on his own as he usually would?"

The room quieted as each student struggled to fathom the motives of the faculty. An occasional nervous cough echoed through the stony silence.

One of the rowdies said, "I think we should vote her in."

All laughed. Some threw pillows and cushions at the speaker.

"No, I'm serious. It might be a lark to have a woman around to cheer the place up. More importantly, if the faculty wanted us to vote 'no,' I say we vote 'yes,' and turn the joke back on them."

Shouts of "Bravo!" and "Here, here!" filled the room.

"This will be a joke to laugh at for a hundred years!" shouted someone.

Stratton pounded his gavel. "It has been suggested that we play an enormous joke on the faculty and vote 'yes.' All in favor?"

"Aye!" The massed shout of 129 voices rang the rafters and rattled plates in the cupboard.

When Theodore Stratton announced the unanimous vote in Dean Lee's office, the dean buried his face in his hands. The other faculty paled and lost their taste for cigars. Several felt to weak too stand.

Slowly shaking his head, Dean Lee muttered, "Good Lord, we actually have to let her in. We're ruined. Whose idea was this?"

"Maybe she won't really come," suggested Dr. Kingsly with a nervous grin.

"At least Dr. Warrington will probably give generously to the school again," added sarcastic Dr. Webster, the anatomy professor.

Acceptance letter still clutched in her hand, Elizabeth Blackwell hailed a buggy from the train station to college. Word flashed across campus that the "lady" had arrived. One hundred twenty-nine men hid behind trees or poked out of windows to see this imagined hulk stomp into their lives. Each crouched ready to jeer, hoot, and howl at their joke. Laughter froze in their throats. Mouths dropped open. Eyes widened. This was no mannish freak, no Amazon monster. Could this petite, attractive lady in the long gray coat and laced gray Quaker bonnet be *their* Elizabeth Blackwell?

Overflowing with excitement and pride, Elizabeth forced herself to march calmly across wide grassy courtyards to the administration building, her head and eyes always straight ahead, her back straight and as tall as she could make it.

Inside she wanted to leap, shout, turn cartwheels, and kiss every tree on this wonderful campus. But from the corners of her eyes she had caught the watching faces. She knew she'd have to prove herself and act like a true lady as well as an eager student to be accepted into this prestigious school.

Dr. Kingsly taught the first class of the afternoon that November 6, 1947. The very room seemed supercharged with electricity. Each student seemed to tremble on the verge of gushing explosion.

Kingsly sighed. This motley rabble was worse than usual today. He'd get little teaching done this hour.

Then the door swung open. Dr. Charles Lee entered. Every person in the lecture hall froze and stared. Behind Lee walked Elizabeth Blackwell. One hundred and twenty-nine ruffian rowdies blushed simultaneously and lowered their eyes, toeing nervously at the floor. Almost as one they leapt from their seats and pulled back chairs, hoping this suave, sophisticated Miss Blackwell would sit in the seat they offered.

Elizabeth trained her eyes straight ahead, knowing that if she glanced either right or left and saw their faces, she'd blush and expose herself as a rank amateur in the presence of this collection of the finest scholarly minds in America.

Dr. Lee motioned to a seat in the middle of the front row. Elizabeth gladly accepted, knowing she wouldn't have to look at the other students from here.

Dr. Lee turned to face the class. "Gentlemen. You voted for her. I present Miss Elizabeth Blackwell." He nodded to Kingsly. "Dr. Kingsly you may proceed with your class."

For the first time in his three-year career at Genoa College, Dr. Kingsly delivered an entire ninety-minute lecture without having to yell for quiet even once. The Genoa rowdies sat still as stone, listening, gazing transfixed at their new student. Elizabeth was the only one to take notes on Kingsly's lecture. The others were too rapt to notice.

At the faculty meeting next morning, most of the professors agreed bringing in a female student was the best idea they had ever had. Classes were finally orderly and quiet. Students finally went quickly and silently to their assigned lab tables and actually conducted assigned experiments. The professors puffed contentedly on cigars and mused that they should have brought Miss Blackwell in much sooner. Dr. Lee smugly smiled, "As I contended all along, there is considerable value to female medical students after all."

The other students quickly realized Elizabeth was an eager, serious, intelligent, and gifted student. Many asked to review her class and lab notes before tests, because hers were so much better than theirs. Others found that she was a quick and easy talker, an understanding listener, and pleasant to be around.

Elizabeth's one remaining hurdle at school was Dr. Webster and his Anatomy and Dissection Class. Webster still spluttered that, "It just isn't proper for a woman to see certain body parts. I can't very well uncover and open up cadavers in front of a woman. It's scandalous. What would my wife say?"

He stopped Elizabeth in the hall outside the medical amphitheater, where students watched surgeons operate on dummies, cadavers, and real patients, to request that she skip anatomy class all together; that it would be improper, immodest, and unladylike for her to attend.

Elizabeth's heart skipped a beat. She knew that she couldn't pass medical school without anatomy class. If Dr. Webster refused to allow her in, all her struggles were worthless. She would never become a doctor. It was a time to bend, so as not to break. She offered to always sit in the far back corner of the amphitheater and to never utter a word, so that the male students might be able to concentrate. Reluctantly Webster agreed.

Elizabeth's greatest resistance, however, came from the citizens of Genoa. Genoa's men thought a woman medical student humorous and probably a publicity stunt by the college. They shrugged and agreed that, "No one here would ever go to a female doctor. But maybe things were different in big cities."

It was the women of Genoa who turned on Elizabeth most bitterly. They shunned her on the streets and refused to serve her in local stores. They called her "wicked," and said she should be ashamed of herself for trying to act like a man. Elizabeth was turned away from a dozen boarding houses before she found one that grudgingly let her take a small, attic room. The town's women wrote letters to the college demanding that she be dismissed, and then to the mayor, urging that she be thrown out of town. A woman trying to be a doctor, they said, was immoral and offensive.

It wasn't until Elizabeth Blackwell graduated number one in her class in January 1849, and received a standing ovation from students and faculty alike, that the town's women grudgingly acknowledged her accomplishment.

Alone, attacked and discouraged from all sides, Elizabeth Blackwell still found the courage and perseverance to fight her way into and through medical school. In so doing, she smashed down a major barrier to women's choice in careers. She was the first woman to graduate from an American medical school. She was the first American woman to become a doctor. By 1900 over 10 percent of the nation's annual medical school graduates were women. Before 1850 there was only one.

Being awarded the title "Dr. Elizabeth Blackwell" did not end Elizabeth's struggles. No hospital would hire her. No male doctors wanted to work with a female on staff. Patients, especially women, refused to be seen by a female doctor. To practice at all, Dr. Elizabeth Blackwell had to open a free clinic for the poor in New York City. But her practice quickly spread from that humble beginning by word of mouth alone. But that is another story.

Questions to Explore

As female doctors began to appear by the late 1800s, do you think people wanted to go to a female doctor? Why or why not? Do you think this attitude has changed?

Do your grandparents prefer a male or female doctor? Why? Which do your parents prefer?

Are there still obstacles facing women today who want to go into some professions?

Identify some of the obstacles girls still face in becoming engineers or scientists. How can these attitudes be changed?

References for Further Reading

- *In the Children's Library*

Brown, Jordan. *Elizabeth Blackwell, Physician.* New York: Chelsea House, 1989.

Green, Carol. *Elizabeth Blackwell, First Woman Doctor.* Chicago, IL: Childrens Press, 1991.

Schleichert, Elizabeth. *The Life of Elizabeth Blackwell.* Frederick, MD: Twenty-First Century Books, 1992.

Wilson, Dorothy. *I Will Be a Doctor!* Nashville, TN: Abingdon Press, 1984.

- *In the Adult Library:*

Sahli, Nancy Ann. *Elizabeth Blackwell, M.D.: A Biography.* Salem, NH: Arno, 1982.

Smith, Senator Margaret Chase, and H. Paul Jeffers. *Gallant Women.* New York: McGraw-Hill, 1968.

See your librarian for additional titles.

Barton's Bandages

A story about Clara Barton, America's first army nurse

About This Story:

At the beginning of the American Civil War there were no women in either the federal or the confederate armies. A few women followed each camp, providing needed services like laundry, sewing, and operating retail stores. But none of these women were attached to, or part of, any unit. Even those few medical orderlies and nurses each regiment could muster were all men. No one thought women could survive the rough conditions and dangers of life on the march.

But during the early months of that terrible war, the prohibition on women serving as medical aids and unit nurses began to break down. Necessity and the determination and bravery of individual women began the process, then the gratitudel of the units they served finally changed official policy.

This is a story about one of the first women to attach herself to an army regiment as a much-needed nurse, a lady who became America's most famous nurse.

"Oh, look! A parade," called eighteen-year-old Juliet Thomas, pointing out the window of the cramped fourth-floor office in a government building in Washington, D.C. The early afternoon sun shown bright and crisp. The promise of spring hung in the sweet scent of the air. The long winter of 1862 was finally ending.

Thirty-five-year-old Marjorie Walsh bounded up from her typewriter and peered over the windowsill. "Pooh. Just more soldiers," she scoffed. "That's all you see in Washington anymore—soldiers, soldiers, soldiers. I'm sick of blue uniforms."

"I think uniforms are very handsome," sighed Juliet.

The third typist in the boxy room of the U.S. Patent Office also rose to gaze out the window. At barely five feet tall, she had to stand on her chair to see down to the street below. Her look was one of longing. "If I were a man, I'd *be* a soldier," she said more to herself than to the other two women.

Marjorie wrinkled up her nose. "Being a soldier is all mud, sore feet, rotten food, being sick, and being yelled at by sergeants. No thank you!"

Petite Clara Barton shrugged, still gazing at the marching column of Union infantry. "I'd still do it if I could."

Marjorie shook her head, again. "Dreariest life in the world, and then you get shot for your trouble. Not me!"

Then all three gasped as a new regiment rounded the corner into view and started down Massachusetts Avenue toward the Union army campground. Marjorie laughed, "That's the raggediest scrap of soldiers I ever saw."

The color drained from Juliet's face and her knees grew weak. She grasped the windowsill for support. "Those poor men look horrid. I bet they've been in a terrible battle."

Clara's plain, solemn face was etched with concern. "They look worse than my brother, David, when he had smallpox. I had to take care of him for six months." Leaning farther out the window on her toes, straining to read the tattered flag hanging limp in the still air, she asked, "Who are those poor, bedraggled men?"

Below them, three battalions of men in threadbare, mud- and dust-smeared uniforms limped and shuffled down the wide avenue. The wounded leaned heavily on neighbors. The sick staggered along with gaunt, gray faces.

Marjorie waved out the window as she laughed. "Yoo-hoo. Hello boys."

"Stop it!" cried Clara. "I recognize that flag. Those men are from Massachusetts."

"So?" asked Marjorie.

"So, *I'm* from Massachusetts. I could know some of them."

"All right, ladies. Back to work," snarled a tall, balding man from the doorway. "The government pays you to type, not gossip at the windows."

Marjorie and Juliet sank back into their chairs. But Clara Barton couldn't tear her eyes away from the spectacle below. "They need help," she murmured, feeling a powerful pull toward the Massachusetts men.

"You too, Miss Barton. Back to work!"

"They need help," she repeated, still staring. And timid, forty-year-old Clara Barton rushed away from the window and brushed past her supervisor.

"And just where do you think you're going?" he bellowed. "Your break doesn't come for another forty minutes. Miss Barton?"

Clara raced down the long flights of echoing stairs and darted out onto the street. She rushed along the straggling line of dreary men behind the Massachusetts flag until she reached the lone major marching at the column's head.

"Excuse me for asking," called Clara, falling in step beside the officer, "but where in Massachusetts are your men from?"

"Worcester area mostly, ma'am," he replied in a tired, flat voice without even glancing in her direction. "But we're spread out from Clinton to south of Oxford. I'm Major Fielding from just above North Oxford."

Clara gasped. Her feet seemed rooted in cement.

"Out of the way, please, ma'am," growled a grizzled sergeant just behind her. "Troops comin' through."

Clara recovered and lifted her long skirts to run and catch up with Major Fielding. "*I'm* from North Oxford," she said. "I know some of the Fieldings. I must know your mother! What happened that you look this way?"

The major turned his head and smiled wearily. "Pleased to meet ya', ma'am. We're just back from action in the Shenandoah Valley."

Behind her several sergeants laughed. "These boys seen most of their action in the outhouse."

"Quiet in the ranks!" yelled the major. Then he tipped his hat to Clara. "I apologize for the men's language, ma'am. But they're right. What with an epidemic of dysentery, I could only muster 30 percent of my unit onto the field for our fight two days ago."

Clara exclaimed, "Have you no doctors and nurses?"

"One doctor," came the reply. "He's our surgeon. His time's pretty well taken up with the wounded. Besides, he's usually got no supplies. Nothing comes from the army, and no blankets, clothes, bandages, or food come from back home." He slowly shook his head and added, "We're kind of out-of-touch with home."

"Aren't any of the families sending aid?" asked Clara.

"No one ever organized any aid for this unit, ma'am."

Clara's mind raced. "But don't you have any volunteer orderlies?"

"Had two, ma'am. One got shot. Other left for home."

Clara began to swing her arms energetically as she mimicked a proud march. Taking care of these men would be so much more important than typing in the patent office, she couldn't imagine going back to her crowded office. Her shoulders squared and she smiled broadly as she marched with her new unit. "If I may ask, Major Fielding, what unit are we in?"

"*We*, ma'am, are the 22nd Massachusetts," replied the major, glancing skeptically at the trim, smiling woman beside him.

Clara extended her right hand as they marched. "Pleased to meet you, Major. I'm Clara Barton, your new nurse."

Again the sergeants laughed behind her. "No women allowed in the army," they growled.

Clara still gazed at the major. "I don't need to officially join up. I'll be your volunteer nurse."

Major Fielding smiled and reached out to shake her extended hand. "Glad to have you, Miss Barton. We'll take whatever help we can get."

Long before they reached the regiment's bivouac area fifteen blocks farther down the avenue, Clara had forgotten her job in the patent office. Now she had something that felt important in her life. She had over 800 souls to take care of in the 22nd.

Within a week, Clara had written to the mother of every man in the regiment, organizing needed supply shipments. Through spring and summer, battles and skirmishes, Clara traveled to the front to join the 22nd with gathered medical supplies and to act as a vital regimental nurse.

• • •

It was still an hour before dawn on the morning of September 17, 1862, when Clara wiped the muggy dew out of her short, curly hair and tried to brush some of the caked mud off her hands and dress. She sat on the seat of her medical supply wagon in an endless train of wagons creaking through the night toward the town of Sharpsburg, Maryland.

"How can you smile at a time like this, Miss Barton?" asked Benjamin, the seventeen-year-old, shaggy-haired orderly driving Clara's wagon over the rutted roads. "I'm positively miserable."

Clara's stomach growled from lack of food. Her legs were numb and her joints ached from countless hours bouncing on the front seat of this wagon. "I'm smiling because I just remembered how a friend of mine once described army life: mud, bad food, and sore feet. She was pretty much right."

Benjamin fidgeted nervously. "I hear there's gonna' be a BIG fight today along that Antietam Creek that flows by Sharpsburg. I hear Lee's got 70,000 Rebs over there just spoiling for a fight. I guess our General McClellan's gonna' hit 'em with everything we've got."

Clara laughed again and shook her head. "I've been a nurse with this army for six months now. McClellan's never hit anybody with everything he has. More likely, he won't hit at all. Besides, I heard there are only half that many Confederates."

The young man gulped and wiped his hands on his pants. "Are you afraid of battles, Miss Barton?"

"Once a battle starts, Benjamin, you'll be too busy caring for the wounded to be afraid. What scares me is snakes."

"Snakes?" repeated Benjamin.

Clara nodded and laughed softly. "When 20,000 men tramp across a field and a hundred roaring cannon rattle the ground, it scares the snakes. They all seem to scurry back to wherever I am. I hate snakes."

As dawn painted bright stripes of red and yellow on the eastern horizon, the wagons began to scatter amongst a sea of tents and soldiers. Clara pointed her wagon toward the front until a colonel with a handlebar mustache, sword dangling from a thick gold sash, and a large plume rising from his hat, held up his hands to stop her.

"No women up to the front, ma'am. You'll have to turn back."

Patiently Clara explained, "I'm Clara Barton, a nurse with the 22nd Massachusetts. They're up in the middle of the line and I have their medical supplies. So I have to be up there too."

"No women," growled the colonel. "Wait here and move up to do your nursing work when the fighting's over."

Clara Barton rose up in her wagon. Her small, solid frame stood rock hard and straight over her mound of supplies. Her fists were clenched at her sides. Her eyes smoldered like burning coals at the man.

"Colonel, I've been in six battles already this year. At Cedar Mountain, Major Jefferies, the regimental surgeon, ran out of bandages and thread until I arrived. Men lay dying of thirst because there was no one to tend to them until I arrived, rushing out into the field with two other women within a hundred yards of the fiercest fighting. A cannonball killed five wounded men lined up near me before I could reach them with water and bandages. I was called the 'angel of Cedar Mountain.'

"At Second Bull Run, a colonel, much like yourself, held me back near Washington. I secretly hopped an army supply train to Fairfax Station. The sight before my eyes as I stepped off that train was appalling. A whole hillside of wounded and dead lay in long, muddy rows in the pounding rain with no one to care for them. It looked as if someone had planted a crop of mangled human forms.

"I grabbed three male orderlies and started up and down the rows, giving sips of water, propping up wounded so they wouldn't drown in muddy pools, bandaging what I could.

"A lieutenant raced through on horseback ordering everyone to retreat. He said the Rebs were coming hard on his heels. I yelled at him to rally some troops to save these thousands of helpless men from enemy hands. The fighting raged on three sides of us before the Rebs were driven back. All the while, I dashed up and down the rows offering such help as I could provide. One of my orderlies was hit and crumpled face down into the mud before my eyes."

Clara seemed to rise taller on the front of her small wagon. "So don't you tell me, Colonel, that I can't be up at the front with my boys. If the 22nd Regiment is up there, I will be up there too."

The colonel fidgeted with his sash, unsure of what to do. "Go ahead, then. But don't blame me if you get shot. I warned you."

Clara snapped the reins and her two horses lurched down the long slope to Antietam Creek. She found the 22nd crouched in long rows, listening to the rumbling din of the early morning battle off in a wide cornfield to their right. Sulfur smoke rose thick from the battle area and drifted over Clara as she stepped from man to man, checking their rations of water and bandages.

At eleven o'clock, the regimental commander galloped down from the Command Post and called the regiment to attention. For half a mile in either direction, the same call was yelled to other regiments. Cannons suddenly erupted just behind. Shells screeched overhead and across muddy Antietam Creek.

The colonel's sword rose into the air. "Forward!"

Clara waited a few minutes and then followed her regiment, a thick satchel of bandages across one shoulder, water canteens draped across the other. She splashed across the shallow waters of Antietam and scrambled up the west bank.

In orderly rows, the soldiers before her marched toward a sunken road fifty yards ahead where countless Reb muskets poked through a split rail fence. Thirty yards to go, now twenty yards. As one, the Reb muskets exploded. As if chopped down by a giant mower, whole sections of the marching Union line crumpled to the grass.

A messenger rushed back, yelling that men were getting shot faster than they could fall. Clara ran forward to see if she could get close enough to help.

The Union line wavered and fell back. Clara was pushed back with them. At the creek they rallied and charged again. Again deadly Confederate fire pushed them back. By now, the field in front of that sunken road was covered with crumpled bodies, grass barely showing through.

Again and again, Union forces rushed the Confederate line. Clara Barton steadily worked in the bloody field. Almost half her regiment had been hit. She scurried, head low, from man to man, applying bandages, giving comfort, aid, and water.

Clara no longer heard the bullets whining past her as the battle raged back and forth. A captain, galloping full out on his horse, yelled for her to get back and said she might be overrun. Clara answered that she'd get back when these wounded went back. The captain muttered and rode off in a great rush.

A bullet nicked Clara's left arm and killed the man she was tending. It was the second bullet to graze her that day. She felt the pain of neither until long after sundown.

As the sun sank low against the western hills, hundreds of other orderlies and medical corpsmen wandered the battlefields helping as best they could. The fighting at Antietam was over. The nursing and bandaging would go on for weeks, the healing for years.

After the Civil War ended in 1865, Clara Barton organized an effort to locate dead and missing soldiers for distraught families back home. In four years she discovered the location or fate of more than 30,000 soldiers.

She traveled to Europe, supposedly for a vacation, but soon volunteered as a nurse in the Franco-Prussian War raging across the plains of Germany. Here she met the founders of the new European Red Cross Corps of Medical Aids.

In 1881 Clara returned to the United States and founded the American Red Cross, the deed for which she is best known. Her Red Cross has aided millions of Americans in times of war, natural disaster, and other need. But that's another story.

Questions to Explore

Do you think nursing is "men's work" or "women's work?" Why?

Has nursing work always been thought of as you think of it today? In past times? In other countries? How could you find out?

References for Further Reading

- *In the Children's Library*

  Sonneborn, Liz. *Clara Barton*. New York: Chelsea House, 1992.

  Mann, Peggy. *Clara Barton: Battlefield Nurse*. New York: Coward-McCann, 1969.

- *In the Adult Library*

  Pryor, Elizabeth. *Clara Barton: Professional Angel*. Philadelphia: University of Pennsylvania Press, 1987.

See your librarian for additional titles.

7

Stories About Military Service

Water and Fire

A story about Mary Hays ("Molly Pitcher") and her bravery during the Battle of Monmouth

About This Story:

If you read most history books you'll think the American Revolutionary War was strictly a man's struggle. We hear little of women's efforts and contributions to the founding of the United States. Politics and war were both considered "men's work." Still, many women struggled heroically to support their fledgling army and the ill-equipped effort to become a free and separate country. Women traveled with the armies, especially during winter, to cook, sew, and clean. They gathered supplies, and tended the wounded.

One of those women became the first real heroine of the struggle for American independence. This is a story about that woman.

"A blanket. I'd give anything for a blanket this cold won't seep through," complained twenty-three-year-old Molly Hays as she huddled around a tiny fire. Her breath puffed into the night air and instantly froze into tiny clouds of ice.

"Ha! You'd have to stand in line for *that* blanket," moaned Susan Hollings through chattering teeth. She hunched as close as she dared to their carefully tended fire. But the small tongues of flame were no match for the bitter cold that had settled in like it owned the whole of Pennsylvania.

This winter of 1777-1778 was as cold as any that could be remembered. Valley Forge seemed to be the very heart of this frozen invasion. These two women, and a hundred more like them, huddled in the wives' camp, a quarter mile down from the main winter camp of General Washington's Continental Army. The army depended on wives coming to winter camp to cook, clean, sew, and tend to sick and wounded soldiers.

Susan shivered. "I swear, this winter and this dismal camp make me think the revolution isn't worth it. British rule and my warm Philadelphia house seem a bargain compared to freedom if it comes with this cold!"

"Hush with such talk," rebuked Molly. Her brown eyes flashed under thick eyebrows. Her dark hair, piled onto her head in summer, now flowed loose over her ears and shoulders for warmth, framing a pale, pretty face. "Nothing is more important than freedom. Don't you see? We're part of the great struggle for freedom—us, right here at this campfire. Because of us, people in this country may be free for all generations to come. And because of us, I think the men are holding up right well."

Susan grunted in the flickering firelight. "What about *us*? I'd hold up much better, too, if someone would cook and clean for me once in a while."

"Don't be silly, Susan," answered Molly, lightly shaking her head. "Campwork is the only part we can play in a war. Besides, we won't have to tramp around and be shot at come summer."

"Ah, summer. Such a lovely word."

With a slight wrinkle of her nose, Molly dismissed Susan's complaints. "I, for one, wish I could do more to help General Washington." Molly rose and stretched her petite, five-foot-tall body. Then she rubbed her arms, aching from having hauled firewood all day. "Do you think this war will ever become famous? Just think. Some day, people might even remember this bitter winter camp and all the work we do." She sighed. "I think I'll see if I can do anything for the men."

"Sit back down and keep yourself warm," commanded Susan. "They're no worse off than we are. And remember, *they* volunteered. You're only here because you got married."

"No. I'm here because I *want* to be, because it's important," insisted Molly.

Another woman laughed, "She's here to be close to her sweetheart soldier husband."

A dreamy look flashed across Molly's face. "Yes, John Hays. He's a gunner with the 1st Pennsylvania Artillery."

Another woman in the circle laughed and pointed a thumb at Molly. "Look at her. Married eight years and she still gets goosebumps at her husband's name."

Susan shrugged, "It's so bloody cold, my goosebumps have goosebumps."

Molly trembled as a finger of icy cold slithered down her spine, and she stamped her foot in frustration. "It makes me positively angry. I know we can beat the British. But this weather, this awful weather. It may just beat us all."

"Is Molly your real name?" asked Susan.

"No. Mary, Mary Ludwig—well, now Mary Hays. But everyone has always called me Molly because it livelier, like me."

"That's you, for sure," agreed the other women.

At the door of the shack she shared with four of these women, Molly paused. "What day is today?"

"Who cares? They're all the same—cold," answered one of the women.

"I'm serious," said Molly.

Susan sighed and dug for a paper in her pocket. Unfolding it, she said, "February 3, 1778. We've only been in this frozen camp two months. It feels more like twenty years."

Molly stamped her foot again. "Still two full weeks till our anniversary. I wish I could wrap up a victory over the British all by myself and hand it to John as an anniversary present."

By early April, 1778, the winter-that-would-never-end finally inched toward spring. The dreary camp bustled with the whispered promise of change. Wildflowers rose up, tall and proud. Green-tipped buds poked out from the fingers of trees. Deep winter snows retreated to frozen gray patches. Paths and roads thawed to splashy spring mud.

Washington's Continental Army rose up from winter hibernation itching to burst onto the muddy road. Mud and marching seemed delightful alternatives to the dreary, monotonous, bone-chilling cold of winter at Valley Forge. The anticipation of summer campaigns warmed each soldier's heart.

Captains and lieutenants raced back and forth, shouting excited orders, thick layers of mud clinging to their boots and leggings. "Strike the tents!" "Prepare for march!"

Swords rattled at officers' sides as they strutted past their troops. "All gear to supply wagons!" "Attach artillery to caissons!" "Bring up the horses!"

Molly watched with mixed feelings as the bustling men slowly arranged themselves into long, even ranks of soldiers. Like everyone else, she longed to escape the bitter cold and monotony of this awful camp. But she had loved spending so much time with John. Now he sat tall and eager on a wagon pulling caisson and cannon. He was leaving her for the dangers of summer war.

She stood alone and silent long after the last commander shouted, "Company! At the rout-step, march!"; after the last column struggled through pools of mud to begin their summer of foot-weary marching and battle; after the last sounds of the men faded around a bend in the road.

Molly sighed. There was nothing for her to do now but ride home to her parent's farm and wait. Waiting was what Molly hated most. She had always been a "doer," not a "waiter." She burned with as much patriotic spirit as any soldier in the army. She wanted to strike the blow that drove King George out of America as much as any man. Why did they get to fight for their country while she had to sit at home and wait?

It was mid-June when word spread along the farm roads south of Trenton that armies were on the move nearby. A British army under General Clinton was scurrying for the safety of New York. General Lee, one of Washington's deputies, was in hot pursuit. Locals said they could smell a big fight coming in the same way they could smell a coming rain.

In the late afternoon heat of June 25, the first blue-coated units, scouts, and lead guards marched past the Ludwig farm. Their grim faces remained hidden in the thick dust they raised from the parched road.

On June 26, General Washington's main army marched by. Almost 12,000 bluecoats with long French muskets, horses, sabers, wagons, and 500 French soldiers under General Lafayette, all rushed through the choking dust to catch General Clinton.

Molly ran to the road to watch and wave, hoping for a glimpse of John. Her parents sat in the shade on the front porch, dabbing the back of their necks with cool washcloths.

Molly raced back to the porch. "Oh, isn't it exciting? John's bound to come by soon!"

"Awful hot to be marching all day," said her father.

"They're liable to drop of heatstroke 'fore noon," said her mother.

In her excitement Molly hadn't noticed. It was hot, brutally hot. The temperature was fast pushing 100 degrees. A thick, muggy haze made the very land seem to suffer, and made even breathing a chore.

"Oh, dear," sighed Molly. "I hope John's all right in this heat. He's never worked outside, you know. He's a barber."

With a clatter of horses and the creaking of wagons, the 1st Pennsylvania Artillery rode by, cannons rolling backward up the road, tied on behind.

"John! John!" Molly cried as her husband stood, waving on his buckboard seat. He leapt to the ground and ran to his wife.

"Back on your mount, Private Hays," yelled a captain. "We're racing to catch the British, and got no time for family visits."

"I'll follow and see you in camp tonight," said Molly.

"No. As much as I'd love to see you, you shouldn't," he answered. "Women can't be around during a fight."

Molly stood gazing down the road as the billows of dust slowly settled back to earth. "Why not?" she called after her husband. Long after the columns of soldiers marched over the rise and faded into the shimmering heat she stood, still waiting for an answer.

Then she turned to the porch, her eyes burning with determination. "They'll all be exhausted when they catch the redcoats. And the heat's just getting worse. If they have to fight in this awful weather, John will collapse. I know it. I'm going after them."

"But what for?" asked her mother.

"A woman'd just be in the way during a fight," said her father.

"I can at least carry water to the men, when they're thirsty. I have to do something. This is my country, too. This is my chance to help."

"You could get killed," said her father.

"Maybe I could. But I *know* I can help."

By late afternoon, Molly rode hard to the north through the oppressive heat still shimmering off field and road. A large pewter water pitcher hung from the saddle of her father's horse. "Drat this weather," she muttered to herself. "It always seems to fight against us harder than the British."

By sunset on the 27th, Washington caught the British at Freehold, New Jersey, and forced them to turn for a fight.

At noon, on June 28, 1778, both armies squared off for battle. Washington's artillery lined along the crest of a low hill on the south side of the field between the two armies. Their orders were to rake the British lines and disrupt their formations, and not to stop for anything until the British collapsed in retreat.

The stifling, humid day was the hottest of the whole summer, as the Continental Army started across that field. Molly found a small spring and a wooden bucket with rough rope handles just across the dirt highway from the battlefield. She filled both bucket and pitcher and crouched, waiting, as the first cannon shells smashed into trees, just in front of a line of advancing redcoats.

British and American cannon roared with a steady, "Boom! Boom! Boom!" The sound rumbled like the pulse beat of the earth. Boom! Boom! Boom! Each cannonball whined as it raced overhead.

Long, steady ranks of British redcoats emerged from a thin line of trees at the east end of the field. Boom! Boom! Boom! Mounted couriers raced back and forth between the units and Washington's command post overlooking the field. Sweat pouring down her own face, Molly crept across the road with her supply of water.

Now several American units broke from the lines and ran to the right to counter a British regiment trying to break around the American flank. Now American units ran back to their left to mass for a charge at the British right side. Boom! Boom! Boom!

By one o'clock, heat accomplished what the British could not. Continental soldiers began to drop to the parched grass, pale and feverish with heatstroke.

Molly Hays raced onto the battlefield with her precious cargo of water. Many of the fallen men were too weak to lift their heads. She propped them up while they gulped long drinks. Always she said, "If you need more, just call for Molly."

Her pitcher and heavy bucket soon ran dry. Molly dashed to the spring across the road, below the small hill where the Continental artillery roared.

The rough rope handle rubbed Molly's hands raw as she started back into the smoky battlefield. Caught between a need to race as fast as her legs could run, and a prudent desire not to splash any of her precious water onto the ground, she half jogged, half waddled into the field.

Mounted on horseback on a hill just behind the American lines, the general staff watched in fascination as one skirted and white-capped woman zigzagged across the field as if connecting fallen blue dots.

"Who is *she*?" demanded General Lee to an aide. "What's she doing down there?"

"The only name I've heard, sir, is, 'Molly.' She's carrying water to the men."

Lee angrily pointed at Molly. "That foolish woman could get herself killed. And I won't change my battle tactics just to save her!"

"Foolish?" scoffed General Washington next to him. "I'd call her brave . . . *very* brave."

Soon the cry, "Molly. Molly. Pitcher. Pitcher!" could be heard from fallen voices across the width of the American line. Volleys of musketballs whined thick through the air and thudded into the earth. Cannonballs mowed down whole sections of the brave soldiers dashing back and forth. Smoke from musket and cannon drifted across the field to sting the eye and burn the throat.

Through it all one lone woman ran from fallen bluecoat to bluecoat.

"Molly! Pitcher! Molly! Pitcher!"

Others picked up the chant, thinking Molly Pitcher was the name of this amazing woman. "Molly Pitcher! Molly Pitcher!"

The American cannonfire faltered and slowed, like an engine running on only three cylinders. Boom! . . . Boom! . . . Boom!

Molly dropped her bucket and climbed the hill on the south side of the battlefield to find many American cannoneers wounded or dead. Many more had dropped from the withering heat and the fiery exhaust of red-hot cannons.

"John! John Hays!" cried Molly over the roar of battle as she ran down the line of cannon. She found her husband's cannon fallen silent. Two of it's four man crew were down and wounded. John had collapsed from the heat and could not be revived. The fourth gunner slumped, panting against a cannon wheel.

A messenger galloped up from Washington. "Why has this cannon ceased fire?" he demanded. "All cannons must fire. General's orders!"

"But sir," mumbled the wobbly gunner, "I'm all alone."

"No, you're not," cried Molly. "I watched you practice at Valley Forge. I'll be the rammer."

Both weary gunner and mounted messenger eyed Molly warily and then shrugged. It seemed the only option at the time.

Molly lifted the long ramrod from where it had fallen next to her husband. She grunted in surprise, finding the iron rod much heavier than she expected. "Swabbing the bore," she called as she ran the ramrod's padded end down the cannon barrel to clear it before firing. Her one remaining cannonmate loaded the powder charge.

"Ramming home!" called Molly as she jammed that charge to the bottom of the barrel with her ramrod. He loaded the cannonball and wadding. She rammed it down. He primed, aimed and, "Fire!" The cannon erupted, belching a fireball flash and smoke. Molly jumped and screamed at the deafening explosion.

"Swab!" commanded her cannonmate.

Molly shook her head to ease the painful ringing in her ears, and ran the ramrod down the barrel. "Swabbing the bore!"

Ram home the powder. Ball and wadding. Ram it down. Prime. Aim. Fire! Their cannonball streaked through the afternoon heat and crashed into the British line. Four more redcoats fell inert to the ground.

"Swabbing the bore! Ramming the powder home!" Ball and wadding. Prime. Aim. Fire! Swab. Ram. Fire! Swab, ram, fire!

A British cannonball screeched out of the sky and passed right between Molly's legs, tearing away a great hunk of her dress and petticoats. Molly stood frozen in shock until her cannonmate yelled, "Swab!" Molly looked down to realize in surprise that she was unhurt, except for a painful burn on one calf from the sizzling cannonball. Her legs were still there, attached to her body.

"Swab!" yelled her cannonmate.

"Right," answered Molly shaking her head to recover. "Swabbing the bore. Ram the powder home." Ball and wadding. Prime. Aim. Fire!

The Battle of Monmouth raged back and forth across the field all afternoon until darkness forced the weary armies apart. All that time, Molly Pitcher worked her husband's cannon, the first woman to fire an American cannon, the first dress on an American battlefield. By twilight almost 500 Americans lay dead or wounded. Nearly 1,000 had dropped from the heat. The British had lost far more.

Molly's face, hands, and dress were black from the thick, smudgy smoke. As the "cease fire!" order was yelled and repeated down the line, Molly sank down next to her husband to hold his hand until a stretcher came to carry him to the field hospital. Too tired to eat, she slept in the grass next to her cannon.

By first light on the 29th, the British were gone. They had fled, defeated, during the night.

A messenger rode up and stopped in front of Molly. "Are you Molly Pitcher?"

"Molly who?" she answered, trying to stretch and rub the grimy sleep out of her eyes.

"Come with me. General Washington wants to see you."

"Now? Me? I can't. I must look dreadful."

General Washington said Molly had been a pillar of strength and courage for his whole army. He called her an angel of mercy to his suffering men. He said she was one of the best gunners he had ever seen. He said she had saved hundreds of men with her water, and had done as much or more than any man in the army to defeat the British. He made Molly an honorary Sergeant of Artillery, and said she could tell her grandchildren that she had won this battle along the road to freedom. Molly blushed as French and American soldiers cheered and saluted.

Molly Pitcher was the first American heroine of the Revolutionary War. The legend of Molly Pitcher quickly spread through the entire Continental Army.

"Sergeant Molly," the heroine of the Battle of Monmouth, became an inspiration for soldiers from the Carolinas to Vermont. No one knew her real name was Mary Hays, or that she was a simple barber's wife from Carlisle, Pennsylvania. But everyone knew that a remarkable woman had sped tirelessly across the battlefield to save American soldiers with her water, and had then beaten back the British with her cannonfire.

After the war, Molly and John returned to Pennsylvania. When she retired from her job working for the Pennsylvania Legislature in 1824, Molly was granted an annual pension of forty dollars per year for her bravery during the war, the only woman during the Revolutionary War to receive a military pension. Of course, forty dollars went a lot farther in 1824 than it would today. But that's another story.

Questions to Explore

Besides soldiers holding guns and sabers, who and what does an army need to sustain itself? Who provided all those services during the Revolutionary War?

Can you find stories about how armies have gathered the supplies and services they needed throughout history? How are those services provided today?

What roles do women play in today's military?

References for Further Reading

- *In the Children's Library*

  Stevenson, Augusta. *Molly Pitcher: Young Patriot.* New York: Alladin Books, 1960.

- *In the Adult Library*

  Clyne, Patricia Edwards. *Patriots in Petticoats.* New York: Dodd, Mead, 1976.

See your librarian for additional titles.

Surrendering to a Woman

A story about Deborah Sampson, America's first fighting woman

About This Story:

The American Revolutionary War was a small, desperate struggle fought across all of the original thirteen colonies, from the Canadian border to South Carolina. Battles were often fought between hundreds of soldiers, rather than between armies of thousands. The British could spare few of their mighty military forces to subdue the colonial uprising as they had far bigger problems on the Continent. So they used Mohawk Indians and Loyal Militia (colonists who supported British rule, or Tories) to fill their ranks.

The Continental Army was perpetually under-manned, under-supplied, and under-funded. They were often forced to rely on dedication and patriotic zeal when stocks of new clothes and food ran low. They were usually out-gunned and out-matched in clashes with British and Tory forces. Patriot Local Militia often rushed to the Continental Army's assistance at the first sound of gunfire.

Precious few men volunteered to take up the uniform of the Continental Army. To the best of our knowledge, only one woman did. This is a story about that woman.

Though her blond hair was now streaked with gray, forty-two-year-old Deborah Sampson still stood tall and straight behind the lectern on March 24, 1802, at Federal Hall in Boston; her blue eyes still sparkled. A standing room only crowd crammed into every nook and cranny to hear what she would say. A French Charleville flintlock rifle with gleaming bayonet leaned against the lectern. It was smaller than American-made muskets, and was typical issue for the Continental Army's Light Infantry and Ranger Units.

Staring at this sea of faces, Deborah took in a slow, deep breath. "How odd," she thought. "I feared I'd be jailed, flogged, or shot if anyone found out. Now everyone knows. But instead of throwing eggs, they cheer. And they come out in droves to hear me speak. How very odd."

She thumbed through the stack of cards on which audience members had jotted down questions for her, and arranged the ones she wanted to answer first on top. She drew one more deep breath and began.

"Good evening ladies and gentlemen. I must admit I am a trifle overwhelmed to see all of you here. The only thing that marked me as different from so many other soldiers was that I had to lie to gain the uniform. I always feared I would be prosecuted and despised if found out. Instead I am honored by having all of you come to hear me talk. I will now try to answer some of the questions you have asked."

She held up the top card on the stack and read, "Why did you want to join the Continental Army knowing you'd have to hide your true identity?"

A murmur blew through the crowd as heads nodded in agreement with the question. Deborah thought for a moment before answering. "Many of you here made great sacrifices to help create these United States. Many of you committed yourselves in whatever way you could to winning the war. So did I. It is far too simple to say that I impersonated a man and joined the army only to escape the complete dolt my mother'd picked out for me to marry, even though it is true that I was glad to get away from him."

A murmer of laughter rippled through the room.

"It is also too simple to say I joined because the delight, freedom, and sense of adventure I felt by shedding the limits imposed on womanhood outweighed my sadness at having to give up my beautiful, long hair and my feminine identity, even though they did. I knew I would face great dangers every day—and not only from British muskets. Rather, I risked being found out by my fellow soldiers. I knew I would have to be ever vigilant not to slip, and that I would have to carry this great secret all alone and never be able to relax or get close to the soldiers around me.

"But this is my country too. And I couldn't stand by and watch it struggle through a difficult birth without pitching in. I am five feet, nine inches tall and sturdy from years of farmwork, and have a naturally deep voice. In 1781, Washington called for 30,000 new volunteers. Only 8,000 men signed on. I did what I had to do to join the army because my country needed me and because it is *my* country."

A great wave of applause met Deborah's answer. This rousing response put a flush on Deborah's cheeks, and confidence in her voice as she snatched up the next card. "Why did you pick the name, 'Robert Shurtleff' when you enlisted?"

Deborah smiled. "Those were my brother's first and middle names. He died in the same year I was born, so I never met him. But my mother misses him dearly, so I know he was a good person and his name deserved to live again."

Again her answer fetched a generous round of applause. Deborah beamed. Speaking tours might be more enjoyable than she had thought. She read the third card. "What was your scariest moment with the army?"

"Two incidents stand out in my memory. One was a moment not of fear for myself, but for the poor victims of the first Mohawk Indian raid I came across. Children had been scalped and left to slowly bleed to death. Women's bodies had been butchered. Men were hacked to pieces. I never forgave the Mohawks for that raid, and I was glad to volunteer for the forty man . . . er, person . . ."

A roll of laughter skipped across the fascinated horror of the crowd.

" . . . Ranger Unit that captured more than 500 Mohawks during the winter of 1782-83.

"The other moment was my first battle. I enlisted in May of 1782. Things were going very much our way. Cornwallis had surrendered at Yorktown in October of '81, but the war was far from over. The British still held New York City with a strong force, and had a large army fighting its way south down the Hudson River from Canada. If those two forces met, the colonies would be cut in half and the tide would turn back to favor the British. Complicating things, many thousands of Tories, organized into cutthroat brigades, and bands of Mohawks raided Patriot houses and posts throughout the lower Hudson River Valley.

"Our one stronghold was the narrows where the Hudson makes two abrupt turns around the bluffs called West Point. That's where I was stationed. My division of Rangers was first assigned to push back the Tories, and then to stopping the Mohawks.

"I had been in camp three weeks, in the army only one month, when we marched out for our first extended patrol. Until that moment, my whole focus had been getting through the normal daily routine of a soldier without being discovered—figuring how to sleep, eat, bathe, and use the facilities without being recognized as a woman.

"Now as part of a company of fifty Rangers, I marched out with flintlock, stuffed haversack, and cartridge boxes to go to war. On our third day out, we crossed a field just north of Tarrytown, deep in territory controlled by Tory brigades. Suddenly a volley of musketballs whizzed over our heads. We whirled to see that we had been ambushed by a large company of Tories on horseback led by two redcoats.

" 'Form your lines!' shouted our sergeant.

"A second volley screamed past us. One ball punched a hole in my hat and split my feather in two. Two of our lads dropped to the ground, blood flowing out across the grass.

" 'Prepare to fire!' yelled the sergeant, waving his sword.

"The Tories charged down the hill with fierce yells as they tried to reload on horseback.

" 'FIRE!'

"Four of the Tories fell from the saddle. Two Tory horses went down.

" 'Reload and hold your line!'

"Feverishly, I ripped open the paper around a cartridge and poured the powder into my pan. I wheeled over my musket and dropped powder and ball in.

"The Tories regrouped and fired. The man next to me cried out in surprise and pain and crumpled to the ground. The earth trembled as the Tory horses charged again.

"I rammed the powder down hard and replaced my ramrod. It felt like it took hours to reload. But I was the third Ranger to re-shoulder my piece and wait for our sergeant's command.

" 'FIRE!'

"Our muskets exploded with a thunderclap roar and a cloud of smoke. Six more Tories fell dead. The others wavered and hesitated.

"We heard a loud commotion off to our left. Two long lines of infantry Loyalists under direction of a redcoat sergeant broke from the woods ready to fire. There must have been eighty of them closing in on our flank. We had walked into a trap and were badly outnumbered.

" 'Volunteers to shield that flank,' yelled the sergeant.

"Reflexively, I stepped forward.

" 'Good. You, Shurtleff, take ten men and stall that infantry until we've regrouped in the woods,' the sergeant commanded. 'Then rejoin us as fast as you can.'

"With ten uniformed Rangers, I sprinted to our left flank to face the lines of oncoming Tories. I wondered what the hardened Rangers behind me would think to know a woman led them into battle.

" 'Line here!' I yelled, coming to a stop. 'On one knee. Prepare to fire!'

"We saw the smoke rise as a forest of Tory muskets exploded. Balls whined past my head. One man in my line collapsed backward, a gaping hole in his chest.

" 'FIRE!' I yelled. Our few muskets erupted in red flames, smoke, and thunder. Five Tories fell, but the rest continued to march down upon us.

" 'Reload!'

"Desperately we tore open the paper of our powder charges and rammed ball and powder home.

"The redcoat sergeant yelled, 'Fire!' Two more of my line fell silent on the field.

" 'FIRE!' I screamed as soon as I saw all muskets up and shouldered. 'Retreat for the woods!' I called, and we scurried for the safety of the trees before the next Tory volley could rip into us. I turned to see four new Tories lying crumpled on the field. The rest broke ranks and charged at a full run after us, bayonets gleaming.

"We rejoined our company amongst the first trees of the woods just as the mounted Tories charged in on top of us. All was a sea of confusion: smoke, shouts of pain, neighing horses, the roar of muskets, the clash of steel bayonets. And then I saw the wondrous sight of redcoats and Tories streaming back to the field in retreat.

"The ranks of our besieged company had suddenly swelled. Two volunteer Patriot units had rushed up from Tarrytown at the first sound of gunfire. Now nearly 200 Patriot muskets tore into the Tory ranks. And the Tories fled.

" 'Fire at will and pursue with bayonet!' cried our sergeant. 'Charge!'

"It was my first bayonet charge. With a shout of triumph, I raced out of the trees after the Tories and bounded across the field. We poured a flood of musket-balls into the fleeing Tories as we ran.

"Suddenly I stumbled into a small cluster of Tories who had formed in a protected pocket around a fallen friend. A Tory bayonet swung at my head. I had no time to think, nor even to scream. Instinctively, as we had been trained, I raised one arm to deflect the blow and lunged forward, low and straight, with my own bayonet.

"The eyes of the Tory before me winced in pain, then shot open in shocked surprise. He trembled for a moment and collapsed to the grass, blood spilling out of the ragged gash across his coat. The rest of the men in the pocket threw down their arms and surrendered as other Rangers rushed in to support me.

"My legs turned to rubber. My breath came in rapid gasps. I couldn't stand, and collapsed to the grass next to my wounded enemy as the terrible emotion of the moment caught up with me. My only thought had been to stay alive. Now at its end, the horror of this battle and of striking my fellow man flooded over me. I began to weep. Then my sobs turned to laughter. Six fierce Tories had just surrendered to a woman."

The dead silence of Federal Hall was broken first by appreciative laughter, then by thunderous applause and a wave of relief, as if every person had held their breath throughout the tense story and finally was able to breathe again.

Deborah raised the next card. "What is the most humorous moment you can recall?"

Deborah's brow furrowed in thought, and then she suddenly brightened. "The wrestling match," she answered.

"In October of '82, things were slow in camp and we all had time to kill. Some of the boys in our Ranger company started a wrestling contest. As I walked past, unaware, two of the lads dragged me in. 'Shurtleff takes on the winner,' they cried, and everyone cheered.

"I tried to back out. I said I was in a rush, but then couldn't think of where to or what for. I complained of a sore back and said I had just eaten. Nothing worked. I was pushed forward into the ring. My only thought was, 'Oh, no. They'll find out I'm a woman for sure.'

"The man I was to wrestle was a thick, powerful brute from Kentfield. 'Ah,' he smiled. 'This should be a real match. You're a fighter. I remember you from the battle at Tarrytown.'

"Then to my horror he stripped off his shirt to fight bare chested. 'Come on, Shurtleff, strip off that shirt and wrestle man to man.'

"In the midst of my protests, he bolted forward, snatched me up, spun me high in the air, and slammed me to the ground on my back.

"The crowd roared at how he had tricked me. 'You're not as quick as I thought,' he said.

"Another challenger leapt in to try his luck. I lay on my back for a long moment, joints aching, eyes closed, silently whispering to the heavens, 'Thank you, thank you, thank you!' It had been close. But I had escaped and my secret was safe."

Boston women blushed at this story. Men howled with laughter. All cheered and demanded another answer. Deborah lifted the next card. "What are you most proud of in your service as America's first woman soldier?"

"That's an easy one," said Deborah. "There are two things. First, I successfully hid my true identity from every soldier and officer around me for over a year. I never slipped up, and no one found out until the war was over. It was a greater, and more demanding effort than any can imagine.

"Second, I proved myself to be a worthy and competent soldier, and was selected over many others (all men I might add) for assignment to our Ranger Division. I earned the respect of officers and fellow soldiers alike as a brave fighter and reliable worker. It is very gratifying for me to know that, even though women are not allowed to join the army, I proved that they are fully qualified to do so."

Having said this, Deborah Sampson stepped aside from the lectern, snatched up her flintlock, and smartly ran through the manual of arms. She finished by loading and firing in less than twenty seconds.

Ears rang. As the great thunderclap roar of her musket slowly faded from the hall, a surprised murmur of voices was slowly replaced by a standing ovation, as voice after voice acknowledged Deborah Sampson's place as a hero of the American Revolution.

Deborah Sampson was the first American woman soldier, and one of the first American women to make a lecture tour. A street is named in her honor in Sharon, Massachusetts. A monument stands in her honor in Plympton, Massachusetts.

Even more than her military deeds and honors, however, Deborah Sampson should be remembered by us all as an early example of that unshakable American spirit that lets no obstacle, no matter how great, stand in the way of a worthwhile goal. That spirit has been an essential ingredient in the growth of America. But that is another story.

Questions to Explore

Do you think it was right for a woman to lie in order to join the army?

Research the arguments for and against women in military service. Which of these arguments do you believe?

Have women always had to join armies by pretending to be men? Have there ever been countries that allowed women to fight alongside men? Are there such countries today?

References for Further Reading

- *In the Children's Library*

  Clyne, Patricia. *Patriots in Petticoats*. New York: Dodd, Mead, 1976.

  Stevens, Bryna. *Deborah Sampson Goes to War*. Minneapolis, MN: Carolrhoda Books, 1984

- *In the Adult Library*

  Freeman Lucy, and Alma Bond. *America's First Woman Warrior*. New York: Paragon House, 1992.

See your librarian for additional titles.

Private Petticoat

A story about Sarah Edmonds, a female spy and soldier in the American Civil War

About This Story:

When we think of the Civil War, we typically think of long lines of dusty soldiers charging through the smoke of a hundred roaring cannons. We think of Lee, Grant, Stonewall Jackson, Lincoln, and Jefferson Davis. We usually think of men.

But women played a variety of important roles in that great struggle. They provided food, clothes, shoes, and aid for army units. They picked up farm, manufacturing, and retail jobs, and continued running the country's homes, farms, and businesses while their husbands went to war. They did the fund-raising to support the huge armies. And they may well have accomplished the most important work of all; they organized and lead much of the abolition movement.

But some women burned with the same call that drove many men into uniforms—the need to be part of the great struggle itself. More than 400 women took up arms and fought in the Civil War—some in infantry units, some in artillery units, many as medical corpsmen. But women were not allowed to join the army in the 1860s. Each of those women had to disguise herself as a man. They not only had to brave the devastating effects of war on the mind and body, they also had to bear the burden of a lonely, secret double life to fight for the causes they believed in. This is a story of one of those women.

Gray-haired Mrs. Butler, wife of the chaplain for the Union Army of the Potomac sank into a chair. "Let me get this straight. You're going to *pretend* to be a woman so you can spy on the Confederates?"

"Exactly," nodded the figure standing before her with sparkling, gray eyes.

Mrs. Butler rubbed her forehead in confusion. "But . . . but . . . how can you pretend to be a woman? I mean, you *are* a woman."

The gray-eyed woman smiled. "Of course. But you're the only one who knows that."

Mrs. Butler drew with her fingers in the air, trying to understand. "So now *you*, a woman who has successfully disguised herself as a *man* named Franklin Thompson so you could join the army, are going to pretend to be this man disguising himself as a *woman* so you can go on a spying mission?"

Sarah (Emma) Edmonds smiled. "Exactly."

The other woman fanned herself. "It's dizzying! A woman disguised as a man disguised as a woman."

Emma adjusted her red wig and stared into a mirror. "I think I should do pretty well acting like a woman. Do you think I should look plumper? Maybe I should stuff a pillow or two inside my dress."

Mrs. Butler shook her head. "You don't want to wear pillows on a spying mission, Emma. You'll do just fine without."

Emma broke into her mischievous laugh. In a thick Irish brogue she said, "Me name's no longer Emma. Besides, you're the only one in this whole army knows that name. Now me name's Miss Bridget O'Shea."

Mrs. Butler slowly shook her head. "Bridget, Sarah, Franklin . . . You've got too many names!"

Sarah stepped out of the chaplain's small house into a sea of white, canvas tents. The date was May 20, 1862, and this was the mighty Army of the Potomac, the biggest of the Union forces locked in America's Civil War. Endless ranks of blue coats, tall muskets, and gleaming bayonets stretched out like fields of wheat. Rows of carefully aligned cannon and mortars stretched far into the hazy blue morning.

Twenty-two-year-old Emma turned past the hospital tents where she worked as the medical orderly, Private Franklin Thompson, and headed for the command tents of U.S. Army of Potomac, dressed as an Irish peddler with all the swish and sway to match.

"Colonel Shrub, sir. There's . . . well . . . a woman . . . to see you." Major Milton stood just inside the flaps of Colonel Shrub's tent, glancing periodically over his shoulder at the red-headed woman smiling outside.

Colonel Shrub slammed down his pen and growled. "I'm a busy man. General McClellan's taken Yorktown and is eager to attack Richmond. I have to plan the troop movements for 110,000 men. I got no time. Send her away!"

"But sir," pleaded the Major, dabbing at the sweat trickling down his neck on this muggy Virginia day. "She says she's Private Franklin Thompson."

Colonel Shrub glared at his aide through steel-gray eyes and chomped on an unlit cigar stub. "Well, which is it, Major? Is this she really a 'he,' a medic named Thompson, or is this she a 'she' come to pedal her wares?"

Major Milton grimaced and pulled on his muttonchop sideburns. "Well, yes, sir, she is. I mean, of course she's a 'she.' Just look at her, sir. But she says . . . Oh, if you would just see her for a moment, sir?"

Colonel Shrub ran both hands through his short salt-and-pepper hair. Then he leaned back in his folding chair with a deep sigh. "Send her in, Milton. I guess the attack of the United States army on the capital of the Confederacy will have to wait for a peddler woman."

Before Milton could gratefully salute and step back outside, a slender, red-headed Irish woman swept past him with a gracious smile and curtsied. "Bridget O'Shea, a peddler from County Clare in Ireland at your service, Colonel."

Colonel Shrub's eyes darted from the woman to Major Milton. Milton shrugged. Shrub chewed harder on his cigar and roughly rubbed his unshaved chin. "How may I help you, madam?"

She laughed merrily. "Why, Colonel, darlin', it is I who can help you. Don't you recognize your own spy?"

With that, Thompson lifted the wig revealing his own shaggy, brown hair, and saluted. Colonel Shrub gasped so hard he almost swallowed his cigar and doubled over in a coughing fit.

"Thompson?" he wheezed between coughs. "Egad, you look just like a woman. That's a great disguise."

"Thank you, sir," answered the private. "I thought it might fool the Rebs."

Colonel Shrub cleared the last of the cigar out of his throat and settled back into his chair. "That disguise would fool Jeff Davis, himself, Thompson. But to fool the Confederates you'll have to *act* like a woman."

"I think I can act like a woman, sir," interrupted Thompson with a mischievous grin. Slim built for a Michigan farm boy, Thompson stood just five and a half feet tall with brown hair and clear gray eyes.

Colonel Shrub shook his head. "I'm not convinced. You're a medic, not an actor."

"I can do it, sir," insisted Thompson.

"All right. Show me," said the colonel, turning his chair and folding his arms across his barrel chest. "Walk. No, no, no. More swish, more flare, Thompson. Get your skirts flowing like my wife does. Think like a woman, not like a soldier!"

Thompson couldn't hold back a laugh. "I'm trying, sir."

"Concentrate, Thompson. There, that's better. Now sit. No! You sit like a farmer. Use more finesse, man, dainty and helpless, like a woman."

Again Thompson laughed. "Do you really think women are helpless, sir?"

Again and again Colonel Shrub corrected his spy. Finally he shook his head. "I don't think you'll ever look natural as a woman, Thompson. But I'm desperate for information, so I'm sending you out, anyway."

"Thank you, sir," answered Thompson with a broad smile.

Colonel Shrub rose from his writing desk and fished a fresh cigar from a uniform coat pocket. He unrolled a large map on the trampled grass floor of his tent. "Memorize this, Thompson."

Stabbing with his cigar at the map, Shrub continued. "We've got 100,000 men slogging their way through these wretched Virginia swamps, heading past Yorktown, here, and up to Richmond. But in several key areas, we don't know what Confederate forces are in front of us. Here," he stabbed the map leaving a brown smudge from the cigar, "and especially here."

Now his cigar jabbed at a thin blue line called the Chickahominy River. Private Thompson craned his head around to read the name. "Chick—a—home."

"Chickamahoginy, or some such thing," broke in the colonel. "I can't read these Southern names either. But that's where you're going. You'll cross the river . . . here . . . tonight. Find out what units the Rebs got in this sector. Find out their plans."

Private Thompson nodded and saluted. "Bridget O'Shea can do that, sir."

"Who?" asked the colonel.

Thompson plopped the wig back on his head. His voice rose an octave. "Why, Bridget O'Shea, darlin' Colonel." And she curtsied.

Colonel Shrub grunted and turned back to his writing. "Good luck, Thompson. Be back in two days with whatever you can learn—no later. Oh, and I, ah, admire your bravery for this. If you're caught, you'll be hanged for sure, impersonating a woman. It's mighty brave."

"Oh, not as brave as other things I've done," muttered Thompson.

"What was that?" asked Colonel Shrub.

"Nothing. Thank you sir." And Private Franklin Thompson backed out of the tent.

At ten thirty that night, the mists began to swirl into dense fog. A lone rowboat softly sculled its way through pitch-black darkness on the swollen Chickahominy River and silently nosed into the far shore. A trim Irish woman stepped out. The corporal at the oars eagerly turned back through the dark to the safety and warmth of Union campfires.

Sarah closed her eyes and pictured Colonel Shrub's maps. The road toward Richmond should be off to her right. She lifted her skirts and started through soggy underbrush. With each step her heart beat a little faster, a little harder. Her breath came in deep gasps, more from nervous fear than from the effort of her hike.

How could she discover the Confederate plans? How could she talk her way into Confederate Headquarters? What if they discovered she was a spy? Sarah's dream had never been just to join the army. It had always been much more. Sarah dreamed that she would somehow make a difference in the outcome of the war. Here was her chance, maybe her only chance. She *had* to succeed. But how?

The mist thickened into drizzle; the drizzle into sheets of rain. As soon as she stumbled into the deeply worn ruts that were the Richmond road, Sarah sought shelter. An abandoned house with a crumbled porch loomed off to her right. She raced for it.

She forced her way past a badly rusted door, and heard a low moan from the kitchen. A Confederate soldier, a captain, lay shivering on the floor, the side of his gray coat stained crimson, his fevered face covered with sweat. In an instant Sarah knew that he was very sick and badly wounded, and that he was dying.

What could she do all alone in this stormy night? She gave him water. She held his hand. She softly sang him songs. As rain and wind howled outside, as shutters banged and water plopped through a leaky roof into puddles on the floor around them, Sarah sang. Then the Confederate captain died.

Before he died, he passed a golden pocket watch to Sarah. In whispered voice he begged her to tell Major McKee at General Ewell's Headquarters that it came from Captain Hall.

Sarah's heart skipped a beat. General Ewell was the Confederate General whose plans she was supposed to steal. All evening she had struggled to think of how she'd talk her way into Ewell's headquarters. Here was her answer, a lump of softly ticking gold laying heavy in her hands.

By noon, three Confederate sentries escorted Bridget O'Shea through half a dozen security checkpoints to a tall flagpole at the edge of a sea of white canvas tents. To Sarah this tent city look just like the one she had left the day before. These boys looked no different than the ones she left on the other side of the Chickahominy River. If it weren't for the color of their coats, she'd never be able to separate Union from Confederate soldiers.

In an orderly semicircle around one side of the flag stood larger tents. There the sentries stopped in front of a lean, kindly looking man with a sad face, soaking in a moment of sunshine.

"Major McKee, sir. This Irish woman says she's lookin' for you."

The sentries saluted, just like Union sentries saluted, and turned for their posts.

The lines in Major McKee's face deepened as he clutched the golden watch and sadly shook his head. "Hall was my nephew and a fine boy." Then he added, "This war will kill us all 'fore it's done."

He clicked his heels and courteously bowed. "I am deeply indebted to you, Miss O'Shea. It's a kind and brave thing you've done."

"Not as brave as other things I've done," she muttered.

Bridget O'Shea was given free rein to Ewell's camp. She wandered from company to company, from regiment to regiment. The Confederates were gracious and kind. Many offered her tours of their camp. Soon Sarah had memorized the identity and strength of each unit under Ewell's command. The little impish voice in her was growing cocky. Spying was easy.

But what were their plans? Sarah had less than one day left to uncover the Confederate plans and then escape back across the Chickahominy River.

Major McKee found her talking with several young officers near the camp photographer's tent. He bowed gallantly. "Miss O'Shea, ma'am. Would you do us the honor of staying for our victory party?"

A bolt of fear ricocheted through Sarah. Was she too late? Had there already been a battle? Had the Union lost without her information? She was barely able to smile as she repeated, "Victory party, Major? Has there been a fight today?"

Major McKee's eyes glowed with excitement. "Not yet madam. But the Yankees will cross the Chickahominy soon, and I have just hidden and fortified two brigades with heavy guns in those dense thickets as an ambush. As the Yanks come ashore, they won't stand a chance, and we *will* hold a grand victory party."

Sarah trembled with excitement. So that was the Confederate battle plan! But she still had to escape. She curtsied, forced a wide smile, and fluttered her eyelashes at Major McKee. "And at that party I hope you'll save a dance for me, Major, darlin'."

Then Major McKee's face lost it's luster. His eyes saddened. "Before this coming scrap, I'd like to recover my nephew's body. Could you possibly ride out with a detachment and show them where that house sits?"

A wave of relief swept through Sarah. Riding with this detail would get her through Confederate roadblocks and back near the river. Every time she needed something, the enemy stepped up and offered it. Again she curtsied and smiled to Major McKee. "I would truly be honored, sir."

With this four-man detail, Sarah easily rode through guardposts, sentries, and picket lines that otherwise would have greeted her with that fearful word, "Halt!"

That impish voice inside Sarah laughed mischievously. Spying was exciting and came easily to Sarah. "I'll have to do it again," she told herself.

But still Sarah's heart pounded. How would she get away from these four armed men? If she bolted, they'd surely chase her down. But if she could catch all four off their horses while she was still on hers, she might get enough of a jump to make a break.

A sergeant leaned nearer Sarah and said, "Mind where you ride, Miss O'Shea. Troops are dug in just ahead itchin' for a fight. If you ride up there, they're liable to think you're a spy."

"I'll remember that, Sergeant."

At the crumbling, mournful house, the four men dismounted and stepped toward the collapsed porch. Sarah lingered in the saddle. Her heart roared up in her ears as the four men pried open the rusted door. A voice inside her screamed, "Now!"

Sarah kicked her horse and bolted, flying as fast as she could make the Confederate horse run.

"Miss O'Shea, not that way," yelled the sergeant. "It's less than half a mile to the front!"

The detail leapt to their horses and raced after Sarah.

Ahead Sarah saw three armed men step into the road and wave for her to stop. Again she kicked the horse, "Yee-haw!" and leaned down close to it's neck. They thundered forward.

One of the sentries raised his gun to fire. Before he could, Sarah's red wig flew off, spinning through the air, looking like the whole top of her head had flown off. The sentry stared, too startled to pull the trigger. Sarah smashed through the guardpost.

Shots rang after her as she dashed for the river. She clung tight to the horse's neck, her body tense waiting for a shot to find its mark. Bullets whizzed past her and thudded to the ground like heavy drops of rain.

Sarah's dangers were not all behind her. Nervous Union sentries and sharpshooters waited just across the Chickahominy River, more likely to shoot at her than not. She splashed her horse noisily into the river, both hands raised high over her head, screaming over and over, "I have important information for Colonel Shrub! I have important information for Colonel Shrub!"

How many Union lives would have been lost the next day had they crossed the Chickahominy without Sarah Edmonds' information? We'll never really know. But history does record that very few were actually lost, and that the crossing was smooth and bypassed major Confederate resistance.

Before serious illness forced her out of the army, Sarah Edmonds spied for the Union as a contraband slave named Cuff; as the Irish peddler, Bridget O'Shea; as a black washerwoman; as Southern gentleman and businessman, Charles Maybery; and even as a Confederate soldier from Kentucky, all while posing as Private Franklin Thompson behind Union lines.

In each of these spying disguises Emma collected valuable information for the Union army. But surely her best deception was in fooling that same Union army. For it was not until the war had been over for many years that the army discovered that its decorated spy hero, Franklin Thompson, had really been a woman all along. But that is another story.

Questions to Explore

Why was the Civil War fought? Did the Confederacy fight for the same reasons that the Union did?

Do you think women have the same right to fight for their country and their beliefs that men have?

How many women fought in the Civil War? Can you find stories about them?

References for Further Reading

- *In the Children's Library*

Reit, Seymour. *Behind Enemy Lines*. San Diego, CA: Harcourt Brace Jovanovich, 1988.

Dawson, Sarah. *A Confederate Girl's Diary*. Bloomington, IN: Indiana University Press, 1960.

- *In the Adult Library*

Dannett, Sylvia. *Noble Women of the North*. New York: Thomas Yoseloff, 1959.

Hoehling, Adolph. *Women Who Spied*. New York: Dodd, Mead, 1967.

See your librarian for additional titles.

8

Stories About Business

Red, White, and Betsy

A story about Elizabeth ("Betsy") Ross, who was one of America's first successful businesswomen and the designer of the American flag

About This Story:

We have all heard that Elizabeth ("Betsy") Ross sewed the first American flag. Interestingly enough, it is virtually impossible to prove whether that story is true, although it is very plausible. It is true, however, that Betsy Ross was a determined, successful businesswoman, having owned, managed, and expanded a thriving upholstery shop from 1773 to her retirement in 1827. It is also true that Betsy Ross was a staunch patriot and sewed many American flags once the design was approved by the Continental Congress. She was an interesting, skilled, and successful woman. This is a story about her.

A crackling fire radiated cozy warmth throughout the living room of the spacious, brick Philadelphia house. Six children drew, played, and wrestled on the floor. Six women sewed, talked, and laughed at the long table by the kitchen.

A seventy-five-year-old, white-haired woman eased herself into the comfortable rocker that had been "her chair" for almost fifty years. It sat where it always sat—close to the fire, but not too close; back a bit so she could see everything, but not back so far that she was stuck in a corner. Slowly she surveyed the happy, noisy home with a deep sense of pleasure and pride. This was a house filled with life. This was a house filled with love. Surely this was the old woman's greatest achievement. Certainly it was a greater joy than any of her more famous accomplishments.

She began to rock as she loved to do, and looked down at her hands. Gnarled and arthritic now, they had once been quick and nimble. Once they had been champion sewers, these old hands. But that didn't matter now. Her eyes were going bad, and she couldn't see to sew anyway.

Even that didn't matter tonight. Tonight two of her three daughters, four granddaughters, and six great-grandchildren had gathered for a celebration. Tomorrow was Betsy Ross's last day working at the family upholstery shop she had owned and operated for fifty-four years. This was her retirement party.

Seven-year-old Melissa stopped her drawing and flopped over at her great-grandmother's feet. Her chin rested on the long skirt covering Betsy's knees. Her glowing face shone with wonder and excitement. That face reminded Betsy very much of her own seven-year-old face. The thought made her smile as she reached out to stroke the child's hair, yellow as wheat waving in the field.

"Tell us a story, Granny Betsy," Melissa asked.

"That's *Great*-Granny to you, Melissa," teased Betsy.

"Great-Grandmother Betsy's too long," complained six-year-old Joshua. "Granny Betsy is bad enough."

"*Please* tell us a story," Melissa begged.

In a flash all six great-grandchildren crowded at their great-grandmother's feet chanting, "Story, story, story!"

"All right," Betsy laughed. "A story it shall be."

"Yea!" cheered six young voices.

One of Betsy's granddaughters at the table leaned back and called, "Joshua. Back up and give Granny Betsy some room."

"Yes, Mother."

A daughter, Clarissa, chuckled, "Here she goes. I've got a feeling *all* the old stories will be coming out tonight."

Betsy rocked contentedly back and forth. "Let me see. A story . . . Ah, here's a good one. Way back in 1760 when I was only eight—just the same as you Melissa."

"I'm only seven, Granny Betsy," interrupted Melissa.

"Is that so?" asked Betsy in mock amazement. "Why, I thought you'd have had two or three birthdays by now and already be ten."

"Gran-nny," protested Melissa.

"Now where was I," continued Betsy, gently patting the girl's head. "Oh, yes. When I was only eight, I entered my first needlepoint contest—at the county fair. I was so excited I couldn't sleep for a week. Not because I was nervous about the contest, mind you. I knew I was plenty good enough. I was excited about going to the fair.

"My family were Quakers, you know, and we rarely got to leave the farm. Now I was traveling twenty miles to Lancaster! My entry was rolled up in a basket as we bounced along the dirt roads in the family buggy. The needlepoint was a pretty Dutch design with flowers around the border. In the middle it read, 'Good girls never waste their time. Here you see how I used mine.' I had worked on it for three months and was very pleased with the results."

"Gran-nny, tell us a *good* story," complained Joshua.

"Yeah, you know the one we want to hear," called two of the others.

Betsy pretended to pout. "I won second place, I'll have you know—at eight years old! Father said to be thankful, not proud, and to tuck my ribbon away in a drawer instead of tacking it on the kitchen wall as I wanted."

"Gran-nnny!"

"All right! I'll tell a different one. Did you know I was a real rebel when I was young?"

"You mean in the Revolutionary War?" asked Melissa.

"Oh, way before that," said Betsy with a wave of her hand. "I drove my father crazy."

The children giggled. This sounded like a much better story.

"When I was sixteen, I hounded my parents to let me work outside our home. My parents were fit to be tied! 'It isn't proper for a Quaker girl,' they said. I told them I didn't care a hoot for proper.

"My father crossed his arms and said, 'Industry itself is enough reward, whether the job be new or old.'

"I said that if it didn't matter if the job was new or old, I'd pick new, and somewhere new besides. Father would throw his hands into the air and mutter, 'Ach! That girl!' "

The children all laughed at Betsy's imitation of her stern Quaker father.

"When I turned eighteen, they finally let me get a job in town in an upholstery shop, because everyone knew I was a champion seamstress. And that's where I met John Ross. He worked beside me, and was only three years older than I was. John was kind, bright, and funny and he loved America with all his heart and soul. Of course, he wasn't nearly as precise and neat at his work as I was. But he was faster and stronger.

"In 1773, we wanted to marry. My parents wouldn't even discuss it because John wasn't Quaker. Quakers aren't allowed to marry outside the faith. But remember, I told you I was a rebel. John and I eloped!

"Father was furious when I told them I was married and moving to Philadelphia with John to start our own upholstery shop. Father exploded! He jammed his fists on his hips and said slowly enough to emphasize each separate syllable, 'Thou shouldst not have done this thing!' "

One of the boys laughed, "That's not even angry, Granny Betsy."

"You never met my father. 'Thou shouldst not have done this thing,' was *furious* for him."

The children howled at Betsy's exaggerated impersonation of her father. Several tried to imitate her with little fists wedged on hipbones. Then they laughed all the harder.

"Life in the city was exciting for a sheltered country girl like me. Everywhere was something new and different to see and do. Business was brisk in our shop, and we soon established a reputation for fast and exceptionally good work. It felt wonderful to walk out our front door and see the sign, 'Ross Upholstery Shop,' and know it was *my* shop!

"Philadelphia was still peaceful in 1773, not like Boston where it had grown tense and ugly. In Philadelphia, we were still friends with the British and believed we could find peaceful ways to resolve any differences we had with England.

"Then in 1775, John joined the Continental Army. There were secret meetings, sudden drills, and John's musket was hidden under a wide bolt of cloth in our shop. I thought it all very exciting, but a bit silly—until John began to tell me about the Stamp Act."

"What's the Stamp Act, Granny?" asked Joshua.

"That's a good question, and I asked John to tell me exactly what the Stamp Act was and what the British had done to make him so angry. That's one lesson my father taught me that I still follow: 'If you don't know, ask. If you have an idea, say it.'

"John told me of all the unfair and burdensome taxes England had imposed on the colonists, of colonists being forced to buy from only British merchants, and of the bad roads and other neglect of the British government. England was squeezing extra taxes and profits from the colonies here, so she could carry on wars and ventures all over the world. The most recent of these taxes was the Stamp Act, which required every legal or commercial document to be "stamped" by the British government, for a fee, of course. The taxes from the Stamp Act were so expensive that normal business was almost impossible. 'It's not fair,' John said, 'and I'll fight to stop it.' I agreed with him. It wasn't fair at all. And I was as fighting mad as John.

"Then in early 1776, John was killed when an explosion destroyed a secret ammunitions warehouse he was guarding. I was devastated. But there was the shop to manage, my three girls (your grandmothers) to care for, and at night I secretly forged musketballs for the army."

"But Granny," interrupted Joshua. "When are you going to get to how you made the flag?"

"Oh, that," smiled Betsy with false modesty at being asked to tell her favorite story. "I suppose, if you insist."

"Yea!" cheered the children.

"Time for bed, children," called one of Betsy's granddaughters leaning back from her quilting to stretch.

"Not just yet," said Betsy. "They can stay up for one more story. After all, it's a celebration night."

"YEA!" cheered the children.

"Now where was I?"

"The flag, Granny Betsy," reminded Melissa.

"Oh, yes. The flag. But first, don't you want to hear about how through two wars and three husbands, I, a woman, owned and operated a thriving business for fifty-four years right here in downtown Philadelphia? And all that time women weren't supposed to be able to own, much less run, a business. Hogwash! There was no reason why a woman couldn't do it then. And there's no reason a woman can't do it now. You remember that, each one of you, as you grow. Tell yourself: 'If it's a good thing to do, I know I can do it if I try.' "

Her finger wagged in mock seriousness at them as she spoke. The children erupted in giggles at hearing their great-grandmother say something like "hogwash."

Betsy settled back in her rocker and surveyed the beaming faces before her. "Now where was I? Oh, yes, the flag. I remember the visit as clear as yesterday. It was just at dusk; the sky still glowed pink and orange. It was early June of 1776. June the tenth if I recall correctly."

One of the women leaned back from her sewing and smiled. "You always told me it happened on the twelfth, Mother."

The children giggled.

Betsy's eyebrows shot up and her hands thudded into her lap. "I'm afraid your memory is starting to slip, Clarissa. If I can remember the whole visit clear as yesterday, I can surely remember the date."

Betsy turned back to the children as the women laughed among themselves. "Now, where was I? Ah, yes. I was just tidying up the shop, getting ready to come in and fix supper for my three girls when I heard an urgent knocking on my door—on that very front door behind you.

"I thought to myself, 'Now who is it comes a 'calling, pounding so hard on my door at *this* time of day?'

"I opened the door to three gentlemen huddled in the shadows. The first was Colonel George Ross, your Great-Grandfather John's uncle. He often came to see me. Just behind him stood Robert Morris, a close friend of his. And behind him, gold-fringed epaulettes glowing in the twilight, stood General George Washington, himself!

"My mouth dropped open. I'm sure I stared shamelessly at him. I didn't know what to do. I felt like I should curtsy, or bow, or some such. *The* general of the whole Continental Army standing at my door!

"Colonel Ross asked, 'May we come in?'

"I remember I turned beet-red with embarrassment, making three such important gentlemen stand waiting. They stepped into this very room. General Washington started to sit on that bench by the bookcase. I grabbed his arm, saying, 'Oh, no. Sit here, General. The rocker's more comfortable.'

"He said that the bench would be fine, and sat right there in that very spot."

As Betsy spoke, she pointed at the middle of a bench across the room. All the children turned to look, half expecting to see the general materialize before their eyes.

"The general's face was kind, but tired, as he spoke. He told me that each colony had its own flag. Most generals had their own flag, or pennant. Many army units had their own. But if these colonies were going to be a nation, we needed one single flag everyone could follow. It had to be a flag that symbolized this new country, a flag that included everyone, a flag that would inspire every soldier, and stir the heart of every citizen.

"As I recall, I said that was a pretty tall order for one piece of cloth. But he pulled a paper from a coat pocket and said that he had made some sketches of what he thought would do the trick, and would I be willing to make the first one so he could take it to Congress and get their approval?

"He unfolded a piece of paper and smoothed it over his knees. On it was a sketch for a square flag. The bottom two-thirds had thirteen alternating red and white stripes. Across the top was a blue field with a circle of thirteen white stars in the middle. The men were all very excited about this design, and rubbed their hands together as they talked.

" 'Do you see?' asked Colonel Ross. "One star and one stripe for every state, all equal, and the stars in a circle, a perfect union. It's perfect!'

"But General Washington was watching my face and could tell I didn't think the idea was as perfect as they did.

" 'Do *you* have any ideas for improving this design?' he asked.

"I'm sure I blushed again, and got very nervous. After all, who was I to tell General Washington what was wrong with his very own design? But you know what my father taught me: If you have an idea, say it. So I said, 'It's a fine flag, General. But if you moved the field of blue over to one corner, then you could make the circle of stars bigger and you wouldn't have these empty blue patches on either side.'

"My heart was pounding, half expecting General Washington to tell me to mind my own business. But he didn't. The general nodded, stroked his chin thoughtfully."

The children at Betsy's feet giggled as she imitated the famous founder of the country.

"General Washington asked me if I had any other ideas. I answered, 'As long as you've asked, General, I think five-pointed stars would look better in the circle than six-pointed ones. Besides, I know a nifty trick for making perfect five-pointed stars.' "

"What's the trick, Granny Betsy?" asked Melissa.

Betsy beamed. "Well, as long as you've asked. Clarissa, could you hand me scissors and a piece of paper?"

Betsy's daughter nodded and rose from the table.

"Thank you, dear," said Betsy, taking the paper. "Now watch. Fold once, twice, three times. Snip here, snip there. Unfold, and there you are, a perfect five-pointed star."

The children whispered, "Wow!" and then all cheered.

"Now where was I?" continued Betsy. "Oh, yes. By this time General Washington was getting a bit annoyed with all my changes to his carefully thought-out flag design. He crossed his arms and asked, 'Any *more* changes, Mistress Ross?'

" 'Just one more,' I answered trying to smile as sweetly as I could. 'A square flag doesn't flutter as well in the wind as one that's wider than it is tall.'

"Mr. Morris tried to hide a smile behind a polite cough. Colonel Ross shrugged. 'I told you she was the best, General.' Now mind you those were his exact words. 'I told you she was the best.'

"General Washington just grunted and stared at his flag sketch. Finally he rose, letting his sketch flutter to the floor. 'So be it, Mistress Ross. We'll use your design. One final question. Can you make the flag?'

" 'I've never made one, General,' I said. 'But it's a good thing and I know I can if I try.'

"And that, children, is how the American flag came to be the way it is today."

Clarissa smiled again, "Mother, you always told me you were afraid to mention changing the flag's shape to General Washington, that you secretly made it a rectangle, and that he liked it when he saw it.

Betsy's eyebrows arched. "Fiddle-dee-dee, Clarissa. I worry about how poor your memory has become. If I made the flag, you'd think I'd remember what the General and I agreed to." She turned back to the children, "Now off to bed, all of you."

Betsy Ross loved to tell the story of making the first American flag, and told it many times. It's a fact that General Washington, Colonel Ross, and Robert Morris were all in Philadelphia and not otherwise accounted for on the night Betsy claimed they visited her shop. Additional bits of family evidence also support the claim. But we'll probably never know for sure. There is no absolute proof that Betsy Ross sewed that first American flag.

Nonetheless, this story has become part of our national heritage, our myth of national origin. More importantly, whether or not she sewed the *first* flag, Betsy later sewed many American flags and ran a steady, successful business for over half a century at a time when very few women could claim to do so. But that is another story.

Questions to Explore

Why was it so unusual for a woman to own a business in the 1700s and early 1800s?

How many women own businesses in America today?

What has changed to make it easier for women to own businesses today?

References for Further Reading

- *In the Children's Library*

  Mayer, Jane. *Betsy Ross and the Flag.* New York: Random House, 1952.

  Spencer, Eve. *A Flag for Our Country.* Austin TX: Raintree-Steck-Vaughn, 1993.

  Weil, Ann. *Betsy Ross: Designer of the Flag.* Indianopolis, IN: Bobbs-Merrill, 1983.

- *In the Adult Library*

  Morris, Robert. *The Truth About the Betsy Ross Story.* Beach Haven, NJ: Wynnehaven, 1982.

See your librarian for additional titles.

Wild West Whip

A story about Charlene ("Charley") Parkhurst, a female stagecoach driver and the first woman in the United States to vote in a presidential election

About This Story:

The stagecoach of the nineteenth century was like today's trains, trucks, and airplanes all rolled into one. The stage was the lifeblood of the early West. It was the only cross-country transportation available. Stagecoach drivers were heroes, as big as sports superstars today.

During the California gold rush (1849-1860) regular stagecoach runs sped throughout the gold country and down to port cities like Stockton and San Francisco. One of the most famous of all California stage drivers was named Charley Parkhurst. This is a story of Charley.

William Gantly felt a sudden vibration in the wooden sidewalk under his feet. Then a thunderous, clanging roar exploded around the corner and raced toward him. William looked toward this magnificent spectacle, and then lurched after his lanky nine-year-old daughter, who had already skipped out into the dusty Mariposa, California, street.

"Caroline, get back!" screamed her father as he stretched frantically to snatch his daughter back to safety.

"Yee-haw!" cried a voice. A whip snapped. Racing horse hooves pounded the dirt.

The curly, red-headed girl froze, staring in terror at the whirlwind racing straight at her. All color drained from her freckled face. William Gantly grabbed his daughter by the scruff of her coat and yanked back as hard as he could. Caroline sprawled onto the wood plank sidewalk as, in a swirling cloud of dust, six horses and the bright yellow wheels and red Concord coach of the Wells Fargo Stage thundered toward the stage office, two blocks farther down the street.

William lifted his trembling daughter and helped brush the dirt from her clothes. Then his eyes narrowed and his finger wagged right in the girl's face. "Caroline, you could have been killed by that stage. You know you have to look both ways before you dash into the street! These are modern times—1858—and you have to be careful. I've told you a thousand times the stage drivers always race into town for the dramatic effect."

"Sorry, Papa."

Then Mr. Gantly's face softened into a grin. "Did you happen to see who was driving that stage, Caroline?"

The girl slowly shook her head. "You pulled me so hard I couldn't see anything."

"That was Charley Parkhurst."

Two gray-bearded men lounged on a bench against the dry goods store behind them. One studied his pocket watch. "Yep, right on time. Just what you'd expect from Charley Parkhurst."

The girl's mouth dropped open, and she stared in reverent awe at the still-settling dust cloud. "Wow! Charley Parkhurst! Can we go watch, Papa?"

Mr. Gantly tipped back his hat and nodded. "Why not? Let's go."

Like a stone fired from a slingshot, Caroline shot down Main Street. "Yaaahoo! It's Charley Parkhurst!" Her near brush with death at the hands of this same stage driver was instantly forgotten.

Caroline Gantly skidded to a stop at the hitching post beside the dust-covered stage just as its driver rose, stretched, and began to slap thick layers of Sierra dust from his pants and jacket. His gloves were of the finest buckskin, with bright Indian beads and embroidery decorating wide gauntlets. A red bandanna was wrapped around his neck as protection from road dust. His wide-brimmed hat was made of soft felt with a fancy snakeskin band.

Charley grabbed the cash box from under the driver's seat with powerful arms and swung it down to the local Wells Fargo agent. Then Charley followed, hopping lightly to the ground right in front of Caroline. At five and a half feet, Charley was only three inches taller than his young fan. But the three-inch heels on his custom boots raised him up to a respectable height.

Charley paused, nodded to the growing crowd, and adjusted the ever-present wad of chewing tobacco in his lip. Then he spit a stream of brown tobacco juice into the street and gently patted Caroline on the head. "Howdy, kid." He glanced down at the glow in Caroline's eye as she looked at him and his stagecoach.

"You'd like to drive one of these?" he asked and smiled.

Caroline blushed and dropped her eyes. "But I'm a girl."

Charley chortled. "Don't you ever let 'em tell you you can't do somethin' jes' cause you're a girl. You hear me?"

And the legendary driver swaggered toward the office.

Caroline stared dreamily after him. A shop owner in the crowd turned to a blacksmith neighbor, shaking his head admiringly. "Charley Parkhurst can chew, spit, drink, cuss, and gamble with the very best of the whips. And he's a darn sight better driver."

"Whip" was a common term meaning "stagecoach driver," because each driver used a whip to control his six headstrong horses.

The blacksmith and the man next to him both turned on the shop owner. "You're loco, Harvey. Everyone knows Hank Monk is the best whip alive."

The bartender next to him nodded in agreement. "Even the famed newspaperman, Horace Greeley, wrote an article saying Hank was the best after Hank raced him to Placerville through a terrible storm and got him there on time."

Charley heard these comments and turned from the Wells Fargo office door. "Any blind fool could have driven through the drizzle that night. Why you had to run around just to get wet that rain was so puny. And as for Horace Greeley, I say he isn't worth readin' if'n he don't know better than to ride behind six swayback plow horses and a jackass."

The crowd laughed and cheered. The men who had stood up for Hank Monk turned bright red. Charley winked at Caroline and held up his hands for quiet. "Sugarfoot tried to hold up my stage again this trip. He *tried*."

Charley started into the office, but the crowd yammered for details. Sugarfoot was one of the most feared highwaymen roaming the gold country. Charley leaned against the door frame and spit again before continuing. "It was almost the exact same spot as a couple months ago when he snatched my gold box. This time happened two days back on my way down to Stockton with a heavy gold shipment in my express box."

In 1849, gold was discovered in Sutter's Miller in California, beginning the great California gold rush. By 1858, an army of miners had played out most of the mother lode deposits. Still, there was a steady flow of gold dust and flakes trickling down from the mines for shipment to port.

Charley shifted against the door frame and continued. "Just around a tight curve near the bottom of the hills, two masked men jumped out waving rifle and shotgun. 'Throw down the box Charley,' says one of 'em.

"I says, 'I take it you're that same yellow-livered, lowdown snake venom that hit me two months ago?'

"One of the two tips his hat real polite and says, 'Don't be a dead hero, Charley. Just throw down the box.'

"'Course I had my loaded '45 under the seat. But that's no match for the shotgun and rifle already pointing in my face. I needed a distraction to give me an edge.

"I says while I eyes 'em both good and hard, 'You shouldn't ought to push yer luck this-a-way, Sugarfoot. You'll wind up dead.'

"He points that shotgun right at my head. 'Ain't luck, Charley,' he says. 'I'm just smarter'n you. Now throw down the box.'

"Well, sir, I'm not about to take that kind of talk from some no-account, two-bit pile of road dust. As I pretended to reach down for the express box, I yanked hard on the reins. The lead team reared high, neighing and pawing the air. The bandits turned toward the horses.

"Before they turned back, Blam! Blam! I grabbed that Colt '45 and fired two quick shots. One bandit dropped his shotgun and doubled over, clutching his stomach. The other skeedaddled into the bushes and leapt on his horse.

"The wounded one staggered after his compadre into the bushes and onto a second horse. Stockton sheriff rode out next day—that'd be yesterday—and found a body beside the road, a '45 slug in his stomach. It was Sugarfoot."

At first the crowd murmured in stunned awe. Then they exploded in wild cheers. Charley was a hero! Out numbered and out gunned, he had shot down a notorious highwayman.

Charley shrugged, spit, and swaggered into the office as if it was all in a normal day's work.

William Gantly knelt next to his daughter, still chuckling. "That man is something. I tell you *that*, Caroline, he is something! Did I ever tell you the story about Charley Parkhurst and the Big Oak Flats Bridge on the Tuolumne River? Now that was a *real* storm that night."

"Yes, Father," huffed Caroline, slowly rolling her eyes, " 'bout a million times."

Twenty-one years later, on January 1, 1880, Caroline Gantly, now married and named Caroline Beacher, sat in her San Francisco home reading the *San Francisco Call* when she gasped and dropped her china teacup to the floor in surprise. On page three, she found an article announcing the death of longtime stagecoach driver Charley Parkhurst. The article said Charley had retired in poor health to Aptos, California (near the coastal resort town of Santa Cruz), in 1870. There he lived as a recluse, refusing all medical aid until a friend found Charley's body on the morning of December 28, 1879.

The county coroner's cursory autopsy determined that the cause of death was mouth cancer from the long years of chewing tobacco. But it was not the death of Caroline's longtime hero that shocked her. It was something else discovered during that autopsy that drained the color from her face.

Caroline called to her own daughter. "Charlene. Come here, sweetheart."

Eight-year-old Charlene took one look at her mother and ran over. "What's wrong, Mommy?"

Misty-eyed, unable to choose between laughing, cheering, and crying, Caroline asked, "Have I ever told you about Charley Parkhurst and the Big Oak Flats Bridge on the Tuolumne River?"

The girl wrinkled up her nose and shook her head. "Who's Charley Parker?"

"Parkhurst," corrected her mother. "He was the best whip that ever lived."

"The best *what*?"

"A whip is a stagecoach driver, Charlene."

The girl nodded. Her mother continued. "It was one of those monstrous spring storms with thunder, lightning, and buckets of rain, and it had been coming down hard for over a day. Combined with the runoff from the thick snowpack that year."

"What year?" interrupted the girl.

"1856, as I recall. No, '57," answered her mother. "I was no older than you are now. Almost all the drivers stopped their stagecoaches to wait out the storm. But not Charley Parkhurst. No, sir. There was a printed schedule he was supposed to keep, and no spring rain was going to prevent him from keeping it.

"With all that rain and the heavy runoff, the Tuolumne River had swollen way over its banks, and savagely cut away at the walls in the narrow canyons leading down from the Sierra Mountains. The blasting force of that river was far more destructive than even the mighty hydraulic hoses miners used to wash away whole hills during the gold rush days. Trees were ripped up and swept along by the river, speeding downstream like five-ton arrows. Huge boulders crashed along the riverbed.

"The stationmaster warned Charley against trying to cross the Big Oak Flats Bridge. Rocks, branches, and trees had pounded on the supports. The swollen river had eaten away the riverbank at the bridge's foundation. It could collapse any minute. Charley just snapped his reins and galloped his six horses into the driving rain. The coach slid and careened down the narrow, switchback road toward the boiling flood far below.

"About fifty yards shy of the bridge, a stranger appeared, frantically waving his arms and shouting over the roar of the torrent. Charley pulled his horses to a sliding stop.

" 'She's about to go!' screamed the frightened man, wildly waving his arms toward the bridge.

"Charley looked back at his single, wide-eyed passenger who stared, transfixed at the raging river. No one could survive a dunking in the Tuolumne that day. He pleaded, 'I can wait. Let's go back, please.'

" 'Go back?' Charley curled his lip and spit the words out with scorn. Charley let out a screeching rebel yell, cracked his whip, and with a quick twist of his wrists, took a tight double hitch on the reins.

"The bright red coach shot forward, down toward that swaying span. Logs and brush had piled up against the weakened bridge. Water already surged up over its deck.

"Nostrils wide and ears laid back, Charley's six horses blasted onto the rickety boards of that bridge as one. The coach wheels skidded, fishtailing wide before snapping back into line and racing onto the bridge. Support pillars groaned. Planks rattled and popped. The bridge railing and curb collapsed into the river, instantly splintered like a balsa wood dollhouse.

"The coach slid to a stop on the far side. With a wrenching screech, the bridge shuddered, ripped loose from its moorings, and disintegrated into the churning fury of the river.

"Charley's passenger craned his head out the side window, staring ashen-faced at the gaping hole they had just crossed, and whispered, 'I thought for sure we were goners, that you and me were going down into that deadly water.'

" 'Naw,' snorted Charley. 'I'd never let it happen. I'm too particular about who I take a bath with.' The passenger and gold box were delivered right on schedule.

"That's the kind of whip Charley Parkhurst was," concluded Caroline to her mesmerized daughter as she tapped one finger on the article in the *Call*.

"Is that what the article is about, Mommy?"

Again Caroline smiled that misty, far-off smile. "No, the article is mostly a description of the time Charley decided to vote in a presidential election."

Again Charlene interrupted her mother. "Who cares if some old geezer votes?"

"Let me finish," said her mother, "and you will, too. It was in the presidential election in 1868, when Charley voted in the town of Soquel, California. Article says Charley always hinted that he voted for Grant. What makes that vote significant is the incredible secret Charley carried right to his death. You see, when the Santa Cruz County coroner performed an autopsy on Charley, he not only found the cause of Charley's death, he also found the secret Charley had hidden from the whole world. Charley Parkhurst was a woman."

"A woman?" exclaimed Charlene. "But women aren't allowed to vote."

Caroline shrugged. "That's the kind of person Charley Parkhurst was. Everyone else said, 'can't.' Charley just went ahead and did it."

Then she quickly added, "I suppose we should say, *Charlene* Parkhurst. Paper says that's the name she was born with back in New Hampshire. Says she ran away at ten wearing boy's clothes as a disguise. I guess she just never changed back."

"Her name was Charlene, just like mine?" asked the girl.

Again her mother shrugged. "I told you Charley Parkhurst was my hero, and I couldn't name you, 'Charley,' when you were born a girl. But just think, Charlene Parkhurst was the very first woman to ever vote in this country. And I knew her! She even patted me on the head once. And now she'll be famous forever."

She added, "And she was a darn sight better whip than any man who ever mounted a stage!"

"And she was named after *me*," added her daughter.

Charlene ("Charley") Parkhurst was one of the finest stagecoach drivers in California history, maintaining one of the best on-time records of the famed Wells Fargo crew of drivers. More importantly, she did with her life exactly what she most wanted to do (work with the horses she loved and drive a stagecoach) even though it violated every rule, custom, and regulation of the time, and even though she had to adopt an elaborate disguise to do it. But Charlene didn't seem to mind, and neither did her employers, passengers, or fellow drivers, because none knew her secret.

She also voted fifty years before a constitutional amendment made it legal for women to do so. Charlene Parkhurst represented the vital and vibrant "go-for-it" spirit so essential in conquering the West, a spirit we so desperately need on so many fronts, and to conquer so many problems today. But that is another story.

Questions to Explore

We've all seen Old West stagecoaches on movies and television. Where were the routes they really ran? What did they carry?

Why was the stage so important to the development of the West?

Why do you think there weren't women stagecoach drivers?

References for Further Reading

- *In the Children's Library*

  Lee, Hector. *Heroes, Villains, and Ghosts: Folklore of Old California.* Santa Barbara, CA: Capra Press, 1984.

- *In the Adult Library*

  Sheafer, Silvia Anne. *Gold Rush Women.* Sacramento, CA: Historical California Journal Publications, 1978.

  Reiter, Joan Swallow. *The Women (The Old West).* New York: Time-Life Books, 1978.

See your librarian for additional titles.

A Hair-Brained Idea

A story about Sara Breedlove ("Madam C. J.") Walker, America's first self-made, female millionaire

About This Story:

The twentieth century did not dawn for American blacks with any of the rights, hope, and freedom promised by emancipation and the end of the Civil War. Few blacks could read or write, education for blacks was difficult to obtain and even then of generally poor quality. Banks wouldn't loan money to black people, and blacks earned less than half of what their white counterparts received for the same work.

Worst off were black women. Few black women at the turn of the century earned more than a dollar and a half a week at a time when the average unskilled white worker earned around 11 dollars for the same week's work. Opportunities for black women to better their lot were few and far between. But they were not nonexistent. This is a story about the black woman who made it possible for thousands of other black women to earn a decent living and proudly raise their heads with a diploma and the title of "professional."

Newfangled automobiles, some electric and some gasoline powered, puttered along busy Wylie Street on the west side of the Susquehanna River in the heart of Pittsburgh's black community. The constant "toot, toot!" of their horns sent pedestrians scurrying and made horses whinny nervously.

By April, 1915, the promise of "better times ahead," finally held a faint glimmer of reality for black Americans. Jobs were easier to find. And while black women in Pittsburgh still averaged just above 2 dollars a week, black men were averaging over 5 dollars for their labor. Both pay rates were far better than what could be expected back in the South where most of these blacks had started.

A decent life finally felt like a dream that might become reality. Wylie Street alone boasted twenty businesses owned by blacks. More were tucked along neighboring streets. The smell of bustle and opportunity drifted in the air and forced a more hopeful rhythm into the feet that walked along Wylie Street.

This background of upbeat city noise and activity made the young woman hunched, sobbing, on one corner of the front steps of the two-story building that housed Lelia College seem all the more dismal. An elegantly dressed, middle-aged black woman stood quietly watching. Her luxurious hair was swept to the top of her head, as was the style of the day.

With a slight shake of her head and muttering to herself, "My, my, my. What have we here?" the lady plopped down onto the steps beside the weeping teenager. Extending a linen handkerchief, she said, "You're about to cry yourself to death, girl. What's made you weep this way?"

Startled and embarrassed, the girl looked up through red, bloodshot eyes. Her thin arms wrapped aroung her body. "They won't let me in," she said between gulping sobs.

"What? You mean the door's locked?" asked the woman, trying hard now not to smile.

"No," cried the girl. "They won't let me into the school!"

"This school?" asked the woman, pointing with her thumb over her shoulder at Lelia College. "The beauty school?"

The girl nodded and wiped her nose on her sleeve. "And now I have to wait a whole month for the next class."

The older lady now shook the handkerchief so it couldn't be overlooked. "Here. Wipe your eyes, girl. What's your name?"

"Marjorie Joyner, ma'am," answered the girl, blowing her nose hard before wiping her eyes.

The lady studied Marjorie for a long moment. "Why do you want to go to beauty school, anyway, Marjorie Joyner?"

"Why?" gasped the girl, as surprised as if she'd been asked why she wanted to be happy. "Why? Just look at this."

Marjorie rummaged through the bottom of her purse and produced a ripped newspaper page, beginning to yellow. Smoothing the paper on her leg, she pointed to a large ad. "Read that."

The elegantly dressed lady leaned across and pointed with her finger as she read, "A diploma from Madam C. J. Walker's School of Hair Culture at Lelia College is your passport to prosperity."

The lady shook her head and smiled. "My, my, my. So you want to learn that fancy hair care stuff, and become rich. Is that it?"

Marjorie nodded vigorously.

"And you believe what it says in that ad?" asked the lady.

"Oh, yes ma'am, I do," answered the girl. "Just read this part." Marjorie pointed to a quote from a Mrs. William James of Columbus, Ohio. Slowly, having to sound out each word, Marjorie read, " 'Before I became a hair care professional at Madam C. J. Walker's school, I barely earned 2 dollars a week. Now I average over 25 dollars a week. We even bought our own house.' There! And my aunt in Cleveland knows a woman who studied with Madam Walker and now earns 30 dollars a week. Can you imagine that much money? She gets to buy new clothes and everything!"

The lady seated next to Marjorie shrugged. "So wait one month and get in on the *next* class."

Marjorie began to sob again. "But I don't have any money to live on. I don't even have the 17 dollars to pay for school."

Marjorie paused to blow her nose again. "I already spent every penny I had to go to a white women's beauty school. I did real well and learned all kinds of fancy stuff. I can even do the French Marcel Wave."

"Um hmm," nodded the lady, suddenly impressed. "Do tell."

"But then I find out a black woman can't get jobs in a white ladies' shop. And most of the stuff they taught me won't work on black women's hair, so I can't get a job in a black women's shop either. I got no money, no job, no place to stay. I got nothin'!"

The lady eased one arm around Marjorie's thin shoulders. "There, there. You think this Madam Walker sat crying on some doorstep waiting for someone to walk along and hand *her* a job?"

Marjorie leaned back and looked at the lady as if she were crazy. "Madam Walker don't need somebody to give her no job. She's probably got a zillion dollars."

Hands on hips, the lady's voice was tinged with sarcasm. "And you think she's *always* been rich?"

"I don't know," shrugged the girl. "I guess so. She owns stores and schools and everything."

"Girl. You got things figured out all upside down and backwards," laughed the lady. "Let me tell you about Madam C. J. Walker." The lady dramatically cleared her throat. "Sarah Breedlove was born . . ."

"Who?" interrupted Marjorie.

"That was Madam Walker's name when she was a child. Now stay up with me, girl. Sarah Breedlove was born in Louisiana to penniless sharecroppers. She had to work the fields Monday to Friday, and help her mama with washing for white folks on Saturday starting at the age of five. She was orphaned when yellow fever took both parents at seven, married at fourteen, and widowed by a work accident at twenty. There she was in Vicksburg, twenty years old, already worked hard fifteen years, no education, a two-year-old daughter to care for, and dead, flat broke without a penny for the third time in her life.

"You think she sat on some doorstep and cried for a job?"

Marjorie sullenly looked at her bony knees. "No. She invented hair care products and got rich."

"Girl!" snapped the lady, hands on hips again. "You don't just—poof—invent something. First you got to know what you want to invent, and then you got to have time to work on it and make it work. When you're broke, alone, and scared, all you know is you got to scramble to find a way to eat.

"Sarah took in wash seven days a week for over two years to save enough money to buy tickets for her and her daughter, Lelia, to St. Louis, where folks in Vicksburg said life was better."

Marjorie interrupted, "Is that the Lelia this school is named for?"

The lady laughed. "Now you're thinking, girl. But don't get ahead of my story. Sarah arrived, broke *again*, in St. Louis, and mighty disappointed to find no streets of gold and honey like she'd dreamed back in Vicksburg.

"You think she sat weeping on some step waiting for a handout?"

Angrily Marjorie crossed her arms, and said with singsong sarcasm, "No. She invented hair care products and made a million dollars."

"Girl, you just don't listen," replied the lady, slowly shaking her head. "She had no time and no money for such foolishness. What she did was the only thing she knew, she took in wash. For twelve years her arms stayed buried in soapsuds up to the elbow. At night, two neighbors helped her learn to read and write."

The lady nodded solemnly and sat back as if finished with her story.

Marjorie Joyner squealed, "But how'd she invent hair care products and get to own everything?"

"Oh, *that*," said the lady, pretending to be very serious. "Compared to spending twenty years as a scrubwoman bent over a washtub, the rest was easy.

"One night it just hit Sarah like a flash that she was thirty-seven years old and couldn't stay bent over a washtub forever."

"So *then* she became a rich inventor," interrupted Marjorie.

The lady's eyebrows arched. "Girl, *you* want to tell this story, or you want me to?"

"Sorry," whispered Marjorie.

After a short, icy stare, the lady continued. "Sarah realized if she was ever going to be anything better than a scrubwoman, she had to *look* better than a scrubwoman. For Sarah, that mostly meant doing something about her hair. As was true for many black women, Sarah's hair was broken, stringy, frizzy, and was rapidly falling out to reveal her scalp in several places.

"Sarah decided that if she could fix her hair, the rest of her would somehow fix itself. She tried everything she could get her hands on: Queen Pomade, Ford's Original Oxidized Ox Marrow, La Creole Hair Restorer, even Poro Wonderful Hair Grower. Nothing worked. Not even a little.

"And that's when it happened. This was early 1905 by now. Sarah had a powerful dream. In it a huge black man told Sarah what to mix up to make her own, better, hair tonic. Some of the ingredients were easy to get. But some were only grown in Africa. Sarah had to use almost all her savings—over 10 dollars—to have them shipped in. And she did it on blind faith because of what she was told in a dream!

"Oh, how exciting it was for Sarah to mix that first batch when all the ingredients finally arrived. Just like in her dream, it whipped up smooth, cool, and creamy. First Sarah tried it on herself, hands trembling with anticipation as she worked that first dab in.

"Within two weeks, her hair grew in faster than it had ever fallen out. Even better, it grew in thick and luxurious, not stringy and frizzy. Sarah tried it on her daughter and neighbors. It worked for them just as well. Sarah decided right then to stop calling herself a scrubwoman, and call herself a 'manufacturer of hair care products.' "

Marjorie clapped her hands together. "And she sold a zillion jars of the stuff and became rich."

"There you go again, girl," snapped the lady. "Jumping straight to the rich part, and skipping right over the work part. You think it's easy to make a truckload of something and get people to plunk down their money for it just because you say it works? No, it is not. The work was just beginning."

Marjorie sank back onto the step and muttered, "I hate the work part."

The lady started to count Sarah's problems on her fingers. "Sarah had no money for advertising like the other companies. She had no money for a factory. She had no money to hire saleswomen or workers. She wasn't even sure she had the best formula yet.

"She moved to Denver to get away from the St. Louis competition. Sarah arrived there . . ."

"I know," interrupted Marjorie with a sigh. "She arrived flat broke again."

"Naw," laughed the lady. " 'Taint so. She arrived in Denver with her daughter, her formula, and a whole dollar fifty, all that was left of her savings. So it was back to doin' what she knew best: washing clothes to pay rent and food. She also cooked for a druggist. But every night she experimented with the formula. It was over a year before Sarah had her first three products ready to go: Wonderful Hair Grower (the dream formula), Glossine Conditioner, and Vegetable Shampoo.

"Sarah mixed them up one small batch at a time, then carried the jars all over town, selling door to door to get money to make the next batch. After a year she was able to quit the cooking job and spend more time giving free demonstrations and walking the Denver streets making door-to-door sales. After two more years she put aside her scrub tub forever. The hair care products alone brought in 10 dollars a week now.

"Then Sarah spent two whole years on the road getting women to try her stuff in new cities, new states. Then she came here, to Pittsburgh, and founded this college to train more women to use her products and to carry them out into every state and city in the country.

"In 1912, Sarah set up a factory near the rail center in Indianapolis to fill mail orders. Now more than 2,000 women earn good salaries either working for Madam C. J. Walker or as agents with their own home salons."

"And *now* do we get to the part where Madam Walker becomes rich and famous?" asked Marjorie.

The lady smiled, nodded, and then laughed out loud. "Well, now that you mention it, Marjorie, I guess I am."

Marjorie's eyes grew wide and she stumbled to her feet, trying to straighten her dress, wipe her tear-streaked face, and smooth her hair, all in one frantic motion. "You're Madam C. J. Walker? You're her? I didn't mean to say anything bad about your school. Honest. I want to go there more than anything!"

Madam C. J. smiled and reached out her hand to shake. "Howdy do, Marjorie Joyner. It's mighty nice to make your acquaintance. There's something I learned a long time ago I want you to always remember . . ."

"I will!" blurted Marjorie.

"Hold your horses, girl. You're jumpin' ahead of me again. What I want you to remember is: 'Don't ever sit and wait for something to happen. Nothing ever happens while you sit. If you want to *get* a start; give *yourself* that start.' "

Madam C. J. Walker reached into a pocket for something and handed it to Marjorie. "Here. You save this for your tuition next month and a little living money while you're in my school."

Marjorie's mouth dropped open, and her hands trembled holding the bill. She raised it up against the sunlight and snapped it in her hands a few times, "Oooweee! I never saw a 20 dollar bill before! Oh, thank you, Mrs. Madam Walker. This is the most money I ever saw at one time in my whole life!"

Marjorie was transfixed by the crisp new bill, and couldn't take her eyes or hands off it as she bounced up and down. "I'll be the best student you ever had, Mrs. Madam C. J. I did good in white ladies' beauty school. But I'll do even better here!"

Sarah reached out and patted the girl's shoulder to calm her down. "I believe you will, Marjorie. I believe you will."

As she sank back dreamily to the steps, Marjorie reached out and lightly rubbed her hand across the cement. "These are the steps to *my* school and to *my* success!" Then she looked up, confused. "If your name is Sarah Breedlove, where did the name 'Madam C. J. Walker' come from?"

"While I lived in Denver, I married again, to Mr. C. J. Walker. That made me Mrs. C. J. Walker. But I thought *Madam* C. J. Walker was a name folks would be more willing to buy from."

After graduating, Marjorie Joyner ran her own salon for eight years. Then she became the National Supervisor for all the Walker Beauty Schools and opened over a dozen schools at colleges across the country.

Sarah Breedlove (Madam C. J. Walker) became the first self-made female millionaire in America. She was also the first self-made black millionaire in the country. At its height, the Madam C. J. Walker Company provided far-above-average working salaries to more than 5,000 black women. Mrs. Walker also tirelessly used her time and her resources to support education for black women, to encourage and create opportunities for black women, and to advance and promote legislation guaranteeing the rights of blacks, women, and especially black women. Few business*men*, no matter how successful, can claim to have done as much. But that is another story.

Questions to Explore

There are four steps to creating an invention: identifying a need; getting an idea for something that will fill that need; developing a working model of that idea, and marketing, or selling, the device to manufacturers and to the public. Which of these four do you think is the hardest?

Which have inventors said was the hardest for them?

References for Further Reading

- *In the Children's Library*

  Bundles, A'Lelia. *Madam C. J. Walker: Entrepreneur*. New York: Chelsea House, 1991.

- *In the Adult Library*

  Lommel, Cookie. *Madam C. J. Walker*. Los Angeles, CA: Melrose Square, 1993.

See your librarian for additional titles.

9

Stories About Visual, Written, and Performing Arts

Second-Best Sister

A story about the sisters Catherine Beecher and Harriet Beecher Stowe and their efforts for abolition and women's rights

About This Story:

Relatively few individuals have been influential enough to have been able to affect the course of America's history. Only a very few of this number come from the same families. Rarest of all are sisters who have each been able to touch the nation in a unique way and change the way it thinks and acts. This is a story of one such pair of sisters, both of whom deserve the attention of whole books.

Two elderly sisters sat in silence at opposite ends of an ornate couch in the sitting room of a plush Washington hotel. Both women were dressed in finery to match the elegance of the hotel, which had successfully resisted the worn and shabby look most hotels had taken on since 100,000 Union soldiers had moved into Washington, and since the Civil War still went poorly for the North in this October of 1862.

Neither sister could quite find the words to bridge the awkward silence between them. But then, neither ever had. There had always been a greater distance between them than just the eleven year difference in their ages.

From her end of the red, crushed-velvet couch, fifty-one-year-old Harriet studied her sister. At sixty-two, Catherine's hair was nearly snow white. But Harriet saw no frailty, no lessening of the charge-ahead, adventuresome, get-it-done spirit that had always possessed Catherine. No, it was something else Harriet felt.

Then it hit her. From the far end of the couch Catherine now looked at her with the same look of longing and yearning with which Harriet had for years gazed at Catherine. It was a look that cried out, "Why should I feel like second-best around her? When will it be my turn?"

Harriet secretly smiled. It felt wonderful to be on the receiving end of that gaze for a change. How could the tables have turned so completely? Harriet's mind drifted back over countless times that same look had covered her own face.

Pictures of their father, Reverend Lyman Beecher, in his Congregational Church in Litchfield, Connecticut, flashed through Harriet's mind. One Sunday morning in particular stood out. Harriet was sixteen that bright spring of 1828. She had worn a pretty new dress. Catherine had neither noticed nor cared. She had been too busy discussing the financing for a new building at her girl's school.

• • •

Father's sermon droned on, as they so often did, enjoining his listeners to apply their talents to God's work, to act now and use their gifts. Catherine sat, looking impatient, as if to say, "Doesn't everybody already do that? Why in heaven's name not?"

Harriet had gazed at her sister with that look, thinking, "Will it ever be my turn to do something important?" At twenty-seven, Catherine had become one of the nation's top female educators. She had started her own successful school for girls. She lectured all over the East. She bubbled with enthusiasm and flowed through life, casually leaving works of brilliance and value swirling in her wake. Harriet thought her sister was far too intelligent and quick to be real flesh and blood.

What had plain, big-nosed Harriet done? "Nothing," she told herself. "I'm shy and quiet, and everyone thinks I'm just a lump."

And that's when that look of envy and yearning filled Harriet's face, as if to shout to her sister, "I have ideas. I have meaningful, passionate feelings. I just can't get them out to others as you can. I don't know what to do with them."

There stood her father, pounding on the pulpit and commanding his flock not to wait, not to make excuses, but to act now to put their talents to work for God's purpose. There sat Catherine smugly overflowing with new ideas on reforming women's education and work, planning to improve the life of every woman in America. Sixteen-year-old Harriet wanted to cry and run from the church in frustration.

• • •

Harriet shifted on the hotel couch and glanced at the gilded wall clock. The carriage would be here soon. Again she smiled. The president's carriage was not coming to pick up Catherine for a trip to the White House. It was coming for her.

Harriet thought back, trying to find the moment when it had changed. She easily remembered when she felt the most desperate, the most ineffective: Cincinnati in the early 1840s. That was the low point for Harriet. It was a time when greatness seemed to flow all about her, but Harriet couldn't grab hold of any herself.

• • •

Catherine was busy revolutionizing the lives of every woman in America in those years. She had concluded that women must professionalize the home just as men had used science and technology to professionalize the workplace. These male efforts were called the "industrial revolution," and had shaken the very fabric of the working world. Catherine said women must do the same at home, and invented such exciting terms as "home science," and "home economics." Women all over the country gushed praises for Catherine. She had forever changed their lives and added pride and dignity to their work.

Every new and lofty idea Catherine had turned into action and into success, while Harriet watched from the sidelines, the simple, uninspiring, and unoriginal wife of Reverend Calvin Stowe, a mother, and part-time teacher at Catherine's school.

The Underground Railroad ran through Cincinnati where the Beecher sisters now lived. Runaway slaves crept through the ghetto alleys, the terror of hunted animals fixed in their eyes. Brave whites and freed blacks daily risked all they had to shelter and aid these slaves along their desperate race to freedom. Harriet was then thirty-two and had gained a passionate belief that slavery was wrong and evil. But what had she done about it? Nothing. But then, what *could* she do?

Harriet could remember sitting in church in Cincinnati in 1843. What was that awful preacher's name? Ah yes, Reverend Lester. His were the most boring sermons Harriet ever heard. She used to drift off into an imaginary world that stirred her soul with grand heroes and noble struggles. To Harriet, those Sunday imagined scenes felt far more real than her drab daily life.

As Reverend Lester rose to the pulpit and rambled into another endless sermon, Harriet sank deeper into her pew and let her imaginary world flow over her. In her mind, she saw a young slave girl of eighteen or nineteen somewhere in Kentucky. The girl was running wildly through frozen thickets and mounded snows. She was running away.

The girl—Harriet decided her name was Eliza—clutched a baby tight to her chest with one arm, the other beating desperately at tangling vines and gouging thorns. Fear and panic shone in her eyes. Poor Eliza was alone, hunted, in a fierce and dangerous winter world.

It was her own baby Eliza carried. She was running away with her baby. The cruel plantation owner had agreed to sell the baby to a plantation in Georgia. So Eliza had run. Her feet pointed north, always north, as she flailed her way through frozen swamp and tangled wood.

Far behind, Eliza could hear the baying of dogs as they picked up her scent. Their howls struck icy shafts of terror through Eliza's heart. Her legs felt leaden after miles of struggling. Her whole being was numb with cold and burning with desperation. They were coming after her, dogs with bared fangs and men with whips and guns. She had to run faster, faster. Her breath came in ragged gulps. Her heart pounded so fiercely it hurt.

Eliza gasped in shock as she broke into the open at the banks of the wide Ohio River. Churning ice floes spun, groaned, and raced downstream with the swift current, thick as a swarm of locust.

Now she could hear horses and the yells of men. They'd nab her in another minute. She had to get away! She had to run. This time it would be her life. But she was trapped at the edge of this frozen river.

Tears of terror freezing to Eliza's cheeks, she stepped onto the nearest of the treacherous blocks of bobbing ice. She gasped as the ice chunk shifted, nearly tumbling her into icy waters. Stumbling, sliding, but always racing north, Eliza leapt from floe to floe, from chunk to chunk, as she raced the desperate course of fools into the very heart of the frozen river, running either to freedom, or to certain death in the swirling cold of the hungry dark waters below.

"There she is!" cried the men back on the bank.

"Shoot her," commanded the owner.

"Run, Eliza! Run!" thought Harriet, fists clenched tight in her pew.

"All rise for a closing hymn," droned Reverend Lester.

Still lost in her imaginary world, Harriet bolted to her feet. "Run, Eliza!" she cried.

Then meek Harriet turned beet-red and her eyes dropped to the floor as everyone turned to stare.

Harriet glanced at Catherine, sitting up in the front row. Her "hurry-this-service-up-I-have-a-lot-of-important-things-to-do" look was chiseled on her face.

Harriet thought, "Slavery is against God's will. I know it is. I know every person in Cincinnati, in all these United States, should be totally opposed to all slavery. If only I could convince them. Why must it always be Catherine who has great ideas, who changes the world, who makes things happen? When will it be my turn?"

• • •

Sixty-two-year-old Catherine took a final sip of tea and set her cup back in its saucer on the table at her end of the couch. "I do not begrudge you your success, Harriet," she said finally. "On the contrary, you have written a great book and have moved a nation. You should be proud. You have had a great impact on our collective consciences. But . . ."

A young couple rushed toward the sisters with nervous giggles. Together they reverently carried a copy of Harriet's book.

"Excuse me, please. But my wife was wondering . . ." the man began.

The woman blushed and giggled again. "You *are* Harriet Beecher Stowe, aren't you?" she asked.

Harriet smiled and nodded.

"I knew it. I just *knew* it," gushed the woman. "I loved *Uncle Tom's Cabin*! I read it three times."

"We *both* think it is the greatest literary work of our time," added her husband. "Would you be so kind as to sign our copy?"

Harriet Beecher Stowe signed her name on the inside cover as the young woman excitedly twirled one of her long curls. Then the couple rushed off with repeated "Thank you's."

Harriet nodded to her sister. "Sorry. But that happens a lot anymore. Please continue."

Catherine took in a deep breath as she re-gathered her thoughts. "You have obviously had a great impact, dear sister. But I feel your sudden fame has come because your book has touched the world of men. Others of us . . ."

A portly man in overcoat and top hat interrupted from a chair across the room. "Excuse me . . ." He had been reading a newspaper when the couple approached Harriet, and had peered around his paper to watch. "Excuse me, but are you really the little lady that's made the whole world buzz about the evils of slavery?"

"The whole *male* world," muttered Catherine under her breath. "Women have been working to rid the world of slavery for a hundred years."

The man shook his head and laughed. "Well, I say, extraordinary writing, madam. You certainly stirred up this man's thinking with that story. They say your book is what really started the Civil War."

"There," snapped Catherine. "That is exactly what I mean. Your book stirred *men's* thinking. If your book had reached only women, you would not be waiting here for the president's carriage so you could traipse off for tea with President Lincoln."

Then she took another deep breath and held up her hands to calm herself. "I apologize, Harriet. That was uncalled for. You richly deserve all the honors and praise you receive. It is just frustrating to see lavish honors heaped upon those who affect the world of men, while those who affect the world of women are ignored. You have done much to make blacks free and equal citizens of this nation, and you deserve your reward. But it is just that so many of us have toiled long years to free the women of this nation and make them real and equal citizens. President Lincoln neither knows, nor cares to know any of our names.

"I have revolutionized the attitudes of American housewives. I made them each a proud professional in her home. No man seems to notice or care. Others fight for the rights of women to own property, be educated, vote, and travel freely. Our work is unheard and unnoticed. When will it be our turn for fanfare, for autographs, for recognition?"

Harriet smiled with warmth and affection and reached out to pat her sister's arm. "Dear Catherine, if I thought it would help, I would give you every accolade I have received, for you have earned them more that I. I am sure your time, and women's time, will come."

Catherine Beecher was not only one of the great female educators of the nineteenth century, she revolutionized the attitude with which American housewives approached their work. She transformed them from unskilled kitchen slaves to professional homemakers. Her "home economics," and "home science" gave housewives a career.

Her little sister, Harriet Beecher Stowe, gave the world shocking and dramatic images and characters that have lived in our conscience for over a century: desperate Eliza, the cruel Simon Legree, proud and noble Uncle Tom, sweet and sickly Eva. Her book swept the world, selling over 600,000 copies the first year. In it she made slavery inescapably tangible to comfortable white people, and forced each reader to take a stand on the issue.

President Lincoln called her, "the little lady that started this big war." He also credited her and her writings with keeping the British from joining the war in support of the South (an act which did more than any battle to win the war for the North). Finally, Lincoln claimed that no literary work had so inflamed a nation since Tom Paine's *Common Sense* in 1776.

Two sisters, each of whom had a profound impact on the development and shape of our country; each of whom asked the same question: "When will it be my turn?" Maybe more of us should ask that same question, and then work with equal vigor to make our time happen. But that's another story.

Questions to Explore

Does every good idea get equal attention from the public? What factors affect whether or not an idea becomes popular?

How do people hear about new ideas today? Is that how ideas have always been spread?

Why do you think Harriet's book caught so much more attention than Catherine's work had?

References for Further Reading

- *In the Children's Library*

  Gerson, Noel. *Harriet Beecher Stowe*. New York: Praeger, 1976.

  Scott, John Anthony. *Woman Against Slavery: The Story of Harriet Beecher Stowe*. New York: Thomas Crowell, 1978.

  Smith, Senator Margaret Chase, and H. Paul Jeffers. *Gallant Women*. New York: McGraw-Hill, 1968.

- *In the Adult Library*

  Adams, John. *Harriet Beecher Stowe*. Bloomington, IN: Indiana University Press, 1989.

  Stowe, Harriet Beecher. *Uncle Tom's Cabin*. Boston: Houghton, Osgoos, 1878.

See your librarian for additional titles.

Pigtails and Buckshot

A story about Annie ("Oakley") Moses, the world's best trick shooter

About This Story:

In the mid-1800s, many parts of western Ohio were still considered part of the "frontier." Small settlements and one-street towns were surrounded by vast tracts of wild and unsettled land.

Life in these small settlement towns tended to organize itself along very traditional roles. Men hunted, farmed, and protected the homestead. Women washed, cleaned, raised the children, and tended garden. Breaking these expected patterns was more than frowned upon.

Still, one teenage girl did exactly that. She supported her family as a hunter, and rose to become a household name across the western world. This is a story about her.

Annie leaned back, resting in her saddle. Her small pinto horse snorted and pawed the ground under her, eager to burst out from this backstage cover.

A tall, slender man with wavy, brown hair ran over wearing fancy western clothes, long leather fringe dangling everywhere. "Annie, Annie! Did you double-check your guns? Is everything loaded and ready?"

Tightly curled ringlets of chestnut hair framed twenty-three-year-old Annie's smiling face. Her cool gray eyes sparkled. "Relax, Frank. I've done this show a thousand times."

"Not *this* show for *this* audience," he answered.

Echoing across the giant stadium, Annie could hear the English accented voice of the royal announcer. "Ladies and gentlemen . . ."

Annie was actually surprised not to feel nervous. She didn't bite her nails. Her heart didn't pound. She had performed these tricks a thousand times. This felt like any other show. It didn't seem to matter that they were on the other side of the ocean.

"Dukes and Earls. Please stand one and all for the Queen!"

Weren't you supposed to feel nervous when you were requested to perform for the Queen of England?

Waiting for the introductions and opening band number, Annie remembered back to the very first time she'd shot in front of a crowd. She hadn't felt nervous then, either.

• • •

The last yellow leaves had fluttered slowly to the ground in the crisp November wind. The blue Ohio River curved in a great crescent around Cincinnati's south side, with the blue hills of Kentucky rising beyond. Viewed from the

263

heights surrounding the sprawling bee-hive city, Cincinnati glowed with the sparkle of gas lamps and rang with music: the clanging bells of steamboats, the steady gongs of buoys, the accordion oompahs rising from the German quarter and evening clubs, the moos and squeals from the sprawling stockyards of "Porkopolis," and the countless clanking chains of the mules pulling barges up and down the Erie Canal.

Standing at the head of Main Street at twilight on November 8th, 1875, the endless sights and sounds of Cincinnati seemed a fairyland to fifteen-year-old Annie Moses. She couldn't tear her eyes away from the spectacle as she clutched at her twenty-three-year-old sister, "Oh, Lydia, it's so big, and bright!"

Lydia scoffed, "*Everything* is big and bright compared to North Star Township."

"Is not," answered Annie, fists on hips. "I like North Star Township."

Lydia shook her head. "North Star is a tiny speck lost in the woods. I moved to the city as soon as I could, and even that was ten years later than I'd have liked."

Lydia's husband, Joe Stein, stood next to her. Their three silhouettes rose against the fading western sky like a human stair step. Tall, lanky Joe stood over six feet. Lydia, in the middle, reached five feet five inches when she stood up straight. Little Annie on the end couldn't top five feet on her tiptoes.

Slowly Annie's dazzled gray eyes clouded. "But Lydia. It's just miles and miles of buildings and houses down there. Where do you gather hickory nuts and sassafras bark?"

Lydia's eyes rolled as she slowly shook her head and sighed. "We buy them at a store, Annie."

Annie wrinkled up her nose and stared suspiciously at her older sister. "You buy something you can get fer free?"

Joe laughed. "Welcome to the city, Annie."

"Annie Moses!" snapped Lydia. "You are a hopeless country hick. You've lived fifteen years in the lost, wild woods, and that's sixteen years too many."

Lydia reached up and fluffed a handful of her sister's thick chestnut hair. "Just look at this. Your hair just . . . lies there."

Annie shrugged. "That's the way it grows."

"You should get it styled while you're visiting here in the city."

Annie laughed. "Livin' in the woods we never heard of styling hair."

"That's my point," said Lydia with a sharp nod of her head. "You look like you dragged the backwoods to town with you. It's like you're wearing a big sign, 'Country hick.' "

And for the first time in her life, Annie Moses glimpsed what she wore through the eyes of polite society: a faded and patched boy's shirt and pants, and her brother's too-big, floppy boots. Her cheeks reddened and she shrugged defensively, "I put shoes on special fer you. Normal, I jes go barefoot. Besides, these clothes are comfortable and better fer walking than a silly ole dress."

"Well, you embarrass me. You're visiting your sister in the city. Try to act decent. And especially, don't drag your gun around like you tried to do this afternoon. Girls don't shoot!"

The remaining shreds of Annie's lighthearted smile evaporated. "It's not a 'gun.' It's a brand new Remington, single-action, repeating rifle." Self-conscious and angry, she added, "And why not carry my rifle? Lots of men do."

Joe laughed. Lydia glared at him and jabbed him with her elbow. "Owww! That hurt."

"Then don't laugh at my sister." She turned to Annie. "You're a fifteen-year-old girl. Girls don't carry rifles in Cincinnati! You've lugged that thing around for eight years and that's ten too many."

Annie pleaded, "But I'm a hunter. That's how I support Mama and the little ones. That's how I paid fer coach fare to get here."

Lydia shook her head solemnly, like a judge passing sentence on the condemned. "Girls don't shoot."

Annie brooded. Her forehead tightened into a mass of wrinkles. She had heard those words before, not more than a month ago. Tramping barefoot into the small town of Greenville in western Ohio, her callused feet shuffling through the dust, she had proudly hoisted a rich bundle of furs over one shoulder. Her gleaming rifle swung over the other with a thick roll of marsh grass dangling underneath.

"Hey, Annie Moses, what you bring me?" called Frenchie La Motte with his donkey laugh from the porch of his fur trading shop. His eyes and hands were always moving, darting this way and that, his clay pipe always clamped between his teeth.

"Mostly beaver, Mr. La Motte, and some muskrat," she'd called back.

Next door, Charlie Katzenberger had stepped out of the swinging double doors of the Katzenberger Brother's General Store wiping his hands on his stained white apron. "Annie. Did you bring pigeons and quail? The hotel I supply for needs both."

"Two dozen, Mr. Katzenberger. In this roll of marsh grass to keep 'em fresh."

He'd warily crossed his arms. "None of the meat's damaged with shot, is it, Annie?"

Frenchie let loose his loud, braying laugh. "What you talkin' 'bout, Charlie? That's Annie Moses. She never brought in a bird wasn't shot clean, through the head. She's the only one in the county who can shoot that good."

Annie had swelled with pride. And then it happened. Two of Greenville's society women stepped out of the dry goods shop, their long dresses sweeping the ground, their laced-up bodices forcing their torsos stiff and straight. One of the women glared down her long nose, curled her lip and said those same words. "Girls don't shoot, young Miss Moses. You look ridiculous and should be ashamed."

Her friend sneered, "Some girls obviously don't know how to be girls."

Then they haughtily brushed past Annie with a "Humph!" instead of a "How do you do?"

Annie had been left in the dust of Greenville's Broadway Street feeling ashamed.

Gazing down over the twinkling twilight lamps of Cincinnati from the top of Main Street next to Joe and her sister, Annie tasted that same bitter shame, as if something was very wrong with her, and she was the only one who didn't know what or why.

Lydia merrily squeezed her arm around Annie's shoulders. "Don't you worry, little sis. This very night we're going to fix you up good and proper."

"Fix me up how?" asked Annie.

Joe's face lit up. "Vine Street."

"Perfect!" exclaimed Lydia, locking arm in arm with her husband on one side, and sister on the other. "Dress shops, restaurants, clubs. We'll make a whole night of it!"

German music flowed from the bright clubs lining the canal: the Pacific Gardens, the Melodeon, Schuler's, Wielert's, the Coliseum. Sparkling gowns glowed in the flicker of soft gas lamps in dress shop windows.

Annie stopped, cocking her head. "I hear shooting."

Joe pointed down around the corner. "It's the Germania Schuetzen Association in the beer garden. They're crazy about target shooting."

Annie's face lit up. "Can we go?"

Joe shook his head. "But we could swing over to Charlie Stuttelberg's."

Lydia held up both hands. "No! Girls don't shoot, and Annie has got to start acting like a girl."

Joe smiled and twirled his wife around on the sidewalk. "Don't be a spoilsport. Just this once. It'll be fun."

Stuttelberg's shooting gallery was empty when Joe, Lydia, and Annie came in. Charlie, himself, sat reading a newspaper in one corner.

Joe lifted one of the target rifles. "I'm a pretty good shot. I'll show you what to do." He squeezed off six shots. Three miniature metal ducks in the nearest row of seven collapsed backwards.

He handed the gun to Annie. "You try it. Oh, wait, maybe I should let you use a smaller one."

Annie snatched the heavier, longer rifle, weighed it in her hand, and sighted down the barrel. "Do they give prizes?"

Without glancing up from his evening paper, Stuttelberg said, "No charge if you ring the bell five times."

"What bell?" Annie asked.

"Center of the farthest bull's eye," continued Charlie's bored monotone as he sat, still lost to sight behind his *Cincinnati Post*.

"Go for the ducks I shot," said Joe, pointing to the front row of targets. "That bull's eye is way too far away."

Annie swung the gun to her shoulder. Bong! The gleaming metal speck of a bull's eye rang.

Charlie glanced over the top of his paper.

Joe nodded, impressed. "Lydia said you hunted some. But I never thought you'd hit . . ."

Annie pumped in a new shell and fired fast, shot after shot. Bong! Bong! Bong! Bong! Bong! Bong! It sounded like a fire alarm bell clanging at the far end of the gallery.

Annie laid the gun back on the counter of the gallery and nodded. "Not a bad rifle. Pulls a might to the left, though."

Mouths dropped open, Joe and Lydia stared at the distant, still-vibrating bell.

Charlie dropped his newspaper and stumbled from his stool. Rushing over, he grabbed another rifle. "Do that again. No charge."

Annie swung the rifle to her shoulder and fired six shots. Six tin quail in the very last row went down like a row of dominoes on their moving metal track. Annie smiled, " 'Course, real quail are a lot harder to hit than tin ones."

Charlie Stuttelberg stared, dumbfounded at the missing quail as he lifted another gun. "Do the bell again," he ordered.

Annie shrugged. "Won't be any harder the second time than the first." Up swung the rifle. Bong! Bong! Bong! Bong! Bong! Bong!

The last ringing "Bong!" of the bell slowly faded into silence as Charlie rubbed his chin and stared at the petite girl before him. Her foot tapped to the beat of a German polka across the street, her thick chestnut hair flowed over her shoulders. "You don't look like a marksman. Where'd you learn to shoot?"

Lydia interrupted. "I know. She's a girl, and girls aren't supposed to shoot guns. I've been trying to get her to stop . . ."

"Stop?" bellowed Charlie. "This girl's a natural. She's got a gift. She's something special!"

Annie shrugged. "When it feels right, I just squeeze the trigger."

Charlie Stuttelberg slid another rifle down the counter to Annie and rummaged underneath for a deck of cards. He snatched one card, the five of diamonds, walked to the back wall, and tacked it up near the ceiling. "See if you can hit that card, little lady."

Annie swung the rifle to her shoulder and fired five quick shots.

Charlie walked the card back to the counter with trembling hands. Each of the five diamonds on the card had been neatly shot away. He held it up to show the small crowd that had gathered at the door. In a hoarse whisper he gasped, "I never seen anything like it in my life. She's better'n Frank Butler."

"If you don't mind, I'd rather shoot with my own rifle next time," said Annie. "Frenchie La Motte rebuilt the sights just right."

"Who's Frank Butler?" asked Lydia.

"Just the best professional shooter in these whole United States," answered Joe. "He does shows at the Coliseum."

"Butler's never been beat," said someone in the crowd.

"I'll put 50 dollars on the girl," shouted someone else.

"So will I," added Charlie Stuttelberg.

A procession made its way down Vine to the Coliseum Club, where Frank Butler usually held court in the evenings. Charlie Stuttelberg slapped a 100 dollar bill on Frank's table. "I got a crack shot from Drake County. This hundred says you'll lose."

Butler's blue eyes twinkled. "Bring him on. I'm always ready to win money from you, Charlie."

"Not him," smiled Charlie. "*Her*." And he pointed at Annie.

Frank Butler was a tall man and almost fell out of his seat. "*Her*? She's too small to lift a gun. Besides, she's a girl. Girls don't shoot."

Annie stamped her foot. "I can *too* shoot, and just maybe a darn sight better'n you."

Butler rose, towering over the tiny bundle of fire and conviction that was Annie. "At the Fairmont Shooting Club. Tomorrow. Three o'clock sharp."

Without another word he turned and left.

The Fairmont sat at the top of Shooter's Hill. Spectators crowded into every open spot up and down the slope. Frank Butler arrived by carriage wearing a blue-eyed smile, a belted shooting coat, and a green felt hat with a feather.

Annie Moses walked up the hill in a dress Lydia had insisted she wear, her hair braided with pink bows. She was given her choice of guns from the club's rack. She chose one with a long, polished barrel and sighted down it's length.

Frank Butler took his stance at the firing line. "Pull!" he called.

A spring-loaded catapult hurled a clay disk, called a pigeon, high into the air and far down the field.

Blam! First Frank's gun, and then the clay pigeon exploded.

"Dead!" cried the referee, signaling a hit. The crowd applauded.

Annie stepped to the line. "What did you say to get them to throw a disk? Pull?"

Twang! At the mention of that word the disk whined into the Ohio sky. Annie's gun still rested in the crook of her arm; she was not at all ready to shoot.

Frank Butler began to protest, demanding that she be given a second chance.

But whiplash fast, Annie spun her rifle to her shoulder and locked her cheek against the stock. Blam!

"Dead!" cried the referee.

Lydia, Joe, and Charlie Stuttelberg screamed support from the front row. The crowd roared.

Frank stared in awe at the pigtailed wisp of a girl next to him. Could he have made that shot? He wasn't at all sure. This girl was something.

Annie shrugged. "These clay pigeons fly a lot slower than real ones."

Butler tightened his grip on his rifle and turned back to the line. "Pull!"

Blam!

"Dead!"

The crowd cheered

It was Annie's turn again. And she realized that she wasn't the least bit nervous. She should have been, shooting against the best shot in America in front of this huge crowd in a funny-feeling dress instead of her regular clothes. She had every right to be. But she wasn't. She felt calm, relaxed, and confident.

"Pull!" Blam! "Dead!"

"Pull!" Blam! "Dead!"

"Pull!" Blam! "Dead!"

• • •

"You're on next, Miss Oakley. The Queen's just taking her seat," called the English stage manager, scurrying back and forth behind the curtain.

The crowd cheered and cheered as an orchestra played "God Save the Queen" and the Queen of England took her seat. The announcer's voice rolled over the standing-room-only crowd in Earl's Court, London. "And now the star of the Wild West Show, Miss Annie Oakley!"

Annie was calm and relaxed. Having her guns at her side always made her feel that way. She dug her spurs into the pinto's sides, let out a sharp whoop, and charged, pig-tails flying, into the arena. Five seconds and six quick shots later, all six candles on a rotating wooden disk in center ring went out. The crowd roared. Another show had begun.

After beating Frank Butler twenty-five pigeons to twenty-four on that November afternoon in 1875, Annie Moses rose quickly to be recognized as the best shooter in America. Using the name Annie Oakley, she thrilled most of the crowned heads of Europe. She shot against and beat the Archduke of Russia, supposedly the best shot on the Continent.

Annie could routinely make shots no one else could make at all. She had an incredible gift, a talent, and enough show business flare to be a true world-class entertainer.

Far more importantly, Annie refused to listen to family, neighbors, and a society all eager to tell her what a girl couldn't and shouldn't do. Their customs and moral codes said it was wrong for Annie, a girl, to practice shooting a gun. Women weren't supposed to do that. Annie refused to listen. She was good, she knew it, and she wouldn't give up. As a result, she became the best known trick shooter in the world.

So where did the name "Oakley" come from? It was the name of a town where Annie Moses performed with Frank Butler during the summer of 1877. Annie liked the town, she liked the name, and she liked the shows they performed there. It's also where Annie and Frank were married. But that's another story.

Questions to Explore

Do you think there are things boys should do but girls should not? What are they? Why do you believe this?

Can you think of things girls should do but boys shouldn't?

Do people in other countries think the same as you? What about people in other times?

Annie learned to use a gun from necessity, she had to help feed her family. How much of a role do you think necessity has in changing society's opinions about gender roles? Can you think of modern examples?

References for Further Reading

- *In the Children's Library*

   Bennett, Wayne, ed. *Women Who Dared to Be Different*. Champaign, IL: Garrard, 1973.

   Quackenbush, Robert. *Who's that Girl with the Gun: A Story of Annie Oakley*. New York: Prentice-Hall, 1987.

- *In the Adult Library*

   Havighurst, Walter. *Annie Oakley of the Wild West*. Lincoln, NE: University of Nebraska Press, 1954.

   Kasper, Shirl. *Annie Oakley*. Norman, OK: University of Oklahoma Press, 1992.

See your librarian for additional titles.

A Pen for the Pain

A story about Elizabeth Cochran Seamen ("Nellie Bly") and her work as an undercover reporter

About This Story:

As America roared toward the twentieth century, there was building and bustling everywhere, cities bulged at the seams and buildings poked higher and higher, until they fairly scraped the sky. It was a time overflowing with energy and optimism. A seemingly endless supply of land stretched out to the west, and there were endless opportunities for any who would reach out and snatch them up. Everything seemed good today and promised to be better tomorrow.

Overlooked and ignored by this great forward rush were those in need. None were either more in need, or more ignored, than the mentally ill, urban poor. The "hospitals" built to care for them looked and acted more like medieval dungeons. Their "care" often amounted to no more than being locked away and forgotten.

One reporter ripped away the veil of secrecy surrounding New York's dismal treatment of the mentally ill poor, and shocked a nation into action on their behalf. This reporter also happened to be America's first woman newspaper reporter. This is a story about her.

Clang! The echo of the steel door slamming reverberated up and down the stark cement hall. Suddenly the woman felt trapped, hemmed in, unable to breathe.

"Quit gawkin' and start movin'." The orderly in dingy whites roughly jabbed her with his nightstick and laughed as Elizabeth cried out in pain and fear. Her own cry seemed to disappear in the flood of moans, wails, and sobs that poured from every metal cage along the hallway.

Fear rose in her. Her heart pounded as if it would burst. In an effort to control her growing sense of panic, Elizabeth Cochran softly repeated to herself as she was shoved toward the cage that would be her home, "I am not crazy. I will get out. I am not crazy. I will get out."

But her mind couldn't focus on the words. All she heard were the jangling keys of the orderly. They almost played a tune as he stomped down the hall behind her. It was a tune that filled Elizabeth with fear.

Just days ago this had seemed a lark. Elizabeth, whose pen name was Nellie Bly, called it a "madcap" adventure to her friends. It had seemed somehow glamorous when she'd presented the idea to Mr. Pulitzer, her editor at *The World,* a major New York newspaper.

But as Elizabeth was flung into a ten-by-fifteen-foot cage with thick metal bars, any remaining intrigue and glamour evaporated. Here, locked in this zoo cage with three other women, Elizabeth felt only terror and a deep longing to see the light of day. Getting her scoop story was forgotten.

"This is all a mistake," pleaded Elizabeth. "I have to get out of here right away."

Again the orderly laughed. "This is Blackwell Island State Hospital, lady. Once you're here, you never get out."

Suddenly lacking the strength to stand, Elizabeth collapsed into a tight ball in one corner. "I am not insane. I will get out. I am not insane. I will get out."

Three other women shared Elizabeth's "room." Two shuffled back and forth with vacant stares, mumbling to themselves. The third, a stringy-haired and sickly looking woman even younger than Elizabeth, squatted in front of Elizabeth peering at her, and would alternate between a screamed cackle and a sobbing whimper.

To reassure herself, Elizabeth recited the facts to her predicament. "My pen name is Nellie Bly. My real name is Elizabeth Cochran. I am twenty-four years old and a new reporter for *The World* newspaper. My editor is Joseph Pulitzer. Today is October 18, 1888. I am here to get an inside scoop about how poor, mentally ill women are treated in this city. Mr. Pulitzer will get me out in one week. I am not crazy. He will get me out."

Elizabeth tried to smile at the poor woman squatting before her. "Hello, my name is Elizabeth. What's yours?" The woman only stared and moaned.

"Are you hurt?" asked Elizabeth, becoming concerned. "Do you need to see a doctor?"

The reply came from the next cage-like room. "She never talks. Just stares."

Elizabeth turned to find an alarmingly thin, white-haired woman with deep set, hollow eyes smiling at her. "But she's all right. Good thing too, 'cause these doctors wouldn't come even if she were dying."

Elizabeth was shocked. "But don't the doctors take care of you?"

A thin laugh escaped around the old woman's black and rotting teeth. To Elizabeth it sounded very sad. "We're poor here. To fancy doctors, we're not worth caring for. They just keep us stuffed away cheap and out of everyone's way till we pass on. Oh, and my name's Sarah."

Elizabeth realized this woman didn't sound crazy at all. "Why are you here, Sarah?" she asked.

The woman shrugged. "I'm old and I'm poor. I got no family to take care of me. In this city being old, poor, and helpless is a crime. If you're a man, you go to jail. If you're a woman, they say you're crazy and send you here."

"Quiet!" The voice boomed down the hall and made Elizabeth jump. Then she heard the keys jangling their tune of fear. Elizabeth shivered.

"Ah, dinner's comin'," whispered Sarah.

A gruff orderly unlocked the cage door and shoved a plate at each of the women. On each was a cup of thin tea, five prunes, and a piece of bread with a thin smear of rancid butter.

"That's it?" exclaimed Elizabeth.

"Quiet!" growled the orderly.

A small spider crawled out of Elizabeth's bread. The tea tasted like dishwater. Elizabeth couldn't make herself eat any of it.

" 'Bout average," whispered Sarah with a satisfied nod as she munched a prune.

Deep inside, Elizabeth's fear suddenly turned to anger. From her research, she knew that state law required that adequate care and housing be given to all mental hospital patients and that Blackwell Island Hospital was well paid by the city to feed, house, and care for New York City's poor, mentally ill women. But it was now painfully clear to Elizabeth that very little of that money was ever used to help the patients. *But it will be once I'm through with this place*, she thought.

Elizabeth glanced toward the next cage and found Sarah studying her. The old woman shook her head. "You're young and pretty, and you're not one bit crazy. How did you get here?"

Nellie smoldered with indignation over the horrid way Blackwell Island cared for its patients. "I'm an undercover reporter," she whispered. "I'm going to tell the world what really goes on in here."

Sarah chuckled and shrugged. "My mistake. You *are* crazy."

"No, I'm not," insisted Elizabeth. "I really am a reporter. I'm Nellie Bly."

Sarah's eyes widened. "You got yerself in here on purpose?" Then she grinned and nodded. "Very brave. But no one cares what happens to us in here."

"Oh, they'll care, all right," answered Elizabeth.

"Quiet!" The orderly slammed his nightstick against the bars. Elizabeth screamed and jumped. Her heart raced.

After dinner, attendants herded the women into freezing baths. Elizabeth's teeth chattered and her lips turned blue. Then they were locked in tiny individual cells for the night. A deep chill filled Elizabeth's room. Her bed was rock hard. She had a thin mattress and one threadbare blanket to protect her from the cold. *If it's this bad in October*, thought Elizabeth, *how could any woman survive here in January?*

Elizabeth Cochran lay back on her bed, staring at the bars on her window and at the heavy metal cell door, and she thought back over this incredible day. Her stomach rumbled from hunger. She shivered from cold. She trembled from fear of the brutal orderlies.

Then she smiled. "You must be very brave," Sarah had said. Now Elizabeth added, "Very brave or very crazy."

But then, this wasn't the first time she had done something both brave and foolhardy. Three years before, at twenty-one, Elizabeth Cochran had bravely barged into the editor's office of the *Pittsburgh Dispatch* and demanded a chance to write. To her great surprise, after he scanned several examples of her writing, George Madden had given her a trial article.

Elizabeth wrote a forceful and heartfelt argument that women should not be forced into marriage, that they should be allowed to have meaningful careers, and that they should be allowed to divorce abusive husbands.

George Madden read the piece and nodded. "Very well written. But plenty of people will hate you when I publish this."

An assistant editor walked past Madden's office whistling a Stephen Foster tune about a girl named . . .

"Nellie Bly!" shouted Madden. "That'll be your pen name, so you can write, and folks can't track you down."

Elizabeth nodded. "Nellie Bly will do nicely—as long as it comes with a full-time job and a paycheck."

With that agreement, the *Pittsburgh Dispatch* made Elizabeth Cochran America's first female news reporter. The year was 1885.

Elizabeth also remembered bursting into the office of Joseph Pulitzer, editor of *The World*, when she'd first moved to New York City earlier that year. She told him she wanted to work for *The World*.

He told her to leave. She refused. He tried to throw her out. Elizabeth gripped her chair and refused to leave.

He barked that he'd have her arrested. She said she'd write a great exposé about being dragged out of his office and sell it to all his competitors.

He said that there was no room for a female reporter at *The World*. Elizabeth held tight to her chair and said it was about time he made room.

And now she was on her first assignment as an undercover reporter for *The World*. Her first task had been to get herself committed to Blackwell Island. Elizabeth rented a room in a cheap boarding house and then pretended fits of total memory loss until the landlady called the police. The police called a doctor, who took one look at Elizabeth's behavior and at her tattered clothes and committed her to Blackwell Island on the spot.

Just before Elizabeth drifted into a fitful sleep, she whispered to herself, "As soon as Mr. Pulitzer gets me out of here, I'll write an article that will have the whole country enraged at the conditions in this place. Just as soon as he gets me out."

The next morning, each woman was herded back into the central cages for a breakfast even more meager than the previous night's dinner. "How could anyone survive on this diet?" wondered Elizabeth.

One of the women in the next cage lay on the cement floor shivering, her clothes were wet with sweat. She called out over and over to go home. Two orderlies burst into the cage and yelled at her to "Shut up!" When she didn't, they slapped her.

Elizabeth was outraged. "She's sick. Find a doctor," she said.

One of the orderlies spun around, an angry snarl on his face. "Quiet!"

Elizabeth couldn't tolerate such abuse. "I am a reporter," she announced. "You treat her properly or you will be the lead in my article for *The World* newspaper."

Both orderlies laughed. "Yeah, and I'm Napoleon. Now quiet, or you're next."

Elizabeth burst into tears of helpless rage and frustration. The sound of the orderlies' keys drove desperate fear deep into her heart.

When Elizabeth finally opened her eyes, she looked from cage to cage and saw reflected in the face of every other woman there the same feeling that had descended on her: utter, lost hopelessness.

"This is no hospital," she said out loud. "There is no healing or caring here. This is no better than the city pound where lost dogs are crammed together, waiting their turn to die." Then her eyes hardened. "But I will stop it! As soon as I get out, I will."

Sarah slowly shook her old head and cackled. "You tell 'em, girl. But remember, nobody cares about poor, sick women."

"I do," said Elizabeth. "And if I do, others will."

Elizabeth's second and third days dragged by with the same starvation diet, the same numbing cold, the same brutal atmosphere of fear, and the same dulling routine. Elizabeth began to wonder how long a sane woman could survive here without being driven crazy. She found that by the fourth day, she paced constantly, back and forth across her cage. By the fifth day she found herself carrying on long conversations with people who weren't there. By the sixth, she bit her nails, chewing them so fiercely they bled.

"Sarah," she hissed through the bars. "How do you keep your sanity in this horrid place?"

"It's the only thing I got left," answered the old woman with a shrug. "I don't dare lose the last thing I got."

By Elizabeth's seventh day at Blackwell Island, it felt that she'd been here all her life. Then something clicked way back in her mind. The seventh day. Mr. Pulitzer was supposed to get her out today.

Elizabeth paced extra fast across her cement cage all day, anxious to see her publisher's friendly face. Lunch came and went. The afternoon drifted by in endless pacing and nail-biting.

Dinner arrived as the last rays of day faded from the walls. Panic began to rise through Elizabeth. Something had gone wrong. Pulitzer hadn't come.

By noon of the eighth day, Elizabeth began to scream, "I don't belong here. Let me out! I don't belong here!"

The orderlies yelled and banged on her cage. When she wouldn't stop, they locked her in one of the little sleeping cells. By nightfall, Elizabeth's hope faded from a steady beacon to a dim glow, and then flickered out like a snuffed-out match. Dark closed in tight around her.

Elizabeth never heard a sound as sweet as the voice of Mr. Pulitzer's lawyer on the afternoon of her tenth day saying there had been a snag, but that he had finally signed all the papers and she was free to leave.

Elizabeth never saw a sight as sweet as that late afternoon sun sinking low over the Manhattan skyline. She gulped in huge breaths of the sweet, fresh air of freedom, her energy and anger rekindling brighter and brighter with every breath.

"I've got a carriage to take you to your apartment," said the lawyer.

"No!" commanded Elizabeth, her eyes and heart on fire. "There are too many women still in there. Take me to *The World* office. I have writing to do."

Before the presses had been cleaned from printing Nellie Bly's scathing page one article, the clamor began. Citizens were outraged. The mayor demanded an explanation. The governor launched an investigation.

The director of Blackwell Island Hospital and several staff doctors were fired. A system of cruel abuse and neglect began to change. Care, feeding, and treatment of the patients improved. Nellie Bly was an instant hero and star reporter.

America's first woman reporter in articles, editorials, and undercover assignments successfully attacked many of the great social injustices of her time. For this work she well deserves both fame and our thanks. However, her real fame didn't arrive until she challenged a fictional character, Phileas Fogg, to a race. In Jules Verne's book, *Around the World in Eighty Days*, Fogg had circumnavigated the world in eighty days. Nellie decided she could do better. She made it in seventy-two days. But that is another story.

Questions to Explore

Nellie Bly lied and deceived officials of New York City and State to gain access to Blackwell Island State Hospital and get her story. Do you think it's okay for reporters to do whatever they have to do to get an important story? Even break the law?

What kind of story would be that important? What wouldn't you let reporters do to get a story?

How do you think we should balance the public's right to know with individual rights and with national security?

Can you find stories about times when a reporter went too far in trying to get a story? Can you find stories about times when a reporter broke the law to get a story, and the end result was considered "good?"

Also, after the work of Dorothea Dix and others, laws existed mandating humane care for the mentally ill. How did Blackwell Island get away with mistreating its patients? Has such mistreatment happened elsewhere? Where and by whom?

References for Further Reading

- *In the Children's Library*

  Bennett, Wayne, ed. *Women Who Dared to Be Different.* Champaign, IL: Garrard, 1973.

  Quackenbush, Robert. *Stop the Presses, Nellie's Got a Scoop.* New York: Simon & Schuster, 1992.

- *In the Adult Library*

  Kroeger, Brooke. *Nellie Bly: Daredevil, Reporter, Feminist.* New York: Random House, 1994.

See your librarian for additional titles.

Chance to Dance

A story about Isadora Duncan, who was America's first modern dancer

About This Story:

Formal dance in the nineteenth century was almost always a very stiff, structured form of ballet with elaborate costumes and formal, stylized movements. It was an art form locked in the chains of tradition, needing to break free. Freedom came in the person of a lone American dancer. This is a story about her.

I first saw her dance in my hometown of Budapest, Hungary, in May, 1903. It was a performance that changed my life. All my beliefs about dance were exploded. I was left forever enriched and enchanted. I have watched many dancers and many dances. I have seen the best companies, choreographers, and ballerinas in Europe. They were good. They were talented. They displayed precise and exquisite technique.

But never has anyone shaken my very soul until I watched Isadora Duncan. I am Alexander Gross, an impresario, or producer, of ballet and opera events.

Why did I go to the opera house that night? I suppose I thought it would be a lark, a chance to see this American oddity they called "the California fawn." There are no serious dancers or dance companies in America. How could a new sensation arise from that artistic desert across the Atlantic?

Perhaps I went because of the scandalous talk of her dance costume—bare arms clear to the shoulder, and bare legs to the knee! Even bare feet! No tights, no corset. That alone was shocking enough to make the evening's journey worthwhile.

And then she danced—with no scenery, no elaborate costume, no supporting company, no partner. Just Isadora in her Greek gown, flowing and gliding in gauzy veils of fabric. To me it appeared as if a dryad from Mount Olympus had awakened to dance a magical dream. Others dance *to* the music. She unites with the music, becomes the music. With just the rhythmic, graceful movements of her arms, legs, head, and body, she showed me what the music meant.

She danced to Mendelssohn's "A Welcome to Spring." I could see the brilliant flowers, soaring birds, and lambs at play. I understood how they reveled in this first warm, sunny day of spring. I saw how it made them rejoice.

Then I realized these emotions, these feelings, had been in the music all along. But I was unable to see them, to feel them, to understand them, until Isadora expressed each one in her dance.

Traditional ballet dancers use stiff gesture or pantomime to signify the words of a song. A dancer might point to her head to signify "the prince." Then she'd point to her eye to mean "has seen," then pull both hands to her heart "the

277

girl he loves," point to the floor to mean "here," and finally spread both hands overhead to mean "this evening." Isadora simply, naturally becomes what the music is written about. By comparison ordinary ballet moves appear dull and lifeless.

Then Isadora danced to a poem. As I watched, the words took form and motion. They became charged with electric energy and flow. The poem took life. "If I were a bird, I would soar with clouds . . ." I could feel the desire for flight, the frustration of being earthbound, the need to break free.

Isadora used none of the rigid, artificial movements and exaggerated postures ballet dancers have perfected over the centuries. She let her body swirl, flow, run, slide, frolic, whirl, float, slither, creep, soar, and slide as the music directed her.

She closed with a passionate dance to Strauss's "The Blue Danube," the river that winds through the heart of Budapest, the river that is our heartbeat and soul. But I had never really known or cared for the river until I saw it through Isadora's dance. Watching her flow with rippling arms across the stage, I could see, smell, hear, and feel our beloved river better and more deeply than when I'd stood on its shore.

Words cannot describe the magic she performed. I could see from the yearning in the eyes around me that everyone was touched as I was. Our standing ovation lasted for twenty minutes. People cheered, wept, and screamed for more.

I was so moved, so shaken by her performance, I did not trust my legs to hold me up until the theater had nearly emptied. I couldn't just leave that magical event and walk into the cool Budapest night as if this were an ordinary performance, an ordinary May evening. I had to meet this genius.

I forced my way backstage, past theater ushers posted at the stage apron, claiming, as an impresario, to be arranging a tour for Isadora. A sea of people were wedged into the small backstage area and corridor to the dressing rooms. The din from hundreds of voices all cheering, screeching, screaming to be heard over the others made my ears ring. My eyes watered from the intense fragrance of pile after pile of expensive bouquets, tossed in loving admiration onto the stage at concert's end, and now being swept roughly into higher and higher heaps by the janitor's push broom.

A young woman just ahead of me successfully begged and poked her way through the crowd toward the star's dressing room. I stepped up tight behind her, and was sucked along, unseen, in her wake.

Two scowling brutes blocked the dressing room door, letting no one through. "I'm Isadora's sister, Elizabeth," she yelled into one guard's ear. He grunted and inched to one side so she could squeeze past. I slid through behind her, smiling broadly and pointing at the other woman as the guard reached out to block me. "I'm with Elizabeth," I yelled. After a moment's hesitation, he shrugged and let me pass before re-blocking the door.

Elizabeth joined her and Isadors's mother by the bright makeup table. I pressed my back to the wall and crept away from the door, unnoticed, as all eyes were locked on twenty-five-year-old Isadora.

Isadora sat on the arm of a long, ornate couch. More than thirty starry-eyed young people crowded at her feet gazing with love and admiration as their hero lectured them on movement and the body. Family and older friends perched on chairs and counters beyond this tight-packed circle.

Her smooth, brown hair, which had been worn up on top of her head for the recital, now flowed gracefully to her shoulders. Isadora's was a delicate face: soft blue eyes, small mouth, slightly upturned pug nose. But my first impression at this close distance was not of her beauty. All else was overwhelmed by her supreme, unshakable self-confidence, by her uncompromising belief that she was right, and the whole rest of the dance world was wrong.

"Dance is movement art based on nature," she said as I entered, answering some student's question. "Do not look to music to learn about rhythm. Go to the ocean and learn from the waves. Don't dance *to* music. *Experience* the music, and dance your experience. Dance to express the experience of your being, your life."

As she spoke, each movement of finger, arm, or eyelash seemed perfectly and gracefully chosen to accent and explain her words. Even here, sitting on a couch, her body danced as if each moment had been carefully choreographed and rehearsed.

Rising to her feet, pacing along the couch, she continued, "Motion cannot be taught straining at a balance bar in some smelly, horrid studio with glaring mirrors all round. Study motion from bees, and clouds, and wind."

The dressing room door opened again and a waiter staggered in with trays of food and drink. The roar from outside flooded the room. I missed the next question from the ring of students. The door slammed shut as Isadora began her answer.

"No, no, no. The center of motion is not at the base of the spine as ballet would falsely teach. It is here in the chest. Move forward with the front of the chest and all else naturally follows. It is the same with gravity. Awkward and ugly ballet leaps, points, and twirls pretend to conquer gravity. They cannot and so look ridiculous. Use gravity. Use your connection to the floor. Step, run, even jump. But always know your base is the floor, and gravity is what gives you that base."

Some college-aged friends suggested that they spend the rest of the evening dancing at local nightclubs. Isadora's mother cried, "No, Isadora. You need to rest."

With an impulsive giggle, Isadora and a dozen of her followers slipped out a window to avoid the crowd in the hall and were swallowed up by the dark for a night of dancing on tables, chairs, and bars.

Such an odd combination, I thought. This brilliant artist is totally focused on, and dedicated to her dance. And yet, she seems forever controlled by the whims and impulsive fancies of each individual moment. Maybe, I decided, that is the key to her magic after all.

I followed Isadora to Berlin where she was scheduled to perform next. It seemed I could not rest until I had seen her weave her magic again. Outside the massive Kroll Opera House early in the afternoon of Isadora's evening performance, I saw Elizabeth Duncan, her sister, leaving by a side entrance. Impulsively, I rushed over and introduced myself. "May I speak with you about Isadora as you walk?" I asked. "She has totally captivated me."

Twenty-one-year-old Elizabeth smiled shyly and shrugged. "She does that to everyone." Elizabeth turned down WilhelmStrasse toward the market district. "You may walk with me if you like."

We passed fashionable clothing stores and ornate office buildings. Newfangled automobiles puttered down the street, happy drivers blaring aoogha horns that frightened the horses. I asked, "Where did Isadora come from? How did she suddenly appear in Budapest as an overnight wonder?"

Elizabeth laughed. "Overnight? You are very funny. For ten years our family has teetered on the edge of starvation, barely able to survive on the little money brought in by Isadora's dancing, waiting for your 'overnight' success."

"Ten years?" I stammered. "How is that possible?"

"First in San Francisco where father left us, then in Chicago, New York, London, and finally Paris; in every city, Isadora would proclaim, 'This is the city that will recognize my talent.' She would manage to land a few private recitals in high society parlors that paid little or nothing. The rest of her time, she either studied Greek statues, figures, and writings or danced in studios, parks, streets, or beaches.

"The four of us—Mother, Isadora, me, and brother Raymond—lived in tiny, damp flats, because there was never any money. We'd move constantly to avoid being thrown out when mother couldn't pay rent. All we carried from place to place were a few clothes and our piano. Eventually, Isadora would scrounge financing for a local stage performance.

"And always the critics would ridicule her work, her look, her costume, her style, her everything. Isadora never cared. She didn't just *think* she'd be a star, she *knew* she'd be a star. Each review that said otherwise (and they all did) was obviously written by someone who didn't know what he was talking about. Isadora knew with absolute certainly that she was right and thousands of ballet dancers and critics around the world were wrong."

Elizabeth and I reached the busy market district with its pungent aroma of countless shops baking, cooking, preparing food for a hungry Berlin. Elizabeth happily plunked item after item into her wide shopping basket. "It's so nice after Isadora has a good show. For a few weeks we have money to buy whatever food we want."

I asked, "Has Isadora always been so sure of herself, and so set in her views?"

Again Elizabeth laughed, a light and carefree sound. "Even as a child. I was too young to remember. But I have heard the story often. When Isadora was ten, Mother enrolled her in a ballet class. In the middle of her first session the teacher angrily clapped her hands to stop the class. 'Stop, stop, stop! What, child, are you doing?'

" 'I'm being a cloud,' answered Isadora, 'because that's what the music is about.'

" 'The music is about ballet,' snapped the teacher, 'and you are being a pest!'

"Isadora was sent home early.

"During the third lesson, the teacher told everyone to rise up on their toes. Everyone did except Isadora. She asked, 'Why?'

" 'Because it's beautiful, and it's important.'

" 'It's ugly and unnatural,' answered Isadora. 'This isn't dance. This is stiff and commonplace gymnastics.'

"And she stormed out, never to return."

Elizabeth laughed again as she finished her story, and then she took her shopping back to the theater. I went to my hotel to await the beginning of the evening's performance.

That evening the immense Kroll Opera House overflowed with spectators: the devoted, the curious, and the skeptical. The highlight of the two-hour performance came when Isadora presented her new masterpiece, "The Dance of the Future," based on a fifteenth century painting, "Primavera" (Spring). The soft, subtle, and marvelous movements of the birth of spring came to life before our eyes.

The Kroll Opera House rocked with thunderous shouts, cheers, and applause when Isadora bowed her close at center stage. After that came a string of encores that we eagerly demanded, and she graciously presented. During the last, hundreds of young students swarmed onto the stage. Isadora was in danger of being crushed to death by so much adoration. Guards helped her escape to the wings.

Headlines around the world the next morning proclaimed the overnight emergence of an American dance sensation, the rapid rise to stardom of the "California fawn."

Single-handed, Isadora Duncan changed the look and direction of dance in the Western world. She was a true pioneer who brushed aside an early lack of success, poverty, and ridicule, to follow her inner vision of the nature and purpose of dance.

Isadora established no school, and left behind no concrete set of techniques. All she left us with is the memory of her inspired performances and her many lectures on dance and movement. Still, Isadora is considered the founding mother of modern dance and modern movement theory. She is also credited with reshaping the look of modern ballet. Isadora's revolutionary dance laid the foundation for other great twentieth century dancers and choreographers: Martha Graham, Ruth St. Denis, Twala Tharp, and Merce Cunningham. But each of those is another story.

Questions to Explore

What makes a dance or other art form "revolutionary?"

What do you think made Isadora Duncan's dancing unique?

When and where have other new dance forms emerged? What were some of the most revolutionary changes to dance or the other arts since Isadore Duncan?

Do the art forms of a period reflect the character of the time? How?

References for Further Reading

- *In the Children's Library*

   Kozodoy, Ruth. *Isadora Duncan.* New York: Chelsea House, 1988.

- *In the Adult Library*

   Duncan, Isadora. *My Life.* New York: Liveright, 1927.

   Loewenthal, Lillian. *The Search for Isadora.* Pennington, NJ: A Dance Horizons Book, 1993.

   Walter, Terry. *Isadora Duncan: Her Life, Her Art, Her Legacy.* New York: Dodd, Mead, 1963.

See your librarian for additional titles.

Aim, Focus, Shoot

A story about Margaret Bourke-White, America's first female industrial photographer and photojournalist

About This Story:

The science and chemistry of photography were first developed in the early 1800s. Those early prints were called ferrotype and then tintype. By the early 1900s photographers lugged bulky box cameras and used heavy four-by-five-inch glass plates as negatives. These plates and cameras were very cumbersome to set up and required long shutter times, so that anything that moved while the photograph was being taken was blurred in the final picture. Prints were grainy and didn't allow as many gray tones between pure black and pure white.

The work was physically demanding and slow, and the field was dominated by a handful of men. This began to change in the late 1920s with the advent of industrial photography, and then in the 1930s with an explosion of photojournalism and photo-rich magazines such as Fortune *and* Life. *One person happened to be on the cutting edge of the development in both fields. She was also the first woman to enter the field of photography. This is a story about her.*

Crisp yellow leaves swirled into the gutters on a cloudy October morning in 1927. A tall, twenty-three-year-old woman swept into a downtown camera shop in Cleveland, Ohio, and adjusted her flowing red scarf. "I need to borrow *both* Graflex cameras today, Beme."

"Both?" he spluttered, nervously pushing his glasses back up to the middle of his balding head. "My boss will kill me if he finds out you borrowed both Graflexes from the store. Why both?"

The woman's brown eyes danced with a look that hinted of both innocent girl and confident huckster. Her stylishly short, brown hair was tight against her head, a wide curl climbing up over one cheek. Her mouth spread into a mocking Cheshire cat smile. "I've never photographed a live steer before. I may need to use the camera with a wide-angle lens, and I may want the one with a telephoto."

"You'll want flash powder and tray, too. Right, Peggy?" asked short, stocky Alfred Bemis leaning on the counter. Only Margaret White got away with calling him "Beme." Only Beme got away with calling her "Peggy."

"I hate flash powder," she groused. "Maybe it'll work without it."

Alfred stopped and stared at Margaret, his hands frozen still reaching for the second bulky Graflex camera. With her flashing smile and commanding voice, Margaret always looked so self-assured, so confident, so professional. But, Beme realized that for someone who called herself a photographer, she had only a vague idea of how film and cameras really worked.

"You're in way over your head here. Aren't you?" he cautioned.

Margaret shrugged. "That's how you learn to swim, Beme. Besides, a bank's paying me for this one. It's for a promotion."

"An assignment? Impressive. How much?" he asked.

"Ten dollars for just one photo of a steer!" Margaret's smile was wide with excitement.

Alfred whistled. "That much?" He wagged a warning finger at her. "Then you better make this photo come out right! I'll call Earl and see if he can tag along. You may need him."

Photography in the early 1900s was still heavy equipment, smelly, corrosive chemicals, and long hours of guesswork throughout the very imprecise process of film developing and printing. Photographers spent far more time hunched in darkrooms working with enlargers and chemical trays and guessing at chemical proportions and temperatures than they did outside manhandling bulky cameras.

In this traditionally male field, Margaret's twinkling eyes and alluring smile seemed like a breath of fresh air. A sense of drama and excitement buzzed around her, and quickly netted Margaret two champions: Alfred Bemis, knowledgeable equipment expert and supplier, and Earl Leiter, one of the best photo6finishers and printers in the business. They were the safety net that let Margaret's creative eye and imagination soar free without being dragged down by worrying about all the technical details.

Piece by piece Beme lugged the bulky camera equipment into the blustery Cleveland morning.

"Load it in Patrick, please," said Margaret, slipping on a pair of gloves that matched her red scarf, hat, and shoes. Patrick, a five-year-old Chevrolet coupe, sat waiting at the curb.

Alfred mopped his forehead as he closed the trunk over the last of his loads. "Earl will meet you at the bank. I gave you an extra box of film plates. You all ready for your first assignment shoot?"

Margaret nodded, mentally ticking through her inventory. "Hat, gloves, scarf, matching red camera cloth. I'm ready."

Bemis scowled. "I meant film plates, shutter release cables, flash sync cables, and tripods. You're going to work, not to a dance. Why dress up like you're going to a party?"

Margaret chortled. "This is also a business. I have to look as professional as the bank president in order to be treated professionally. I'm dressed to look like I'm the best and the most expensive photographer in America," she added with a sharp nod.

Alfred shook his head admiringly. "You just might make it as a photographer— in spite of being the only woman in the field."

"No," she corrected, her eyes beaming, a snickering smile dancing on her lips. "I'll succeed *because* I'm a woman, and because I know the secret of being a great photographer."

Exasperated, Alfred huffed, "I've studied photography for six years and I'm *still* learning about film emulsions, paper contrasts, enlarger settings, and developing and printing techniques. Earl has studied for twice that long. He's the best printer around. He knows more about photo chemicals than anyone. Still we're not good enough to earn a living as photographers. How do you know already?"

Margaret scoffed. "That's all technical junk, Beme. Professor White at the University of Michigan told me techies are a dime a dozen. He said real photography is all in the eye and the imagination. That's my strong suit. That's why I get paid 10 bucks a photo."

As Margaret slid into Patrick's front seat, Alfred leaned in the window with a pleading look. "You *will* have the equipment back before we close tonight, won't you?"

"Relax, Beme," she smiled, revving the engine. "It's only a picture of a steer."

Margaret White was an exceedingly bright student, and had planned to follow her scientist-inventor father into the world of science. But cameras kept dragging her attention and imagination away from her original goal, herpetology, the study of reptiles and amphibians.

The one course she treasured at the University of Michigan was a photography course. After she transferred to Cornell University in Ithaca, New York, she could no longer deny her passion for photographing campus buildings.

She'd skip classes to spend a whole day waiting for the light to fall "just right" across an ivy-covered hall. She'd spend hours removing trash and unwanted details from her scene before she'd shoot. She'd consume long winter hours making just the right tracks in the snow in front of some tower, and rubbing out all the others—all to let her transform campus classrooms into enchanted castles on photographic paper. And she loved every minute of it.

Word quickly spread that Margaret White's pictures made the buildings look better than the architects who conceived them had dreamed. Only one thing could lure Margaret's camera away from buildings: smoke-belching, steam-blasting, fire-hissing, iron-clanging factories. To Margaret White's eye, the strong angles, hard steel, fire, and smoke of factories were the most beautiful sights in the world.

Margaret's dearest dream was to photograph noisy, smelly factories. But in the 1920s, the world of factories was closed to women, as was the tiny, exclusive field of industrial photography.

Now she had moved to Cleveland and hung out her shingle. Driving in her loaded car, she said to the busy downtown traffic, "Now, let's see if I can create a dream image of a steer."

Lanky Earl Leiter paced the sidewalk outside the Union Trust Bank building while Margaret parked Patrick.

They crossed the open, echoing bank lobby and approached two armed bank guards standing on either side of an 1,800 pound champion longhorn steer: a hulking, jet-black animal, surrounded by a sea of blindingly white marble.

Margaret's heart sank. Her unflappable composure faltered as she whispered, "I can't photograph a black blob in the middle of pure white. The film will never get it."

The first glimmerings of fear for the success of her photographic career edged into her heart. "What can I do, Earl?"

Earl thoughtfully circled the steer as it pawed the marble stand to which it was tied. A tiny, blood-red eye bulged from each side of it's head, frantically glaring back at Margaret. "Double pans of magnesium flash powder," Earl suggested. "One here. One over there."

Margaret sadly shook her head. "Even that won't help. There's nothing interesting here. I need strong lines and angles in the background."

Earl shook his head. "Shoot the flash. Get detail in the mangy steer. Forget the background."

"No," insisted Margaret. "If it's part of my picture I have to make it right."

She dragged a lobby chair nearer to the steer and dropped into its upholstered cushions, staring at the solid marble walls surrounding the beast. Suddenly she brightened and sprang to her feet, adjusting her tripod and camera way down low, close to the floor, where she liked to shoot buildings.

Slowly, she focused on the steer. Then she sighed and flopped back into her chair. "If only there were three strong diagonal lines across that wall . . ."

Earl's eyes widened. "Don't you *dare* scribble on those marble walls, Margaret White!"

Margaret's eyes began to dance with their usual confidence. "I won't have to. In about three hours, the sun ought to be low enough to shine through the front windows and onto that wall. My lines will be the shadows of the dividers in the window."

Impressed by her creative vision, Earl dragged a second chair next to hers. "And I'll set up and run the flash pans for you."

"Thanks, Earl. But you better make it look like *I* did everything."

When his eyes narrowed questioningly she simply said, "They hired *me* as their photographer. They have to think I know it all."

The pair sat, watching the steer and waiting. Mr. Joseph Hill, the bank's president, came over and demanded to know why they weren't working.

"We are," answered Margaret with her most alluring smile. And they waited.

Customers, who had crowded three and four deep to watch, drifted slowly away. And still Margaret and Earl waited.

Finally Margaret rocked forward to her knees and shoved her head under her matching red camera cloth. "Perfect!" she cried. "Set up the flash pans fast. We've got to shoot before a cloud spoils my lines."

"Ready!" called Earl as a new crowd gathered tight around.

"Get the steer to turn toward me," called Margaret, head still buried behind the camera and under her cloth.

Earl clapped, stomped, yelled, and whistled. The steer stubbornly refused to move.

Earl threw an eraser at it. Nostrils flaring, the animal spun to lunge at its tormentor.

"Now!" cried Margaret.

Click, the shutter opened. Blam! Both trays of magnesium powder exploded with a blast of light and a thunderous roar. The steer bellowed in fright and frantically ripped at his restraining ropes. A gentle rain of ash swirled down over steer and camera cloth.

"Again!" cried Margaret. "Hurry!"

"Ready," shouted Earl as he refilled both trays with magnesium powder.

The steer bucked and savagely slashed its horns toward Margaret.

"Now!" she cried.

Click. BLAM! The second blast echoed through the building. Customers covered their ears and screamed. The steer roared in terror and bucked like a wild

Brahma bull. One kick chipped a marble stand, another cracked a floor tile. Restraining ropes groaned. The guards dove for cover.

Bank personnel rushed from offices, thinking the bank had been bombed. Outside, sirens wailed as three police squad cars skidded to a stop, having been automatically summoned when the first flash triggered the bank's security system.

"What, in heaven's name, is going on here?" demanded Mr. Hill, storming out of his office.

Margaret, having recovered her composure, smiled cordially and extended a gloved hand to the president. "I'm Margaret Bourke-White, your photographer. I'm afraid if you've come to watch me work, the session's over. I've already gotten the picture. You'll see a print in the morning."

With a final wave to acknowledge the applause of the crowd, Margaret and Earl packed up their gear and left the bank and enraged steer.

Outside Earl asked, "Where did the new name come from?"

Margaret shrugged. "Bourke is my mother's maiden name. It suddenly occurred to me that a hyphenated last name sounds more professional."

At nine o'clock the next morning Mr. Hill and his senior vice presidents passed Margaret's proof print (which Earl had printed because he was a much better printer than Margaret) around the fourth floor conference table as Margaret discretely glowed.

"Extraordinary!" exclaimed one.

"Looks much better than the foul animal does live," said another.

"Makes the steer appear proud, fierce, and commanding," concluded Joseph Hill. "All the things we want people to think of when they think of Union Trust Bank. Remarkable work, Miss Bourke-White."

Not wanting any of her genius overlooked, Margaret leaned over the president's chair. "Be sure to notice the fresh and unique angle of the camera and my powerful composition."

Twenty minutes later, the bank had ordered more than 500 prints of the picture. Margaret Bourke-White was on her way. Now she felt like a professional photographer. She had been hired to take a specific picture, and she had delivered better than her client expected.

Margaret raced from the bank clutching a crisp 10 dollar bill and a 200 dollar print order. She was sure the elation she felt was better than anything she would ever feel again.

A phone call one week later proved her wrong. A gravelly voice like a human bulldog introduced itself as Elroy Kulas, president of the Otis Steel Company. Had she heard of Otis Steel?

Margaret's heart skipped a beat. She could barely cough out a whispered, "Yes." Otis Steel owned a monstrous factory with two dozen soot-covered smokestacks by the railroad tracks in Cleveland. Margaret had often longingly photographed the plant from outside its high wire mesh fences.

Mr. Kulas told her that the company needed a new brochure and some factory pictures to make Otis Steel appear elegant and dependable.

Margaret's knees turned to rubber. Her hands trembled so that she could scarcely hold the phone. Steel factory pictures?

Frankly, he continued, he didn't care much for photography and didn't think it would work. But his banker, Joseph Hill at Union Trust, had recommended Margaret. So Kulas decided to give her a shot, if she wanted to take on a steel plant.

"Oh, yes!" said Margaret. "Oh, yes, indeed!" It was a dream come true. Steel mills were the most incredible factories of all. Even Margaret hadn't dare dream of being allowed into a steel mill. And now the offer fell into her lap as her very first industrial assignment. No one had successfully photographed a major industrial plant in full operation. Margaret wanted to yell for joy. She would be the first.

Kulas barked, "You aren't a fainter, are you? We allowed one woman in the plant. She fainted dead away from the heat."

"I don't faint," Margaret assured him.

"You're not afraid of noise, steam, sparks, smoke, and fire are you?" he continued. "I won't have any squeamish woman crying for help in my plant."

Margaret answered that noise, steam, sparks, smoke, and fire were her very favorite elements to work with.

Kulas grunted. "You've got free run of the plant. I'll be back from Europe in two months. If you show me something decent, you get whatever price you ask. If you don't, you get nothing."

And he hung up before Margaret could tell him there was nothing more beautiful, artful, and elegant than molten steel.

Joy turned into urgent phone calls to Beme and Earl Leiter, and then into sixty days of frantic work for the trio. All day, every day they shot in the factory: distance shots, close-ups, wide-angle and telephoto. They built protective barriers, so Margaret could hang out over 120 ton ladles of bubbling, molten steel.

She crawled closer to the inferno fire pits than any plant worker dared to go, close enough that sparks showered around her and she blistered her face and melted the cover and mounts on her camera. She shinnied up narrow girders and beams seventy feet above blast furnaces, waves of fiery heat billowing up around her, just to find an interesting angle.

Through the wee hours every night Earl and Beme developed and printed her day's work.

For fifty-five days in a row the results were the same: total failure. The plant was too dark. The molten steel glowed too bright. There was more contrast than film, equipment, and paper could handle. Every picture was jet black with white blobs.

They tried different cameras, different lenses, different kinds of film, different sets of processing chemicals, different kinds of printing paper. They tried double, triple, and quadruple pans of magnesium flash powder.

Nothing helped. The plant was so dark and massive, while the molten slag and steel so bright and so intensely white-hot, that nothing could match the two together.

On day fifty-six, a salesman stopped in Beme's camera shop to demonstrate a new product: high intensity photo flares straight from Hollywood. One of these flares, the man said, would light up half the holes in Hades for thirty seconds. Beme said he'd like to test four dozen, all the salesman carried with him.

On the same day, Earl found a new German printing paper that was especially designed to handle high contrast printing.

On day fifty-eight they found that simultaneously firing five flares lit the steel mill well enough for Margaret's camera to capture the breathtaking beauty and elegance her creative mind and imagination had been seeing for two months.

They had enough flares left for five shots. Two months grueling work came down to less than half a dozen clicks of the shutter.

Tensions ran high as Beme developed the glass plate negatives. The three heads stared in hushed silence in the soft, red light of the darkroom as Beme washed the glass plates through the fixer solution.

"We did it!" cried Margaret.

The five negative images before them were stunning.

Earl took over for the printing. As the print images slowly appeared in the developer tray, everyone's high hopes were dashed. The prints were flat and uninteresting.

Through day fifty-nine, Earl experimented with different combinations of chemicals and temperatures to force the new German paper to live up to its potential. Beme and Margaret paced outside the darkroom.

On day sixty, Margaret was ushered into Elroy Kulas's mahogany-lined office with her five sixteen-by-twenty-inch prints. He gazed at them for less than a minute and told Margaret that whatever she asked for the prints was acceptable, because they were worth more.

They were, he said, masterpieces. She had captured the power, majesty, gracefulness, and elegance of steel on paper. She had made a steel mill look like art.

She started to ask for $100 a print, then gulped and changed it to $200. Kulas paid her on the spot. Margaret Bourke-White instantly became the most famous industrial photographer in the country. And she owed her chance to prove her worth to two loyal friends, some lucky timing, and a promotional steer.

Over the next thirty years, Margaret Bourke-White's photographs came to be cherished by millions. She was the star photographer for *Fortune Magazine* and shot the first cover for *Life*. She produced some of the most moving and influential photographic series ever taken.

More importantly, she was always a pioneer, a leader in the emerging major photographic fields of industrial photography and photojournalism. She helped to define and shape these important fields as well as the profession of photography, not just for women, but for all photographers. By the time Margaret hung up her camera in the early 1960s, she was chosen as one of the top ten living American women of the twentieth century. But that is another story.

Questions to Explore

How do a camera and photographic film really record the scene before them?

What is the simplest camera you can use?

See if you can find articles in the library describing how a camera works.

References for Further Reading

- *In the Children's Library*

  Ayer, Eleanor. *Photographing the World: Margaret Bourke-White.* New York: Dillon Press, 1992.

  Sternsker, Bernard, ed. *Women of Valor.* Chicago: Ivan Dee, 1990.

- *In the Adult Library*

  Goldberg, Vicki. *Margaret Bourke-White.* Reading, MA: Addison-Wesley, 1987.

See your librarian for additional titles.

Appendix A

Timeline of Stories and Major Events in American History

The following brief timeline of major events in U.S. history is intended to provide some framework and context for the stories in this book. It is not intended to be a comprehensive summary of American history.

Historical Event	Year	Figure
Jamestown Colony founded	1607	Pocahontas
First African slave sold in Virginia	1619	
Plymouth Colony founded in Massachusetts	1620	
French and Indian War begins	1754	
Boston Tea Party	1773	
First Continental Congress	1774	
Revolutionary War begins	1775	
Declaration of Independence adopted	1776	
	1778	Mary Hays ("Molly Pitcher")
	1781	Elizabeth ("Mumbet") Freeman
	1782	Deborah Sampson
U.S. Constitution adopted	1788	
George Washington elected as first president	1789	
Thomas Jefferson makes the Louisiana Purchase	1803	
Louis and Clark expedition	1805	Sacajawea
Robert Fulton invents the steamboat	1807	
War of 1812 begins	1812	
Erie Canal opens up the "West" (Ohio)	1825	
	1827	Elizabeth ("Betsy") Ross (retires)
	1828	Sojourner Truth
Underground Railroad begins	1830	
Texas revolt and the Battle of the Alamo	1836	
	1840	Elizabeth Cady Stanton
Oregon Trail crosses the continent	1843	
Telegraph invented	1844	Dorothea Dix
	1847	Elizabeth Blackwell
California gold rush	1849	Harriet Tubman

Historical Event	Year	Figure
	1850	Sarah Winnemucca
	1851	Amelia Bloomer
Kansas-Nebraska Act and "Bloody Kansas"	1854	
	1858	Charlene ("Charley") Parkhurst
First oil is discovered in Titusville, Pennsylvania	1859	
Pony Express begins	1860	
Civil War begins	1861	
Uncle Tom's Cabin is published	1862	Harriet Beecher Stowe; Catherine Beecher; Clara Barton; Sarah Edmonds
First cattle drive. Indian wars begin	1866	
Transcontinental railroad completed	1869	
	1872	Susan B. Anthony
	1875	Annie ("Oakley") Moses
Alexander Graham Bell patents the telephone	1876	
The Battle of the Little Bighorn (Custer's Last Stand)	1876	
Thomas A. Edison invents the lightbulb	1879	Fannie Farmer
	1884	Belva Lockwood
	1887	Annie Sullivan
	1888	Elizabeth Cochran Seamen ("Nellie Bly")
Oklahoma land rush	1889	
First skyscraper (Chicago)	1890	Jane Addams
The massacre at Wounded Knee ends Indian Wars	1890	
	1896	Queen Liliuokalani; Carrie Nation and Francis Willard
First modern movie	1903	Isadora Duncan
The Wright brothers fly at Kitty Hawk	1903	Mary Harris ("Mother") Jones
	1904	Mary Bethune
Ford begins mass-production of the Model T	1908	
NAACP founded	1909	
	1915	Sara Breedlove ("Madam C. J.") Walker

Historical Event	Year	Figure
United States enters World War I	1917	Jeanette Rankin
Nineteenth Amendment (Prohibition) ratified	1919	Edith Wilson
Twentieth Amendment (Women's Suffrage) ratified	1920	
First public radio broadcast	1920	
George Washington Carver invents peanut butter	1921	Eleanor Roosevelt
	1925	Margaret Mead
	1926	Gertrude Ederle
	1927	Margaret Bourke-White
Television invented	1928	
Stock market crash; Great Depression begins	1929	
	1932	Amelia Earhart (disappears)
	1938	Jacqueline Cochran
United States enters World War II	1941	
A-Bomb dropped on Japan; Nuclear age begins	1945	
United Nations founded	1945	
Korean war begins	1950	
Racial segregation declared illegal	1954	
Interstate highway system begins	1956	
	1958	Rachel Carson
Civil Rights Act passed	1960	Jane Goodall
Vietnam War begins	1964	
First man on the moon	1969	
	1973	Maria Pepe

Appendix B

Additional Significant Women in American History

Hundreds of women have made significant contributions to American history at a national level. Thousands more are significant at regional, state, and local levels. Below is an alphabetical list of an additional 100 women who made important contributions on a national level. Certainly this list is not exhaustive. Each reader can find many additional women that merit national recognition. But this list is a beginning, a crosssection of women not included in this book who helped to shape our national heritage. See how many names you can add to this list. Create a similar list for your state and for your local area.

Name	Life Span	Field
Bella Abzug	1920-	Politician
Abigail Adams	1744-1818	Politician/First Lady
Louisa May Alcott	1832-1888	Author
Florence Allen	1884-1966	Lawyer and Judge
Blanche Mae Armwood	1890-1939	Educator
Sarah Bagley	1806-1880?	Women's Rights Activist
Jo Ella Baker	1903-1986	Civil Rights Activist
Emily Greene Balch	1867-1961	Nobel Peace Prize Winner
Alva Belmont	1853-1933	Labor Activist
Mary Ann Bickerdyke	1817-1901	Civil War/Frontier Nurse
Helen Gurley Brown	1922-	Writer and Publisher
Pearl S. Buck	1892-1973	Writer
Martha Jane Burk ("Calamity Jane")	1848?-1903	Wild West Personality
Nannie Burroughs	1878-1961	Educator
Hattie Caraway	1878-1950	First Elected Female Senator
Anna Ella Carroll	1815-1894	Political Activist
Carrie Chapman Catt	1859-1947	Women's Rights Activist
Maria Chapman	1806-1885	Abolitionist
Julia Child	1912-	Chef
Shirley Chisholm	1924-	Politician
Eugenie Clark	1918-	Biologist
Septima Clark	1898-1987	Civil Rights Activist
Jane Croly ("Jennie June")	1829-1901	Newspaper Columnist
Laura Cross	1962-	First Girl to win National Soapbox Derby
Nancy Dickerson	1927?-	First Female TV News Anchor
Emily Dickinson	1830-1886	Poet
Mary Mapes Dodge	1831-1905	Educator/Writer
Mary Baker Eddy	1821-1910	Religious Founder
Crystal Bird Fauset	1893-1965	First Black Woman Elected to State Legislature

Name	Life Span	Field
Rebecca Latimer Felton	1835-1930	First Seated Female U.S. Senator
Edna Ferber	1885-1968	Writer
Geraldine Ferraro	1935-	First Female Vice Presidential Nominee by a Major Party
Williamina Fleming	1857-1911	Astronomer
Jessie Ann Fremont	1824-1902	Abolitionist and Political Activist
Betty Friedan	1921-	Women's Rights Activist
Margaret Fuller	1810-1880	Literary Critic
Sarah Bradlee Fulton	1741-1835	Revolutionary War Activist
Matilda Gage	1826-1898	Women's Suffrage Activist
Charlotte Gilman	1860-1935	Early Women's Movement Leader
Martha Graham	1894-1991	Dancer and Choreographer
Rose O'Neal Greenhow	1815-1864	Civil War Spy
Sarah Hale	1788-1879	Early Magazine Writer and Editor
Fannie Lou Hamer	1917-1977	Civil Rights Activist
Alice Hamilton	1869-1970	Industrial Medicine Specialist
Pearl Hart	1875?-1924?	Last Female Desperado in the Wild West
Lillian Hellman	1905-1984	Playwright
Oveta Culp Hobby	1905-	Founded Women's Army Corps
Billie Holiday	1915?-1959	Singer
Julia Ward Howe	1819-1910	Women's Suffragist and Writer
Dolores Huerta	1930-	Labor Organizer
Anne Hutchinson	1591-1643	Social and Religious Activist
Barbara Jordon	1936-	Politician
Sarah Knight	1666-1727	Frontier Woman
Blanch Wolf Knoph	1894-1966	Business Woman and Publisher
Rose Knox	1857-1950	Inventor and Business Woman
Elizabeth Koontz	1919-1989	Educator and First Black President of NEA
Dorothea Lange	1895-1965	Photographer
Mary Ashton Livermore	1820-1905	Nurse and Women's Rights Activist
Juliette Low	1860-1927	Founded Girl Scouts
Mary Mason Lyon	1797-1849	Educator
Dolley Madison	1768-1849	Politician and First Lady
Barbara McClintock	1902-1985	Botanist
Aimee Semple McPherson	1890-1944	Infamous Gospel Preacher
Edna St. Vincent Millay	1892-1950	Poet
Maria Mitchell	1818-1889	Astronomer
Esther Morris	1814-1902	First American Woman to Hold an Official Government Office
Anna Mary ("Grandma") Moses	1860-1961	Painter
Lucretia Mott	1793-1880	Women's Rights Activist
Sandra Day O'Connor	1930-	First Female Supreme Court Justice
Georgia O'Keeffe	1887-1986	Painter

Name	Life Span	Field
Leonora O'Reilly	1870-1927	Labor Organizer
Alice Palmer	1855-1902	Educator
Maud Wood Park	1875-1955	First President of the League of Women Voters
Rosa Parks	1913-	Civil Rights Activist
Eleanor ("Cissy") Patterson	1881-1948	Publisher
Mary Jane Patterson	1840-1894	First Black Woman to Graduate from a U.S. College
Alice Paul	1885-1977	Women's Suffrage Leader
Frances Perkins	1880-1965	First Female Cabinet Officer
Mary Pickford	1893-1979	First Female Movie Superstar
Lydia Pinkham	1819-1883	Inventor and Business Woman
Emily Post	1872-1960	Social and Etiquette Commentator
Harriet Quimby	1875?-1912	First American Woman Licensed to Fly a Plane
Ellen Richards	1842-1911	Scientist and Educator
Sally Ride	1951-	First American Woman in Space
Nellie Ross	1876?-1977	First American Woman Governor
Margaret Sanger	1879-1966	Birth Control Activist
Saint Elizabeth Ann Seton	1774-1821	First American-Born Catholic Saint
Bessie Smith	1894-1937	Blues Singing Pioneer
Margaret Chase Smith	1897-	Politician
Gertrude Stein	1874-1946	Writer
Lucy Stone	1818-1893	Women's Rights Activist
Mary Eliza Church Terrell	1863-1954	Founded National Association of Colored Women
Dorothy Thompson	1893-1961	Early Feminist and Journalist
Mary Heaton Vorse	1874-1966	Labor Writer and Activist
Maggie Walker	1867-1934	First Black Female Bank President
Ida Bell Wells-Barnett	1862-1931	Civil Rights Writer and Lecturer
Phillis Wheatley	1753?-1784	Poet and First Black American to Publish a Book
Emma Hart Willard	1787-1870	Educator
"Babe" Didrickson Zaharias	1911?-1956	Female Athlete

INDEX

About the Author

The only West Point graduate to ever become a professional storyteller, Kendall Haven also holds a master's degree in oceanography and spent six years as a senior research scientist for the United States Department of Energy before finding his true passion for storytelling and a different kind of "truth." He has now performed for more than 1.5 million children and adults in 38 states, and has presented workshops to more than 15,000 teachers on the practical, in-class teaching power of storytelling. Haven has won numerous awards both for his story-writing and for his storytelling. He has become one of the nation's leading advocates for the educational value of storytelling, is director of the National Whole Language Umbrella Storytelling Action Group, and is on the board of directors of the National Storytelling Association.

Haven has published five audio tapes and two picture books of his original stories; created a three-hour high-adventure radio drama for National Public Radio on the effects of watching television, which has won five major national awards; and is the author of the extremely popular *Marvels of Science: 50 Fascinating 5-Minute Reads* (Libraries Unlimited, 1994).

Haven has used his writing talent to create stories for many nonprofit organizations including The American Cancer Society, the Institute for Mental Health Initiatives, several California crisis centers, the Children's Television Resource and Education Center, a regional hospital, and the Child Abuse Prevention Training Center of California.

He lives with his wife and nephew in the rolling Sonoma County grape vineyards of rural northern California.

MORE GREAT READS!

MARVELS OF SCIENCE: 50 Fascinating 5-Minute Reads
Kendall Haven

Ideal for both read-alouds and reading assignments, these 50 short stories take just minutes to read but amply illustrate scientific principles and the evolution of science through history. **Grades 3 and up**.
1994 xxii, 238p. paper ISBN 1-56308-159-8

GREAT MOMENTS IN SCIENCE: Experiments and Readers Theatre
Kendall Haven

Bring significant moments and characters in the history of Western science to life with these 12 scripts and experiments based on the stories in *Marvels of Science*. **Grades 4–9**.
xii, 227p. 8½x11 paper ISBN 1-56308-355-8

MAGIC MINUTES: Quick Read-Alouds for Every Day
Pat Nelson

Seasonally arranged, this collection of 170 short, short stories covers everything from multicultural folktales, historical accounts, biographical sketches, and real-life stories to math and science problems and anecdotes. **All levels**.
xv, 151p. paper ISBN 0-87287-996-8

DAY OF THE MOON SHADOW: Tales with Ancient Answers to Scientific Questions
Judy Gail and Linda A. Houlding

Brief, understandable, and fascinating scientific explanations to a multitude of questions are coupled with related ancient folktales or myths. A sure way to stimulate interest in natural science and in other cultures. **Grades 2–6**.
xx, 287p. 8½x11 paper ISBN 1-56308-348-5

WONDER BEASTS: Tales and Lore of the Phoenix, the Griffin, the Unicorn, and the Dragon
Joe Nigg

Focusing on the phoenix, the griffin, the unicorn, and the dragon, this multicultural folklore collection and sourcebook is a wonderful supplement to world history courses and a great resource for reports. **All levels**.
xxvi, 160p. ISBN 1-56308-242-X

OF BUGS AND BEASTS: Fact, Folklore, and Activities
Lauren J. Livo, Glenn McGlathery, and Norma J. Livo

Covering a variety of nature's least-loved animals, from insects to mammals, this book offers folk stories, folklore, natural histories, learning activities, and problem-solving projects for the classroom, library, or home. **All levels**.
Learning Through Folklore Series; Norma J. Livo, Ed.
xxi, 217p. 8½x11 paper ISBN 1-56308-179-2

For a free catalog or to place an order for any of our titles, please contact:
Libraries Unlimited/Teacher Ideas Press, Dept. B9
P.O. Box 6633, Englewood, CO 80155
Phone: 1-800-237-6124 Fax: 1-303-220-8843 E-mail: lu-books@lu.com